BULLWHIP DAYS

Also by James Mellon

THE FACE OF LINCOLN

AFRICAN HUNTER

Bullwhip Days

THE SLAVES REMEMBER

Edited and with an Introduction by

JAMES MELLON

Weidenfeld & Nicolson

New York

PUBLISHED BY WEIDENFELD & NICOLSON, NEW YORK
A DIVISION OF WHEATLAND CORPORATION
841 BROADWAY
NEW YORK, NY 10003-4793

PUBLISHED IN CANADA BY GENERAL PUBLISHING COMPANY, LTD.

LIBRARY OF CONGRESS CATALOGING-IN-PUBLICATION DATA

BULLWHIP DAYS : THE SLAVES REMEMBER / EDITED AND WITH AN INTRODUCTION BY
JAMES MELLON. — 1ST ED.
P.   CM.
ISBN 1-55584-210-0
1. SLAVES—UNITED STATES—BIOGRAPHY.   2. SLAVERY—UNITED STATES—
CONDITION OF SLAVES.   3. AFRO-AMERICANS—HISTORY—TO 1863.
I. MELLON, JAMES.
E444.B95   1988
973'.0496073022—DC 19
[B]   88-4967
                                                                              CIP

MANUFACTURED IN THE UNITED STATES OF AMERICA
THIS BOOK IS PRINTED ON ACID-FREE PAPER.
FIRST EDITION
1   3   5   7   9   10   8   6   4   2

For
All The Slaves
White And Black, Living And Dead,
And Especially For Those
Whose Suffering Was Never Known
Or Has Been Forgotten

Contents

Contents

Illustrations

———◆———

Introduction

HUMAN emotion, we are often reminded, is universal and timeless. Yet few of us pause to consider that innumerable human feelings and experiences have vanished forever because the conditions that gave rise to them no longer exist.

This book is about an entire range of human feelings that can no longer be experienced: the feelings that arose from the condition of being a statutory slave, of being owned, physically, by one's fellow man as a piece of property.

Men and women who have been imbruted and stripped of their human rights in these times by some mindless authoritarian government rightfully consider themselves enslaved. Theirs is a merely figurative form of slavery, however, for even the most brutal, most unabashedly nihilistic tyrants of the twentieth century have stopped short of claiming to own their victims as personal property. That this crassest of all claims was indeed advanced by hundreds of thousands of farmers in the American South until 1865 is a sobering, riveting fact. This book invites the reader to meditate upon that fact.

In the year 1619, only a decade after the founding of England's first successful colony in the Americas, a number of black Africans were put ashore from a ship at Jamestown, Virginia. Some form of cosmic thunder would have been appropriate at that epochal juncture, but as Thomas Jefferson later lamented, "Heaven remained silent." A laconic diarist merely noted without comment that "there came in a Dutch man-of-warre that sold us 20 negars." American slavery had begun.

Kidnapped by their tribal enemies in Africa or by the white sea captains who ferried them to these shores, despoiled of their customs, torn from their families and villages, countless African tribesmen were shunted across the Atlantic in the squalid holds of the slave ships. This nefarious traffic in human flesh, which had begun as a trickle, quickly became a torrent, until by 1860 Abraham Lincoln felt compelled to declaim with distress and foreboding that almost one-sixth of the people then living in the so-called "land of the free" were in fact slaves.

By the mid-1930s, however, the four million black men and women who had been born in slavery and had subsequently been freed at the close of the Civil War had dwindled to a few thousand aged individuals scattered mainly throughout the Southern states. These were the last surviving Americans who had endured the cosmic arrogance of statutory slavery—who could bear personal witness to the now extinct feelings that arise from being physically owned by one's fellow man like a chair or table, like a dog or cat.

Aware that the memories of these former slaves amounted to an incomparable treasure trove of American history, and one that was quickly vanishing, the Federal Writers' Project, an adjunct of the Works Progress Administration, dispatched a number of interviewers—men and women, whites and blacks—to seek out and question the former slaves.

A typical interview would have occurred on the rickety porch of a former slave's shack, situated either in the country or in the ramshackle, colored section of a Southern town. There, the interviewer and his subject might have been seen slouched into rockers, drinking coffee, and chatting informally about antebellum days.

The interviewer would prompt the former slave with queries about his origins and family, his former masters and overseers, his daily routine of work, his food, cooking, and living quarters, his superstitions and religious beliefs, the medicines he made and used, the abuse he suffered, the songs he sang, the music he danced to. The former slave's responses to these questions were collated into a narrative account of his life, and this book consists primarily of twenty-nine such narratives—actual life stories of former slaves—chosen from some two thousand similar accounts recorded by the interviewers between 1934 and 1941. Also included are nine collections of excerpts from the narratives, each of which relates to one or more

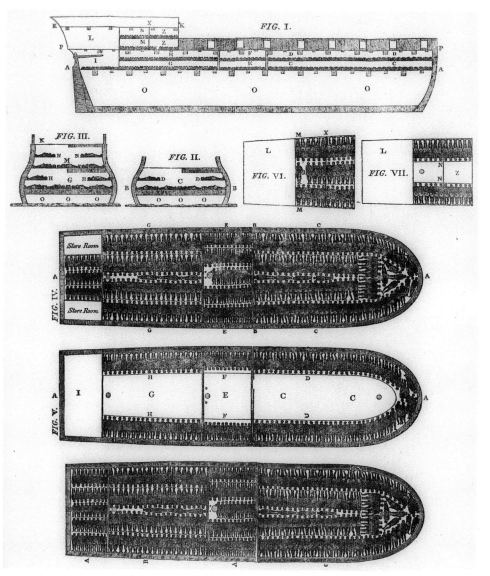

PLATE I: Schematic plan of a slave ship.

particular aspects of slave life. The text has been lightly edited to improve readability.

The slave narratives bear eloquent witness to the trials that awaited the slaves in America. Sitting, as it were, in judgment upon their masters, the former bondsmen describe the feeling of being sold away from one's wife and children in a public auction, of being rented out, borrowed, traded for a mule or cow, insured for loss, willed to the master's relatives, seized as payment for debts, put up as collateral for loans, or simply lost by one's owner in a card game. We hear how some slaves were whipped for "fun," raped, or made to fight one another like gladiators; how runaways were hunted by their masters on horseback and treed by packs of hounds; how a few bondsmen were rolled down bumpy hillsides in barrels that had nails driven through the sides, while others were boxed up in wooden crates and shipped to neighboring states.

Yet these life stories also reveal how widely the conditions of human bondage could vary. The experience of slavery was predicated upon the interplay of two personalities—that of the slave and that of his master—and just as the personality of each could vary as widely as human nature itself, so the experience of being a slave could assume an infinite variety of forms. Not surprisingly, then, the chilling brutalities recalled by some of these aged witnesses are interspersed with tales of kindness, courage, loyalty, generosity, self-sacrifice, and occasional downright heroism. We read how many of the masters treated their slaves with unfailing humanity and accepted them almost as family members; how others continued to assist their bondsmen in adverse times, long after Emancipation; and how still others acknowledged the equality of men, denounced slavery as an outrageous injustice, and treated their slaves like free laborers. We read too of slaves who fought valiantly beside their masters in the Confederate army, defended their owners from outlaws or plundering Yankee soldiers, and remembered the master's death as their first sorrow.

The dominant theme that threads the Gordian weave of these narratives and lends them so much relevance to contemporary America is racism. We ignore this theme at our peril, for no other social problem has cast so long a shadow over our history or cost us so dearly in lives ruined and treasure lost. Indeed, whoever would understand the black community in America today must seek to understand not only the conditions of slavery in which that community was born, but also the experience of racism. For it was racism that gave American slavery its distinctive character.

The twenty-nine life stories recorded here, in which racism either bristles overtly or smolders subliminally, should provoke the thoughtful reader to ask himself some difficult questions:

First and foremost, what, in essence, *is* racism? How closely are racial antipathies related to the perceived physical differences between races? Abraham Lincoln insisted repeatedly that "there is a physical difference between the white and black races which will forever forbid the two races living together on terms of social and political equality." If this is so, can America's relentless march toward complete racial equality proceed any faster than the glacial pace at which the two races are mixing blood?

Or, is racism, more subtly, an antipathy to certain cultural attitudes and tendencies that are rightly or wrongly attributed to a race—attitudes and tendencies the racist hates in others because he fears them in himself?

Furthermore, are racial reactions unpremeditated, like our spontaneous reactions to different foods, wines, or works of art? If so, is race the only sphere of life in which we are not entitled to any personal preferences? Are we, then, to include among racists any and all who profess to be attracted to another race, as for instance those who feel that "black is beautiful"? And if racial feelings are not spontaneous—if to feel racial antipathy "you have to be carefully taught," as the song goes—then who "taught" those who feel racial attraction?

Finally, just when and where did the kind of racism peculiar to America originate? If even the earliest colonists—those who themselves had immigrated to these shores—already shared a pervasive conviction that black people are fundamentally inferior to white people, could American racism have originated in America? And, allowing that it originated in the Old World, why was racial antipathy so much deeper and more pronounced among the British and northern European colonists than among immigrants from the Mediterranean world?

That the slave narratives invite us to grapple with these thorny questions and to ponder the enigma of racism in all its formidable depth, antiquity, and intransigence lends particular relevance and urgency to these life stories. And their historical significance is augmented by the fact that they dash forever the fantasy that white and black Americans would speedily merge into effectively unified communities, integrated both spiritually and socially, if only racial discrimination were to cease altogether.

By baring the granitic foundations of black society in America, these narratives offer a sobering glimpse of the cultural abyss that yet separates the two races. Among the final impressions that emerge from these pages and linger indelibly is that of the white man and the black, each doggedly confronting the other, each torn between rage and sardonic laughter at the ultimate preposterousness of their confrontation, both timelessly frozen in an attitude of mutual rejection, like the figures of two pugilists painted on a Grecian urn. It remains to be asked whether a nation thus divided against itself can realize the Jeffersonian promise of equality in any reasonable time frame.

At first glance, certain aspects of these memoirs are likely to strain the reader's credibility. Why, indeed, should any educated person expect to find important truths in a succession of life stories related by superannuated illiterates who earnestly insist that rusty nail water will cure warts and who speak without apparent guile of having been leered at by ghosts and ridden by witches?

Clearly, we must read these narratives with the heart, not merely with the cold light of reason. While so much in them has the ring of *sincerity,* we must often perceive the *truth* refracted through one or more layers of distortion.

Bear in mind that we, Western men educated in the Greek philosophical tradition, tamely—indeed unconsciously—acquiesce in the fierce Aristotelian distinction between what we can see with the eye and what we can "see" only with the mind's eye or imagination. That which is visible to the naked eye is for us real and must be said to exist. That which we imagine, or can see only with the mind's eye, is for us essentially unreal, does not exist, and must be branded as a kind of mental fabrication. Thus, we are trained to bridle our imaginations and to sharpen our capacities for empirical perception.

The former slaves were not accustomed to view the world so simplistically. Descending from African societies that were steeped in superstition and tribal lore, these witnesses, who lacked formal education, had nonetheless been conditioned to accord a heightened sense of reality to the spooks and hobgoblins that hooted in the green forests of their imaginations. Not surprisingly, the phantoms they imagined appeared more "real" to them than the mundane tangibles that they could see empirically.

That the former slaves were interviewed in the middle years of the Great Depression when they were among the oldest, poorest, and hungriest of Americans has also influenced these narratives profoundly. Hence the frantic preoccupation of the informants with food and cooking. Hence, also, the loving exaggeration with which the sumptuous "eats" on Old Master's plantation are frequently described. It is no wonder, surely, that these victims of history who had little or nothing to show for their sixty years of free labor, following Emancipation, should look back with misconceived nostalgia upon the certainties of life under slavery and entertain some illusions about the distant spring of their lives when they were strong and healthy.

Today, just as authoritarianism is the prevailing form of government on earth, so slavery, continually redefining and adapting itself, is alive and well in our midst. For while the physical ownership of human beings appears at last to have petered out worldwide, the execrable stratagems by which one man robs another of his bread and freedom linger tenaciously and vary but little. They include the oppressor's studied efforts to humiliate his victims, to brutally demonstrate his physical power over their bodies, to overawe them with fatuous displays of his own "natural" superiority, and, perhaps above all, to convince them, and more subtly himself, that without his benevolent despotism they would all be hopelessly lost. Such were the attitudes and practices which, over long usage, had merged in the minds of the slaveowners to form a classic repressive mentality. That these narratives afford so many candid glimpses of this mentality in operation is the final guarantee of their lasting historical importance.

To view these life stories exclusively from an ethical standpoint, however, is to rob them of their poignancy. True, the former slaves were, in a sense, testifying before the court of history, and most of them appear to have been aware of it; but, appropriately, their testimony is not primarily a catalogue of injuries. The quality of men's lives depends far more upon their spiritual resources than upon their circumstances, and the slaves had spiritual resources to spare.

More significantly, these memoirs are a window on the lost world of the Southern plantations. They afford us glimpse after candid glimpse of daily life in these feudal, self-sufficient communities, where a subject people and its masters wrought the necessities of life from the earth in an endless grinding race against the seasons. Etched out in these pages is an intricately rich and convincing mural of vanishing preindustrial America, which was soon to be swept away.

These narratives are indeed "the short and simple annals of the poor," and in their brevity and simplicity they are epigrammatic. Figuratively, they form a stage across which parades an arresting medley of personalities. Heroes and cowards, scoundrels and men of principle, the generous, the greedy, the meek and the truculent— each speaks his lines, walks through his little act. And the reader, as he frets his own hour upon the stage of life, may find it edifying to reflect upon this variegated parade that has preceded him.

Recorded in the picturesque vernacular of these ancient witnesses is a resounding triumph of the human spirit over one of history's most brazen crimes and most lamentable follies. Grievances abound in these pages, but there is little whimpering. The testimony of these venerable survivors stands forever as a thundering affirmation of life, regardless of the conditions under which it is lived.

James Mellon

In all the books that you have
studied, you never have studied
Negro history, have you? You studied
about the Indians and white folks,
but what did they tell you about the
Negro? If you want Negro history,
you will have to get it from somebody
who wore the shoe, and by and by, from
one to the other, you will get a book.

MR. REED, *former slave*

What I come through in life,
if I go down in meself for it, I could
make a book.

J. W. WHITE, *former slave*

Narratives

———◦┼ ┼◦———

GEORGIA BAKER

MARY REYNOLDS

KATIE ROWE

GEORGIA BAKER

WHAR was I born? Why I was born on de plantation of a great man. It was Marse Alec Stephens' plantation 'bout a mile and a half from Crawfordville, in Taliaferro County, Georgia. Mary and Grandison Tilly was my ma and pa. Ma was cook up at de big house and she died when I was jus' a little gal. Pa was a field hand, and he belonged to Marse Britt Tilly.

Dere was four of us chillun: me, and Mary, and Frances, and Mack. Marse Alec let Marse Jim Johnson have Mack for his bodyguard. Frances, she wukked in de field, and Mary was de baby; she was too little to wuk. Me, I was fourteen years old when de War was over. I swept yards, toted water to de field, and played round de house and yard wid de rest of de chillun.

De long log houses what us lived in was called "shotgun" houses 'cause dey had three rooms, one behind de other in a row lak de barrel of a shotgun. All de chillun slept in one end room and de grown folks slept in de other end room. De kitchen whar us cooked and et was de middle room.

Beds was made out of pine poles put together wid cords. Dem wheat straw mattresses was for grown folks mostly, 'cause nigh all de chillun slept on pallets. How-some-ever, dere was some few slave chillun what had beds to sleep on. Pillows! Dem days, us never knowed what pillows was. Gals slept on one side of de room and boys on de other, in de chillun's room. Uncle Jim, he was de bed maker, and he made up a heap of little beds lak what dey calls cots now.

Becky and Stafford Stephens was my grandma and grandpa. Marse Alec bought 'em in Old Virginny. I don't know what my grandma done, 'cause she died 'fore I was borned, but I 'members Grandpa

PLATE 2: A former slave.

Stafford well enough. I can see him now. He was a old man what slept on a trundle bed in de kitchen, and all he done was to set by de fire all day wid a switch in his hand and tend de chillun whilst deir mammies was at wuk. Chillun minded better dem days dan dey does now. Grandpa Stafford never had to holler at 'em but one time. Dey knowed dey would git de switch next if dey didn't behave.

Now dere you is axin' 'bout dat somepin'-t'-eat us had dem days! Oh, yessum! Marse Alec had plenty for his slaves to eat. Dere was meat, bread, collard greens, snap beans, taters, peas, all sorts of dried fruit, and just lots of milk and butter. Marse Alec had twelve cows and dat's whar I learned to love milk so good. De same Uncle Jim what made our beds made our wooden bowls what dey kept filled wid bread and milk for de chillun all day. You might want to call dat place whar Marse Alec had our vegetables raised a gyarden, but it looked more lak a big field to me, it was so big. You jus' ought to have seed dat dere fireplace whar dey cooked all us had to eat. It was one sho'-'nuf big somepin', all full of pots, skillets, and ovens. Dey warn't never 'lowed to git full of smut neither. Dey had to be cleant and shined up atter evvy meal, and dey sho' was pretty hangin' dar in dat big old fireplace.

Marse Alec growed all his corn on his Cougar Crick plantation. He planned for evvything us needed and dere warn't but mighty little dat he didn't have raised to take keer of our needs.

On Sundays, whenever Marse Alec was home, he done lots of readin' out of a great big old book. I didn't know what it was, but he was pow'ful busy wid it. He never had no parties or dancin' dat I knows 'bout, but he was all de time havin' dem big 'portant mens at his house talkin' 'bout de business what tuk him off from home so much. I used to see Lawyer Toombs dere heaps of times. He was a big, fine-lookin' man. Another big lawyer was all de time comin' dar too, but I done lost his name. Marse Alec had so awful much sense in his haid dat folkses said it stunted his growin'. Anyhow, long as he lived he warn't no bigger den a boy.

De fust time I ever seed Marse Alec to know who he was I warn't more'n six years old. Uncle Stafford had went fishin' and cotched de nicest mess of fish you ever seed. He cleant 'em and put 'em in a pan of water, and told me to take 'em up to de big house to Marse Alec. I was skeered when I went in de big house yard and axed what looked like a little boy whar Marse Alec was. And I was wuss skeered when he said, "Dis is Marse Alec you is talkin' to. What you want?" I tole him Uncle Stafford sont him de fishes, and he tell me, "Take 'em to de kitchen and tell Liza to cook 'em for me." I sho' ain't never gwine to forgit dat.

One day, dey sent me wid a bucket of water to de field, and I had to go through de peach orchard. I et so many peaches I was 'most daid when I got back to de house. Dey had to drench me down wid sweet milk, and from dat day to dis I ain't never lakked peaches. From den on, Marse Alec called me "de peach gal."

Marse Alec warn't home much of de time, but when he was dar he used to walk down to de cabins and laugh and talk to his niggers. He used to sing a song for de slave chillun dat run somepin' lak dis:

> Walk light ladies,
> De cake's all dough,
> You needn't mind de weather,
> If de wind don't blow.

Us didn't know when he was a-singin' dat tune to us chillun dat when us growed up us would be cakewalkin'* to de same song.

George and Mack was de hunters. When dey went huntin' dey brought back jus' evvything: possums, rabbits, coons, squirrels, birds, and wild turkeys. Yessum, wild turkeys is some sort of birds, I reckon, but when us talked about birds to eat, us meant part'idges. Some folkses calls 'em quails. De fishes us had in summertime was a sight to see. Us sho' et good, dem days. Now us jus' eats what-some-ever us can git.

Summertime, us jus' wore what us wanted to. Dresses was made wid full skirts gathered onto tight-fittin' waisties. Winter clothes was good and warm; dresses made of yarn cloth made up jus' lak dem summertime clothes, and petticoats and draw's made out of osnaburg.† Chillun what was big enough done de spinnin', and Aunt Betsey and Aunt Finny, dey wove most evvy night till dey rung de

---

*A popular dance in the antebellum South.
†A durable cloth.

bell at ten o'clock for us to go to bed. Us made bolts and bolts of cloth evvy year.

Us went bar'foots in summer, but bless your sweet life us had good shoes in winter and wore good stockin's, too. It tuk three shoemakers for our plantation. Dey was Uncle Isom, Uncle Jim, and Uncle Stafford. Dey made up holestock shoes for de 'omans [women] and gals and brass-toed brogans for de mens and boys. Lordy, didn't I tell you what sort of shoes holestock shoes is? Dey was de shoes de 'omans wore, and dey had extra pieces on de sides so us wouldn't knock holes in 'em too quick.

Us had pretty white dresses for Sunday. Marse Alec wanted evvy-body on his place dressed up dat day. He sent his houseboy, Uncle Harris, down to de cabins evvy Sunday mornin' to tell evvy slave to clean hisself up. Dey warn't never give no chance to forgit. Dere was a big old room set aside for a washroom. Folkses laughs at me now 'cause I ain't never stopped takin' a bath evvy Sunday mornin'.

Did I tell you dat de man what looked atter Marse Alec's business was his fust cousin? Marse Lordnorth Stephens was de boss on Marse Alec's plantation. 'Course, Marse Alec owned us and he was our sho'-'nuf marster. Neither one of 'em ever married. Marse Lordnorth was a good man, but he didn't have no use for 'omans. He was a sissy. Dere warn't no marster nowhar no better den our Marse Alec Stephens, but he never stayed home enough to tend to things hisself much, 'cause he was all de time too busy on de outside. He was de President* or somepin' of our side durin' de War.

Uncle Pierce went wid Marse Alec evvywhar he went. His dog "Rio" had more sense den most folkses. Marse Alec, he was all de time havin' big mens visit him up at the big house. One time, out in de yard, him and one of dem 'portant mens got in a argyment 'bout somepin'. Us chillun snuck up close to hear what dey was makin' such a ruckus 'bout. I heared Marse Alec say, "I got more sense in my big toe dan you is got in your whole body." And he was right: he did have more sense den most folkses. Ain't I been a-tellin' you he was de President or somepin' lak dat, dem days?

Ma, she was Marse Alec's cook and looked atter de house. Atter she died, Marse Lordnorth got Mrs. Mary Berry, from Habersham

*Vice President of the Confederacy.

County, to keep house at de big house, but Aunt Liza, she done de cookin' atter Mis' Mary got dar. Us little niggers sho' did love Mis' Mary. Us called her "Mammy Mary" sometimes. Mis' Mary had three sons and one of 'em was named Jeff Davis. I 'members when dey come and got him and tuk him off to war. Marse Lordnorth built a four-room house on de plantation for Mis' Mary and her boys. Evvybody loved our Mis' Mary, 'cause she was so good and sweet, and dere warn't nothin' us wouldn't have done for her.

No, Lord! Marse Lordnorth never needed no overseer or no carriage driver neither. Uncle Jim was de head man what got de niggers up evvy mornin' and started 'em off to wuk right. Marse Lordnorth never had no certain early time for his slaves to git up nor no special late time for 'em to quit wuk. De hours dey wukked was 'cordin' to how much wuk was ahead to be done. Folkses in Crawfordville called us "Stephens' free niggers."

De big house sho' was a pretty place, a-settin' up on a high hill. De squirrels was so tame dar dey jus' played all round de yard. Marse Alec's dog is buried in dat yard.

No, m'am, I never knowed how many acres dere was on de plantation us lived on, and Marse Alec had other places, too. He had land scattered evvywhar. Lord, dere was a heap of niggers on dat place, and all of us was kin to one another. Grandma Becky and Grandpa Stafford was de fust slaves Marse Alec ever had, and dey sho' had a passel of chillun.

One thing sho': Marse Lordnorth wouldn't keep no bright-colored nigger on dat plantation, if he could help it. Aunt Mary was a bright-colored nigger and dey said dat Marse John, Marse Lordnorth's brother, was her pa; but anyhow Marse Lordnorth never had no use for her, 'cause she was a bright-colored nigger.

Us minded Marse Lordnorth—us had to do dat—but he let us do pretty much as us pleased. Us never had no sorry piece of a marster. He was a good man and he made a sho'-'nuf good marster. I never seed no nigger git a beatin', and what's more, I never heared of nothin' lak dat on our place. Dere was a jail in Crawfordville, but none of us niggers on Marse Alec' place warn't never put in it.

No, Lord!—none of us niggers never knowed nothin' 'bout readin' and writin'. Dere warn't no school for niggers, den, and I ain't never been to school a day in my life. Niggers was more skeered of newspapers dan dey is of snakes now, and us never knowed what a Bible was, dem days.

Niggers never had no churches of deir own den. Dey went to de white folkses' churches and set in de gallery. One Sunday, when me and my sister Frances went to church, I found fifty cents in Confederate money and showed it to her. She tuk it away from me. Dat's de onliest money I seed durin' slavery time. 'Course, you knows dey throwed Confederate money away for trash atter de War was over. Den us young chaps used to play wid it.

I never went to no baptisin's nor no funerals neither, den. Funerals warn't de style. When a nigger died dem days, dey jus' put his body in a box and buried it. I 'members very well when Aunt Sally and Aunt Catherine died, but I was little den, and I didn't take it in what dey done 'bout buryin' 'em.

None of Marse Alec's slaves never run away to no North, 'cause he was so good to 'em dey never wanted to leave him. De onliest nigger what left Marse Alec's place was Uncle Dave, and he wouldn't have left 'cept he got in trouble wid a white 'oman. You needn't ax me her name, 'cause I ain't gwine to tell it, but I knows it well as I does my own name. Anyhow, Marse Alec give Uncle Dave some money and told him to leave, and nobody never seed him atter dat.

Oh, yessum!—us heared 'bout 'em, but none of us never seed no patterollers* on Marse Alec's plantation. He never 'lowed 'em on his land, and he let 'em know dat he kept his slaves supplied wid passes whenever dey wanted to go places, so as dey could come and go when dey got good and ready. Thursday and Sa'day nights was de main nights dey went off. Uncle Stafford's wife was Mis' Mary Stephens' cook, Uncle Jim's wife lived on de Finley place, and Uncle Isom's belonged to de Rollises; so dey had regular passes all de time and no patterollers never bothered 'em none.

Whenever Marse Alec or Marse Lordnorth wanted to send a message, dey jus' put George or Mack on a mule and sont 'em on. But one thing sho': dere warn't no slave knowed what was in dem letters.

Most times, when slaves went to deir quarters at night, de mens rested, but sometimes dey holped de 'omans cyard [card] de cotton

*Patrollers.

9

and wool. Young folkses frolicked, sung songs, and visited from cabin to cabin. When dey got behind wid de field wuk, slaves sometimes wukked atter dinner Sa'days, but dat warn't often.

But, oh, dem Sa'day nights! Dat was when slaves got together and danced. George, he blowed de quills,* and he sho' could blow good dance music on 'em. Dem niggers would jus' dance down. Dere warn't no foolishment 'lowed atter ten o'clock no night. Sundays we went to church and visited round, but folkses didn't spend as much time gaddin' 'bout lak dey does now'days.

Christmas Day! Oh, what a time us niggers did have dat day! Marse Lordnorth and Marse Alec give us evvything you could name to eat: cake of all kinds, fresh meat, lightbread, turkeys, chickens, ducks, geese, and all kinds of wild game. Dere was allus plenty of pecans, apples, and dried peaches, too, at Christmas. No, m'am, us never knowed nothin' 'bout Santa Claus till atter de War.

Marse Alec would call de grown folkses to de big house early on Christmas mornin' and pass round a big pewter pitcher full of whiskey. Den he would put a little whiskey in dat same pitcher and fill it wid sweetened water and give dat to us chillun. Us called dat "toddy" or "dram." Marse Alec allus had plenty of good whiskey, 'cause Uncle Willis made it up for him and it was made jus' right.

De night atter Christmas Day, us pulled syrup candy, drunk more liquor, and danced. Us had a big time for a whole week, and den, on New Year's Day, us done a little wuk jus' to start de year right. Us feasted dat day on fresh meat, plenty of cake, and whiskey. Dere was allus a big pile of ash-roasted taters on hand to go wid dat good old baked meat. Us allus tried to raise enough taters to last all through de winter, 'cause niggers sho' does love dem sweet taters.

No, m'am, dere warn't no special corn-shuckin's and cotton-pickin's on Marse Alec's place. But, of course, dey did quilt in de winter, 'cause dere had to be lots of quiltin' done for all dem slaves to have plenty of warm kivver. And you know, lady, 'omans can quilt better if dey gits a passel of 'em together to do it. Marse Alec and Marse Lordnorth never 'lowed deir slaves to mix up wid other folkses' business much.

*A musical instrument.

Oh, Lord!—us never played no games in slavery times, 'cept jus' to run around in a ring and pat our hands. I never sung no songs, 'cause I warn't no singer. And don't talk 'bout no Raw Head and Bloody Bones* or nothin' lak dat. Dey used to skeer us chillun so bad 'bout dem sort of things dat us used to lay in bed at night a-shakin' lak us was havin' chills.

I've seed plenty of ha'nts right here in Athens. Not long atter I had left Crawfordville and moved to Athens, I had been in bed jus' a little while one night and was jus' dozin' off to sleep when I woke up and sat right sprang up in bed. I seed a white man, dressed in white, standin' before me. I sho' didn't say nothin' to him, for I was too skeered. De very last time I went to a dance, somepin' got atter me and skeered me so my hair riz up till I couldn't git my hat on my haid, and dat cyored [cured] me of gwine to dances. I ain't never been to no more sich doin's.

Old Marster was powerful good to his niggers when dey got sick. He had 'em seed atter soon as it was 'ported to him dat dey was ailin'. Yessum, dere warn't nothin' short 'bout our good marsters, 'deed dere warn't! Grandpa Stafford had a sore laig and Marse Lordnorth looked atter him and had Uncle Jim dress dat pore old sore laig evvy day. Slaves didn't git sick as often as niggers does now'days. Mammy Mary had all sorts of teas made up for us, 'cordin' to whatever ailment us had. Boneset tea was for colds. De fust thing dey allus done for sore throat was to give us tea made of red oak bark wid alum. Scurvy grass tea cleant us out in de springtime, and dey made us wear little sacks of assfiddy† round our necks to keep off lots of sorts of miseries. Some folkses hung de left hind foot of a mole on a string round deir babies' necks to make 'em teethe easier. I never done nothin' lak dat to my babies 'cause I never believed in no such foolishment. Some babies is jus' natchelly gwine to teethe easier den others, anyhow.

I 'members jus' as good as if it was yesterday what Mammy Mary said when she told us de fust news of our freedom. "You all is free now," she said. "You don't none of you belong to Mister Lordnorth nor Mister Alec no more. But I does hope you will all stay wid 'em,

---

*Mythical horror figures parents told stories about in order to scare children into obedience.
†Asafoetida.

'cause dey will allus be jus' as good to you as dey has done bin in de past." Me, I warn't even studyin' nothin' 'bout leavin' Marse Alec, but Sarah Ann and Aunt Mary, dey throwed down deir hoes and jus' whooped and hollered 'cause dey was so glad. When dem Yankees come to our place, Mammy Mary axed 'em if dey warn't tired of war. "What does you know 'bout war?" dey axed her right back. "No, us won't never git tired of doin' good."

Whilst Marse Alec was President or somepin', he got sick and had to come back home, and it warn't long atter dat 'fore de Surrender. Allen was 'pinted to watch for de bluecoats. When dey come to take Marse Alec off, dey was all over de place wid deir guns. Us niggers hollered and cried and tuk on pow'ful, 'cause us sho' thought dey was gwine to kill him on account of his bein' such a high-up man on de side what dey was fightin'. All de niggers followed 'em to de depot when dey tuk Marse Alec and Uncle Pierce away. Dey kept Marse Alec in prison off somewhar a long time, but dey sont Uncle Pierce back home 'fore long.

I seed Jeff Davis when dey brung him through Crawfordville on de train. Dey had him all fastened up wid chains. Dey told me dat a nigger 'oman put pizen in Jeff Davis's somepin'-t'-eat and dat was what kilt him. One thing sho': our Marse Alec warn't pizened by nobody. He was comin' from de field one day when a big old heavy gate fell down on him, and even if he did live a long time afterwards, dat was what was de cause of his death.

I seed Uncle Pierce 'fore he died and us sot and talked and cried 'bout Marse Alec. Yessum, us sho' did have de best marster in de world. If ever a man went to Heaven, Marse Alec did. I sho' does wish our good old marster was livin' now.

I stayed on wid my two good marsters till three years atter de War, and den went to wuk for Marse Tye Elder, in Crawfordville. Atter dat I wukked for Miss Puss King, and when she left Crawfordville I come on here to Athens and wukked for Miss Tildy Upson, on Prince Avenue. Den I went to Atlanta to wuk for Miss Ruth Elliott. Miss Ruth was a niece of Abraham Lincoln's. Her father was President Lincoln's brother,* and he was a Methodist preacher what lived in Mailpack, New York. I went evvywhar wid Miss Ruth. When me

*The narrator is mistaken. President Lincoln had no brother.

12

and Miss Ruth was in Philadelphia, I got sick and she sent me home to Athens, and I done been here wid my daughter ever since.

Lordy, Miss!—I ain't never been married, but I did live wid Major Baker eighteen years, and us had five chillun. Dey is all daid but two. Niggers didn't pay so much 'tention to gittin' married dem days as dey does now. I stays here wid my gal, Ida Baker. My son lives in Cleveland, Ohio. My fust child was borned when I warn't but fourteen years old. De War ended in April and she was borned in November of dat year. Now, Miss, I ain't never told but one white 'oman who her pa was, so you needn't start axin' me nothin' 'bout dat. She had done been walkin' evvywhar 'fore she died when she was jus' ten months old, and I'm a-tellin' you de truth when I say she had more sense dan a heap of white chillun has when dey is lots older den she was.

Whilst I was off in New York wid Miss Ruth, Major, he up and got married. I reckon he's daid by now. I don't keer nohow, atter de way he done me. I made a good livin' for Major till he married again. I seed de 'oman he married once.

Yes, m'am, I sho' would rather have slavery days back if I could have my same good marsters, 'cause I never had no hard times den lak I went through atter dey give us freedom. I ain't never got over not bein' able to see Marse Alec no more. I was livin' at Marse Tye Elder's when de gate fell on Marse Alec, and he was crippled and lamed up from dat time on till he died. He got to be Governor of Georgia whilst he was crippled. When he got hurt by dat gate, smallpox was evvywhar and dey wouldn't let me go to see 'bout him. Dat most killed me, 'cause I did want to go see if dere was somepin' I could do for him.

Lord have mussy, Miss! I had a time jinin' up wid de church. I was in Mailpack, New York, wid Miss Ruth when I had de urge to jine up. I told Miss Ruth 'bout it and she said, "Dere ain't no Baptist church in ten miles of here." "Lord have mussy!" I said. "Miss Ruth, what I gwine do? Dese is all Methodist churches up here and I jus' can't jine up wid no Methodists." "Yes you can," she snapped at me, " 'cause my own pa's a-holdin' a 'vival in dis very town, and de Methodist Church is de best anyhow."

Well, I went and jined de Reverend Lincoln's Methodist church, but I never felt right 'bout it. Den us went to Philadelphia, and soon as I could find a Baptist church dar, I jined up wid it. Northern churches ain't lak our Southern churches, 'cause de black and white folkses all belong to de same church dar and goes to church together. On dat account, I still didn't feel lak I had jined de church. Bless your sweet life, Honey, when I come back to de South, I was quick as I could be to jine up wid a good old Southern Baptist church. I sho' didn't mean to live outdoors, 'specially atter I dies.

Miss, I done told you all I knows 'bout Marse Alec and dem days when I lived on his plantation. I thanks you a lot for dat purty yaller dress, and I hopes you comes back to see me again sometime.

MARY REYNOLDS

M Y PAW'S name was Tom Vaughn and he was from the North, born free man and lived and died free to the end of his days. He wasn't no eddicated man, but he was what he calls himself, a piano man. He told me once he lived in New York and Chicago, and he built the insides of pianos and knew how to make them play in tune. He said some white folks from the South told him if he'd come with them to the South he'd find a lot of work to do with pianos in them parts, and he come with them.

He saw my maw on the Kilpatrick place and her man was dead. He told Dr. Kilpatrick, my massa, he'd buy my maw and her three chillun with all the money he had, iffen he'd sell her. But Dr. Kilpatrick was never one to sell any but the old niggers who was only part workin' in the fields and past their breedin' times. So my paw marries my maw and works the fields, same as any other nigger. They had six gals: Martha and Pamela and Josephine and Ellen and Katherine and me.

I was born same time as Mis' Sara Kilpatrick. Dr. Kilpatrick's first wife and my maw come to their time right together. Mis' Sara's maw died and they brung Mis' Sara to suck with me. It's a thing we ain't never forgot. My maw's name was Sallie and Mis' Sara allus looked with kindness on my maw. We sucked till we was a fair size and played together, which wasn't no common thing. None the other li'l niggers played with the white chillun. But Mis' Sara loved me so good.

I was jus' 'bout big 'nuf to start playin' with a broom, to go 'bout sweepin' up and not even half doin' it, when Dr. Kilpatrick sold me. They was a old white man in Trinity and his wife died, and he didn't have chick or child or slave or nothin'. Massa sold me cheap, 'cause he didn't want Mis' Sara to play with no nigger young-un. That old man bought me a big doll and went off and left me all day, with the door open. I jus' sot on the floor and played with that doll. I used to cry. He'd come home and give me somethin' to eat and then go to bed, and I slep' on the foot of the bed with him. I was scairt all the time in the dark. He never did close the door.

Mis' Sara pined and sickened. Massa done what he could, but they wasn't no peartness in her. She got sicker and sicker, and Massa brung 'nother doctor. He say, "You li'l gal is grievin' the life out her body and she sho' gwine die iffen you don't do somethin' 'bout it." Mis' Sara says over and over, "I want Mary." Massa say to the doctor, "That's a li'l nigger young-un I done sold." The doctor tells him he better git me back iffen he wants to save the life of his child. Dr. Kilpatrick has to give a big plenty more to git me back than what he sold me for, but Mis' Sara plumps up right off and grows into fine health.

Then Massa married a rich lady from Mississippi and they has chillun for company to Mis' Sara, and seem like for a time she forgits me.

Massa Kilpatrick wasn't no piddlin' man. He was a man of plenty. He had a big house with more style to it than a crib, but it could room plenty people. He was a medicine doctor, and they was rooms in the second story for sick folks what come to lay in. It would take two days to go all over the land he owned. He had cattle and stock and sheep and more'n a hundred slaves and more besides. He bought the bes' of niggers near every time the spec'lators come that way. He'd make a swap of the old ones and give money for young ones what could work.

He raised corn and cotton and cane and taters and goobers,* 'sides the peas and other feedin' for the niggers. I 'member I helt a hoe handle mighty onsteady when they put a old woman to larn me and some other chillun to scrape the fields. That old woman would be frantic. She'd show me and then turn 'bout to show some other li'l nigger, and I'd have the young corn cut clean as the grass. She says,

*Peanuts.

PLATE 3: Slave nurse with young master.

"For the love of Gawd, you better larn it right, or Solomon will beat the breath out you body." Old man Solomon was the nigger driver.

Slavery was the worst days that was ever seed in the world. They was things past tellin', but I got the scars on my old body to show to this day. I seed worse than what happened to me. I seed them put the men and women in the stock with they hands screwed down through holes in the board and they feets tied together and they naked behinds to the world. Solomon the overseer beat them with a big whip and Massa look on. The niggers better not stop in the fields when they hear them yellin'. They cut the flesh 'most to the bones, and some they was, when they taken them out of stock and put them on the beds, they never got up again.

When a nigger died, they let his folks come out the fields to see him afore he died. They buried him the same day—take a big plank and bust it with a ax in the middle 'nuf to bend it back, and put the dead nigger in betwixt it. They'd cart him down to the graveyard on the place and not bury him deep 'nuf that buzzards wouldn't come circlin' round. Niggers mourns now, but in them days they wasn't no time for mournin'.

The conch shell blowed afore daylight and all hands better git out for roll call or Solomon bust the door down and git them out. It was work hard, git beatin's, and half-fed. They brung the vittles and water to the fields on a slide pulled by a old mule. Plenty times they was only a half barrel water—and it stale and hot—for all us niggers on the hottes' days. Mostly we ate pickled pork and corn bread and peas and beans and taters. They never was as much as we needed.

The time I hated the most was pickin' cotton when the frost was on the bolls. My hands git sore and crack open and bleed. We'd have a li'l fire in the fields, and iffen the ones with tender hands couldn't stand it no longer, we'd run and warm our hands a li'l bit. When I could steal a tater, I used to slip it in the ashes, and when I'd run to the fire I'd take it out and eat it on the sly.

In the cabins it was nice and warm. They was built of pine boardin', and they was one long row of them up the hill back of the big house. Near one side of the cabins was a fireplace. They'd bring in two, three big logs and put them on the fire and they'd last near a week. The beds was made out of puncheons [poles] fitted in holes bored in the wall, and planks laid 'cross them poles. We had tickin' mattresses filled with corn shucks. Sometimes the men built chairs at night. We didn't know much 'bout havin' nothin', though.

Sometimes Massa let niggers have a li'l patch. They'd raise taters or goobers. They like to have them to help fill out on the vittles. Taters roasted in the ashes was the best tastin' eatin' I ever had. I could die better satisfied to have jus' one more tater roasted in hot ashes. The niggers had to work the patches at night and dig the taters and goobers at night. Then, if they wanted to sell any in town, they'd have to git a pass to go. They had to go at night, 'cause they couldn't ever spare a hand from the fields.

Once in a while they'd give us a li'l piece of Sat'day evenin' to wash our clothes in the branch. We hanged them on the ground in the woods to dry. They was a place to wash clothes not far from the well, but they was so many niggers they couldn't all git round to it on Sundays. When they'd git through with the clothes on Sat'day evenin's, the niggers which sold they goobers and taters brung fiddles and guitars and come out and play. I was plenty biggity and liked to cut a step.

We was scairt of Solomon and his whip, though, and he didn't like frolickin'. He didn't like for us niggers to pray, either. We never heared of no church, but us have prayin' in the cabins. We'd set on the floor and pray with our heads down low and sing low, but if Solomon heared, he'd come and beat on the wall with the stock of his whip. He'd say, "I'll come in there and tear the hide off you back." But some the old niggers tell us we got to pray to Gawd that he don't think different of the blacks and the whites. I know that Solomon is burnin' in hell today, and it pleasures me to know it.

Once my maw and paw taken me and Katherine after night to slip to 'nother place to a prayin'-and-singin'. A nigger man with white beard told us a day am comin' when niggers only be slaves of Gawd. We prays for the end of trib'lation and the end of beatin's and for shoes that fit our feet. We prayed that us niggers could have all we wanted to eat, and special for fresh meat. Some the old ones say we have to bear all, 'cause that all we can do. Some say they was glad to [wished for] the time they's dead, 'cause they'd rather rot in the ground than have the beatin's. What I hated most was when they'd beat me and I didn't know what they beat me for, and I hated them strippin' me naked as the day I was born.

When we's comin' back from that prayin', I thunk I heared the nigger dogs and somebody on horseback. I say, "Maw, it's them nigger hounds, and they'll eat us up." You could hear them old hounds and sluts a-bayin'. Maw listens and say, "Sho' 'nuf, them dogs am runnin' and Gawd help us!" Then she and Paw talk, and they take us to a fence corner and stands us up 'gainst the rails and say, "Don't move, and if anyone comes near, don't breathe loud." They went to the woods, so the hounds chase them and not git us. Me and Katherine stand there, holdin' hands, shakin' so we can hardly stand. We hears the hounds come nearer, but we don't move. They goes after Paw and Maw, but they circles round to the cabins and gits in. Maw say it's the power of Gawd.

In them days I weared shirts, like all the young-uns. They had collars and come below the knees and was split up the sides. That's all we weared in hot weather. The men weared jeans and the women gingham. Shoes was the worstes' trouble. We weared rough russets when it got cold, and it seem powerful strange they'd never git them to fit. Once, when I was a young gal, they got me a new pair with all-brass studs in the toes. They was too li'l for me, but I had to wear them. The brass trimmin's cut into my ankles and them places got mis'ble bad. I rubs tallow in them sore places and wrops rags round them, and my sores got worser and worser. The scars are there to this day.

I wasn't sick much, though. Some the niggers had chills and fever a lot, but they hadn't discovered so many diseases then as now. Dr. Kilpatrick give sick niggers ipecac and asafoetida and oil and turpentine and black fever pills.

They was a cabin called the spinnin' house, and two looms and two spinnin' wheels was goin' all the time, and two nigger women sewing all the time. It took plenty sewin' to make all the things for a place so big. Once Massa went to Baton Rouge and brung back a yaller gal dressed in fine style. She was a seamster nigger. He builds her a house 'way from the quarters and she done fine sewin' for the whites.

Us niggers knowed the doctor took a black woman quick as he did a white, and took any on his place he wanted, and he took them often. But mostly the chillun born on the place looked like niggers. Aunt Cheyney allus say four of hers was Massa's, but he didn't give them no mind.

This yaller gal breeds so fast she gits a mess of white young-uns. She larnt them fine manners and combs out they hair. Once't two of them goes down the hill to the dollhouse where the Kilpatrick chillun am playin'. They wants to go in the dollhouse, and one the Kilpatrick boys say, "That's for white chillun." They say, "We ain't no niggers, 'cause we got the same daddy you has, and he comes to see us near every day and fetches us clothes and things from town." They is fussin' and Missy Kilpatrick is listenin' out her chamber window. She heard them white niggers say, "He is our daddy and we call him 'Daddy' when he comes to our house to see our mama."

When Massa come home that evenin' his wife hardly say nothin' to him, and he ask her what the matter, and she tells him, "Since you asks me, I'm studyin' in my mind 'bout them white young-uns of that yaller nigger wench from Baton Rouge." He say, "Now, Honey, I fetches that gal jus' for you, 'cause she a fine seamster." She say, "It look kind of funny they got the same kind of hair and eyes as my chillun, and they got a nose looks like yours." He say, "Honey, you jus' payin' 'tention to talk of li'l chillun that ain't got no mind to what they say." She say, "Over in Mississippi I got a home and plenty with my daddy, and I got that in my mind."

Well, she didn't never leave and Massa bought her a fine new span of surrey hosses. But she don't never have no more chillun and she ain't so cordial with the Massa. Margaret, that yaller gal, has more white young-uns, but they don't never go down the hill no more to the big house.

Aunt Cheyney was jus' out of bed with a sucklin' baby one time, and she runs away. Some say that was 'nother baby of Massa's breedin'. She don't come to the house to nurse her baby, so they misses her and old Solomon gits the nigger hounds and takes her trail. They gits near her and she grabs a limb and tried to heist herself in a tree, but them dogs grab her and pull her down. The men hollers them onto her, and the dogs tore her naked and et the breasts plumb off her body. She got well and lived to be a old woman, but 'nother woman has to suck her baby, 'cause she ain't got no sign of breasts no more.

They give all the niggers fresh meat on Christmas and a plug tobacco all round. The highes' cotton picker gits a suit of clothes, and all the women what had twins that year gits a outfittin' of clothes for the twins and a double warm blanket.

Seems like after I got bigger, I 'member more 'n more niggers run away. They's most allus cotched. Massa used to hire out his niggers for wage hands. One time he hired me and a nigger boy, Turner, to work for some ornery white trash named Kidd. One day Turner goes off and don't come back. Old man Kidd say I knowed 'bout it, and he tied my wrists together and stripped me. He hanged me by the wrists from a limb on a tree and spraddled my legs round the trunk and tied my feet together. Then he beat me. He beat me worser than I ever been beat before, and I faints dead away. When I come to, I'm in bed. I didn't care so much iffen I died.

I don't know how much time passed, but Mis' Sara come to me. Some white folks done git word to her. Mr. Kidd tries to talk hisself out of it, but Mis' Sara fetched me home when I'm well 'nuf to move. She took me in a cart and my maw takes care of me. Massa looks me over good and says I'll git well, but I'm ruin' for breedin' chillun.

After while I taken a notion to marry, and Massa and Missy marries us same as all the niggers. They stands inside the house with a broom held crosswise of the door, and we stands outside. Missy puts a li'l wreath on my head they kept there, and we steps over the broom into the house. Now that's all they was to the marryin'. After freedom I git married and has it put in the Book by a preacher.

One day we was workin' in the fields and hears the conch shell blow, so we all goes to the back gate of the big house. Massa am there. He say, "Call the roll for every nigger big 'nuf to walk and I wants them to go to the river and wait there. They's gwine be a show and I wants you to see it." They was a big boat down there, done built up on the sides with boards and holes in the boards and a big gun barrel stickin' through every hole. We ain't never seed nothin' like that. Massa goes up the plank onto the boat and comes out on the boat porch. He say, "This am a Yankee boat." He goes inside and the water wheels starts movin' and that boat goes movin' up the river and they says it goes to Natchez.

The boat wasn't more'n out of sight when a big drove of sojers comes into town. They say they's Fed'rals. More'n half the niggers goes off with them sojers, but I goes on back home 'cause of my old mammy.

Next day them Yankees is swarmin' the place. Some the niggers wants to show them somethin'. I follows to the woods. The niggers shows them sojers a big pit in the ground, bigger'n a big house. It is got wooden doors that lifts up, but the top am sodded and grass growin' on it, so you couldn't tell it. In that pit is stock, hosses and cows and mules and money and chinaware and silver and a mess of stuff them sojers takes.

We jus' sot on the place doin' nothin' till the white folks comes home. Mis' Sara come out to the cabin and say she wants to read a letter to my mammy. It come from Louis Carter, which is brother to my mammy, and he done follow the Fed'rals to Galveston. A white man done write the letter for him. It am tored in half, and Massa done that. The letter say Louis am workin' in Galveston and wants Mammy to come with us, and he'll pay our way. Mis' Sara say Massa swear, "Damn Louis Carter. I ain't gwine tell Sallie nothin'." And he starts to tear the letter up, but she won't let him and she reads it to Mammy.

After a time Massa takes all his niggers what wants to go to Texas with him and Mammy gits to Galveston and dies there. I goes with Massa to the Tennessee Colony and then to Navasota. Mis' Sara marries Mr. T. Coleman and goes to El Paso. She wrote and told me to come to her and I allus meant to go.

My husband and me farmed round for times, and then I done housework and cookin' for many years. I come to Dallas and cooked seven year for one white family. My husband died years ago. I guess Mis' Sara been dead these long years. I allus kep' my years by Mis' Sara's years, 'count we is born so close.

I been blind and mos' helpless for five year. I'm gittin' mighty enfeeblin', and I ain't walked outside the door for a long time back. I sets and 'members the times in the world. I 'members now clear as yesterday things I forgot for a long time. I 'members 'bout the days of slavery and I don't 'lieve they ever gwine have slaves no more on this earth. I think Gawd done took that burden offen his black chillun and I'm aimin' to praise him for it to his face in the days of Glory what ain't so far off.

KATIE ROWE

I CAN set on de gallery, whar de sunlight shine bright, and sew a powerful fine seam when my grandchillun wants a special purty dress for de school doings, but I ain't worth much for nothing else, I reckon.

These same old eyes seen powerful lot of tribulations in my time, and when I shets 'em now I can see lots of li'l chillun, jest lak my grandchillun, toting hoes bigger dan dey is, and dey pore little black hands and legs bleeding whar dey was scratched by de brambledy weeds, and whar dey got whuppings 'cause dey didn't git done all de work de overseer set out for 'em.

I was one of dem little slave gals my own self, and I never seen nothing but work and tribulations till I was a grown up woman, jest about.

De niggers had hard traveling on de plantation whar I was born and raised, 'cause Old Master live in town and jest had de overseer on de place, but iffen he had lived out dar hisself, I speck it been as bad, 'cause he was a hard driver his own self.

He git biting mad when de Yankees have dat big battle at Pea Ridge and scatter de 'Federates all down through our country all bleeding and tied up and hungry, and he jest mount on his hoss and ride out to de plantation whar we all hoeing corn. He ride up and tell old man Saunders—dat de overseer—to bunch us all up round de lead row man—dat my own uncle, Sandy—and den he tell us de law!

"You niggers been seeing de 'Federate soldiers coming by here looking purty raggedy and hurt and wore out," he say, "but dat no sign dey licked! Dem Yankees ain't gwine git dis fur, but iffen dey do, you all ain't gwine git free by 'em 'cause I gwine line you up on de bank of Bois d' Arc Creek and free you wid my shotgun! Anybody miss jest one lick wid de hoe, or one step in de line, or one clap of dat bell, or one toot of de horn, and he gwine be free and talking to de Debil long befo' he ever see a pair of blue britches!"

Dat de way he talk to us, and dat de way he act wid us all de time.

We live in de log quarters on de plantation, not far from Washington, Arkansas, close to Bois d' Arc Creek, in de edge of de Little River bottom. Old Master's name was Dr. Isaac Jones, and he live in de town, whar he keep four, five house niggers, but he have about two hundred on de plantation big and little, and old man Saunders oversee 'em at de time of de War. Old Mistress' name was Betty, and she had a daughter name' Betty about grown, and then they was three boys, Tom, Bryan, and Bob, but they was too young to go to de War. I never did see 'em but once or twice till after de War. Old Master didn't go to de War, 'cause he was a doctor and de onliest one left in Washington, and purty soon he was dead anyhow.

Next fall, after he ride out and tell us dat he gwine shoot us befo' he let us free, he come out to see how his steam gin doing. De gin box was a little old thing 'bout as big as a bedstead, wid a long belt running through de side of de gin house out to de engine and boiler in de yard. De boiler burn cord wood, and it have a little crack in it whar de nigger ginner been trying to fix it.

Old Master come out, hopping mad 'cause de gin shet down, and ast de ginner, Old Brown, what de matter. Old Brown say de boiler weak and dat it liable to bust, but Old Master jump down off'n his hoss and go round to de boiler and say, "Cuss fire to your black heart! Dat boiler all right! Throw on some cordwood, cuss fire to your heart!"

Old Brown start to de wood pile grumbling to hisself and Old Master stoop down to look at de boiler again, and it blow right up and him standing right dar!

Old Master was blowed all to pieces, and dey jest find little bitsy chunks of his clothes and parts of him to bury. De wood pile blow down and Old Brown land way off in de woods, but he wasn't killed. Two wagons of cotton blowed over, and de mules run away, and all de niggers was scared nearly to death 'cause we knowed de overseer gwine be a lot worse, now dat Old Master gone.

PLATE 4: A former slave.

Before de War, when Master was a young man, de slaves didn't have it so hard, my mammy tell me. Her name was Fanny and her old mammy name was Nanny. Grandma Nanny was alive during de War yet.

How she come in de Jones family was dis way: Old Mistress was jest a little girl, and her older brother bought Nanny and give her to her. I think his name was Littlejohn; anyways we called him Master Little John. He drawed up a paper what say dat Nanny allus belong to Mis' Betty and all de chillun Nanny ever have belong to her, too, and nobody can't take 'em for a debt and things like dat. When Mis' Betty marry, Old Master he can't sell Nanny or any of her chillun, neither.

Dat paper hold good, too, and Grandmammy tell me about one time it hold good and keep my own mammy on de place.

Grandmammy say Mammy was jest a little gal and was playing out in de road wid three, four other little chillun when a white man and Old Master rid up. The white man had a paper about some kind of a debt, and Old Master say for him to take his pick of de nigger chillun and give him back de paper.

Jest as Grandmammy go to de cabin door and hear him say dat, de man git off his hoss and pick up my mammy and put her up in front of him and start to ride off down de road.

Pretty soon Mr. Little John come riding up and say something to Old Master, and see Grandmammy standing in de yard screaming and crying. He jest jab de spur in his hoss and go kiting off down de road after dat white man.

Mammy say he ketch up wid him jest as he git to Bois d' Arc Creek and start to wade the hoss across. Mr. Little John holler to him to come back wid dat little nigger 'cause de paper don't kivver dat child, 'cause she Old Mistress' own child, and when de man jest ride on, Mr. Little John throw his big old long hoss-pistol down on him and make him come back. De man was hopping mad, but he have to give over my mammy and take one de other chillun for de debt paper.

Old Master allus kind of techy 'bout Old Mistress having niggers he can't trade or sell. One day he have his whole family and some more white folks out at de plantation. He showing 'em all de quarters when we all come in from de field in de evening, and he call all de niggers up to let de folks see 'em. He made Grandmammy and Mammy and me stand to one side, and den he say to the other niggers, "Dese niggers belong to my wife, but you belong to me, and I'm de only one you is to call Master. Dis is Tom, and Bryan, and Bob and Mis' Betty, and you is to call 'em dat, and don't you ever call one of 'em Young Master or Young Mistress, cuss fire to your black hearts!" All de other white folks look kind of funny, and Old Mistress look 'shamed of Old Master.

My own pappy was in dat bunch, too. His name was Frank, and after de War he took de name of Frank Henderson, 'cause he was born under dat name, but I allus went by Jones, de name I was born under.

Long about de middle of de War, after Old Master was killed, de soldiers begin coming round de place and camping. Dey was Southern soldiers, and dey say dey have to take de mules and most de corn to git along on. Jest go in de barns and cribs and take anything dey want, and us niggers didn't have no sweet taters nor Irish taters to eat on when dey gone, neither.

One bunch come and stay in de woods across de road from de overseer's house, and dey was all on hosses. Dey bugle go jest 'bout de time our old horn blow in de morning, and when we come in dey eating supper, and we smell it and sho' git hungry!

Before Old Master died he sold off a whole lot of hosses and cattle and some niggers, too. He had de sales on de plantation, and white men from around dar come to bid, and some traders come. He had a big stump whar he made de niggers stand while dey was being sold, and de men and boys had to strip off to de waist to show dey muscle and iffen dey had any scars or hurt places, but de women and gals didn't have to strip to de waist.

De white men come up and look in de slave's mouth jest lak he was a mule or a hoss.

After Old Master go, de overseer hold one sale, but mostly he jest trade wid de traders what come by. He made de niggers git on de stump, though. De traders all had big bunches of slaves and dey have 'em all strung out in a line going down de road. Some had wagons and de chillun could ride, but not many. Dey didn't chain or tie 'em 'cause dey didn't have no place dey could run to, anyway.

I seen chillun sold off and de mammy not sold, and sometimes de mammy sold and a little baby kept on de place and give to another woman to raise. Dem white folks didn't care nothing 'bout how de slaves grieved when dey tore up a family.

Old Man Saunders was de hardest overseer of anybody. He would git mad and give a whipping some time, and de slave wouldn't even know what it was about.

My uncle Sandy was de lead row nigger, and he was a good nigger and never would tech a drap of likker. One night, some de niggers git hold of some likker somehow, and dey leave de jug half full on de step of Sandy's cabin. Next morning, old man Saunders come out in de field so mad he was pale.

He jest go to de lead row and tell Sandy to go wid him, and he start toward de woods along Bois d' Arc Creek wid Sandy follering behind. De overseer always carry a big, heavy stick, but we didn't know he was so mad, and dey jest went off in de woods.

Purty soon we hear Sandy hollering and we know old overseer pouring it on. Den de overseer come back by hisself and go on up to de house.

Come late evening he come and see what we done in de day's work, and go back to de quarters wid us all. When he git to Mammy's cabin, whar Grandmammy live, too, he say to Grandmammy, "I sent Sandy down in de woods to hunt a hoss. He gwine come in hungry purty soon. You better make him a extra hoe cake," and he kind of laugh and go on to his house.

Jest soon as he gone, we all tell Grandmammy we think he got a whipping, and sho' 'nuf he didn't come in.

De next day some white boys find Uncle Sandy whar dat overseer done killed him and throwed him in a little pond. And dey never done nothing to old man Saunders at all.

When he go to whip a nigger he made him strip to de waist, and he take a cat-o'-nine-tails and bring de blisters, and den bust de blisters wid a wide strap of leather fastened to a stick handle. I seen de blood running out'n many a back, all de way from de neck to de waist!

Many de time a nigger git blistered and cut up so bad dat we have to git a sheet and grease it wid lard and wrap 'em up in it, and dey have to wear a greasy cloth wrapped around dey body under de shirt for three, four days after dey git a big whipping.

Later on, in de War, de Yankees come in all around us and camp, and de overseer git sweet as honey in de comb. Nobody git a whipping all de time de Yankees dar.

Dey come and took all de meat and corn and taters dey want, and dey tell us, "Why don't you poor darkeys take all de meat and molasses you want? You made it and it's yours much as anybody's." But we know dey soon be gone, and den we git a whipping, iffen we do. Some niggers run off and went wid de Yankees, but dey had to work jest as hard for dem, and dey didn't eat so good and so often wid de soldiers.

I never forget de day we was set free.

Dat morning we all go to de cotton field early, and den a house nigger come out from Old Mistress on a hoss and say she want de overseer to come into town, and he leave and go in. After while, de old horn blow up at de overseer's house, and we all stop and listen, 'cause it de wrong time of day for de horn.

We start chopping again, and dar go de horn again.

De lead row nigger holler, "Hold up!" And we all stop again. "We better go on in. Dat our horn," he holler at de head nigger, and de head nigger think so, too, but he say he afraid we catch de Debil from de overseer iffen we quit widout him dar, and de lead row man say maybe de overseer back from town and blowing de horn hisself, so we line up and go in.

When we git to de quarters we see all de old ones and de chillun up in de overseer's yard, so we go on up dar. De overseer setting on de end de gallery wid a paper in his hand, and when we all come up, he say come and stand close to de gallery. Den he call off everybody's name and see we all dar.

Setting on de gallery in a hide-bottom chair was a man we never see before. He had on a big broad black hat lak de Yankees wore, but it didn't have no yaller string on it lak most de Yankees had, and he was in store clothes dat wasn't homespun or jeans, and dey was black. His hair was plumb gray and so was his beard, and it come way down here on his chest, but he didn't look lak he was very old, 'cause his face was kind of fleshy and healthy looking. I think we all been sold off in a bunch, and I notice some kind of smiling, and I think they sho' glad of it.

De man say, "You darkies know what day dis is?" He talk kind, and smile.

We all don't know, of course, and we jest stand dar and grin. Pretty soon he ask again and de head man say, "No, we don't know."

"Well dis de fourth day of June, and dis is 1865, and I want you all to 'member de date, 'cause you allus going 'member de day. Today you is free, jest lak I is, and Mr. Saunders and your mistress and all us white people," de man say.

"I come to tell you," he say, "and I wants to be sho' you all understand, 'cause you don't have to git up and go by de horn no more. You is your own bosses now, and you don't have to have no passes to go and come."

We never did have no passes, nohow, but we knowed lots of other niggers on other plantations got 'em.

"I wants to bless you and hope you always is happy, and tell you you got all de right dat any white people got," de man say, and den he git on his hoss and ride off.

We all jest watch him go on down de road, and den we go up to Mr. Saunders and ask him what he want us to do. He jest grunt and say to do lak we damn please, he reckon, but git off dat place to do it, less'n any of us wants to stay and make de crop for half of what we make.

None of us know whar to go, so we all stay, and he split up de fields and show us which part we got to work in, and we go on lak we was, and make de crop and git it in, but dey ain't no more harm after dat day. Some de niggers lazy and don't git in de field early, and dey git it took away from 'em, but dey plead around and git it back and work better de rest of dat year.

But we all gits fooled on dat first go-out. When de crop all in we don't git half. Old Mistress sick in town, and de overseer was still on de place and he charge us half de crop for de quarters and de mules and tools and grub.

Den he leave, and we gits another white man, and he sets up a book, and give us half de next year and takes out for what we use up, but we all got something left over after dat first go-out.

Old Mistress never git well after she lose all her niggers, and one day de white boss tell us she jest drap over dead setting in her chair, and we know her heart jest broke.

Next year de chillun sell off most de place and we scatter off, and I and Mammy go into Little Rock and do work in de town. Grandmammy done dead.

I git married to John White in Little Rock, but he died and we didn't have no chillun. Den, in four, five years, I marry Billy Rowe. He was a Cherokee citizen and he had belonged to a Cherokee name Dave Rowe and lived east of Tahlequah before de War. We married in Little Rock, but he had land in de Cherokee Nation, and we come to east of Tahlequah and lived till he died, and den I come to Tulsa to live wid my youngest daughter.

Billy Rowe and me had three chillun: Ellie, John, and Lula. Lula married a Thomas, and it's her I lives with.

Lots of old people lak me say dat dey was happy in slavery, and dat dey had de worst tribulations after freedom, but I knows dey didn't have no white master and overseer lak we all had on our place. Dey both dead now, and dey no use talking 'bout de dead, but I know I been gone long ago iffen dat white man Saunders didn't lose his hold on me.

It was de fourth day of June in 1865 I begins to live, and I gwine take de picture of dat old man in de big black hat and long whiskers, setting on de gallery and talking kind to us, clean into my grave wid me.

No, bless God, I ain't never seen no more black boys bleeding all up and down de back under a cat-o'-nine-tails, and I never go by no cabin and hear no poor nigger groaning, all wrapped up in a lardy sheet no more.

I hear my chillun read about General Lee, and I know he was a good man. I didn't know nothing about him den, but I know now he wasn't fighting for dat kind of white folks.

Maybe dey's dat kind still yet, but dey don't show it up no more, and I got lots of white friends, too. All my chillun and grandchillun been to school, and dey git along good, and I know we living in a better world, whar dey ain't nobody "cussing fire to my black heart!"

I sho' thank de good Lawd I got to see it.

Voices

―――――――◁∻ ∻▷――――――――

SLAVE CHILDREN,

FOOD AND COOKING,

STEALING,

AND FADING REMEMBRANCES OF AFRICA

D<small>E FUS</small>' thing I recollect is living in a slave cabin back o' Marse's big house, along wid forty or fifty other slaves. All my childhood life, I can never remember seeing my pa or ma gwine to wuk or coming in from wuk in de daylight, as dey went to de fiel's fo' day an' wukked till after dark. It wuz wuk, wuk, all de time. My ma wukked in de fiel's up to de day I wuz born. I wuz born 'twix de fiel's an' de cabins. Ma wuz den tooken to de house on a hoss.

—JENNIE WEBB

The riding boss would come round before the day broke and wake you up. You had to be in the field before sunup—that is, the man would. The woman who had a little child had a little more play than the man, because she had to care for the child before she left. She had to carry the child over to the old lady that took care of the babies.

The cook that cooked up at the big house, she cooked bread and milk and sent it to the larger children for their dinner. They didn't feed the little children, because their mothers had to nurse them. The mother went to the field as soon as she cared for her child. She would come back and nurse the child around about twice. She would come once in the morning about ten o'clock and once again at twelve o'clock, before she ate her own lunch. She and her husband ate in the field. She would come back again about three P.M. Then you wouldn't see her anymore till dark that night. Long as you could see, you had to stay in the field.

Then, the mother would go and get the children and bring them home. She would cook for supper and feed them. Maybe, the children

PLATE 5: Slaves working a field on Edisto Island, South Carolina, in 1862.

would be asleep before she would get all that done. Then she would have to wake them up to feed them.

—DICEY THOMAS

On all of Master's plantations, dere was one old 'oman dat didn't have nothin' else to do but look atter and cook for de nigger chillun whilst dey mammies was at wuk in de fields. Aunt Viney tuk keer of us. She had a big old horn what she blowed when it was time for us to eat, and us knowed better dan to git so fur off dat us couldn't hear dat horn, for Aunt Viney would sho' tear us up. Master had done told her she better fix us plenty t'eat and give it to us on time. Dere was a great long trough what went plum 'cross de yard, and dat was whar us et.

For dinner, us had peas or some other sort of veg'tables, and corn bread. Aunt Viney crumbled up dat bread in de trough and poured de veg'tables and pot-licker over it. Den, she blowed de horn and chillun come a-runnin' from evvy which away. If us et it all up, she had to put more vittles in de trough. At nights, she crumbled de corn bread in de trough and poured buttermilk over it. Us never had nothin' but corn bread and buttermilk, at night.

Sometimes, dat trough would be a sight, 'cause us never stopped to wash our hands, and 'fore us had been eatin' more dan a minute or two what was in de trough would look lak de red mud what had come off of our hands. Sometimes, Aunt Viney would fuss at us and make us clean it out.

—ROBERT SHEPHERD

Lan' sakes alive, us chillun, white an' black, had a good time. Us wuz all ober de place, robbin' birds' nests in de orchard, er-fishing an' goin' in washin' in de deep holes, er-riding de plough horses to and from de field—effen us could wangle de ride—runnin' de calves an' colts, an' fightin' de old ganders. All de black chillun wore a long shirt. It come down to de middle ob de legs, an' you couldn't tell a gal from a boy cep'n de white girls. Dey wore great big bonnets, an' dey wuz sewed to deir hair to make 'em keep 'em on to perteck deir faces from de sun.

— WINGER VANHOOK

Marster's chillun tease us when we play wif dem. When dey git real mean, I jus' grab dem by de hair, an' I sure would get dem, den. Dey would call us all kind o' names to tease us—"ole yaller pun'kin," an' sich. We jus' holler "white pun'kin" right back at dem; den dey fro sticks an' stones at us. We sho' uster git mad an' have lots o' fights an' sich. When dey git good an' fightin' mad, I jus' grab dem by de hair, an' den I had 'em. An' when dey bawl an' squall loud, I run an' hide in de quarters.

— LUCY LEWIS

Ole Missus and young Missus told the little slave children that the stork brought the white babies to their mothers, but that the slave children were all hatched out from buzzards' eggs. And we believed it was true.

— KATIE SUTTON

Dere am two womens dat have cha'ge ob de nu'se'y. All de small chilluns am kep' dere, while de mothers am wukkin' in de fiel'. Dey leaves dem in de mo'nin' an' gits dem at night. De marster sho' am pa'ticulah 'bout dem younguns. Dem nu'ses have to ten' to dem right, 'bout de feed an' de sleep an' de play, an' sich. De marster lots ob times looks dem over an' points one out an' says, "Dat one will be wo'th a thousan' dollahs," an' he points to anudder an' says, "Dat one will be a whopper." You see, 'twas jus' lak raisin' de mules: if you don't hurts dem when dey am young, you gits good strong niggers when dey am big.

— WILLIE WILLIAMS

Children were not made to work till dey got twelve or fourteen years old, unless it was some light work around de house—mindin' de table, fannin' flies, an' pickin' up chips to start a fire, scratchin' Master's head so he could sleep in de evenings, an' washin' Missus' feet at night, 'fore she went to bed.

—JOHN SMITH

Mrs. Harris lived alone in a big house. I was the only slave she had. There was no other children, black or white.

I knew I was unhappy, but I thought everythin' was like that. I didn't know there was happiness for nobody—me nor nobody. When I got whipped, I thought that was jus' a part of being alive. I didn't take it like it was my special punishment, jus' comin' to me.

I slep' in Mrs. Harris' own room, on de floor. It was a dark, big house. I now guesses she was scared to be alone, asleep.

When de War broke, I didn't know what it was for. Mrs. Harris was hatin' the North, and I was hatin' the North, too. I thought the North was kind of like a spider in a dream, that was going to come and wipe away the house and carry me off. When I heard of Santa Claus, that was going to come down the chimney, I screamed. I gets a poker and wasn't goin' to let him in. Everythin' was like a tangled dream—jus' opposite to what I found out later it was. I believes now that Mrs. Harris liked to get me thinkin' things weren't like they was.

—KATIE PHOENIX

Ole Marster was good to us. He give us plenty of good food. I git plenty of whippin's, but he neber beat us hard. He had a son what was jis' one mont' ol'er 'n me, and we uster run roun' and play togedder lots, and so I stay on atter freedom come. Ole Marster, he whip me and his son jis' de same. Sometimes, he put me in a sack and whip me in de sack. He done dat mo' to scare me. He didn' whip us no more 'n he orter, though. Dey was some good marsters and some mean ones, and some wuthless cullud people.

—MADISON BRUIN

Well, I was just a little girl, about eight years old, staying in Beaufort at de missus' house, polishing her brass andirons and scrubbing her floors, when one morning she says to me, "Janie, take this note down to Mr. Wilcox' wholesale store, on Bay Street, and fetch me back de package de clerk give you."

I took de note. De man read it, and he say, "Uh-huh." Den, he turn away, and he come back wid a little package which I took back to de missus.

She open it, when I bring it in, and say, "Go upstairs, Miss!"

It was a raw cowhide strap, 'bout two feet long, and she started to pourin' it on me all de way upstairs. I didn't know what she was whippin' me 'bout, but she pour it on, and she pour it on.

Turrectly she say, "You can't say 'Marse Henry,' Miss? You can't say 'Marse Henry'?"

"Yes'm! Yes'm! I kin say 'Marse Henry'!"

Marse Henry was just a little boy 'bout three or four years old—come 'bout half way up to me. She wanted me to say "Massa" to him—a baby!

—REBECCA GRANT

Ise 'membah one slave dat gits whupped so bad hims neber gits up. Hims died. We-uns chilluns would go roun' whar hims was an' look at 'im. De marster lets we-uns do dat, Ise guess, fo' to larn we-uns dat 'tis bes' fo' to min'.

—TESHAN YOUNG

When a slave died, we just dug a hole in the ground, built a fence around it, and piled him in. No singing, no preaching or praying, ever took place during slavery time. Maser would say, "Well, he was a pretty good Negro. Guess he will go to Heaven, all right." And that was about all there was to a Negro funeral, then. We would not even shed a tear, because he was gone where there would not be any more slaves. That was all the slave thought about, then: not being a slave. Because slavery time was hell.

—MARY GAFFNEY

Nights, I allus slept by Missus' bed. Daytimes, my bed was push' up under her'n. Dis was called a trundle bed. She kept me right wid her most ob de time, an' when mealtime come she put me under de table an' I ate out ob her hand. She'd put a piece ob meat into a biscuit an' hand it down to me. Den, she say, "When dat been finished, holler up after some more, Ike." But she allus warn me not to holler if dere been company to dinner. She'd say, "Jes' put you' hand on my knee an' den I'll know you is ready." But seem like my mouth been so big, an' I eat so fast, an' old Mis' so busy talkin' to dem ladies, dat I jes' keep a-touchin' her on de knee, most ob de time.

—IKE SIMPSON

You wants ter know 'bout some ole slavery foods? Well, I'll tell you what I knows.

Did you ever hear of kush? Kush wus corn bread cooked on de big griddle in de fireplace, mashed up with raw onions an' ham gravy poured over it. You might think dat hit ain't good, but hit am.

Fried chicken wus seasoned, drapped in flour, an' den simmered in a big pan of ham gravy wid de lid on hit, till hit wus tender. Den, de lid wus tuck off, an' de chicken wus fried a golden brown, as quick as possible.

De griddle cakes wus flour an' meal mixed, put on a big ole iron griddle in de fireplace an' flipped over two times.

Ash cake wus made of either meal or flour, wrapped in a damp cloth an' cooked in de hot ashes on de ha'th. Taters wus cooked in de ashes, too, an' dey wus good like dat.

Fish, dem days, wus dipped in meal 'fore dey wus cooked, 'cept catfish, an' dey wus stewed wid onions.

Cornmeal dumplin's wus biled in de turnip greens, collards, cabbages, an' so on, even ter snap beans, an' at supper de pot-licker wus eat wid de dumplin's. Dat's why de folks wus so healthy.

Speakin' 'bout sweets, de blackberry or other kind of pie wus cooked in a big pan wid two crusts. Dat made more, an' wus better, to boot. Cakes wus mostly plain or had jelly fillin', 'cept fer special company.

—ANNA WRIGHT

Ise sho' 'joy myse'f on de old plantation, an' we-uns all had a good time. Allus have plenty to eat. Marster used to say, "De cullud folks raised de food, an' dey's 'titled to all dey wants." Same wid de clothes.

— FLORENCE NAPIER

All de rations am measured out on Sunday mo'nin'. What am given have to do till next Sunday. Thar am plenty diffe'nt rations, but 'twarn't 'nuf fo' de heavy eaters. We-uns all have to be real careful, an' den some of de folks goes hongry, sometimes. De marster gives we-uns meat, co'nmeal, 'lasses, p'taters, peas, beans, milk, an' we-uns gits white flouah on Sunday mo'nin'—jus' 'nuf fo' to make one batch of biscuits.

De short rations caused lots of trouble, 'cause de niggers have to steal food. 'Twas a whuppin' if dey gits catched. De cullud folks am in a hell of a fix if dey can't do de wuk 'cause dey am weak, even if dey am hongry. 'Twas a whuppin' den fo' sho'. If dey steals de food so dey stays strong an' can do de task, 'twas a whuppin'. So thar 'twas: mostest of dem steals an' tooks a whuppin' if dey am catched, an' on a full stomach. My folks don't have to steal food, but we-uns am careful. You can jus' bet 'twarn't nothin' wasted.

— BETTY POWERS

I recollect seein' one biscuit crust, one mornin'. Dey throwed it out to de dogs, an' I beat de dog to it.

— ALEX MCCINNEY

Some of de bes' food us ever had was possum an' taters. Us'd go out at night wid a big sack an' a pack of houn's, an' 'twarn't long befo' we done treed a possum. Atter we done treed him, de dogs would stan' aroun' de tree an' bark. Iffen de tree was small, us could shake him out. Iffen it was big, one of de niggers hadda climb up it an' git old Mr. Possum, hisself.

It is sho'-'nuf fun, dough, to go a-railin' th'ough de woods atter a possum or coon. De coon'll give you de bes' chase, but he ain't no good eatin', lak de possum.

—ISAAM MORGAN

They ain't but one sho'-'nuf way ter cook a possum. I'll tell you jes' how I does it.

Firs', you gits the boy ter clean him fer you; scrape him till he git white. Then, you soaks him all night in salten water. Take him out in the mornin' an' dreen him an' wipe him off nice an' dry. Then, you parboils him a while. Then, you takes him out an' grease him all over with butter; rub flour all over him an' rub pepper in with it. Then, you bas'e him with some er the juice what you parboiled him in. Then, you puts him in the stove an' lets him bake. Ever' time you opens the stove do', you bas'es him with the gravy. Peel yo' sweet pertaters an' bake them along with him till they is nice an' sof' an' brown, like the possum hisse'f. Sprinkle in flour ter thicken yo' gravy, jes' like you was makin' reg'lar chicken gravy. When he's nice an' brown, you puts a pertater in he mouf an' one on each side, an' yo' possum is ready ter eat.

Yas'm, I been sailin' right high all my life. When you comin' ter dinner with us again?

—DELLA BUCKLEY

I don't know why, but I remember we didn't have salt given to us. So we went to the smokehouse, where there were clean boards on the floor where the salt and grease dripping would fall from the smoked hams hanging from the rafters. The boards would be soft and soaked with salt and grease. Well, we took those boards and cooked the salt and fat out of them—cooked the boards right in the bean soup. That way we got salt, and the soup was good.

—CHARLEY ROBERTS

Fire was 'bout the hardes' thing fer us to keep. Dere wa'nt no matches in dem days, an' we toted fire from one plantation to 'nother, when hit burned out. We put live coals in pans or buckets an' toted it home.

Sometimes, we put heavy wadding in a old gun an' shot hit out into a brush heap an' den blowed de sparks till de fire blazed. Ever'body had flint rocks, too, but few niggers could work 'em, an' de ones dat could allus had dat job to do.

—HAMP KENNEDY

They would hang pots over the fire . . . and you could smell that stuff cooking. You couldn't cook nothin' then, without somebody knowin' it—couldn't cook and eat in the back while folks sit in the front, without them knowin' it. They used to steal from the old master and cook it, and they would be burning rags or something to keep the white folks from smelling it.

—DICEY THOMAS

The grub I liked best was whatever I could git.

—THE REVEREND LAFAYETTE PRICE

My old boss, he just wouldn't give his hands no meat, at night. He would expect you to steal what you got, at night. If he would read of a reward being out for something that was stolen, he would come around and tell us, and say, "If I catch any of it there, damn you, I'll kill you."

We stole so many chickens that if a chicken would see a darkey he'd run right straight to the house.

—ANONYMOUS

On moonlight nights, yo' could hear a heap of voices, an' when yo' peep ober de dike dar am a gang of niggers a-shootin' craps an' bettin' eber'thing dey has stold from de plantation. Sometimes, a pretty yaller gal er a fat black gal would be dar, but mostly hit would be jist men.

—MIDGE BURNETT

Dere am once dat a nigger gits de whuppin'. Dat am 'cause him stole Marster's favorite pun'kin. 'Twas dis away. De marster am savin' de pun'kin fo' to git de seed. It am big as de ten gallon keg. De co'n field am full ob pun'kins, an dat nigger coulda took what him wants fo' to make sauce, but him took de marster's choice pun'kin. Well, dat cullud gent'man must been awful hongry dat time, 'cause dat pun'kin am so big de nigger have to tussle wid it befo' he gits it to his cabin. 'Twas lak stealin' de elephant; you can't hide it in de watch pocket. Co'se, lots ob de cullud folks see dat cullud gent'man wid de pun'kin, an' 'twarn't long till de marster knows it.

Well, Sar, 'twas a funny sight to see de marster punish dat fellow. Fust, de marster sats him down on the groun' in f'ont ob de cullud quatahs, whar all us can see him. Den, de marster gives him de big bowl ob pun'kin sauce an' a spoon, an' says to him, "Eat dat sauce." De cullud gent'man eats, an' eats, an' eats. Him gits so full dat it am hahd fo' him to swallow, an' him stahts to gag. Den, de marster says, "Eat some mo'. 'Tis awful good." Dat nigger tries again, but him gags an' can't take any mo'. De marster hits him a lick, an' says, "It am good. Eat some mo'," an' den hits sev'ral light licks. Sho' was funny to see. Dere sat de cullud gent'man wid pun'kin sauce smeared on his face an' tears runnin' down his cheeks.

Aftah dat, we-uns younguns would call dat nigger "Marster Pun'kin," an' he sho' chase we-uns ever' time we-uns call him dat. De marster never had any mo' trouble wid de pun'kin stealin'.

—WILLIAM THOMAS

Old Judge bought every roguish nigger in the country. He'd take one home and give him the key to everything on the place and say to help himself. Soon as he got all he wanted to eat, he'd quit being a rogue. Old Judge said that was what made niggers steal: they was hungry.

—MORRIS HILLYER

We were so hongry we were bound to steal or perish. This trait seems to be handed down from slavery days.

—LOUISA ADAMS

Way back in de old days, when de creatures was all people, Br'er Fox give a log-rollin' and invite all de neighborhood. Br'er Possum was dere, and Br'er Rabbit, and all de rest. Old Sis' Fox and some de neighbor women was fixin' de dinner. Dey done de churnin' too, and Sis' Fox go set de bucket of butter in de spring where it be good and cool for de big dinner.

Br'er Rabbit, he keep cuttin' he eye roun' all de time, and he see Sis' Fox put de butter in de spring. At dat, he grin to hisse'f and lick his mouf. When dey start rollin' de logs, Br'er Rabbit was right dar wid he shoulder down, jest a-gruntin'. But he ain't do no wuk.

'Long up in de mornin', when de sun get hot, Br'er Rabbit, he let out a big holler: "Hooee, Br'er Fox, got to run back home a li'l while!"

"What de matta now, Br'er Rabbit?"

"My wife gwine bring me a new heir."

Den, Br'er Rabbit, he run over in de woods like he takin' de shawtcut home. But he jest creep roun' to de spring and take up dat bucket of butter and eat it all. Den, he wipe he mouf and he hands and lay down in de shade to take a nap.

Jest 'fore dinner time, he git up and come out of de woods walkin' slow and proud.

Br'er Fox see him and holler, "Well, has you got de new heir, Br'er Rabbit?"

Br'er Rabbit say, "Uhuh, got a new heir."

Br'er Fox say, "What you name dis-un?"

Br'er Rabbit say, "He name 'Lickbottom.' " Br'er Rabbit tole dat 'cause he done lick de bottom of de butter bucket.

Br'er Fox say, "Well, dat sho' is fine; sho' hope he does well. And now, it's 'bout de middle of de day, so le's knock off and git dinner."

So dey all go up to de house, and Br'er Fox, he go down to de spring to git de butter. When he git dere, he find all de butter gone.

Br'er Fox, he go back to de house and he say, "Somebody done been to de spring and et all de butter. Any of you-all de one what done it?"

Dey all say dey ain't seen no butter. Den, Br'er Fox, he say, "Well, ain't nobody else been roun' heah, so somebody tole a lie. On'y way we kin find out is to hold ever'body up to de fiah and make de butter run out de one what done it."

Dey all 'greed to dat, and den dey start holdin' one 'nother up to de fiah, startin' off wid Br'er Possum. So dey keep on till dey git to Br'er Rabbit, and when dey hold him up, here come all de butter runnin' out.

Den, dey all say, "Uhuh, Br'er Rabbit got de butter. What us gwine do wid him?"

Some say to th'ow him in de fiah, and some say th'ow him in de brierpatch. Br'er Rabbit, he don't say nothin'.

Den, Br'er Fox say, "Br'er Rabbit, which one you ruther us do?"

Br'er Rabbit, he say, "Th'ow me in de fiah, please, Br'er Fox; dem ole briers jest tear my eyes out, if you th'ow me in de brierpatch."

So dey tuk him and th'owed him in de brierpatch. And Br'er Rabbit, he shook he'se'f and jump 'way up on de hill and laugh and say, "Thank you, Br'er Fox. I was bred and born in a brierpatch."

—ANNIE REED

De white folks helped de preachah and de drivah to read and write a little. Uncle Billy wuz our preachah and de garden tendah. Uncle Billy got in trouble once. De missus had three big fine collards in de garden, and she wuz all de time aftah Billy to take good care of dese collards. So, one Sattidy night, aftah church, Billy slips out and cuts dem down. De next mornin', de cook wuz sent to de garden fer vegetables and some of dese collards fer de missus, but dey wuz gone. De cook hurries to de house and tells de missus. She tells Marster, and he come in mad and says, "Who done dis?" De girl dat is de cook says Billy done it. Marster says to get Billy to come here. Billy come to de house, and Marster says, "Billy, you preachah?" Billy says, "Yas, Sah." Marster says, "Billy, you's cut dem collards." Billy says, "Yas, Sah, I's got some greens." Marster says, "Now, Billy, you preachah. Git me de Bible," and he reads, "Thou shall not steal." Den, he hands Billy de Bible and says, "Read dis." He shore hates to, but Marster makes him do it. Den, he shore tear loose on Billy 'bout stealin'. Finally, Billy says, "Now, Marster, I can show you in de Bible why I did not steal." He tells Billy to find it, and Billy finds it and reads, "You shall reap when you laboreth." Marster says to Billy, "Get to hell out'n here."

—JEFF CALHOUN

My masters, the Hudsons, had a rule never to whip old niggers. I never seed an old nigger whipped, except when somethin' was found missin'. Then, they whipped everybody. They said by doin' that they was sure to get the right one.

—ALBERT TODD

Dere wus a song dey used to sing. Yes, Sir—ha! ha!—I wants ter tell you dat song. Here it is:

Some folks say dat a nigger won't steal;
I caught two in my corn fiel';
One had a bushel, one had a peck,
An' one had roas'in ears round his neck.

—KITTY HILL

Dey talks a heap 'bout de niggers stealin'. Well, you know what was de fust stealin' done? Hit was in Africy, when de white folks stole de niggers, jes' like you'd go get a drove o' hosses and sell 'em.

—SHANG HARRIS

My father wuz a full-blooded African. He wuz about eighteen years old when dey brought him over. He come from near Liberia. He said his mother's name wuz Chaney, and dat's whar I gits my name. He said dar wan't no winter whar he come from, and if dey felt like it dey could all go start naked. He wore a slip made of skins of wild animals that come down to his knees. When ships would land in Africa, de black folks would go down to watch dem, and sometimes dey would show dem beads and purty things dey carried on de ship.

One day, when my daddy and his brother, Peter, wuz standing round looking, de boss-man axed dem if dey wanted to work and handed dem a package to carry on de boat. When dey got in dere, dey see so many curious things dey jest wander aroun' looking, and before dey know it de boat has pulled off from de landing and dey is way out in de water and kain't he'p demselves. So dey jest brought

49

'em on over to Georgy and sold 'em. Dere wuz a boat load of 'em, all stolen. Dey sold my daddy and uncle, Peter, to Mr. Holland. Dey wuz put on a block and Mr. Holland buyed 'em. Dat wuz in Dalton, Georgy.

My daddy said in Africa dey didn't live in houses. Dey jest lived in de woods and et nuts and wile honey dey found in trees. Dey killed wile animals, skinned 'em and et 'em, but made slips out of de skins to wear demselves. Dey jest eat dem animals raw. Dey didn't know nothin' 'bout cooking. Dey even et snakes, but when dey found 'em dey cut deir heads off quick, 'fore dey got mad and pizened demselves.

He said dey never heard 'bout God, and when dey died dey always bury dem at night. Dey dig a hole in de groun', and den everybody would git him a torch and march behind de two who wuz carrying de corpse to whar dey dug de grave. Dey didn't know anything 'bout singing and God. Dat was de last of dem.

Dey didn't make crops over dere. Dey jest lived on things dat growed on trees and killed wile animals. Ef dey got too hungry, dey would jest as soon kill each other and eat 'em. Dey didn't know any better.

When my daddy come over here, it went purty hard wid him having to wear clothes, live in houses, and work. So he run away ever' chance he got, and went to de woods and hides hisself. When dey got too hot after him, he'd come home.

—CHANEY MACK

Dey's a place close to where I's bo'n where dey brung de Africy people to tame 'em. Dey uster had big pens where dey put 'em atter dey brung 'em dere in gunships. Dey sho' was wile. Dey hab hair all over 'em, jis' like a dog, and wo' big hammer rings in dey noses. Dey didn' wo' no clothes. Dey have ter chain 'em to keep 'em from runnin' 'way in de woods. Sometime', dey git 'way anyway and run 'way to de swamps, down in Floridy, and git all wile and hairy ag'in. Dey ain' had no houses for 'em, 'cause dey druther live in de woods or in a ba'n.

Dey brung white preachers to help tame 'em. Dey hab two ways of tamin' 'em—wid a whip and wid a preacher. Dey didn' 'low de preacher in de pen by hisse'f, 'cause dey say at times dem preachers don' come back. Some dem wile Africy people done kill 'em and eat 'em. Dey didn' know nothin' 'bout no God or no 'ligion. Dey done worship dem snake as big as a rake han'le, 'cause dey ain' knowed no better. When dey git dem all tame, den dey sole dem all over de lan' for fiel' han's. Dey was jes' like wile Injuns, though. Iffen dey see anybuddy come, dey duck and hide down.

—MARY JOHNSON

If we hadn't been brung over an' made slaves, us an' us chillun dat is being educated an' civilized would be naked savages back in Africa, now.

—TONY COX

Narratives

THOMAS COLE

WILLIAM ADAMS

FANNY CANNADY

THOMAS COLE

I MIGHT as well begin back as far as I can remember and tell you 'bout mahself. I was bo'n in Jackson County, Alabama, August 8, 1845. Mah mother was Elizabeth Cole, her bein' a slave of Dr. Robert Cole. She was a family nurse. She nursed all de six chilluns of Marster Cole. Mah father was Alex Gorrand. He was a slave of John Gorrand. I was of course s'posed ter take mah father's name, but he was sech a bad, honery, no-'count human bein', till I jest taken mah ole marster's name. Mah first name bein' Thomas, Thomas Cole, dat's me.

I only had one brother and one sister dat I knows of, I bein' de oldest one. Mah sister's name was Sarah and mah brother's name was Ben. I was 'bout three or four years older den mah sister, and Ben was still younger den dat. We lived in de house, in one room, wid Marster Cole, as mah mother was de nurse and housekeeper. We always had a good bed ter sleep in and good things ter eat. We would eat at de same table as Marster Cole and his family eat at, only after dey gits through eatin' first.

I was raised up wid de Cole chilluns and played wid dem all de time. We was all de time climbin' trees in de yard, and as I gits older, dey jest gradually puts more work and heavier work on me. Marster Cole started us out workin' by totin' in wood and kindlin' and totin' water and jest sech odd jobs. Den, later on, as we got older, we had ter feed de hogs, de cows, horses, goats, and chickens. All dis kind of work was fer boys too young fer heavy work. Of course, we had ter pick cotton every fall, as soon as we got big enough ter pick, and put de cotton in baskets. Dese baskets would hold 'bout seventy-five ter one hundred pounds. De little chilluns would pick and put de cotton in a basket wid some older person, so de older person could move de basket 'long.

Den, when a slave gets grown, he is jest lak a mule. He works for his grub and a few clothes and works jest as hard as a mule. Some of de slaves on de plantation 'jining our'n didn't have as easy a time as de mules, fer de mules was fed good, but de slaves laks ter have starved ter death; de marster jest gives dem 'nuf ter eat ter keep dem alive.

When I was a young boy, some other boys and I would go possum huntin' and coon huntin' in de daytime, and de men and us boys would go huntin' sometimes at night, and we would skin dem and stretch de hides and de white folks would sell de hides and give us de money. I allus gives mah money ter mah mother and she would save it fer me till I get 'nuf. Den, she would go ter town wid de mistress, to Huntsville, Alabama, and buy me a pair of shoes, a hat, and a pair of Sunday britches. All dese we called Sunday clothes, and we did not wear dem unless we went ter church. Missus Cole allus helped mah mother do de buyin', 'cause mah mother couldn't count money good.

As I done tole you, mah mother was de family nurse fer Dr. Cole's family, and we eat at deir table, and we had plenty ter eat, too—cakes, pies and biscuits, all kinds of meat, sech as pork, beef, fish, venison, and goats and chickens and wild turkeys. We had lots ter eat dat de other slaves didn't have, as mah mother was a nurse and respectable—different from de other Negroes.

Us chilluns 'bout eight years ole went fishin' lots, after our chores was done. De drivah and de marster's boys would go wid us and stay all night, and Sunday we would bring all the fish back, and then we shore would have a big fish fry.

In de wintah, de marster would allus kill from three hundred ter four hundred hogs. We would have two killin's—de first in November and de last one in January. If dis meat runs out 'fore killin' time, we would kill a beef or goats, or some men would be sent out ter git some wild turkeys or deer. Once a week, all de slaves had biscuits. Dere was a orchard of 'bout five or six acres of peaches and apples on de plantation, and we had all de fruit we wanted. We planted pumpkins, and he would let us have 'bout one or two acres fer watermelons, if we would work dem on Satidy evenin's.

One thing 'bout Marster Cole: he shore seed after his slaves when dey was sick. And when he starts doctorin' one of dem, dey usually gits well, too. He never lost but two, and dey was ole people and ready ter die, but he hated ter lose dem just as bad as he would a young stout man. Marster Cole he had one big, stout, healthy-lookin' slave, 'bout six feet four inches tall, and weighed roun' two hundred and ten pounds, dat he gives three thousand dollars fer. Marster Cole and a man from Mississippi and one from Louisiana was all biddin' on dis nigger, and Marster Cole bid him in at three thousand dollars. Dis slave shore was a powerful man and was easy ter control, too. He shore was glad dat Marster Cole bought him. Marster Cole thought lots of dis slave, but he hates ter lose dem ole ones jest as bad.

Dey was a man and his wife. When slaves gits ole, dey gits cheap, just lak a ole mule. Sometimes you couldn't sell dem, 'cause dey wasn't fit fer nothin'. But when dis ole couple died, he had coffins made and carried 'em out and buried 'em. After one of de slave parsons preached de funeral, dey was buried on de plantation, and rocks was put up fer tombstones.

Marster Cole never sole a slave, iffen dey acted half way right. But iffen dey gits unruly, he always carries dem off ter sell dem. He bought six slaves dat I knows of, and he gives from four hundred ter three thousand a piece fer dem.

De first time I married I marries Nancy Eliza Reed, in Chattanooga, Tennessee, right after de War. We lived tergether fer thirty-two years, and she died wid malaria. All dis happened after Freedom. If I had married before Marster Cole died, I would have had ter be married by de parson, 'cause dat was one of Marster Cole's rules: he didn't 'low none of dis jest livin' tergether. When one of de slaves wants ter gits married, he takes dem ter a parson and dey gits married. I has thought 'bout this lots, since Freedom, and I believes Marster Cole was so smart a man he could looks ahead and sees Freedom. Dat is de reason he treated his slaves de way he did.

Marster Cole was a smart man, and he was a good man wid it. He was 'bout five feet ten inches tall, blue-eyed and brown-haired, and weighed 'bout one hundred sixty pounds. Dis man had respect fer other people's feelin's. He treated his slaves lak dey was human bein's, instead of dumb brutes. He 'lowed his slaves more privileges den any other slaveholder round dat part of de country, and he tried ter learn

'em how ter make money and how ter counts money. He tried ter learn
'em all what a person could sell. He was one of de best men I ever
knows in mah whole life, and his wife was jest laks him. Missus Cole
shore was nice ter all de woman slaves. She gives all dem a new dress
every spring jest as shore as de spring rolls around. An' she allus helps
all de slave women wid deir buyin', and sold all deir chickens and
eggs, and gives dem every cent of de money dat was comin' ter dem.

Marster and Missus Cole had six chilluns. De boys' names was
John, de oldest, den Isaac, and de youngest was Isa Lee. I played wid
de boys all de time. Dey was mah young marsters, and when we was
playin', I has ter do mos' anything dey wants me to. One day, we
was playin' roun' de barn and we gits on de rail fence and climbs on
top of de barn, and dey tells me ter jump offen de barn and dey would
follows me. So I jumps off, and it lak ter kill me. Dere was sand down
dere to jump in, but de barn was high, and I was jest a little kid. I
was layin' dere hollerin', and de two oldest boys was jes' standin' up
dere lookin' at me, and de youngest was cryin' and hollerin' fer his
mamma ter come and gits me—dat I was kilt. Missus Cole and mah
mother come runnin' out dere and picks me up and carries me ter de
house and doctors me up wid medicine. And Missus Cole doctors de
oldest two boys wid a switch.

Marster Cole hardly ever keeps an overseer over two years. De
overseer would take his 'structions from Marster Cole when he was
hired, and den Marster Cole would turns him loose, and when de
overseer gits a little outen line, Marster Cole would tells him what ter
do. Marster Cole would tells him a few times, and finally he would
fire him and hires a new one.

De slaves was woke up every mornin' at four thirty by a slave
blowin' a horn. Breakfast is eat, and de men folks goes on ter de fiel's,
and as soon as de women finished up de house work and takes care of
de babies, dey comes ter work, too. All de slaves carried deir dinnah
ter de fiel' wid dem, and iffen you puts it whar de ants or a varmit can
git it, dat is your hard luck. We all works till noon, den we eats our
dinnah in de shade and res' 'bout an hour and half, iffen it is very hot.
Iffen it is cold, we res' 'bout an hour, den we goes back ter work and
stays up wid de lead man all evenin', jest lak we did in de mornin'.

'Tween sundown and night, we takes out, goes ter de quarters, and eats supper, and by dat time we is all ready ter goes ter bed and sleep. You is always tired when you makes a day lak dat on de plantation.

When de slaves leaves de quarters, every mornin', goin' ter work, it was jest lak a bunch of youngsters, nowadays, goin' ter a ball game. Dey was all hollerin', and taggin' each other, and runnin', but dey didn't come in dat way. When we comes in, it was jest lak drivin' an ole give-out mule.

Dar never was but one slave whipped on Marster Cole's plantation, and de overseer whips him 'cause he could not keep up wid de drivah. De drivah was a big slave who could do foah times as much work as de ole slave, but Marster Cole fired de overseer. He says de overseer did not have no foahsight. I don't knows what dat is, but I heard him tell de overseer dat.

Some ob de other plantation owners shore was bad on de poor slaves. Dar was one slave owner next ter us dat didn't have but 'bout fifteen workin' hands, and he tries ter work 'nuf land ter need twenty-five workin' hands. He was beatin' on some of his slaves all de time. Atter strippin' 'em off plum naked, he would have dem tied hand and foot, and bends dem ovah, and runs a pole 'tween de bend in de arms at de elbow and under de legs at de knees, and whip dem wid a cat-o'-nine tails till he bust de hide in lots of places 'cross deir backs, and blood would run offen dem on de groun'. Den he would put salt in dose raw places, specially iffen dey makes out lak dey wants ter fight or sasses him.

A cat-o'-nine-tails is a rawhide leather, platted or woven round a stock [stick] or piece of wood for a handle. Dis piece is short—'bout eight ter ten inches long. De leather is braided on past de stock for quite a piece, and about eight or twelve inches from de end of de whip, all dese strips are tied in a knot, and dey all sprangle out from dis makin' a tassle. Dis is called de "cracker," and it is what splits de hide. Dose cat-o'-nine-tails can be made as long as you want dem. Some people calls dem bullwhips, and dat is right for dem; dey wasn't made ter whip people wid.

Dis man's fiel' 'jined our'n in one place, and I has seed him ride up and down de rows in de fiel' behind his slaves wid dis bullwhip across his saddle or in his hand, and iffen one of de slaves gits on a bad row, he'd ride 'long behind him and holler at him ter ketch up, and iffen he didn't, pretty soon he would hit him wid dis bullwhip a couple of times. When dis man sole a slave, dey was allus glad ter git away. But when he bought one, de first thing he done was bring the slave home and gives him a whippin'. He calls dat puttin' de fear of God in him.

Sometimes de speculaters would come around, but dey never did stop at Marster Cole's place, for he never did paternize any of dem. De speculaters was white men dat sometimes comes around buyin', sellin', or tradin' slaves, jest lak dey do cattle now. Dey would buy, sell, or trade a baby dat was ole 'nuf ter wean, and up ter de ole slaves. Of course, babies and ole folks did not bring much. Babies was too young ter work, and ole folks couldn't do much; besides, dey was liable to die at any time. Dey was mostly considered worthless property, after dey gits feeble.

Dem speculaters would put de chilluns in a wagon, usually pulled by oxens, and de older folks was chained or tied tergether so's dey could not run off, and dey would go from one plantation ter another, all ovah de country. Dis was very common, 'specially in de fall of de year or spring.

Some of de slaves was pretty smart fer de chance dey had ter gits any education. Iffen some of de white folks laks a slave, or dey had some chilluns dat laks a slave, dey would larn him how ter read and write, and dat slave would larn another one ter read and write, iffen he could. But some of dem shore was thick-headed. You jest couldn't larn dem nothin'.

I has an awful time larnin', myself. Marster Cole larned me ter read and write, and I is slow wid it yet, but jest give me more time and I will gits it done. Marster Cole's boys tole me more times dan I got fingers and toes dat I was too thickheaded to larn anything, but I jest kept on tryin' and finally got on ter it, jest gittin' a little at a time.

De way mos' of us larns ter read is de Bible. One of de slaves would larn ter read, and he would read de Bible ter de rest of dem, or as many as wants ter lissen ter him, and finally another one would wants ter larn ter read and he would larn him a little. Marster Cole was awful good about dis. But some of de slave owners would not allow any of de slaves ter own a Bible or have one roun' de plantation. And iffen dey ketched one wid a Bible, dey would takes it away from him.

Mos' every Satidy night and Sunday after dinner, Uncle Dan would read de Bible ter de rest of us and tell de meanin' of it. Uncle Dan was awful ole. He didn't know how ole he was, and Marster didn't know either, but he was grey-headed and his whiskers was jest as white as his hair. Uncle Dan could read good, and he could write good, too, and he knew de Bible about as good as anybody I ever saw. He could sats down wid his Bible, and reads a verse in dar anywhar, and tells you jest what it means.

Marster Cole allus gives all his slaves a pass ter go ter church, and everybody knew it and dey wouldn't bother us. De white folks would let de slaves jine de same church as dey was in, and dey got lots of jiners among de slaves. And I has seed as many as fifty slaves, and I say half dat many white people, baptized at one time. Dey would find a pond or hole in de rivah, shallow enough fer baptizing and where de rest could stan' roun' and look on. All de slaves would stan' outside and hears de parson preach till he calls for jiners, and den dey would goes inside ter jine, and when one goes in another would follow jest lak a flock of goats, and when dey would go ter prayin' yer sins away, dey would all go ter shoutin', and dey would has a good time.

Whar de baptizings comes off, it was almos' lak goin' ter a circus. People comes from ever'whar. Dat was de biggest crowd I ever seed. De baptizings was at a big tank and people was all aroun' it. Dey was all singin' songs, and de preachah preached and prayed, and everybody takes dinnah and has a big time. Dat baptizing was de last one Marster Cole went to, as he took sick right after dat, and he was sick for a long time. Sumpin' was wrong wid his stomach—I believe dey said gallbladder or sumpin' lak dat.

Anyway, Marster Cole was sick fer a long, long time. Mah mother nursed him night and day as long as he was sick. Dey had doctors from all ovah de country ter comes, and dey all gives him medicine and doctored him, but de Lord had called him, I guess, and dose doctors couldn't do him any good, fer de next summah he dies.

Dey has a big funeral sermon fer him at de plantation, and all de slaves was at de house. We all lined up and marched by de coffin and looks in at him. He jest looks lak he was asleep. I guess his soul was in de Great Heaven talkin' wid de angels, for he looks lak he had a peaceful smile on his face, jest lak he did when he was alive and everything pleasin' him.

All de slaves cried jest lak it was one of deir own family dyin'. We all knew our good times was gone, or maybe we would all be sold. We didn't know what was goin' ter happen ter us, but we all knew dat we wasn't goin' ter have as peaceable time and have as much freedom as we had when Marster Cole was alive.

One mornin', Missus Cole comes up ter me afore we goes ter work and says, "Well, well, Thomas, what a big, fine strong boy you is. You ought ter be big enough ter do mos' any kine of work, now. You ain't a baby no more. Thomas, I's goin' ter move offen de plantation and lets Mr. Anderson, the overseah, runs it fer me. He is goin' ter moves in dis house, and I's goin' ter move ter Huntsville. I bought a nice place up dar, so I's goin' ter take your ma wid me, as she has allus been our nurse, but I's goin' ter leave you out here on de plantation. I'm sure Mr. Anderson will take good care of you, and besides, you will be grown in a few more years." Den she turns roun' and goes in de kitchen and leaves me standin' dar.

I thoughts, "Yessum, Mr. Anderson will takes good care of me. He'll give me dat cat-o'-nine-tails de first chance he gits. But I makes up mah mind right dar he wasn't goin' ter gits no chance, 'cause I's goin' ter runs off de first chance I gits. I didn't know much about how ter gits outen dar, but I's goin' ter try it. De first chance I gits, I was goin' north whar dar wasn't no slave owners.

Purty soon, mah mother comes out and tells me ter be good and do all dat Mr. Anderson tells me ter do, and ter stay up wid de rest of de slaves, and dat she would comes ter see me de first chance she gits, and fer me ter do de same thing. 'Bout dat time, de boss hollers fer all of us ter goes ter work, so I tole mah mother good-bye. Dat was de last time I ever seed her. She never did gits ter come back ter see me, and I never could goes in ter see her, and I never seed mah brother and sister anymore. Dey never did brings dem back ter de plantation. I don't knows whether dey was sold er not, after dey gits bigger, and I don't know whether mah mother marries anymore er not.

I got mah dinner and goes on ter de fiel', and de first thing, Mr. Anderson says ter me, "Now Thomas, you got ter do as much work as de rest of dese niggers." I says, "Yassah," and flies in ter it, and I kept up all de time, but from dat day on I didn't has no use fer dat overseah. He wants ter whips me, and I knows it, but I never did gives him a chance.

I worked on, day after day, wantin' a good chance ter run off, and finally dar was talk 'bout de North and South separatin', and dat iffen dey did it would cause a war; dat de North wants de South ter turn de slaves loose, and de South wouldn't do it. I don't know how it all happened, but I thinks de North declares de slaves free, and de South declares their selves free from de North, and den things begins happening.

We begin goin' ter de fiel' earlier and stayin' a little later each day den we did de year befo'. Corn was hauled off, cotton was hauled off, hogs and cattle was rounded up and hauled off, and things begins lookin' bad. Instead of eatin' corn bread made outen cornmeal, we eats corn bread made outen kaffir corn and maize.

Dat wintah, instead killin' from three hundred to four hundred hogs, lak we had allus done befo', we only done one killin' and kilt one hundred and seventy-five, and dey was not all big ones, either.

When de meat supply begins ter runs low in de wintah time er early spring, de overseah, Mr. Anderson, would sends some of de slaves ter kill a deer, wild hogs widout any marks er brand on 'em, er jest any kind of game dey could gits. One day, he calls me up wid some of dem dat had gone befo', and tole us not ter go off de plantation too far, but ter be shore and bring home some meat. All dat bunch of slaves was purty good ter do what dey was tole ter do, and Mr. Anderson wasn't scared dey would run off, but he didn't knows me too well. Dis was de chance I had been wantin'.

So when we all gits ter de hunting groun', de leader says, "Now let's us all scatters out." I tole him me and another man would go north and makes a circle roun' ter de rivah, and I would cross ovah and come down on de east side, and mah partner would come down on de west side, and we would meet back whar we started 'bout sundown. So we started, and when we got roun' ter de rivah, I crossed to de east side, but I didn't go very far east of de rivah till I turns back north, 'steadda goin' south. I was goin' ter a free country—de North, whar dar wasn't no slaves. I traveled all that day and night, up de

PLATE 6: Harriet Tubman (1823–1913), nurse, spy, and scout.

river in de day and followed de North Star dat night. Several times dat night, I thought I could hear de blood houn' trailin' me, and I would gits in a big hurry.

I was hopin' and prayin' all de time dat I could meets up wid dat Harriet Tubman woman. She a colored woman, dey say, dat comes down dar next ter us and gits a man and his wife and takes dem out and dey didn't gits ketched, either. I heard after de War dat she was takin' all dem slaves ter Canada and dat she had a regular town up dar wid jest slaves, Negroes, in it—a good-sized little town, too. She allus travels de undergroun' railroad, dey calls it—travels at night and hides out in de day at different places, and den travels all night again, till she gits whar dey was all safe. She sho' sneaked lots of dem out of de South, but she knowed what she was doin' and who would help her. I never did see dis woman, but I thinks she was a brave woman, anyway.

I traveled dis way fer several nights, hidin' in de daytime in de thickets. I would eats all de nuts I could, as there was lots of dem in de bottoms. I killed a few swamp rabbits and ketched a few fish. I built one fire, puts lots of chunks and logs together, and goes off 'bout half mile and hides in a thicket. Dis thicket lead right up to mah fire, but I goes back 'bout half mile in it and waits fer de fire ter burns down ter coals, and den I goes back and bakes me some fish and a rabbit. I was shakin' all de time, 'fraid I would gits ketched, but I was nearly starved to death and I did not much care iffen I did gits ketched. Maybe I would gits sumpin' ter eat. But I didn't gits ketched and I eats mah rabbit and three er four big fish, and I puts de rest of de fish in mah ole cap and starts out again, feelin' purty good.

I traveled on dat night follerin' de North Star, and hides out de next day and eats de rest of mah fish and some more nuts, and travels all de night again, and hides in a big thicket de next day, and along dat evenin' I hears de guns begin shootin'. I sho' was scared dis time—sho' 'nuf. I's scared ter come out and scared ter stay in dar, and while I was standin' dar thinkin' and shakin', I heard two men say, "Stick yo' hands up, boy. Whar you goin'?" I puts mah hands up as high as I could reach and says, "Ah, ah, ah dunno whar I's goin'. You ain't goin' ter take me back ter de plantation, is you?" Dey said, "No. You want ter fight fer de North?" I tole dem I did, 'cause I could tell by de way dey talked dat dey was Northern men, and dey turns me with dem. Dey was spies fer de North.

Dese spies led me aroun' dis place where dey was shootin', and we walked day and night, and de next day we rode in ter General Rosecrans's camp, and dey took me ter General Rosecrans. Dey thought I was a spy fer de South, and dey ask me all sorts of questions and said dey was goin' ter whip me, dat dey was goin' ter burn mah feet. Dey was goin' ter kill me, if I didn't tell dem who mah general was and what he sent me out for. But I tole dem de truth, and tole it ovah and ovah ter dem, and dey finally believed I was telling de truth, and took me out and puts me ter work. I had ter help wid de cannons, but I got plenty ter eat.

Now, I felt important. I had got off and got me a real man's job, and de rest of de slaves back on de plantation was workin' night and day. But jest right den, I didn't know what was in front of me. I speck if I had, I would have run off again.

I helps set dese cannons on dis Chickamauga Mountain er hill. We was jest settin' 'em roun' in kinda hidin' places. I didn't even know dey was gettin' ready ter fight a battle. I thought we was kinda hidin' 'em ter keeps de Rebels from findin' 'em. But I hads to go to one of dem cannons and stays wid a man and waits on him. I don't know jest what it was he had me doin', er if I ever got it finished. Anyway, de first thing I knows, bang, bang, boom. Den things started, and guns was shootin' faster den de fastest man you ever saw beatin' on one of dese little drums wid two sticks. I's gittin' skeered. I looked roun' ter see which way ter run, but guns was shootin' down de hill in front of me, and dey was shootin' at me, and de men had different colored clothes, and I knew dis was war and dat dey was de Rebels. I looks back and guns was shootin' ovah me, and guns on both sides was poppin'. I tries ter digs me a hole and gits in it, but de first thing I knows dis man was kickin' me, and cussin' me, and wantin' me ter help him ter keep de cannon loaded. Man, I didn't wants no cannon, but I hads ter help him anyway.

We fought dat way till dark; den we quits. De Rebels got more men den we did, so General Rosecrans sends a message ter General Woods ter comes and helps us out. De messenger slips out de back way wid de message. I sho' did wish it was me slippin' off, but I didn't wants no message and I didn't wants ter see no General Woods either. I jest wants ter git back ter de ole plantation and picks mo' cotton. I would have been willin' ter jest do anything jest ter git out of dis mess, but I's stuck. I done tole General Rosecrans I wants ter fight de Rebels, and he sho' was lettin' me do it. He wasn't jest lettin' me do it, he was makin' me do it. I done got in dar, and he wouldn't lets me out.

White folks, dar was men layin' here and dar wantin' help, wantin' water, wid blood runnin' outen dem, and men layin' roun' dead wid de top er sides of de head gone, great big holes in dem. I jest promised de good Lawd if He would jest lemme git out of dat mess, I wouldn't run off no mo', but I didn't know den dat He wasn't goin' ter lets me out wid jest dat battle. He was goin' ter give me plenty more.

But dat battle wasn't ovah yet, fer de next mornin' de Rebels begins shootin' 'way at us again. Dey sho' was killin' lots of our men, too, and General Woods had not come yet, so General Rosecrans ordered us ter retreat, and he did not have ter tell me what he said, either. De Rebels comes after us shootin', and we runs off and leaves dat cannon, what I was wid, settin' on de hill. I didn't wants dat thing, nohow. We kept hot-footin' it till we gits ter Chattanooga, and dar is whar we stops.

After de War was ovah and we was all turned loose, we jest scatters out—no whar ter go and nuthin' ter do, nobody ter goes to fer help. I couldn't go back south, whar I had run off from, ter looks fer work, fer up dar dey calls us traitors, and back farther south, dey would nearly kills us, iffen dey knew we had runs off ter de North ter help dem fight.

I always did hate dat I runs off and leaves de South, fer after de War dey calls us Southern traitors, 'cause we runs off and comes ter de North and risk our lives, same as dey did. If Marster Cole had lived, I never would have run off.

Fer about a year after de War, I jest works any whar I could gits work, and finally I gits work on de railroad. Dey was makin' Chattanooga a big division point on dis railroad and buildin' a big roun' house dar, too. I worked on dis work fer 'bout two weeks, walkin' 'bout town at night wid some of de other boys, befo' I tried ter go wid a girl. I had saw a girl next door, and had thought 'bout tryin' ter break in and go wid her, but I was jest a little bashful and hated to git turned down by any woman. After I gits a payday, I dresses up and ask did she want to goes to a dance wid me. So she tole me she would go, iffen her girlfrien' would go. I tole her I could gits one of de boys fer her frien' ter goes wid, and she said her frien' had a feller.

So we all went ter de dance and danced nearly all de night. Dis dance was a cullud man's dance—in dat part of town—and it was one of de ole-fashioned kind, and we all had a good time, and I buys dem anything dey wants, as I had jest got paid and had more money den anyone at de dance. After dat dance, I went out wid her quite a bit, and went ovah ter her uncle's mos' every night and stays a little while. She lived wid her uncle and aunt, 'cause she was a orphan chile. Dis uncle liked me purty good.

After we sparked fer about two months, her uncle tole Nancy—dat was de girl's name—dat she sho' ought ter marry me, dat I was a railroad man and de railroad paid all deir men good money and gives dem all good jobs, and dat I could make her a good livin'. And she tole me after we marries dat she has been thinkin' 'bout dat herself, 'cause I allus had money. We married after we had courted each other fer quite a while, and de next night her uncle give a dance fer us, and we had a big candy pullin'. We was married at her uncle's by a parson, jest lak Marster Cole allus made his slaves do.

We lived in de house wid her uncle fer 'bout a year er more, and me workin' fer de railroad all de time. Den, we bought a little piece of land in de edge of town, in de cullud part of town, and I hads a little two-room house built on it, and we bought a cow and some chickens and a brood sow and had a big garden broke up and got ready ter live at home. I was makin' purty good money den, and after 'bout two years we had some more built on de house, makin' ours a four-room house, and done some other improvements roun' de place. 'Bout de time we got our home repaired, I got a job as a switchman in de railroad yards in Chattanooga. I worked at dis seven years.

I believe every one—takin' all de slaves dat I knows of as a whole—was really happier and better off after de Emancipation den dey was befo'. Of course, de first few years it was awful hard ter gits adjusted ter de new life dat was in front of dem. All de slaves knew how ter do hard work, fer dey was taught dat from de time dey was big enough ter work till dey died. Dat was de ole slaves' life. But dere was very few dat was taught er knows anything 'bout how ter find a job er how ter depend on demselves fer a livin'. But a few years of scrapin' and scratchin' fer deir own food, and it wasn't so hard. I allus had a good job wid de railroad, wid de exception of de first year after de War, and dat was a hard year fer me. If I had had a family, I don't knows what I would have done.

One thing dat made it so hard, de North was broke and de South was broke, after de War. All de plantation owners had spent all deir money and gives all de stock and feed ter helps win de War and had lost. Dey didn't has nuthin' ter pays anyone ter work fer dem, and dey was mad at de North and has a grudge against de slaves, too— dat is, mos' of dem did—and dey would not gives many of dem work and couldn't work as many as dey did befo' de War.

Some of de slaves thought dat deir marsters ought ter give dem sumpin', but mos' of dem was too glad ter be free and jest wanted ter gits away and didn't wants nothin'. I didn't hears of any of de slaves gittin' anything 'ceptin' a crop on de halves,* after de War. I allus has wondered what Missus Cole done wid her plantation, and would have likes ter have gone back down dere and looks aroun', but I's scared to, after I had run off and jined de North.

After de War, de Ku Klux Klan got purty bad roun' in parts of de South. De KKK was kind of a organization in dem days, jest as it was a few years ago. In dem days, dey puts a mask ovah dem. Dis mask was a big white cloth dat covered dem up, and dey cuts holes in it whar deir eyes is, so dey kin see through, and rides roun' ovah de country on horseback and whips and scares lots of de darkies. Iffen a white man gits behind wid his crop and wants ter give a bushel of potatoes or a bushel of corn fer a days' work—don't make no difference iffen you got plenty of taters er corn—iffen de Ku Klux Klan comes roun' at night and knocks on your do' and tells you ter go and work fer Mr. Brown termorrer fer a bushel of taters, you bettah go and works fer de taters er you gits whipped by de KKK termorrer night. De KKK done lots of things dat wasn't no sense in at all.

And de KKK done lots good things, too. Now, iffen a man was so

*A chance to sharecrop for half the crop.

honery and lazy till he jest wouldn't work and was jest layin' roun' and lettin' his wife and po' little chilluns nearly starve ter death, de KKK would comes roun' and knocks at his door some night and tells him ter git him sumpin' ter do and feeds dat woman and chilluns, and dat iffen he didn't, dey would come back and sees him. And dey sho' would, too, but if you did let them come back the second time, 'tis too bad.

I knows a cullud man what lived about a quarter of a mile from me in Chattanooga dat was sho' lazy. After de slaves was freed, he thought he wasn't supposed ter work fer a livin' atall. Dat nigger would steal from you wid you watchin' him. He would steal anything he could gits his hands on and carries it home. He would even go ter dem white people's fiel's at night and dig deir sweet taters out in de fiel' and steal corn outen de patch. He steals meat outen de smoke-house, and he was livin' bettern anybody. Couldn't nobody ketch him, but everybody knows he was stealin', fer he didn't work enough ter has as much as he has.

So de KKK comes along one night and pulls him right outen de bed beside his wife and carries him off in his underclothes—and it was purty chilly dat night, too. Dey takes dis nigger out and makes him own up ter all he steals and makes him promise ter gits a job and go ter work, and never steal anymore. Den dey whips dis nigger till he couldn't hardly stand up, and turns him loose. He staggers roun' and crawls back home, and as soon as his wife could hears him hollerin' she runs ter him and helps him git home. He sho' was whipped good, and as soon as he could get a job he went ter work.

Dis bunch of KKK was jest a bunch of farmers and businessmen, mostly all plantation owners dressed up in a white robe and deir horses covered up wid a white cloth, too, and eyes cut fer dem and de horses. I's seed dem, and dey did look scary after night, especially iffen it was good and dark, 'cause dis white shows up fer a long ways, and when all de cullud people sees dem comin', dey would go and hide and locks deir door. Dey never did bother me, and I never did bother dem.

Long ago, about two years after me and Nancy was married, our baby boy was born, and 'bout four years later our baby girl was born, de one I am livin' wid now. Me and Nancy was happy all de time, as we had a little better livin' den de mos' of de cullud folks roun' us. Of course we had our little quarrels, as all married people do, but dey didn't even amount ter nothin', as we would gits in a good humor after a while.

I bought me a team and wagon, loaded mah wife and chilluns and a few other things in ter it, and mah wife made a strap outen cloth and puts all de money in it, which was about a thousand dollars, and started out fer Texas.

While we was on de way ter Texas, we fished and hunted every day, and we caught some good fish in some of de rivahs. We traveled on till we got ter Cass County, Texas, and we went ter mah wife's cousins. I bought ninety acres of land. It was all timber. I went in dar and went ter cuttin' logs fer a house and got mah wife's cousin ter help me build a two-room house and a log crib, and I rived out boards ter cover it wid, and we moved in jest as soon as we could.

We cleared up 'bout thirty acres and had plenty of barn and shed room built fer all de feed we could raise. We lived here till mah chilluns was grown. Mah wife died here wid malaria and chills. She had one chill after another. Her health was good when we first moved here, but 'long 'bout five years befo' she died, her health broke and we spent lots of money fer medicine and doctors, but dey didn't do her no good.

We allus has some hogs ter kill ever' wintah, and we kills enough ter have meat and lard ter run us all de year, and we has our cornmeal, milk, and butter and eggs and chickens, so de Depression ain't starved us yet. We all got might near naked during de Depression and mah son-in-law got on de relief dat fall after all our crops got washed away. But when de caseworker comes out here and sees de cows, hogs, mules, and chickens, and a little feed in de barn left ovah from last year, he thought we was nearly rich and cut him off, after givin' us a few clothes, and he couldn't git back on de relief.

We allus goes ter church every Sunday morning and Sunday night and I listens ter every word dat de preachah says. I belongs ter de church ever since mah first wife died, and I reads mah Bible all de time till I lost mah eyesight, and now I has mah daughter ter read it ter me, and I knows it 'bout as well as anybody mah color.

I can't helps do none of de farmin', but I can feeds de hogs and de chickens. Dey gits de feed ready and puts it by de barn door, and I feeds dem night and mornin'. I can't see dem, but I laks ter stand and lissen to dem eatin' de feed and hear de milk hitten de bucket when dey milks. All I can do is jest lissen ter de chickens cackle and all de other things roun' de farm and think back when I was young and done all dis by mahself.

People don't know how well dey is blessed dat has got good eyes, till dey lose dem. Everybody ought ter be more thankful den dey is.

I leans ter de Republicans, but I thinks dat President Roosevelt is de best president dat we ever had. He tries ter help rich man, poor man, and every color and race. If we could gits presidents lak him all de time, de United States and all de people would soon be out of debt and own deir own homes and has good jobs er good farms and git good prices fer everything. Anybody can gits de country in a mess, but it takes a smart man a long time ter cleans things up.

Today, I is broke. I spent all mah money several years ago fer medicine and doctors, but I is in fairly good health now, and I gits a small pension from de government, and I spends it jest as carefully as I did when I was young and made mah own money.

WILLIAM ADAMS

YOU want to know and talk about de power de people tells you I has. Well, sit down here—right there in dat chair—befo' we-uns starts. I gits some ice water and den we-uns can discuss de subject. I wants to 'splain it clearly, so you can understand.

I's born a slave, ninety-three years ago, so of course I 'members de war period. Like all de other slaves I has no chance for education. Three months am de total time I's spent going to school. I teached myself to read and write. I's anxious to larn to read, so I could study and find out about many things. Dat I has done.

There am lots of folks, and educated ones, too, what says we-uns believes in superstition. Well, it's 'cause dey don't understand. 'Member de Lawd, in some of His ways, can be mysterious. De Bible says so. There am some things de Lawd wants all folks to know, some things jus' de chosen few to know, and some things no one should know. Now, jus' 'cause you don't know 'bout some of de Lawd's laws, 'taint superstition if some other person understands and believes in sich.

There is some born to sing, some born to preach, and some born to know de signs. There is some born under de power of de Devil, and have power to put injury and misery on people, and some born under de power of de Lawd for to do good and overcome de evil power. Now, dat produces two forces, like fire and water. De evil forces starts de fire, and I has de water force to put de fire out.

How I larnt sich? Well, I's done larn it. It come to me. When de Lawd gives sich power to a person, it jus' comes to 'em. It am forty years ago now when I's fust fully realize' dat I has de power. However, I's allus int'rested in de workin's of de signs. When I's a little pickaninny, my mammy and uther folks used to talk about de signs. I hears dem talk about what happens to folks 'cause a spell was put on 'em. De old folks in dem days knows more about de signs dat de Lawd uses to reveal His laws dan de folks of today. It am also true of de cullud folks in Africa, dey native land. Some of de folks laughs at dey beliefs and says it am superstition, but it am knowin' how de Lawd reveals His laws.

Now, let me tell you of something I's seen. What am seen can't be doubted. It happens when I's a young man and befo' I's realize' dat I's one dat am chosen for to show de power. A mule had cut his leg so bad dat him am bleedin' to death, and dey couldn't stop it. An old cullud man live near there dat dey turns to. He comes over and passes his hand over de cut. Befo' long, de bleedin' stop, and dat's de power of de Lawd workin' through dat nigger—dat's all it am.

I knows about a woman dat had lost her mind. De doctor say it was caused from a tumor in de head. Dey took an X-ray picture, but dere's no tumor. Dey gives up and says it's a peculiar case. Dat woman was took to one with de power of de good spirit, and he say it's a peculiar case for dem dat don't understand. Dis am a case of de evil spell. Two days after, de woman have her mind back.

Dey's lots of dose kind of cases de ord'nary person never hear 'bout. You hear of de cases de doctors can't understand, nor will dey 'spond to treatment. Dat am 'cause of de evil spell dat am on de persons.

'Bout special persons bein' chosen for to show de power, read you' Bible. It says in de Book of Mark, third chapter, "And He ordained twelve, dat dey should be with Him, dat He might send dem forth to preach and to have de power to heal de sick and to cast out devils." If it wasn't no evil in people, why does de Lawd say to "cast out" sich? And, in de fifth chapter of James, it further say, "If any am sick, let him call de elders. Let dem pray over him. De prayers of faith shall save him." There 'tis again. Faith, dat am what counts.

When I tells dat I seen many persons given up to die, and den a man with de power comes and saves sich person, den it's not for people to say it am superstition to believe in de power.

Don't forget, de agents of de Devil have de power of evil. Dey can put misery of every kind on people. Dey can make trouble with de work and with de business, with de fam'ly and with de health. So

PLATE 7: Uncle Essick.

folks mus' be on de watch all de time. Folks has business trouble 'cause de evil power have control of 'em. Dey has de evil power cast out and save de business. There am a man in Waco dat come to see me 'bout dat. He say to me everything he try to do in the las' six months turned out wrong. It starts with him losin' his pocketbook with fifty dollars in it. He buy a carload of hay, and it catch fire, and he lose all of it. He spends two hundred dollars advertisin' de three-day sale, and it begin to rain, so he lose money. It sho' am de evil power.

"Well," he say. "Dat am de way it go, so I comes to you."

I says to him, "It's de evil power dat have you control', and we-uns shall cause it to be cast out." It's done, and he has no more trouble.

You wants to know if persons with de power for good can be successful in castin' out devils in all cases? Well, I answers dat, yes and no. Dey can in every case, if de affected person have de faith. If de party not have enough faith, den it am a failure.

Wearin' de coin for protection 'gainst de evil power? Dat am simple. Lots of folks wears sich, and dey uses mixtures dat am sprinkled in de house, and sich. Dat am a question of faith. If dey has de true faith in sich, it works. Otherwise, it won't.

Some folks won't think for a minute of goin' without lodestone or de salt and pepper mixture in de little sack, tied round dey neck. Some wears de silver coin tied round dey neck. All sich am for to keep away de effect of de evil power. When one have de faith in sich and dey acc'dently lose de charm, dey sho' am miserable.

An old darky dat has faith in lodestone for de charm told me de 'sperience he has in Atlanta, once. He carryin' de hod and de fust thing he does am drap some brick on he foot. De next thing, he foot slip as him starts up de ladder, and him and de bricks drap to de ground. It am lucky for him it wasn't far. Jus' a sprain' ankle, and de boss sends him home for de day. He am 'cited and gits on de streetcar, and when de conductor call for de fare, Rufus reaches for he money, but he lose it or forgits it at home. De conductor say he let him pay nex' time, and asks where he live. Rufus tells him, and he say, "Why, nigger, you is on de wrong car." Dat cause Rufus to walk further with de lame foot den if he started walkin' in de fust place. He thinks there mus' be something wrong with he charm, and he look for it, and it gone! Sho' 'nuf, it am los'. He think, "Here I sits all day, and I won't make another move till I gits de lodestone. When de chillun comes from school, I sends dem to de drugstore for some of de stone and gits fixed."

How, now, I's been waitin' for dat question 'bout de black cat crossin' de road, and, sho' 'nuf, it come. Let me ask you one. How many people can you find dat likes to have de black cat cross in front of 'em? Dat's right, no one likes dat. Let dis old cullud person inform you dat it am sho' de bad luck sign. It is sign of bad luck ahead, so turn back. Stop what you doin'.

I's tellin' you of two of many cases of failure to took warnin' from de black cat. I knows a man call' Hiller. His wife and him am takin' an auto ride, and de black cat cross de road, and he cussed a little and goes on. Den it's not long till he turns de corner and his wife falls out of de car durin' de turn. When he goes back and picks her up, she am dead.

Another fellow, call' Brown, was a-ridin' hossback, and a black cat cross de path, but he drives on. Well, it's not long till his hoss stumble and throw him off. De fall breaks his leg. So take a warnin': don't overlook de black cat. Dat am a warnin'.

FANNY CANNADY

I DON' 'member much 'bout de sojers an' de fightin' in de War den, 'kaze I wuzn' much more den six years ole at de Surrender, but I do 'member how Marse Jordan Moss shot Leonard Allen, one of his slaves. I ain't never forgot dat.

My mammy an' pappy, Silo an' Fanny Moss, belonged to Marse Jordan and Mis' Sally Moss. Dey had 'bout three hundred niggahs an' mos' of dem worked in de cotton fields.

Marse Jordan wuz hard on his niggahs. He worked dem overtime an' didn' give dem enough to eat. Dey didn' have good clothes either, an' dey shoes wuz made out of wood. He had 'bout a dozen niggahs dat didn' do nothin' else but make wooden shoes for de slaves. De chillun didn' have no shoes a-tall; dey went barefooted in de snow an' ice, same as 'twuz summertime. I never had no shoes on my feets 'twell I wuz pas' ten years ole, an' dat wuz after dem Yankees done sets us free.

I wuz skeered of Marse Jordan, an' all of de grown niggahs wuz too, 'cept Leonard an' Burrus Allen. Dem niggahs wuzn' skeered of nothin'. If de Debil hese'f had come an' shook er stick at 'em, dey'd hit him back. Leonard wuz er big black buck niggah—he was de bigges' niggah I ever seed—an' Burrus wuz near 'bout as big, an' dey 'spized Marse Jordan like pizen.

I wuz sort of skeered of Mis' Sally, too. When Marse Jordan wuzn' roun' she was sweet an' kind, but when he wuz roun', she wuz er "yes, suh, yes, suh," woman. Everythin' he tole her to do she done. He made her slap Mammy one time, 'kaze when she passes his coffee she spilled some in de saucer. Mis' Sally hit Mammy easy, but Marse Jordan say, "Hit her, Sally. Hit de black bitch like she 'zerve to be

PLATE 8: A former slave.

hit." Den Mis' Sally draw back her hand an' hit Mammy in de face, pow. Den she went back to her place at the table an' play like she eatin' her breakfas'. Den, when Marse Jordan leave, she come in de kitchen an' put her arms roun' Mammy an' cry, an' Mammy pat her on de back an' she cry, too. I loved Mis' Sally when Marse Jordan wuzn' roun'.

Marse Jordan's two sons went to de War. Dey went all dressed up in dey fightin' clothes. Young Marse Jordan wuz jus' like Mis' Sally, but Marse Gregory wuz like Marse Jordan, even to de bully way he walk. Young Marse Jordan never come back from de War, but 'twould take more den er bullet to kill Marse Gregory. He too mean to die anyhow, 'kaze de Debil didn' want him an' de Lawd wouldn' have him.

One day Marse Gregory come home on er furlow. He think he look pretty wid his sword clankin' an' his boots shinin'. He wuz er colonel, lootenent, er somethin'. He wuz struttin' roun' de yard showin' off, when Leonard Allen say under his breath, "Look at dat goddamn sojer. He fightin' to keep us niggahs from bein' free."

'Bout dat time Marse Jordan come up. He look at Leonard an' say, "Wat yo' mumblin' 'bout?"

Dat big Leonard wuzn' skeered. He say, "I say, 'Look at dat goddamn sojer. He fightin' to keep us niggahs from bein' free!' "

Marse Jordan's face begun to swell. It turned so red dat de blood near 'bout bust out. He turned to Pappy an' tole him to go an' bring him his shotgun. When Pappy come back Mis' Sally come wid him. De tears wuz streamin' down her face. She run up to Marse Jordan an' caught his arm. Ole Marse flung her off an' took de gun from Pappy. He leveled it on Leonard an' tole him to pull his shirt open. Leonard opened his shirt and stood dere big as er black giant, sneerin' at Ole Marse.

Den Mis' Sally run up again an' stood 'tween dat gun an' Leonard.

Ole Marse yell to Pappy an' tole him to take dat woman out of de way, but nobody ain't moved to touch Mis' Sally an' she didn't move neither; she jus' stood dere facin' Ole Marse. Den Ole Marse let down de gun. He reached over an' slapped Mis' Sally down, den picked up de gun an' shot er hole in Leonard's ches' big as yo' fis'. Den he took up Mis' Sally an' toted her in de house. But I wuz so skeered dat I run an' hid in de stable loft, an' even wid my eyes shut I could see Leonard layin' on de groun' wid dat bloody hole in his ches' an' dat sneer on his black mouf.

After dat, Leonard's brother Burrus hated Ole Marse wus'n er snake. Den, one night he run away. Mammy say he run away to keep from killin' Ole Marse. Anyhow, when Ole Marse foun' he wuz gone, he took er bunch of niggahs an' set out to find him. All day long dey tromped de woods. Den, when night come, dey lit fat pine to'ches an' kept lookin', but dey couldn' find Burrus. De nex' day Ole Marse went down to de county jail an' got de blood houn's. He brung home er great passel of dem, yelpin' an' pullin' at de ropes, but when he turned dem loose dey didn' find Burrus, 'kaze he done grease de bottom of his feets wid snuff an' hog lard so de dogs couldn' smell de trail. Ole Marse den tole all de niggahs dat if anybody housed an' fed Burrus on de sly, dat he goin' to shoot dem like he done shot Leonard. Den he went every day an' searched de cabins; he even looked under de houses.

One day, in 'bout er week, Mis' Sally wuz feedin' de chickens when she heard somethin' in de polkberry bushes behin' de henhouse. She didn' go roun' de house but she went inside an' looked through de crack. Dere wuz Burrus layin' down in de bushes. He wuz near 'bout starved 'kaze he hadn't had nothin' to eat since he done run away.

Mis' Sally whisper an' tole him to lay still, dat she goin' to slip him somethin' to eat. She went back to de house an' made up some more cawnmeal dough for de chickens, an' under de dough she put some bread an' meat. When she went 'cross de yard she met Marse Jordan. He took de pan of dough an' say he goin' to feed de chickens. My mammy say dat Mis' Sally ain't showed no skeer; she jus' smile at Ole Marse an' pat his arm. Den, while she talk she take de pan an' go on to de chicken house, but Ole Marse he go, too. When dey got to de henhouse Ole Marse' puppy begun sniffin' roun'. Soon he sta'ted to bark. He cut up such er fuss dat Ole Marse went to see what wuz wrong. Den he foun' Burrus layin' in de polkberry bushes.

Ole Marse drag Burrus out an' drove him to de house. When Mis' Sally seed him take out his plaited whip, she run upstairs an' jump in de bed an' stuff er pillow over her head.

Dey took Burrus to de whippin' post. Dey strip off his shirt. Den dey put his head an' hands through de holes in de top an' tied his feets to de bottom. Den Ole Marse took de whip. Dat lash hiss like col' water on er red hot iron when it come through de air, an' every time it hit Burrus it lef' er streak of blood. Time Ole Marse finish, Burrus' back look like er piece of raw beef. Dey laid Burrus face down on er plank, den dey poured turpentine in all dem cut places. It burned like fire but dat niggah didn' know nothin' 'bout it, 'kaze he done passed out from pain. But, all his life dat black man toted dem scars on his back.

When de War ended Mis' Sally come to Mammy an' say, "Fanny, I's sho' glad yo's free. Yo' can go now an' yo' won' ever have to be er slave no more."

But Mammy, she ain't had no notion of leavin' Mis' Sally. She put her arms roun' her an' call her "Baby," an' tell her she goin' to stay wid her long as she live. An' she did stay wid her. Me an' Mammy bofe stayed wid Mis' Sally 'twell she died.

Voices

GHOSTS AND CONJURING

I WUZ put in de fields when I wuz big 'nuf to hoe. I's hoed wid de field plumb full ob slaves. Hit wuz wuk, but us got some enjaiment outen hit, too. De slaves would tell tales an' ghos' stories an' all 'bout conjurin' an' hoodooin'. Den, dey would git to singin', prayin', an' a-shoutin'. When de overseer hear 'em, he alwa's go make 'em be quiet lak. You see, de white folks don't git in de spirit. Dey don't shout, pray, hum, an' sing all through de services, lak us do. Dey don't believe in a heap o' things us niggers knows 'bout. Dey tells us dey ain't no ghos', but us knows better'n dat. I's seed ghos' an' haints [haunts] all my life. I's seed 'em right here on dis gallery where I's a-settin'.

—MINERVA GRUBBS

When I was a child, we ust to go to a neighbor lady's to get milk, an' you know, we had to go right by a graveyard. One time, my sister grabbed me an' said, "Law', sister, look at dat woman yonder, all wrapped up in a sheet!" I looked, but I couldn't see it. Den, Ma went down dere, an' my sister said, "Yonder it is!" But Ma said, "Hush, dey ain't no ghos'es." But my sister could see 'em an' we couldn't. She got to where she wouldn't go t'rough dat graveyard atall. I nevah could see 'em, but dem dat is born wid veils ovah deir faces can see 'em. I *know* my sister could see ghos'es, an' I tell you she could scare me to death.

—SARAH HATLEY

I seen some sperrits. Sometime', dey comes right 'long, and den sometime' dey looks kinder vagueish. I kin allus tell when sperrits is

85

PLATE 9: Caesar, a house servant, probably the last statutory slave in New York State (1852).

roun'. Dey got a queer scent. When you walk 'bout twenty feet, steam gwine ter hit you in de face. I kin tell when I's right up on 'em, eben iffen I ain't seen 'em. Dey neber say nuttin', though. Dey jis' pass by. Dey look like men. Dey ain't white, but dey got a pale look. Dey neber look like anybody I knowed.

—ALLEN THOMAS

Sperits? I used to see dem. I's scairt of dem. Sometime', dey looks nat'ral and sometime' like de shadow. Iffen dey look like de shadow, jus' keep on lookin' at dem till dey looks nat'ral. Iffen you walks 'long, dey come right up 'side you. Iffen you looks over you left shoulder, you see dem. Dey makes de air feel warm and you hair rise up, and sometime' dey gives you de cold chills. You can feel it when dey's with you. I's set here and seed dem standin' in dat gate. Dey goes round like dey done when dey a-livin'. Some say dey can't cross water.

—SUSAN SMITH

We-uns younguns once have de fun wid de old niggers. De marster knows 'bout what we-uns am doin' an' sho' have de good laugh. Ise will tell you 'bout it.

'Twas dis away. De old niggers am skeert ob haunts. Well, some ob us younguns took de long rawhide string an' makes de "tick-tack" on de roof ob de cabin whar Tom an' Mandy am a-livin'. Dere am a tree 'bout fifty feet f'om de cabin. Ise climb de tree an' holds de string. When Ise pull de string, it goes "thump" on de roof. 'Twas aftah suppah an' 'bout dahk. Tom an' Mandy, wid sev'ral tudder cullud folks, am sattin' in f'ont ob de cabin, talkin'. De marster am standin' off, to see what happens.

Ise pull de string sev'ral times an' it goes "thump, thump, thump." Den, de cullud folks stop talkin' an' listen. Dey heah nothin', so dey stahts talkin' 'gain, an' den comes de "thump, thump, thump." Dey stop talkin' 'gain. Tom says, "What am dat in de cabin?" an' goes in to look roun'. Him comes out an' reports nothin' dere. So, dey stahts talkin', an' 'gain comes de "thump,

thump, thump." Dis time, dey all stand up an' listen, an' Mandy says, "Gosh fo' Mighty! What am dat?" When she says dat, dere comes de "thump, thump, thump." One ob de persons says, "M'ybe 'tis de haunts." Den, dey heahs de "thump, thump, thump" 'gain.

Well, Sar, dem cullud folks come away f'om dere, right den. Ise sattin' up in de tree an' can't see de marster, but Ise heah him laugh to split de sides. Do you know, Tom an' Mandy—an' 'twas two tudder folks dat stay in dere—wouldn't stay in de cabin dat night. No, Sar, dey sleep in de yahd. De marster passed by dem an' ask, "What fo' you fool niggers lay out heah? Go in de cabin whar you can rest," he tell dem.

"Please, Marster, we-uns sleep out heah. 'Tis haunts in dere. Dis night, we-uns heah dem." An' dere dey sleep all night. When de bell rings in de mo'nin'—'twas befo' daylight—dere dey still am.

—AARON RUSSEL

I nebber believed in ghosts, but I do believe in spirits. Ebbeybody got two spirits. One is the evil spirit and the other your good spirit. All the time, these spirits are wandering about. Do you eber be 'sleep and hear somebody call you and it seems lak you can't answer, right then? Well, that's 'cause your spirit is away from your body and you can't answer till it returns. Have you eber dreamed you wuz off visitin' in a city you neber had been in? Well, that's your spirit gone there while you wuz asleep. Without the presence of the spirit, the body is useless. If a person dies and go ter Heaven, their spirit is at peace. If a person wuz wicked, then their spirit will wander here and there, nebber at peace.

—HENRY MOBLEY

Dat's what ghosts is you know—people dat can't quite git in Heaven, an' dey hadda stroll roun' a little longer on de outside, repentin'.

—CAROLINE HOLLAND

Ghosts? I's used to 'em. I see 'em all de time. Good company! I live over dere by myself, an' dey comes in my house all de time. Sometime', I walk along at night an' I see 'em. An' when you see 'em, you see a sight. Dey play. Dey dance round an' round. Dey happy, all right. But dey'll devil you, too. When dey find out dat you scary, dey'll devil you. Dey don't do nothin' to me; only talk to me. I'll be in my house an' dey'll come talk to me. Or I'll be walkin' down de road an' meet 'em. Dey'll pass de time of day wid me.

Dey all looks alike. You remembers when dat car come down de road jes' now? Well, I seen a bunch of 'em right den. Dey get out de road for dat car to pass. Oh, you can't see 'em. No matter how much I shows 'em to you, you can't see 'em. But me!—dey swell wid me. I see 'em all de time. De big house up dere, it full of 'em. De white folks see 'em, too — dat is, some of de white folks. I see, de other day, a white man dat has to work up here start toward de house when de ghosts was comin' out thick. When I tell him, you ought to seen him turn an' run.

—SOLBERT BUTLER

I is heard people all my life tell 'bout seeing ha'nts and spirits, but I don't believe one word of it. They just thinks they sees them. I know I ain't ever seed even one, and I has lived much longer than them what tells those tales. I has seed many people depart this life what has been mistreated terrible, and if they don't come back to do something 'bout it, 'tain't nobody going to come back.

—REUBEN FOX

I's more scared of live people than I is of dead ones. Dead people ain't gwine to harm you.

—FANNIE GRIFFIN

Does I believe in witches? Sa-a-ay, I knows more 'bout 'em dan to jes' believe. I been *rid* by 'em. Right here in dis house. You ain' never been rid by a witch? Well, you mighty lucky. Dey come in de night, ginnerly soon after you drop off to sleep. Dey put a bridle on your head an' a bit in your mouth an' a saddle on your back. Den dey take

89

off deir skin an' hang it up on de wall. Den dey git on you, an' some nights dey like to ride you to death. You try to holler, but you kain't, counta de iron bit in your mouth, an' you feel like somebody holdin' you down. Den dey ride you back home an' into your bed. When you hit de bed, you jump an' grab de kivvers, an' de witch be gone, like dat. But you know you been rid mighty hard, 'cause you all wet wid sweat, an' you feel plumb tired out.

When mean folks dies, de old Debil sometimes doan want 'em down dere in de bad place, so he makes witches out of 'em an' sends 'em back. One thing 'bout witches: dey gotta count ever'thing 'fore dey can git acrost it. You put a broom acrost your door at night an' de old witch's gotta count ever' straw in dat broom 'fore she can come in.

—JOSEPHINE ANDERSON

My young mistress was allus telling us ghost stories and trying to scare the niggers. She like to got killed at that business. She put a high chair on her shoulder, and kivvered herself with a sheet, and went out in the yard to scare my uncle, Allen. He was the blacksmith, and was going home from the shop carrying a big sledgehammer. When he seed "that tall white thing," he throwed the hammer at it, but missed and hit a big iron pot in the yard and busted it all to pieces.

—LIZZIE HUGHES

I 'members de story 'bout de man what owned de monkey. Dat monkey, he watch and try to do everything a man do. One time, a nigger make up he mind to scare 'nother nigger, and when night time come, he put a white sheet over him and sot out for de place dat nigger pass. De monkey, he seed dat nigger wid de sheet on and he grab de nice white tablecloth and throw it over him and he follow de nigger. Dat nigger, he hear somethin' behin' him and look round and see somethin' white followin' him, and he think it a real ghostie. Den, he took out and run fitten to kill hisse'f. De monkey, he took out after dat nigger, and when he fall 'zausted in he doorway, he find out dat a monkey been chasin' him, and he want to kill dat monkey, but he can't do dat, 'cause de monkey am de massa's pet.

90

So one day dat nigger shavin' and de monkey watchin' him. He know right den de monkey try de same thing, so when he gits through shavin', he turn de razor quick in he hand, so de monkey ain't seein' him, and draw de back of de razor quick 'cross he throat. Sho' 'nuf, when he gone, de monkey git de bresh and rub de lather all over he face, and de nigger, he watchin' through de crack. When dat monkey through shavin', he draw de razor quick 'cross he throat, but he don't know 'nuf to turn it, and he cut he own throat and kill hisse'f. Dat what de nigger want him to do, and he feel satisfy dat de monkey done dead and he have he revengence.

—NAP MCQUEEN

One day, when I wuz a young man, me an' a nigger by de name of Henry wuz huntin' in an old field. In dem days, bear, deer, turkey, and squirrels wuz plentiful, an' 'twan't long befo' we had kilt all we could carry. As we wuz startin' home, some monstrous thing riz up right smack dab in front of us, not more'n a hundred feet away. I asked Henry, "Black boy, does yo' see what I see?" An' Henry say, "Nigger, I hopes yo' don't see what I see, 'cause dey ain't no such man." But dere it stood, wid its sleeves gently flappin' in de wind. Ovah eight feet tall, it wuz, an' all dressed in white. I yells at it, "What does yo' want?" But it didn't say nothin'. I yells some mo', but it jus' stands dere not movin' a finger. Grabbin' de gun, I takes careful aim, but still it don't move. Henry, thinkin' maybe I wuz too scared to shoot straight, say, "Nigger, gib me dat gun!" I gibs Henry de gun, but it don't take but one shot to convince him dat he ain't shootin' at any mortal bein'. Throwin' down de gun, Henry say, "Nigger, let's get away from dis place," which it sho' didn't take us long to do.

—THE REVEREND PRESTON KYLES

If a nigger don't go git too scared, he can fin' out what a haint is. One night, when I wuz a little chap, I wuz sont out in de side yard. De wind wuz a-blowin' a little bit rash; de moon wuz a-shinin' dim lak. I wuz a-goin' easy an' slow, a-lookin' ober fust one shoulder, den de udder one. Seberal big dark objects went an' took on de form ob monsters ready ter spring 'pon me, when I heard a whissin', muffled sound. I rolled my eyes in de direction ob de noise, an' ter my horror, under a clump ob oak trees I saw two or three sho' 'nuf ghos', all white an' bobbing up an' down, swingin' dis way an' dat way, an' a-comin' closer an' closer ter me. I frez in my tracks, felt weak an' trembly, an' jist afore dey cotch me, I runned ober myself, screamin', in de house.

Dis proved ter be swings de white chillun had lef' under de trees, wid big white pillows in dem. De win' an' dim moonlight wuz all a little nigger needed fer a real ghos' scare.

—ALLEN WARD

Did I ever see a spirit? 'Spect I has, and I sho' have felt one more than once. 'Spect I was born wid a caul over my eyes. When de last quarter of de moon come in de seventh month of a seventh year, is de most time you see spirits. Lyin' out in de moon befo' daybreak, I's smelt, I's heard, I's seed, and I's felt Catherine's spirit in de moon shadows. I come nigh catchin' hold of her one night, as I woke up a-dreamin' 'bout her, but befo' I could set up, I hear her pass 'way through de treetops dat I was layin', dreamin' under.

—JESSE WILLIAMS

One time, dey was two boys what went out to git hick'ry nuts. Some of 'em was white—dem dat had de hulls off—and dem what had de hulls on was black. When dey gwine back home, dey drap a couple out de bag by de gate of de graveyard. Warn't long befo' a nigger come by, and he hear 'em sortin' out de nuts, jis' inside de gate. He ain't see 'em, but he hear 'em say, "You tek de black ones and I'll tek de white ones." He t'ink it were de Lord and de Debil tekin' de souls of the white folks and cullud folks what been bury dere, and he lit out and run home and tell de marster.

Marster, he say he gwine see 'bout dat, and if dat nigger lyin' he gwine give him hundred lashes. So he go back wid de nigger, and when dey git to de gate de boys inside was done 'vidin' up deir nuts.

Den, one say, "How 'bout dem two at de gate?" And de other say, "You tek de white one and I tek de black one." Wid dat, de white marster say, "I'm damned iffen you kin tek me. Tek de nigger. I'm gone." And he lit out. But when he git where he gwine, de nigger git dere jis' a leedle bit ahead of him.

—HENRY LEWIS

The old folks told us stories about spirits walking at night—jack-o'-lanterns and all them spooky things that almost scared our growth out of us. All that ain't nothing but foolishness. When a soul once departs this life, it won't never be seen no more. That I can guarantee.

There ain't nothing to none of them hoodoo doctors, neither. They is just highway robbers and should be run out of the country.

—SQUIRE IRVIN

Dey was conjure men and women in slavery days. Dey mek out like dey kin do t'ings to keep de marster from whippin' you. One of dem gib a ole lady a bag of san' and tole her dat keep Marster from whippin' her. Dat same day, she git too uppity and sass de marster, 'cause she feel safe. Dat marster, he whip dat darky so hard he cut dat bag of san' plumb in two. Dat ruint de conjure man's business.

—JOSH HADNOT

Us chillun hang round close to the big house, and us have a old man that went round with us and look after us, white chillun and black chillun, and that old man was my great-granddaddy. Us sho' have to mind him, 'cause iffen we didn't us sho' have bad luck. He allus have the pocket full of things to conjure with. That rabbit foot, he take it out and work that on you till you take the creeps and git shakin' all over. Then there's a pocket full of fish scales, and he kind of squeak and rattle them in the hand, and right then you wish you was dead and promise to do anything.

Another thing he allus have in the pocket was a li'l old dry-up turtle—jes' a mud turtle 'bout the size of a man's thumb. The whole thing jes' dry-up and dead. With that thing he say he could do mos' anything, but he never use it iffen he ain't have to. A few times, I see him git all tangle' up and boddered, and he go off by hisself and sot down in a quiet place, take out this very turtle, and put it in the palm of the hand, and turn it round and round, and say somethin' all the time. After while, he git everything ontwisted, and he come back with a smile on he face and maybe whistlin'.

—ABRAM SELLS

The biggest thing the niggers done was working conjurations. The funny thing 'bout that was they could hoodoo each other, but they sure couldn't hoodoo the white folks.

—JULIUS JONES

My mammy larned me a lot of doctorin' what she larnt from old folkses from Africy, and some de Indians larnt her.

If you has rheumatism, jes' take white sassafras root and bile it and drink de tea.

Eat black-eyed peas on New Year, and have luck all dat year.

When anybody git cut, I allus burns woolen rags and smokes de wound, or burns a piece of fat pine and drops tar from it on scorched wool and binds it on de wound.

For headache, put a horseradish poultice on de head, or wear a nutmeg on a string, round you neck.

If you kills de first snake you sees in spring, you enemies ain't gwine git de best of you dat year.

All dese doctorin' things come clear from Africy, and dey allus worked for Mammy and for me, too.

—HARRIET COLLINS

If you are the first person a cat looks at after he has licked hisself, you are going to be married.

If a woodpecker raps on the house, someone is going to die.

If you cut a child's fingernails before it is a year old, it will steal when it grows up.

If the pictures are not turned toward the wall after a death, some other member of the family will die.

—CASIE BROWN

An' when yuh got sick folks in the house an' yuh heah uh dog howlin' an' carryin' on, jes git ready to give up that person, 'cause it uh sho' sign they'll die. Ef yuh nevuh had rats in uh house an' one comes an' gnaws an' gnaws an' yuh cain' cetch 'em, it's uh sho' sign uh death. Jes' like when yuh heah knockin' an' cain' find it, it's death thet knocks.

An' mark it down, when sick folks thet's been ve'y low gits suddenly bettuh an' wants tuh eat a lot, jes' mark it down, it's death wantin' tuh be fed.

—LULU SCOTT

Aunt Darkas lived in McDonough, Georgia, until a few years ago. She died when she wuz a hundred and twenty-eight years old. But, chile, lemme tell you that 'oman knowed just what ter do fer you. She wuz blind, but she could go ter the woods and pick out any kind of root or herb she wanted. She always said the Lord told her what roots to get, and always, 'fore sunup, you would see her in the woods with a short-handled pick. She said she had ter pick 'em 'fore sunup; I don't know why. If you wuz sick, all you had ter do wuz go ter see Aunt Darkas and tell her.

She had a well, and after listening to your complaint, she would go out there and draw a bucket of water and set it on the floor, and then she would wave her hand over it and say something. She called this healing the water. After this, she would give you a drink of water. As she handed it ter you, she would say, "Now, drink. Take this and drink."

Honey, I had some of that water myself, and believe me it goes all over you and makes you feel so good. Old Aunt Darkas would give you a supply of water and tell you ter come back fer more when that wuz gone. Old Aunt Darkas said the Lord gave her power and vision, and she used to fast fer a week at a time.

—EMMALINE HEARD

I was working and a pilot snake jest up and bit me. First thing, I got a live chicken and split it wide open and put its entrails right next to whar dat snake had done bit me. I bound dat whole chicken to my leg till it got cold. Den, I sont out and had some folks catch me some live toad frogs. Dey throwed off de dead chicken and bound two frogs next to my leg wid de bellies next to my hide. Soon, dey died; den turn't green. Den, my bite was cured. Yes, Sir, live frogs takes out snake poison, when dey dies and turns green. You feels dem a-jumpin' while dey is dying.

—GEORGE BRIGGS

De conjure doctor, old Dr. Jones, walk 'bout in de black coat like a preacher, and wear sideburns, and use roots and sich for he medicine. He larnt 'bout dem in de piney woods from he old granny. He didn't cast spells like de voodoo doctor, but used roots for smallpox, and rind of bacon for mumps, and sheep-wool tea for whoopin' cough. And for snakebite he used alum and saltpeter and bluestone mix' with brandy or whiskey.

He could break conjure spells with broth. He take he kettle and put in splinters of pine or hickory—jes' so dey has bark on dem'—covers dem with water, and puts in de conjure salt.

De big black nigger in de cornfield mos' allus had three charms round he neck—one to make him fort'nate in love, one to keep him well, and one for Lady Luck at dice to be with him.

De power of de rabbit foot am great. One nigger used it to run away with. His old granny done told him to try it, and he did. He conjures hisself by takin' a good soapy bath so de dogs can't smell him, and den say a hoodoo over he rabbit foot, and go to de creek and git a start by wadin'. Dey didn't miss him till he clear gone, and dat show what de rabbit foot done for him.

O, Molly Cottontail,
Be sho' not to fail;
Give me you right hind foot;
My luck won't be for sale.

De graveyard rabbit am de best, kilt by a cross-eyed pusson. De niggers all b'lieved General Lee carried a rabbit foot with him. To keep de rabbit foot's luck workin', it good to pour some whiskey on it once in a while.

—PATSY MOSES

If you got worms, take peach leaves and beat 'em in a poultice and bind it around your stomick, and it will turn 'em back down'ards. I have done tried dat. Peach leaves is good for constipation, too.

When a person's got smallpox, buzzard's grease is de bes'. Stew it up in lard and take de fat.

For warts, you take nine grains of corn, and pick dat wart until it bleed, and take dat corn and git dat blood on dat corn, and wrap it up and drop it in de street. Someone pick it up and dey pick de wart off your hand. De wart really will go 'way, 'cause I had one and done it. 'Nother way is to steal a Irish potato and put it in your pocket. I seen a man done dat, but he oughtn't to have let me see him steal it.

For swellings, you boil mullein and pine tar and rub de swelling. Rusty nail water didn' help much. For fever and swelling, a poultice of cow manure mixed with water and salt is good. Chicken manure tea is good for scarlet fever. You sweeten it jus' a little bit.

—JULIA HENDERSON

When we got sick, we had the best of care. Maser would get us a Negro mama, and she doctored us from herbs she got out of the woods, for cough and colds. She used turpentine gathered from pine trees, honey, and onions, made into a syrup, mixed together. Then, she used red oak, cami weed, and Jerusalem weeds for fever, chills, and malaria. If we did not get better in a hurry, Maser would get the white doctor.

Of course, us Negroes soon learned to play sick lots of times to get out of work, and Maser would let us off until we got better, because if we got worse and died he would lose some money. If Maser caught on to us making out like we were sick, he would sure give us a hard punishment. But we would be very careful not to let him catch us. We knew that old black mama would not tell on us, and if we thought that Maser was going to get the white doctor, we got better right away. It was very seldom that Maser ever caught up with us.

—POLLY SHINE

One young nigger cussed the old conjer man on the place. The old man reached up and cut off some of his hair, put it in a sack, and throwed the sack in the water. That boy acted mighty biggity till that hair started floating downstream. Then, he got scared 'most to death. He ran all day trying to get that hair back. He 'most went crazy, 'fore he got that spell lifted.

—JULIUS JONES

Folks don't kill you like they used to kill you. They used to put most anythin' in you, but now they got so wise, or so afraid that somebody will know 'zactly what killed you, that they do it slick as a eel. I have asked root workers to tell me how they does these things, and one told me that it was easy for folks to put snakes, frogs, turtles, spiders, or most anythin' that you couldn't live with, crawlin' and eatin' on the inside of you. He said these things was killed and put up to dry and then beat up into dust. If any of this dust is put in somethin' you have to eat or drink, these things will come alive like they was eggs hatchin' in you. Then, the more they grow, the worse off you get.

—ESTELLA JONES

My uncle wuz poisoned. Yes, sir, somebody fixed his coffee. He lingered and lingered and finally got so he wuz confined ter bed fer good. Somebody put scorpions in him, and whenever they would crawl under his skin he would nearly go crazy, and it looked lak his eyes would jest pop out. He waited so long ter go ter the conjure doctors, they couldn't do him any good. And the medical doctors ain't no good fer nothing lak that. Yes, sir, them scorpions would start in his feet and run up his leg. He neber did get any better, and he died.

—JASPER MILLEGAN

Let me tell you right here, when you done been conjured, medical doctors can't do you no good. You got ter get anudder conjure doctor ter get it off you.

—ROSA MILLEGAN

Iffen you take butter made on de first day ob May an' mix hit wid de yolk ob an egg an' saltpeter, den roll hit inter small pills an' eat dem, dat will cure conjurin'. Dis is de pow'ful stuff. De cow done bit off de top an' bottom ob ebery herb dat grows in de woods, so in dis May butter you gits de bes' ob ebery plant, an' dar ain't no conjurer kin git de better ob hit.

—ANNIE WARE

In dis house, thar am always de p'otection mixture. To make it, yous do dis way. Put one half teaspoon of red pepper, black pepper, an' salt together. Measure it dat way, as much as yous want to mix. Now, if someone comes to yous house as a friend, but come fo' to cause trouble, sich as flirt wid de wife or de husband, or tries to do somethin' dat will cause separation, use de mixture. When dey leaves de house, yous go to de back doah an' take a pinch of de mixture an' sprinkle it f'om de back to de f'ont of de house, an' at de f'ont doah take a pinch an' throw it aftah dem. If yous do dat, thar won't be any effect f'om de powah. When de husband begins to care fo' a tudder woman, if de wife puts a pinch of de p'otection mixture under de bed befoah gwine to bed, dat will cause de man to fo'get de tudder woman.

—MOSLIE THOMPSON

Many yeahs back, dere wuz a woman who lib right nex' door tuh me. She allus make out lak she wuz my frien' an' talk nice tuh my face, but she wuz really my enemy. She wuz jealous ob what I hab, an' she wuz plottin' how tuh do me ebil.

One mornin', I go ober tuh her house, an' she sittin' down eatin' her breakfast. She say, "Sit down an' hab some coffee wid me."

I hab duh coffee, an' I stay an' talk. Atta a time, I come back home. All ob a sudden, I feel sick. My head wuz dizzy, an' I hab tuh sit down on a chair. Right away, I knowed dat woman hab cunjuh me. Dere wuz a charm in dat coffee.

I goes right out in duh yard an' I gits what I need tuh make a Hell Fire Gun. I hab tuh work fast, fuh dat cunjuh wuz pow'ful strong, an' I wuz feelin' worse all duh time.

In jes' a little time, I hab made duh gun, an' I shoot it off. Stead ob cetchin' one enemy, I cetch t'ree. Dat woman hab git two men tuh he'p her cunjuh me, an' when I shoot off duh gun, it git 'um all. First t'ing yuh know, I heah how first one an' den anudder wuz sick. Dey git worse an' worse, an' atta a time dey all die.

—"MA" STEVENS

Narratives

———⊶⊷———

CHARLEY WILLIAMS

JACK AND ROSA MADDOX

ROSE WILLIAMS

CHARLEY WILLIAMS

IFFEN I could see better out'n my old eyes, and I had me something to work with and de feebleness in my back and head would let me 'lone, I would have me plenty to eat in de kitchen all de time, and plenty tobaccy in my pipe, too, bless God!

And dey wouldn't be no rain trickling through de holes in de roof, and no planks all fell out'n de flo' on de gallery neither, 'cause dis old nigger knows everything about making all he need to git along! Old Master done showed him how to git along in dis world, jest as long as he live on a plantation. But living in de town is a different way of living. All you got to have is a silver dime to lay down for everything you want, and I don't git de dime very often.

But I ain't give up! Nothing like dat! On de days when I don't feel so feeble and trembly I jest keep patching round de place. I got to keep patching so as to keep it whar it will hold de winter out, in case I git to see another winter.

Iffen I don't, it don't grieve me none, 'cause I wants to see Old Master again anyways. I reckon maybe I'll jest go up and ask him what he want me to do, and he'll tell me, and iffen I don't know how, he'll show me how, and I'll try to do it to please him. And when I git it done I wants to hear him grumble like he used to and say, "Charley, you ain't got no sense, but you is a good boy. Dis here ain't very good, but it'll do, I reckon. Git yourself a little piece o' dat brown sugar, but don't let no niggers see you eating it; if you do, I'll whup your black behind."

Dat ain't de way it going be in Heaven, I reckon, but I can't set here on dis old rottendy gallery and think of no way I better like to have it!

PLATE 10: A former slave from Oktibbeha County, Mississippi.

I was a big hulking buck of a boy when de War come along and bust up everything, and I can 'member back when everybody was living peaceful and happy, and nobody never had no notion about no war.

I was borned on the 'leventh of January, in 1843, and was old enough to vote when I got my freedom, but I didn't take no stock in all dat politics and goings on at dat time. I didn't vote till a long time after Old Master passed away, but I was big enough before de War to remember everything pretty plain.

Old Master name was John Williams, and Old Mistress name was Mis' Betty, and she was a Campbell before she married. Young Missy was named Betty after her mommy, and Young Master was named Frank, but I don't know who after. Our overseer was Mr. Simmons, and he was mighty smart and had a lot of patience, but he wouldn't take no talk nor foolishness. He didn't whup nobody very often, but he only had to whup 'em jest one time! He never did whup a nigger at de time de nigger done something, but he would wait till evening and have Old Master come and watch him do it. He never whupped very hard, 'cept when he had told a nigger about something and promised a whupping next time and de nigger done it again. Den dat nigger got what he had been hearing 'bout!

De plantation was about as big as any. I think it had about three hundred acres, and it was about two miles northwest of Monroe, Louisiana. Lots of the plantations had been whacked right out of de new ground and was full of stumps. Master's place was more open, though, and all in the fields was good plowing.

Everything boughten we got come from Shreveport and was brung in by the stage and the freighters, and that was only a little coffee or gunpowder, or some needles for the sewing, or some strap iron for the blacksmith, or something like dat. We made and raised everything else we needed right on the place.

Old Master come out into that country when he was a young man, and they didn't have even so much then as they had when I was a boy. I think he came from Alabama or Tennessee, and way back his people had come from Virginia, or maybe North Carolina, 'cause he knowed all about tobacco on the place. Cotton and tobacco was de long crops on his place, and, of course, lots of hosses and cattle and mules.

De Big House was made out'n square hewed logs, and chinked wid little rocks and daubed wid white clay, and kivvered wid cypress clapboards. I remember one time we put on a new roof, and de niggers hauled up de cypress logs and sawed dem and frowed out de clapboards by hand.

De house had two setting rooms on one side and a big kitchen room on de other, wid a wide passage in between, and den about was de sleeping rooms. They wasn't no stairways, 'cepting on de outside. Jest one big chimbley was all he had, and it was on de kitchen end, and we done all de cooking in a fireplace dat was purty nigh as wide as de whole room.

In de sleeping rooms dey wasn't no fires, 'cepting in braz'ers made out of clay, and we toted up charcoal to burn in 'em when it was cold, mornings in de winter. Dey kept warm wid de bedclothes and de knitten clothes dey had.

Master never did make a big gallery on de house, but our white folks would set out in de yard under de big trees in de shade. They was long benches made out'n hewed logs and all padded wid gray moss and corn shuck padding, and dey set pretty soft. All de furniture in de house was homemade, too. De beds had square posts as big around as my shank, and de frame was mortised into 'em, and holes bored in de frame and homemade rope laced in to make it springy. Den a great big mattress full of goose feathers and two, three comforts as thick as my foot wid carded wool inside. Dey didn't need no fireplaces!

De quarters was a little piece from de Big House, and dey run along both sides of de road dat go to de fields. All one-room log cabins, but dey was good and warm, and everyone had a little open shed at de side whar we sleep in de summer to keep cool.

It wasn't very fancy at de Big House, but it was mighty pretty jest de same, wid de gray moss hanging from de big trees, and de cool green grass all over de yard, and I can shet my old eyes and see it jest like it was before de War come along and bust it up.

I can see Old Master setting out under a big tree smoking one of dem long cheroots his tobacco nigger made by hand, and fanning hisself wid his big wide hat another nigger platted out'n young inside corn shucks for him. And I can hear him holler at a big bunch of white geeses what's gitting in his flower beds and see 'em string off behind de old gander towards de big road.

When de day begin to crack, de whole plantation break out wid all kinds of noises, and you could tell what going on by de kind of noise you hear.

Come de daybreak, you hear de guinea fowls start potracking down at de edge of de woods lot, and den de roosters all start up round de barn, and de ducks finally wake up and jine in. You can smell de sowbelly frying down at de cabins in de "row," to go wid de hoecake and de buttermilk.

Den purty soon de wind rise a little, and you can hear a old bell donging 'way on some plantation a mile or two off, and den more bells at other places, and maybe a horn, and purty soon yonder go Old Master's old ram horn wid a long toot and den some short toots, and here come de overseer down de row of cabins, hollering right and left, and picking de ham out'n his teeth wid a long shiny goose quill pick.

Bells and horns! Bells for dis and horns for dat! All we knowed was go and come by de bells and horns!

Old ram horn blow to send us all to de field. We all line up, about seventy-five field niggers, and go by de toolshed and git our hoes, or maybe go hitch up de mules to de plows and lay de plows out on de side so de overseer can see iffen de points is sharp. Any plow gits broke or de point gits bungled up on de rocks, it goes to de blacksmith nigger. Den we all git on down in de field.

Den de anvil start dangling in de blacksmith shop—"Tank! Deling-ding! Tank! Deling-ding!"—and dat ole bull tongue gitting straightened out!

'Course you can't hear de shoemaker awling and pegging, and de card spinners, and de old mammy sewing by hand, but maybe you can hear de old loom going, "frump, frump," and you know it all right iffen your clothes do be wearing out, 'cause you gwine git new britches purty soon.

We had about a hundred niggers on dat place, young and old. We could make about every kind of thing, 'cepting coffee and gunpowder, dat our white folks and us needed.

When we needs a hat we gits inside corn shucks and weave one out, and makes hoss collars de same way: jest tie two little soft shucks together and begin plaiting.

All de cloth 'cepting de Mistress' Sunday dresses come from de sheep to de carders and de spinners and de weaver. Den we dye it wid "butternut" and hickory bark and indigo and other things and set it wid copperas. Leather tanned on de place made de shoes, and I never see a store-boughten wagon wheel, 'cepting among de stages and de freighters along de big road.

We made purty, long back-combs out'n cow horn, and knitting needles out'n second hickory. Split a young hickory and put in a big wedge to prize it open, den cut it down and let it season, and you got good bent grain for wagon hames and chair rockers and such.

It was jest like dat till I was grown, and den one day come a neighbor man and say we in de War.

Little while, young Master Frank ride over to Vicksburg and jine de Sesesh* army, but Old Master jest go on lak nothing happen, and we all don't hear nothing more until 'long come some Sesesh soldiers and take most Old Master's hosses and all his wagons.

I bin working on de tobacco, and when I come back to de barns everything was gone. I would go into de woods and git good hickory and burn it till it was all coals and put it out wid water to make hickory charcoal for curing de tobacco. I had me some charcoal in de fire trenches under de curing houses, all full of new tobacco, and de overseer come and say to bundle all de tobacco up 'cause he going take it to Shreveport and sell it befo' de soldiers take it, too.

After de hosses all gone and most de cattle and de cotton and de tobacco gone, too, here come de Yankees and spread out all over de whole country. Dey had a big camp down below our plantation.

One evening, a big bunch of Yankee officers come up to de Big House and Old Master set out de brandy in de yard and dey act purty nice. Next day, de whole bunch leave on out of dat part.

When de hosses and stuff all go, Old Master sold all de slaves but about four, but he kept my pappy and mammy and my brother Jimmie and my sister Betty. She was named after Old Mistress. Pappy's name was Charley and Mammy's was Sally. De niggers he kept didn't have much work widout any hosses and wagons, but de

* Secessionist.

blacksmith started in fixing up more wagons and he kep' dem hid in de woods till dey was all fixed.

Den along come some more Yankees, and dey tore up everything we had. Old Master was afeared to shoot at dem on account his womenfolks, so he tried to sneak the fambly out, but they ketched him and brung him back to de plantation.

We niggers didn't know dat he was gone till we seen de Yankees bringing dem back. De Yankees had done took charge of everything and was camping in de big yard, and us was all down at de quarters scared to death, but dey was jest letting us alone.

It was night when de white folks tried to go away, and still night when de Yankees brung dem back, and a house nigger come down to de quarters wid three, four mens in blue clothes and told us to come up to de Big House.

De Yankees didn't seem to be mad wid Old Master, but jest laughed and talked wid him, but he didn't take de jokes any too good.

Den dey asked him could he dance and he said no, and dey told him to dance or make us dance. Dar he stood inside a big ring of dem mens in blue clothes, wid dey brass buttons shining in de light from de fire dey had in front of de tents, and he jest stood and said nothing, and it look lak he wasn't wanting to tell us to dance.

So some of us young bucks jest step up and say we was good dancers, and we start shuffling while de rest of de niggers pat.

Some nigger women go back to de quarters and git de gourd fiddles and de clapping bones made out'n beef ribs and bring dem back so we would have some music. We git all warmed up and dance lak we never did dance befo'! I speck we invent some new steps dat night!

We act lak we dancing for de Yankees, but we trying to please Master and Old Mistress more than anything, and purty soon he begin to smile a little and we all feel a lot better.

Next day de Yankees move on away from our place, and Old Master start gitting ready to move out. We git de wagons we hid, and de whole passel of us leaves out for Shreveport. Jest left de old place standing like it was.

In Shreveport, Old Master git his cotton and tobacco money what he been afraid to have sent back to the plantation when he sell his stuff, and we strike out north through Arkansas.

Dat was de awfullest trip any man ever make! We had to hide from everybody till we find out if dey Yankees or Sesesh, and we go along little old back roads and up one mountain and down another, through de woods all de way.

After a long time we git to the Missouri line, and kind of cut off through de corner of dat state into Kansas. I don't know how we ever git across some of dem rivers, but we did. Dey nearly always would be some soldiers around de fords, and dey would help us find de best crossing. Sometimes we had to unload de wagons and dry out de stuff what all got wet, and camp a day or two to fix up again.

Purty soon we git to Fort Scott, and that was whar de roads forked ever whichaways. One went on north and one east and one went down into de Indian country. It was full of soldiers coming and going back and forth to Arkansas and Fort Gibson.

We took de road on west through Kansas and made for Colorado Springs.

Fort Scott was all run down, and the old places whar dey used to have de soldiers was all fell in, in most places—jest old rackety walls and leaky roofs and a big pole fence made out'n poles sot in de ground all tied together, but it was falling down, too.

They was lots of wagons all around what belong to de Army, hauling stuff for de soldiers, and some folks told Old Master he couldn't make us niggers go wid him, but we said we wanted to anyways, so we jest went on west across Kansas.

When we got away on west we come to a fork, and de best road went kinda south into Mexico, and we come to a little place called Clayton, whar we camped a while and then went north. Dat place is in New Mexico now, but Old Master jest called it Mexico.

About dat time Old Master sell off some of de stuff he been taking along, 'cause de wagons was loaded too heavy for de mountains and he figger he better have de money than some of de stuff, I reckon.

We git to Fort Scott again, and den de Yankee officers come and ask all us niggers iffen we want to leave Old Master and stay dar and work, 'cause we all free now. Old Master say we can do what we please about it.

110

A few of de niggers stay dar in Fort Scott, but most of us say we gwine stay wid Old Master, and we don't care iffen we is free or not.

When we git back to Monroe to de old place us niggers git a big surprise. We didn't hear about it, but some Old Master's kinfolks back in Virginia done come out dar an' fix de place up and kept it for him while we in Colorado, and it look 'bout as good as when we left it.

He cut it up in chunks and put us niggers out on it on de halves, but he had to sell part of it to git de money to git us mules and tools. Den, after while, he had to sell some more, and he seem lak he git old mighty fast.

Young Master bin in de big battles in Virginia, and he git hit, and den he git sick, and when he come home he jest lak a old man, he was so feeble.

About dat time they was a lot of people coming into dat country from de North, and dey kept telling de niggers dat de thing for dem to do was to be free, and come and go whar dey please. Dey try to git de darkies to go and vote, but none us folks took much stock by what dey say. Old Master tell us plenty time to mix in de politics when de young-uns git educated and know what to do.

Jest de same, he never mind iffen we go to de dances and de singing and sech. He allus lent us a wagon iffen we want to borry one to go in, too.

Some de niggers what work for de white folks from de North act purty uppity and big, and come pestering round de dance places and try to talk up ructions amongst us, but it don't last long. De Ku Kluckers start riding round at night, and dey pass de word dat de darkies got to have a pass to go and come and to stay at de dances. Dey have to git de pass from de white folks dey work for, and passes writ from de Northern people* wouldn't do no good. Dat de way de Kluckers keep the darkies in line.

De Kluckers jest ride up to de dance ground and look at everybody's passes, and iffen some darkie is dar widout a pass or got a pass from de wrong man, dey run him home, and iffen he talk big and won't go home, dey whop him and make him go.

Any nigger out on de road after dark liable to run across de

*Yankees.

111

Kluckers, and he better have a good pass! All de dances got to bust up at about 'leven o'clock, too.

One time I seen three, four Kluckers on hosses, all wrapped up in white, and dey was making a black boy git home. Dey was riding hosses and he was trotting down de road ahead of 'em. Ever time he stop and start talking, dey pop de whip at his heels and he start trotting on. He was so mad he was crying, but he was gitting on down de road jest de same.

I seen 'em coming and I gits out my pass Young Master writ so I could show it, but when dey ride by, one in front jest turns in his saddle and look back at t'other men and nod his head, and they jest ride on by widout stopping to see my pass. Dat man knowed me, I reckon. I looks to see iffen I knowed de hoss, but de Kluckers sometime swapped dey hosses round amongst 'em, so de hoss maybe wasn't his'n.

De Kluckers wasn't very bad 'cause de niggers round dar wasn't bad, but I hear plenty of darkies git whopped in other places 'cause dey act up and say dey don't have to take off dey hats in de white stores and such. Any nigger dat behave hisself and don't go running round late at night and drinking never had no trouble wid de Kluckers.

Young Mistress go off and git married, but I don't remember de name, 'cause she live off somewhar else, and de next year, I think it was, my pappy and mammy go on a place about five miles away owned by a man named Mr. Bumpus, and I go 'long wid my sister Betty and brother Jimmie to help 'em.

I live around dat place and never marry till old Mammy and Pappy both gone, and Jimmie and Betty both married, and I was gitting about forty year old myself. Den I go up in Kansas and work around till I git married at last.

I was in Fort Scott, and I married Mathilda Black, in 1900. She is seventy-three years old now and was born in Tennessee. We went to Pittsburgh, Kansas, and lived from 1907 to 1913, when we come to Tulsa.

Young Master's children writ to me once in a while and told me how dey gitting 'long up to about twenty year ago, and den I never heard no more about 'em. I never had no children, and it look lak my wife going outlive me, so my mainest hope when I goes on is seeing Mammy and Pappy and Old Master. Old overseer, I speck, was too devilish mean to be thar!

'Course, I loves my Lord Jesus same as anybody, but you see I never hear much about Him until I was grown, and it seem lak you got to hear about religion when you little to soak it up and put much by it. Nobody could read de Bible when I was a boy, and dey wasn't no white preachers talked to de niggers. We had meeting sometimes, but de nigger preacher jest talk about bein' a good nigger and "doing to please de Master," and I allus thought he meant to please Old Master, and I allus wanted to do dat anyways.

So dat de reason I allus remember de time Old Master pass on.

It was about two years after de War, and Old Master been mighty porely all de time. One day we was working in de Bumpus field and a nigger come on a mule and say Old Mistress like to have us go over to de old place 'cause Old Master mighty low and calling mine and Pappy's and Mammy's name. Old man Bumpus say go right ahead.

When we git to de Big House, Old Master setting propped up in de bed, and you can see he mighty low and out'n his head. He been talking about gitting de oats stacked, 'cause it seem to him lak it gitting gloomy-dark, and it gwine to rain, and hail gwine to ketch de oats in de shocks. Some nigger come running up to de back door wid an old horn Old Mistress sent him out to hunt up, and he blowed it so Old Master could hear it.

Den purty soon de doctor come to de door and say Old Master wants de bell rung 'cause de slaves should ought to be in from de fields, 'cause it gitting too dark to work. Somebody git a wagon tire and beat on it like a bell ringing, right outside Old Master's window, and den we all go up on de porch and peep in. Everybody was snuffling kind of quiet, 'cause we can't help it.

We hear Old Master say, "Dat's all right, Simmons. I don't want my niggers working in de rain. Go down to de quarters and see dey all dried off good. Dey ain't got no sense but dey all good niggers." Everybody around de bed was crying and we all was crying, too.

Den Old Mistress come to de door and say we can go in and look at him if we want to. He was still setting propped up, but he was gone.

I stayed in Louisiana a long time after dat, but I didn't care nothing about it, and it look lak I'm staying a long time past my time in dis world, 'cause I don't care much about staying no longer, only I hates to leave Mathilda.

But any time de Lord want me I'm ready, and I likes to think when He ready He going tell Old Master to ring de bell for me to come on in.

JACK AND ROSA MADDOX

Yes, I was born a slave and so was Rosa. We got out of the chattel slavery, and I was better for gettin' out, but Rosa don't think so. She says all we was freed for is to starve to death. I guess she's right 'bout that, too, for herself. She says her white folks were good to her. But don't you expect me to love my white folks. I love them like a dog loves hickory.

I was settin' here thinking the other night 'bout the talk of them kind of white folks going to Heaven. Lord God, they'd turn the Heaven wrong side out and have the angels working to make something they could take away from them. I can say these things now. I'd say them anywhere—in the courthouse, before the judges, before God. 'Cause they done done all to me that they can do. I'm done past everything but worryin' 'bout Rosa, 'cause she don't get 'nuf to eat and 'cause she feel bad all the time. But they ain't no complainin' in her. [To Rosa] Mama, how you feel in the sun?

Rosa Maddox: Best to be expected this time o' year.

Jack Maddox: I was born in Georgia on a farm. My mother's name was Lucindy. I heard other Negroes say she was a good woman, but she died when I was a little boy, not more than three or four. She left my little brother a crawlin' baby 'bout eleven months old. I can remember a little her dyin'. I can remember her rockin' me on the steps and singin', "Lord revive us. All our help must come from Thee." I can remember cryin' for my mama and bein' lonesome for her. They tried to tell me she was dead, but I couldn't get it through my little head. My little brother was pitiful, plumb pitiful. There was one between me and the baby and all of us was lonesome for Mama. I had a older brother and a older sister. My sister was so good. She wasn't nothing but a chap, but she did what she could for us.

Many times, when she wasn't but nine years old, I have held a pine torch for her to see how to wash our rags at night. Then Judge Maddox's cook was a good woman. She was half-sister to Judge Maddox and was a sister-in-law to my mama. For a long time she let the baby sleep with her in her bed.

But my other brothers and sisters had to sleep on the floor in the cabin, huddled together in cold weather so we wouldn't freeze to death. Our life was a misery. I hate the white man every time I think of us being no more than animals.

Judge Maddox moved into Buena Vista when I was real small. He had a big fine double-run frame house covering a large piece of ground. We used to wait outside the kitchen door of the master's big house. The baby would crawl up by the door and wait with us. The cook would give us what she could. Sometimes she would give us a teaspoon of syrup and we would mix it with water to make something sweet. I used to crave sweet. Or we would eat a biscuit with fried meat grease on it. We used to be too hungry to give the baby his rightful share. We would get the chicken feet where they threw them out and roast them in the ashes and gnaw the bone.

Judge Maddox had about fifty slaves, as I remember, when I was a little boy. Most of them stayed out on the farm and worked out there.

My father was a blacksmith. He could make everything from a horseshoe nail to a gooseneck. He was sold to Judge Maddox from the Burkhalters. My father said the Burkhalters were mean as they come. He said that his master, Mr. Burkhalter, had gone to a war when he was a young man and stayed six months. He told me that there had always been wars and there would always be wars and rumors of wars as long as the world stand.

Rosa never did know nothin' 'bout her father, eh Mama?

Rosa Maddox: That's right, I never did know nothing 'bout my paw, but I looked on my mama like a savior. Her name was Hannah Clemon, and Dr. Andrews, my master, had always owned her. Dr. Andrews was a good man and good liver. He was from Mississippi,

PLATE 11: A slave couple.

but he moved to Union Parish, Louis'ana, when I was such a little girl I don't remember.

My mama said that she remembered when Dr. Andrews came from Louis'ana to Mississippi and got married. He brought her along and told her to piece quilts. She said all the time she had to work in the house and piece quilts so much that she didn't have no time atall. But he moved back to Louis'ana.

Dr. Andrews had 'bout twelve slaves. I had all the time to play until I was 'bout nine years old. We made rag dolls and played dolls—that was me and the other little niggers. I was the baby of my mama. She had eight chillun besides me. We used to play "church." We would play "singin' " and "prayin' " and "dyin'."

We had good little cabins. There was four of them settin' out in the yard. And we had cotton mattresses and blankets. We had 'nuf to eat, too. They 'lowanced it out to us every two weeks. They'ud give us syrup, meal, flour and meat, potatoes, and plenty of milk. The madam, that's Mis' Fannie, Dr. Andrews' wife, had a garden, and she give us fresh greens and onions and things.

The neighbors used to say, "There goes Oat Andrews' free niggers." That's 'cause he never hardly whipped them and give them rest and play time. He doctored us when we was sick and took good care of us. I sho' thought a heap o' Dr. Andrews.

When I was nine or twelve or sech about, I went into the house as a waiting and nurse girl. I had played with one of Mis' Fannie's younger sisters, and she had some more. They used to come and tease me, and I was sassy. Everything I say they'd say, "You done told that once." Then they say they is going to tell Doctor on me, and I don't want that.

The Andrews had two boys and a girl. The girl died and they was awful cut up about it. The boys were good boys. It always seemed they thought a heap of me. 'Course, I thought a heap of them, too. They was smart boys with book learnin' and schoolin'. But they better not ketch any niggers with books. They say that was bad.

Jack Maddox: Now on Judge Maddox's place, if a nigger was caught with a book he got whipped like he was a thief. He had one man named Allen who went to work for a man whose boys taught him to read. When he came back to Judge Maddox's, he would slip off into the woods on Sunday and read a paper or a book. I 'member he told me, "It's a shame that a man couldn' read like he wanted to, cheap as paper is."

When I was about nine or ten years old—it was in 1853—Judge Maddox's family and the Blantons and the Wells and the widow Nutt 'lowed they would come to Texas. Judge Maddox sold off some of his slaves. He sold one man so he could stay with his wife that b'longed to another white man. But three men that I know of came to Texas with Judge Maddox and left wives behind them. One, I know, never saw his wife again. A man didn't have the freedom of a dog in them days. It was pretty good crowd came to Texas. Most of them rode in covered wagons, but 'course us niggers walked.

Judge Maddox settled near Mount Enterprise and built him a good frame house, and little double-room log houses for the niggers. My first real hard work was gathering brush in the fields. Life was pretty hard. There was a cowhide to get you every time you turned your head out of time. They got us up for the fields before day. We used to go to the fields singin'.

We had a overseer. He thought three o'clock the time to get up. Then there was a nigger man was a leader or driver. When they put me to work that ended my play days. I got a little more to eat, but shoes, underwear, a bed, a hat was things I didn't know nothin' 'bout till I was along sixteen years old.

I used to see the little niggers playin' and I wanted to play, too, but I'd have to tote water or somethin'. They played "base," "puss wants a corner," and a game about a old hen fluttering 'round to keep the little chickens from the hawks. They called it playing "shoo shoo." What I always liked, when I used to play, was "William, William Tremble Toe." It goes:

William, William Tremble Toe
He's a good fisherman . . .
Wire briar
Limber lock
Three geese in a flock

One flew east
One flew west
One flew over the cuckoo's nest. . . .

We learned some of them games from Judge Maddox's chilluns. He had eight of them. They were fair to middlin' good chilluns. I can remember them tryin' to comfort me sometimes, when the old lady cut me with a cowhide she kept by her. We didn't see them enough to really get to know them, though.

'Course, we got to go to church in fair weather. They used to fix up a brush arbor in back of the whitefolks' meetinghouse and let the niggers set out there. The white preacher would preach along and then he'ud say, "And you slaves out there, if you want to have the Kingdom Come you got to mind your masters, work hard, and don't steal your master's chickens."

After I was a plumb old man, I read in the papers that there was nine hundred preachers in the penitentiary and I said to myself, "There ought to be nine hundred more there, if they would just ketch them all"—them preachers and their left-handed fellowship.

Rosa Maddox: Now, me, I used to go to church. I used to ride on the horse behind Mis' Fannie. I went and set in the whitefolks' church. But later on I went to a colored church. I thought the singin' was just fine. I got religion when I was pretty little. I just remember that I felt the power of the Lord descend on me. But I was sinful for a long time. I kept on dancing and singin' reels and cotillion songs. But I ain't did that for a long time now. I wanted to do right, but I guess I had a lot of devil in me. One reason I guess was 'cause the Andrews were joyful folks. They just made me joyful.

The niggers on the Andrews place had clothes. The niggers was taught to sew and spin. They knitted socks. Mis' Fannie taught me how to knit and sew and spin. But she used to buy me good calico dresses and make them up for me. Shucks, I had good clothes as anybody. Maybe that was why I had lots of beaus.

Jack Maddox: Well now, Rosa, I believes you disremembers some of those good things. From what I seen, I didn't see much of goodness. I seen speculators coming by with womens and chilluns, as well as men. The older I got, the more I found the taste of they whips with my back layed open. And I seen niggers put in the stocks.

When I got big 'nuf to go fishing I'd go, and the old lady 'ud call me and take my fish away from me. I got tired of it and was hongry for fish. I cooked and ate them in the woods. They quit lettin' me go fishing on Sunday. They put a chain 'round my legs and on my arms. Then they put a stick under my knees and chained me down by the hands to it. I was hobbled worse than a animal.

One Sunday morning, I had on chains and I was mad. The judge had called me early that morning to go to a neighbor's house, and there was heavy frost on the ground. My feet were sore and scabbed over, and going on the frozen ground was worse than a misery, but I had to go. Later on I was building a fire in the fireplace and I kept lettin' the chains clank against the brass firedogs. I knew he didn't like it. But I thought as how I didn't like going in the frost with my sore feet, and I thought to give him a dose of something he don't like. I kept the chain clanking. He come in and got me, and he beat me half to death. Then he put a iron band and chain 'round my neck and it choked me terrible.

Yes, I'm a white folks' nigger. I loves them just like a dog loves a hickory switch.

Seems like there was a lot of speculators got to coming through Texas. Judge Maddox was buying a slave every now and then. One day he brought home a pretty mulatto gal. She was real bright and she had long black straight hair and was dressed neat and good. The old lady come out of the house and took a look and said, "What you bring that thing here for?" The judge said, "Honey, I brung her here for you. She going do your fine needlework." She said, "Fine needlework, your hind leg!"

Well, you know what that old lady done? When Judge Maddox was away from home she got the scissors and cropped that gal's head to the skull. I didn't know no more 'bout that case, but one thing I do know was that white men got plenty chilluns by the nigger women. They didn't ask them. They just took them. I heard plenty 'bout that. Rosa will tell you the same.

Rosa Maddox: Wheee! Nobody needs to ask me. I can tell you that a white man laid a nigger gal whenever he wanted her. Seems like some of them had a plumb craving for the other color. Leastways they wanted to start themselves out on the nigger women. But our master was a good man. I never heard of him bothering any womens. I heard it 'bout others. There was some redheaded neighbors of the Andrews that had a whole crop of redheaded nigger slaves.

Jack Maddox: Judge Maddox bought a nigger man who had a three-string fiddle. I used to hear him play and sing. We had to work at night, too. When I was ten or eleven years old, I had to plait hats out of rice straw and other straw. If we young-uns didn't get as much done as we ought to, they would beat us. But this nigger would play to us as we worked. He played and sang. He had a song for every-thing. His gettin' up song was:

> That old bald nigger
> With the shiny eyes,
> He's too hard for me.
> This old way
> O' gittin' up 'fore day,
> It's too hard for me.

When we went to some neighbors for a corn-shucking and they had some whiskey, the niggers sang:

> All don't form a row shan't drink.
> Come on, all you niggers,
> Stand in a row.
> All don't form a row shan't drink.

It sounded right pretty.

Rosa Maddox: We used to sing songs, too, on Dr. Andrews' place. But I can't never 'member the words. We used to sing songs and kinda imposed the words as we went. "Christmas Time" was the name of a dance song. "Christmas time, Christmas time, it's almost day."

That's all I can remember, but it was a good dance song that we used to sing in the huggin'-up dances.

Jack Maddox: There was a man lived neighbor to Judge Maddox named Ashberry Stegall. He had a name for being a hardhanded man. If one of his niggers did something he didn't like, he put him in a ring made of the other niggers. Then, the nigger would have to run around inside the ring and let all the other niggers hit him with a stick. If a nigger wouldn't hit hard, then he would get it himself. That way, he made the niggers beat each other. Guess he thought that kep' his hands clean.

That man had a old woman who had three daughters, named Liza, Laura, and Charlotte, and he made every one of them gals quit the men they were married to and marry other men that he liked. One of them had a boy fifteen, and one eleven, and one nine, and he made her leave her man and take up with another man. Then he had a old woman not under sixty year old, and he made her marry a man 'bout twenty-four year old. He had 'nother girl who worked in the house for him, and he married her off to a man she didn't have no taste for. That nigger would go to her to sleep with her, and if she wouldn't do it, then he would go to Mr. Stegall and he would whip her. Finally, she had one child by him, but she got many a beating first.

Judge Maddox had three nigger boys run away to go to the free state all at one time. He got the dogs and trailed them, and they caught them, and it was a sorry day for them.

About that time the War come along. I can remember those days very plain. I used to see the men come by to talk it over about the War. When Judge Maddox's boys went, they didn't have time to get new clothes. They just went, and later on got their uniforms.

I was sent with my brother to haul salt from Grand Saline, Texas, 'cause the folks in our parts couldn't get the salt for their vittles. Then I was sent with mules and more niggers to work on the government breastworks [temporary fortifications]. I didn't see it, but I sho' heard the Battle of Vicksburg. And that was something to hear, God knows.

Then I was right close to the Battle of Mansfield, in Louis'ana. I heard it and I got there and seen the dead laying round on the ground. I saw people I knew. I saw J. Bagley, Frank Stamps, Ben

Fuller, Jim Horrow, Will Horrow—he was just a little boy—laying dead, and I saw Theodore and Orlando McFarlin. All these men were dead. I saw where J. Bagley was buried in the big trench that they dug. Later, I helped his folks dig him up and take him home.

I looked inside a tent when I was there and seen a man laying on a table turning green all over, and his tongue hanging out big as my wrist, and his eyes had popped out on his cheeks. That don't look so good.

As I was going home, I stopped by a Mrs. Anderson's place and she had a boy named Bob who was a deserter and was hiding at home. When I was there, some Confederate soldiers came by and told his maw to tell where Bob Anderson was. She said she didn't know 'cause she hadn't seen him. The leader man told her, "You better go tell him that he will come out or we will burn him out." She went into the house and told that unless he give himself up they going to burn him out. So he came out.

They tied him with a rope and tied the other end to the saddle of one of the men. They went off with him trotting behind the horse. His maw sent me following along in the wagon. I followed thirteen miles. After a few miles I seen where he fell down and the drag signs on the groun'. Then, when I comes to Hornage Creek, I seen they had gone through the water. I went across and, after a while, I found him. But you couldn't tell any of the front side of him. They had drug the face off him. I took him home.

I hadn't been at Judge Maddox's very long when he got mad and tied up my shirt over my head and beat me bloody raw. I made up my mind to run away and join with the Federals. I told my brother just littler than me, and in the night we slipped away and went towards the east. We walked and ate and slep' in the woods. One place, we went into a blacksmith shop. We were awful hungry and wanted something to eat. The blacksmith asked us questions and told us to go home to our masters. We got so scared we ran out, and I left my walking stick. I think we walked over a hundred miles.

One night we were in the woods and I heard some men on horseback coming. I went to take a look on the road and I thought they was Federals. I went back to tell my brother. God knows why, but he got up and started running the other way. I had to go and ketch him. The fool ran a good half mile. After I caught him and talked to him, we set out to ketch up with the Federals. We came up to them the next day when they was resting.

That was just above Monticello, Arkansas. They was the kindest folks I ever saw. They gave us some hardtack—something like a hard old cracker—some sowbelly, and the first coffee I ever drank. They gave blankets and let us rest. They let us lay right down by them. We didn't need no kivver-up. I will remember that day long as I live. It was June 25th. I stayed right 'round that bunch of Federals until December in the year '65. I seen the Federals heap corn in piles and burn it. Sure s'prised me to see folks burning good corn. I heard they did it all through lower Georgia.

I went with them to San Antonio. I got arrested there. I guess I got to feeling so good I wanted to make noise. I made noise on the street with a bunch of wild boys and they took me up. I'm proud to say that was the first and last time.

I went and slep' in the Alamo when I was in San Antonio.

A man named Menger who had a hotel in San Antonio gave me a job and a glass of lager beer. First time I ever seen any lager beer. My job was to haul beer down to the Yankee camp at San Pedro Springs, right by San Antonio.

Rosa Maddox: Beer. There ain't no good in beer. He sounds like a drinker, but he ain't never bought but two gallons of whiskey in his life, and that wasn't for hisself.

But we had war where I lived, too. Dr. Andrews' niggers went off to work on the government breastworks. I didn't know what the War was 'bout, but I used to hear guns go off. Every gun goes "boom, boom," so I didn't know who was killing who. When the War was over, Mis' Fannie told me I was free, but she didn't tell me to go away. So I jest stayed, and for a long time I didn't see no difference in anything. Dr. Andrews just went on doctoring people, and folks 'ud say, "There goes Andrews' free niggers." I worked hard, but I got along all right, and I had good times and I had beaus.

Jack Maddox: Rosa didn't see no life like I did. I guess she didn't see no trouble till she saw me, but I'm going to get to that.

The itching heel got a-hold on me and I started back to Arkansas. I worked a while in a sawmill. I rafted for the sawmill. In '68 I went into Rusk County, Louis'ana, and worked for a man opening a new sawmill. In December of '69 I went to a party and that is where I met my wife. I had caught a little look at her before then, and I liked what I saw. I sho' loved her the first time I ever saw her. She was a good dresser, but not as fine a dresser as me.

I had thought I loved a girl before then, but I found out I didn't. I had studied 'bout asking that girl to marry me, and when I found out later that she was the Devil's half-sister I was proud I didn't.

Rosa was doing all them cotillions with her dress spreading out and some of these hug-up dances. A fiddle band was playing. I know they was playing that song about "Christmas time, Christmas time, almost day." I started right out to court Rosa then, but she told me I better go slow with her.

The next year I married Rosa. We decided to buy a farm and make a place for ourselves. We made a payment down on a piece of uncleared land. We went into the woods and Rosa worked like a man. We sawed the trees and split the logs. Rosa cut shingles and together we roofed the house. We dug our own well and together we cleared the land and planted it. We had a baby after we was married 'bout ten months. I thought everything in the world was fine, then. Rosa made all my clothes and knitted my socks, and we was gettin' our place paid for and we was living tol'able well.

Everything went along for three years, and then the man we bought the place from died. We found out the place didn't b'long to us. The children of the first wife of the man who sold us the land took it away from us.

Then we went as tenants to a Louis'ana farmer. Every year, I come out with nothing but owing that man money. After three years he and his son fell out. The son came to me and told me that his paw was beating me on the books. He told me I was a fool not to learn to read and write and know somethin' 'bout figgers. I told Rosa, "I won't be going to bed so early these next nights." That boy helped me, and I got books and papers and, every night by the fire, I studied. When the time for the next agreement come, I told the man that we'd keep double books: he and I would both keep books. At the end of the year, he had me owing him money, but my books showed he owed me nearly a hundred dollars. I told him figgers don't lie, but the hand that made them sho' could. Well, I never got the money, but we parted our ways.

I farmed and did different things. I had five boys and two girls. They were good chillun. All of them dead now but one boy, and he is fifty-one year old.

Rosa and I been like sweethearts all the time. She has been the best woman I could ever have. I never wanted to make no swaps. It's never been too dark, never too cold, never too bad for her to do for me. She was never too tired to set with me at night if I was sick. She was gone from me visiting the chillun for two months once, and that is the only time we ever been separated. I wrote to her every day. I have courted Rosa ever since we been married. 'Course, I ain't always been so virtuous. I have stepped out of the middle of the road. But Rosa didn't take on none. She always caught on to me and womens and got on to me 'bout it a little.

Rosa Maddox: I guess it's a man's nature to do with women, and I guess they can't go agin' their nature. But I always been good. I always been good and religious. But Dada's been a right good man. He was good 'nuf to me.

Jack Maddox: Well, when we was pretty old we knew a woman had a baby. She treated that baby pitiful bad. She said he looked like he was a idiot. I remembered 'bout how miserable I was when I was a little boy, and I said to Rosa if she was willing we would take him. She was willing and the mother give him to us when he was twenty-two months old. He was covered with sores, but a little washing soon cleared it up, and he's been with us ever since, like our boy. He is a smart, nice boy. He is 'bout fifteen now. He knows all the names of the baseball players and the G-men. He knows how to read and gets his lessons fine. He plays baseball and marbles. He has thousands of marbles. I'm sho' proud of him to win the other chillun's marbles. I tole him, "If you don't grab for yourself then nothin' going to help you."

This is the first time I ever told my story.

ROSE WILLIAMS

WHAT I say am de facts. If I's one day old, I's way over ninety and I's born in Bell County, right here in Texas, and am owned by Massa William Black. He owns Mammy and Pappy, too. Massa Black has a big plantation, but he has more niggers dan he need for work on dat place, 'cause he am a nigger trader. He trade and buy and sell all de time.

Massa Black am awful cruel, and he whip de cullud folks and works dem hard and feed dem poorly. We-uns have fer rations de cornmeal and milk and 'lasses and some beans and peas, and meat once a week. We-uns have to work in de field every day from daylight till dark, and on Sunday we-uns do us washin'. Church? Shucks, we-uns don't know what dat mean.

I has de clerrest mem'randum of when de War start. Massa Black sold we-uns right den. Mammy and Pappy powerful glad to git sold, and dey and I is put on de block with 'bout ten other niggers. When we-uns gits to de tradin' block, dere lots of white folks dere what come to look us over. One man shows de interes' in Pappy. Him named Hawkins. He talk to Pappy and Pappy talk to him and say, "Dem my woman and chiles. Please buy all of us and have mercy on we-uns." Massa Hawkins say, "Dat gal am a likely lookin' nigger, she am portly and strong, but three am more dan I wants, I guesses."

De sale start and, 'fore long, Pappy am put on de block. Massa Hawkins wins de bid for Pappy, and when Mammy am put on de block, he wins de bid for her. Den dere am three or four other niggers sold befo' my time comes. Den Massa Black calls me to de block and de auction man say, "What am I offer for dis portly, strong wench. She's never been 'bused and will make a good breeder."

I wants to hear Massa Hawkins bid, but him say nothin'. Two other men am biddin' 'gainst each other, and I sho' has de worriment. Dere am tears comin' down my cheeks 'cause I's bein' sold to some man dat would make sep'ration from my mammy. One man bids five hundred dollars and de auction man ask, "Do I hear more? She am gwine at five hundred dollars." Den someone say, "Five hundred twenty-five," and de auction man say, "She am sold for five hundred twenty-five dollars to Massa Hawkins." Am I glad and 'cited! Why, I's quiverin' all over.

Massa Hawkins takes we-uns to his place and it am a nice planta-tion. Lots better am dat place dan Massa Black's. Dere is 'bout fifty niggers what is growed and lots of chillun. De first thing Massa do when we-uns gits home am give we-uns rations and a cabin. You mus' believe dis nigger when I says dem rations was a feast for us. Dere was plenty meat and tea and coffee and white flour. I's never tasted white flour and coffee, and Mammy fix some biscuits and coffee. Well, de biscuits was yum, yum to me, but de coffee I doesn't like.

De quarters am purty good. Dere am twelve cabins all made from logs, and a table and some benches, and bunks for sleepin', and a fireplace for cookin' and de heat. Dere am no floor, jus' de ground.

Massa Hawkins am good to he niggers and not force 'em too hard. Dere am as much diff'ence 'tween him and old Massa Black in de way of treatment as 'twixt de Lawd and de Devil. Massa Hawkins 'lows de niggers have reason'ble parties and go fishin', but we-uns am never tooken to church and has no books for larnin'. Dere am no edumaca-tion for de niggers.

Dere am one thing Massa Hawkins does to me what I can't shunt from my mind. I knows he don't do it for meanness, but I allus holds it 'gainst him. What he done am force me to live with dat nigger, Rufus, 'gainst my wants.

After I been at he place 'bout a year, de massa come to me and say, "You gwine live with Rufus in dat cabin over yonder. Go fix it for livin'." I's 'bout sixteen year old and has no larnin', and I's jus' a igno'mus chile. I's thought dat him mean for me to tend de cabin for Rufus and some other niggers. Well, dat am de start of de pestigation for me.

I's took charge of de cabin after work am done and fixes supper.

Now, I don't like Rufus, 'cause he a bully. He am big, and 'cause he so he think everybody do what him say. We-uns has supper, den I goes here and dere talkin', till I's ready for sleep, and den I gits in de bunk. After I's in, dat nigger come and crawl in de bunk with me 'fore I knows it. I says, "What you means, you fool nigger?" He say for me to hush de mouth. "Dis am my bunk, too," he say.

"You's teched in de head. Git out," I's told him, and I puts de feet 'gainst him and give him a shove and out he go on de floor, 'fore he know what I's doin'. Dat nigger jump up and he mad. He look like de wild bear. He starts for de bunk and I jumps quick for de poker. It am 'bout three feet long, and when he comes at me I lets him have it over de head. Did dat nigger stop in he tracks? I's say he did. He looks at me steady for a minute and you could tell he thinkin' hard. Den he go and set on de bench and say, "Jus' wait. You thinks you am smart, but you am foolish in de head. Dey's gwine larn you somethin'."

"Hush you big mouth and stay 'way from dis nigger; dat all I wants," I say, and I jus' sets and hold dat poker in de hand. He jus' sets, lookin' like de bull. Dere we-uns sets and sets for 'bout an hour, and den he go out and I bars de door.

De nex' day I goes to de missey and tells her what Rufus wants, and de missey say dat am de massa's wishes. She say, "You am de portly gal and Rufus am de portly man. De massa wants you-uns for to bring forth portly chillun."

I's thinkin' 'bout what de missey say, but say to myse'f, "I's not gwine live with dat Rufus." Dat night when him come in de cabin, I grabs de poker and sets on de bench and says, "Git from me, nigger, 'fore I busts you brains out and stomp on dem." He says nothin' and git out.

De nex' day de massa call me and tell me, "Woman, I's pay big money for you and I's done dat 'cause I wants you to raise me chillun. I's put you to live with Rufus for dat purpose. Now, if you doesn't want whippin' at de stake, you do what I wants."

I thinks 'bout Massa buyin' me offen de block and savin' me from bein' sep'rated from my folks, and 'bout bein' whipped at de stake. Dere it am. What am I to do? I 'cides to do as de massa wish and so I yields.

PLATE 12: A former slave nurse.

When we-uns am given freedom, Massa Hawkins tells us we can stay and work for wages or sharecrop de land. Some stays and some goes. My folks and me stays. We works de land on shares for three years, den moved to other land nearby. I stays with my folks till they dies.

If my mem'randum am correct, it am 'bout thirty year since I come to Fort Worth. Here I cooks for white folks till I goes blind 'bout ten year ago.

I never marries, 'cause one 'sperience am 'nuf for dis nigger. After what I does for de massa, I's never want no truck with any man. De Lawd forgive dis cullud woman, but he have to 'scuse me and look for some others for to 'plenish de earth.

Voices

PLANTATION LIFE,

POOR WHITE FOLKS,

CLASSES OF SLAVES, PATROLLERS,

CHRISTMAS ON THE PLANTATION,

DANCING, CORN-SHUCKINGS, HOG-KILLINGS,

MUSIC, SLAVE MARRIAGES,

AND FORCED BREEDING

DIDN'T evvybody have as good places to sleep as us. I 'members a white fambly named Sims, what lived in Flatwoods. Dey was de poorest white folks I ever seed. Dey had a big drove of chillun, and deir pa never wukked a lick in his life; he jus' lived on other folkses' labors. Deir little log cabin had a partition in it, and 'hind dat partition dere warn't a stitch of nothin'. Dey didn't have no floor but de ground, and back 'hind dat partition was dug out a little deeper dan in de rest of de house. Dey filled dat place wid leaves, and dat's whar all de chillun slept. Evvy day, Mis' Sally made 'em take out de leaves what dey had slep' on de night before and fill de dugout wid fresh leaves. On de other side of de partition, Mis' Sally and her old man slept, 'long wid deir hog, and hoss, and cow. And dat was whar dey cooked and et, too. I ain't never gwine to forgit dem white folks.

—CHARLIE HUDSON

My white folks say the people who didn't have slaves was poor white trash. They upheld me to make light of them.

—SAMPSON WALLIS

We didn't think much of the poor white man. He was down on us. He was driven to it by the rich slave owner. The rich slave owner wouldn't let his Negroes 'sociate with poor white folks. Some of the slave owners, when a poor white man's land joined theirs and they wanted his place, would have their Negroes steal things and carry them to the poor white man and sell them to him. Then, the slave owner, knowing where the stuff was, would go and find his things at the poor white man's house. Then, he would claim his things and take out a writ for the poor white man, but he would give him a chance. He would tell him to sell out to him and leave, or take the consequences. That's the way some of the slave owners got such large tracks of land.

—SAM STEWART

The white folks rode to church and the darkies walked, as many of the poor white folks did. We looked upon the poor white folks as our equals. They mixed with us and helped us to envy our masters. They looked upon our masters as we did.

—THE REVEREND SQUIRE DOWD

Dere was just two classes to de white folks—buckra slave owners and poor white folks dat didn't own no slaves. Dere was more classes 'mongst de slaves. De fust class was de house servants. Dese was de butler, de maids, de nurses, chambermaids, and de cooks. De nex' class was de carriage drivers and de gardeners, de carpenters, de barber, and de stable men. Then come de nex' class: de wheelwright, wagoners, blacksmiths, and slave foremen. De nex' class I 'members was de cow men and de niggers dat have care of de dogs. All dese have good houses and never have to work hard or git a beatin'. Then come de cradlers of de wheat, de threshers, and de millers of de corn and de wheat, and de feeders of de cotton gin.

De lowest class was de common field niggers. A house nigger man might swoop down and mate wid a field hand's good-lookin' daughter, now and then, for pure love of her, but you never see a house gal lower herself by marryin' and matin' wid a common field hand nigger. Dat offend de white folks, 'specially de young misses, who liked de business of matchmakin' and matin' of de young slaves.

—ROSA STARKE

Cook? No, ma'am! I never cooked until after I was married, and I never washed—never washed so much as a rag. All I washed was the

PLATE 13: Returning from the fields.

babies and maybe my mistress's feet. I was a lady's maid. I'd wait on my mistress, and I'd knit socks for all the folks. When they would sleep, it was our duty—us maids—to fan 'em with fans made out of turkey feathers—feather fans. Part of it was to keep 'em cool. Then, they didn't have screens, like we have today, so part of it was to keep the flies off. I remember how we couldn't stomp our feet to keep the flies from bitin', for fear of waking 'em up.

—MATTIE MOOREMAN

I had to do field work. Us slaves had to do a certain amount of tasks a day. Even us kids had to pick a hunnert and fifty pounds of cotton a day, or we got a whoopin'. We picked cotton and put it into lahge and small white-oak baskets. Some of dem baskets would hold more'n a hunnert pounds of cotton. It was accordin' to de way yo' stamped de cotton in. A wagon wid a yoke of oxen hitched to it was standin' in de field ready fo' us to pour our cotton in. When de wagon was full, de oxen pulled de wagon to de hoss-power gin.

Durin' de cotton hoein' time, de overseer wanted all of us—dat is, de biggest ones—to stay right in line and chop along. We had to keep up wid one another. And if we didn't, we jes' got de bullwhoop. De overseer would ride up and hit us over de back, if we didn't do our job right. At times, de overseer would git off'n his hoss, have two other slaves hold another one down, and give him de bullwhoop. They'd give it to him, too.

—JOHN WALTON

In the field was always a big strong nigger to keep peace among the hands. He was called by the other slaves "nigger traitor" behin' his back, and was sorta like a straw boss man. He had to be good with his fists to make the boys who got bad in the field walk the line. 'Course, when Old Massa come to the field, anyone who was actin' up started in to choppin', and everything would get quiet as could be.

—JEPTHA CHOICE

I was a driver [Negro boss of other slaves] during slavery, and I reckons I was about twenty somepin'. I don' remember nothin' in particular dat caused me to get dat drivin' job, 'ceptin' hard work, but I knows dat I was proud of it, 'cause I didn' have to work so hard no mo'. An' den, it sorta made de other niggers look up to me, an' you knows how us niggers is, boss: nothin' makes us happier dan to strut in front of other niggers.

—RUFUS DIRT

The patterollers wus always hanging around at night to catch the niggers that wus visiting away from they own plantations.

And, of course, when they told a nigger he couldn't go away from home, that is just what he wanted to do. Niggers is just like chillun: when you tell 'em they can't do a thing, then they want to know what's in it that you don't want 'em to see.

Patterollers couldn't whip a nigger what had a pass, but the niggers got tired of askin' Old Marster for passes ever' night, so they just lit out anyway.

—LIZZIE BROWN

Slave Song
Run, nigger, run, de patroller ketch you,
Run, nigger, run, it's almos' day;
Dat nigger run, dat nigger flew,
Dat nigger tore his shirt in two;
Dat nigger, he said don't ketch me,
But git dat nigger behind de tree;
Dat nigger cried, dat nigger lied,
Dat nigger shook his old fat side;
Run, nigger, run, it's almos' day.

Over de hill and down de holler,
Patroller ketch nigger by de collar;
Dat nigger run, dat nigger flew,

Dat nigger tore his pants in two.
Run, nigger, run, de patroller git you,
Run, nigger, run, de patroller come;
Watch, nigger, watch, de patroller trick you;
Watch, nigger, watch, he got a big gun.

I 'clare to goodness, patterollers was de Devil's own hosses.
—WILLIAM MCWHORTER

You go off to see somebody at night—jes' like you an' me want to laugh an' talk—an' if dey cetch you, an' you ain't got no pass, den dey gwine to whup you. You be glad to git away, too, 'cause when dey hit you, you wus hit.

I wus down to ole John Brady's place, one night, talkin' to a lady, an' old man Brady slipped up behin' me an' caught me in de collar, an' he say, "What you doin' over here? I'm goin' to give you twenty-five lashes." An' den he say to me, "Come here." He was jus' 'bout as tall as I am, an' when I got to 'im, he say, "Turn roun'," an' I say to 'im dat I ain't doin' nothin'. An' den he say, "Dat's what I'm goin' to whup you fer—'cause you ought to be home doin' sumpin'." 'Bout dat time, when I stooped over to take off my coat, I caught 'im in his pants an' throwed 'im in a puddle o' water, an' den I lit out fer home. If you git home, den dey couldn't do nothin' to you.

He tried to chase me, but he didn't know de way through de woods like I did, an' he fell in a gully an' hurt his arm. De next mornin', when I wus hitchin' up de boss man's horse, I seed 'im comin', an' I tole de boss dat he tried to whup me de night befo'. Den, de boss man say, "Did he have you?" I tole 'im dat he did, but dat I got away. An' den de boss man say, "He had you an' he didn't have you—is dat right?" Den he say, "Don't worry 'bout dat. I can git you out of dat."

'Bout dat time, ole man Brady had done got dere, an' he tole de marster dat I wus on his place de night befo', an' dat I got away when he tried to whup me. An' de marster say to 'im, "Dat wus his game. if you had 'im, you shoulda whupped 'im. Dat's de law. If you had

140

whupped 'im, dat woulda been yo' game. But you let 'im git away, an' so dat wus his game." Ole man Brady's face turned so red dat it looked like he wus gonna bus'.

—BENJAMIN JOHNSON

Atter slaves got in f'om de fields at night, de 'omans cooked supper whilst de mens chopped wood. Lessen de crops was in de grass mighty bad, or somepin' else awful urgent, dere warn't no wuk done atter dinner on Sad'days. De old folks ironed, cleant house, and de lak, and de young folks went out Sad'day nights and danced to de music what dey made beatin' on tin pans. Sundays, youngsters went to de woods and hunted hicker nuts and muscadines. De old folks stayed home and looked one another's haids over for nits and lice. Den, de 'omans wropt each other's hair so it would stay fixed till de next Sunday.

—CHARLIE HUDSON

In de long winter days, de men sat round de fire and whittle wood and make butter paddles and troughs for de pigs, and sich, and axe handles and hoe handles and box traps and figure-four traps. Dey make combs to git de wool clean for de spinnin'. De women sew and knit and de men whittle and told things. Dey talk 'bout charms and sich. You gwine have lots of luck iffen you cotch de rabbit in de graveyard on de dark of de moon, and cut off he hind leg and wear it.

—YACH STRINGFELLOW

After de Halloween, den we has de Christmas, an' hit hard ter tell which dey has de bes' time at. Dey bofe meant a lot ter bofe de niggers an' de white chillun. Dey so excited dey say, "Christmas comin' ternight," whilst dey dance all ober de place.

Our mistis, Mis' Ellen, say, "Harriet, have de servants carry in de Christmas tree an' de holly an' evergreens." Den, dey put de candles on de tree an' hangs de stockin' up fer de chillun, an' fer my chillun, too. Nex' mawnin', all de servants an' de chillun up before hit day, an' de massa, Mr. Johnny, come an' let everybody in ter see what ole Santa brung dem. Dere is sumpin' fer us all, an' fer de men some-time' a keg ob cider er wine is put out on de back porch fer dem all ter have a little Christmas speerit.

De nex' thing dat dey has is de dinner. Hit is served in de big dinin' room. An' dat dinner! De onliest time dat I has ever had so good a dinner wuz when I gits married, an' when Mis' Ellen marry Mr. Johnny. De niggers has deir dinner in de kitchen, an' de white folks has deirs in de dinin' room. After de massa an' de mistis has deir dinner, dey watch de servants have deir dinner.

Dey had de guitar an' de banjo an' de fiddlers, an' dey play de ole Christmas tunes, like "Has Auld Acquaintance Be Forgot," an' all de ole-time songs. Den, dat night, de massa an' de mistis bring de chillun down ter de quarters ter see de niggers have dey dance.

De first thing dey do is ter have deir Christmas supper. Dey has a long table out in de yard in front ob de cabins, an' dey have maybe wild turkey or chicken an' udder good things ter eat. Den, when dey all through eatin', dey has a little fire out in front ob de main cabin, whar de dancin' gwine ter be. Den, dey moves everything out ob de cabin, 'ceptin' a few chairs. Nex' come de fiddlers an' de banjo an' guitar players, an' de young folks gittin' ready ter dance.

De caller begins ter call de dance sets. When de fust tune starts, he calls off like dis, "Heads lead off," an' de fust two go out in de middle ob de floor. All de couples follow, till de cabin is full. Nex', he calls, "Sashay ter de right, an' doe-see-doe." Roun' ter de right dey go. Den, "Han's up 'fore," an' dey hold up deir right han's an' jine dem. Den, he calls, "Swing yo' partners," an dey swing dem roun' twice. An' so hit goes, till daylight come. Den, he begins ter sing dis song:

> Hit's gittin' mighty late, when de guinea hen squall,
> An' yo' better dance now, if yo' gwine ter dance at all.
> If yo' niggers don't watch out, yo'll sing anudder tune,
> Fer de sun'll rise an' cetch yo', if yo' don't go mighty soon,
> An' de stars is gittin' paler, an' de ole gray coon
> Is sittin' in de grapevine a-watchin' de moon.
>
> —HARRIET JONES

Dem corn-shuckin's meant jus' as much fun and jollification as [they did] wuk. Dey gathered Marster's big corn crap [crop] and 'ranged it in long, high piles, and sometimes it tuk sev'ral days for dem corn shuckers to git it all shucked, but evvybody stayed right dar on de job till it was finished. At night, dey wukked by de light of big fires and torches. Den, dey had de big supper and started dancin'. Dey stopped so often to swig dat corn liquor Marster pervided for 'em, dat 'fore midnight folkses started fallin' out and drappin' down in de middle of de dance ring. De others would git 'em by de heels and drag 'em off to one side, till dey come to and was ready to drink more liquor and dance again. Dat was de way dey went on de rest of de night.

—CORDELIA THOMAS

I mus' tell you 'bout dat whiskey and brandy. Massa have he own still and allus have three barrels or more whiskey and brandy on hand. Den, on Christmas Day, him puts a tub of whiskey or brandy in de yard and hangs tin cups round de tub. Us helps ourselves. At first, us start jokin' with each other. Den, us starts to sing and everybody am happy. Massa watches us, and if one us gittin' too much, Massa sends him to he cabin and he sleep it off. Anyway, dat was one day on Massa's place when all am happy and forgits dey am slaves.

—CHARLEY HURT

Now you axed about hog-killin' time? Dat was de time of times. For weeks, de mens would haul wood an' big rocks, an' pile 'em together as high as dis house, an' den have several piles lak dat roun' a big hole in de groun' what had been filled wid water. Den, jus' a little after midnight, de boss would blow de ole hawn, an' all de mens would git up an' git in dem pens. Den, dey would sot dat pile of wood on fire, an' den start knockin' dem hogs in de haid. Us neber shot a hog lak us does now. Us always used an axe to kill 'em wid. Atter knockin' de hog in de haid, dey would tie a rope on his leg, an' atter de water got to de right heat f'om dose red-hot rocks, de hog would be throwed in an' drug aroun' a while, den taken out an' cleaned. Atter he was cleaned, he was cut up into sections an' hung up in de smokehouse. Lawsie, lady, dey don't cure meat dese days; dey jus' uses some kind of liquid to bresh over it. We useta have sho'-'nuf meat.

Den comes cawn-shuckin' time. My goodness, I would jus' love to be dar now. De cawn would be piled up high, an' one man would git on dat pile—'twas usually a kinda nigger fo'man who could sing an' git de work outen de niggers. Dis fo'man would sing a verse somp'n lak dis:

> Polk an' Clay went to wah,
> Polk came back wid a broken jaw.

Den, all de niggers would sing back at him wid a kinda shoutin' sound. Near 'bout all de times, de fo'man made up his own songs. It war de jug dat dey brung aroun' eve'y hour. Dat's de onlies' time de slaves really got drunk.

—JOSEPH HOLMES

De nigger used to sing to nearly everything he did. Hit wuz jes' de way he 'spressed his feelin's, an' hit made him relieved. If he wuz happy, hit made him happier; if he wuz sad, hit made him feel better. An' so, he jes' naturally sings his feelin's.

De timber nigger, he sings as he cuts de logs, 'an keeps de time wid his axe. De women sing as dey bend over de washtub. De cotton choppers sing as dey chops de cotton. De mother sings as she rocks her baby to sleep. An' dey all sing in de meetin's, an' at de baptizin's, an' at de funerals.

Singin' is de niggers' mos' joy an' dey mos' comfort. When dey needs all dese things, dey sing 'bout de joys in de nex' world an' de trouble in dis. Dey first jes' sung de 'ligious songs. Den, dey commenced to sing 'bout de life here. An' when dey sung of bofe, dey called dem de "spirituals." De ole way to sing dem was to keep time wid de clappin' of de han's an' pattin' of de feet. Dey sing dem in different ways fur different occasions. At a meetin', when dey shouts, dey sing joyful, an' when dey sing de same song at a funeral, dey sing hit slow and moanful. When dey sing de same song in de fiel's, hit is sung quick, if dey workin' fas'. If dey is tired, hit is sung slow. If hit is sung at Christmas, den hit is sung gay an' happy.

De days of slavery made de nigger live his life over in de spirituals. Mos' of de real ole-time slaves are gone. Jes' a few, maybe, is lef' who were boys den, but deir song lives on wid bofe de white an' de black folks. We forgets de sorrows an' remembers de happy days, jes' like in de songs.

—VINNIE BRUNSON

During the week, after supper, we would all set round the doors outside and sing or play music. The only musical instruments we had was a jug or big bottle, a skillet lid or frying pan that they'd hit with a stick or a bone. We had a flute, too—made out of reed cane—and it'd make good music. Sometimes, we'd sing and dance so long and loud Old Master'd have to make us stop and go to bed.

—BOB MAYNARD

I can't 'member de old songs, but dese niggers today can't sing lak dat neither, 'cause dey ain't libbed back dere, an' dey can't feel hit lak us old folks. Dem was de good old days all right, an' dey was hard days, too.

—HAMP KENNEDY

My daddy was de onlies' slave er Mister George Rawls, 'n' he come t'rough wid Mister Rawls when he come t' Texas, way back right atter de Mex'can War. My mammy, she de onlies' slave er Mister Andrew Smith, who lib 'bout t'ree er fo' mile' from Mister Rawls' place.

Dey say my daddy was allus gittin' permits t' go ober 'n' see de cook on de Smith place. 'N' de visitin' was gittin' so eb'ry weeken' he was runnin' ober dar, 'n' in 'tween time, too. So dat, at las', Mister Rawls, he say, "Look here, Ned, ain' you wanter marry dat gal ober at

Mister Smith' place?" 'N' when my daddy say he do, Mister Rawls, he say he try t' 'range it. An' dey did. Yes, dey fix it all up purty soon so dey could step ober de broom—dat's what dey uster call it when niggers git marry'.

Well, dey jis' lay de broom down, 'n' dem what's gwine ter git marry' walks out 'n' steps ober dat broom bofe togedder, 'n' de ole massa, he say, "I now pronounce you man 'n' wife," 'n' den dey was marry'. Dat was all dey was t' it—no ce'mony, no license, no nothin', jis' marryin'.

Well, my daddy, he couldn' tek her back t' Mister Rawls wid him, 'cause she b'long t' Mister Smith, 'n' Mister Smith, he wouldn' sell he cook. So dey 'gree dat Mister Smith hire my daddy from Mister Rawls 'n' fix up fo' bofe er dem t' lib togedder at Mister Smith' place, 'n' dat de way dey wuk de t'ing. Den, fo' years 'n' years, my daddy, he wuk right on fo' Mister Smith by de mont' reg'lar, wid him a-payin' Mister Rawls fo' my daddy, jis' like he's a hoss.

—JOE RAWLS

When I growed up, I married Exter Durham. He belonged to Marse Snipes Durham, who had de plantation 'cross de county line, in Orange County. We had a big weddin'. We was married on de front po'ch of de big house. Marse George killed a shoat, an' Mis' Betsy had Georgianna, de cook, to bake a big weddin' cake, all iced up white as snow wid a bride an' groom standin' in de middle holdin' han's. De table was set out in de yard under de trees, an' you ain't never seed de like of eats. All de niggers come to de feas', an' Marse George had a dram for everybody. Dat was some weddin'. I had on a white dress, white shoes, an' long white gloves dat come to my elbows, an' Mis' Betsy done made me a weddin' veil out of a white net window curtain. When she played de weddin' ma'ch on de piano, me an' Exter ma'ched down de walk an' up on de po'ch to de alter Mis' Betsy done fixed.

Uncle Edmond Kirby married us. He was de nigger preacher dat preached at de plantation church. After Uncle Edmond said de las' words over me an' Exter, Marse George got to have his little fun. He say, "Come on, Exter, you an' Tempie got to jump over de broomstick backwards. You got to do dat to see which one gwine be boss of your househol'." Everybody come stan' roun' to watch. Marse George hold de broom 'bout a foot high off de floor. De one dat jump over it backwards an' never touch de handle gwine boss de house, an' if bofe of dem jump over widout touchin' it, dey ain't gwine be no bossin'; dey jus' gwine be 'genial.

I jumped fus', an' you ought to seed me. I sailed right over dat broomstick, same as a cricket. But when Exter jump, he done had a big dram an' his feets was so big an' clumsy dat dey got all tangled up in dat broom, an' he fell headlong. Marse George, he laugh an' laugh, an' tole Exter he gwine be bossed till he skeered to speak less'n I tole him to speak.

After de weddin', we went down to de cabin Mis' Betsy done all dressed up, but Exter couldn' stay no longer den dat night, 'cause he belonged to Marse Snipes Durham an' he had to go back home. He lef' de nex' day for his plantation, but he come back every Saturday night an' stay till Sunday night. We had eleven chillun. Nine was bawn befo' Surrender an' two after we was set free. I was worth a heap to Marse George, 'kaze I had so many chillun.

—TEMPIE DURHAM

When a girl became a woman, she was required to go to a man and become a mother. There was generally a form of marriage. The master read a paper to them telling them they were man an' wife. Some were married by the master laying down a broom and the two slaves, man and woman, would jump over it. The master would then tell them they were man and wife, and they could go to bed together. Master would sometimes go and get a large, hale, hearty Negro man from some other plantation to go to his Negro woman. He would ask the other master to let this man come over to his place to go to his slave girls. A slave girl was expected to have children as soon as she became a woman. Some of them had children at the age of twelve and thirteen years old. Negro men six feet tall went to some of these children.

—HILLIARD YELLERDAY

147

Ise gwine to tell youse how a nigger couple fools Marster Buckham, once. 'Twas a cullud gal—her name was Nancy—'bout seventeen yeahs old, an' her marster tole her to live wid a certain nigger, name' Tip. Dat gal, Nancy, detested dat fellow, Tip. She won't 'low him to come neah her. Tip tole his marster 'bout it, an' de marster gives de gal a whuppin' an' tole her dat him owned her an' dat she must do as him wants. De cullud fellow feels sorry 'bout de gal gettin' de whuppin', so Tip says to Nancy, "Ise don't want to see youse whupped, so Ise sleep on de floah an' youse use de bunk. But youse must promise never to tell de marster." "Ise sho' promise, hope to die," she says.

'Twas 'bout three months aftah, de marster see thar am no chilluns gwine to be bo'n, so he tuks her f'om dat fellow an' 'lows her to stay wid de one she laks. Dat am 'bout five yeahs befo' Surrendah, an' every yeah thar am a chile bo'n to Nancy while she am a slave. De marster never did learn how come thar warn't any chilluns bo'n wid de first man.

—VIRGINIA YARBROUGH

My marster owned three plantations and three hundred slaves. He started out wid two 'oman slaves and raised three hundred slaves. One wuz called "Short Peggy," and the udder wuz called "Long Peggy." Long Peggy had twenty-five chilluns. Long Peggy, a black 'oman, wuz boss ob de plantation. Marster freed her atter she had twenty-five chilluns. Just think o' dat—raisin' three hundred slaves wid two 'omans. It sho' is de trufe, do'.

—JOHN SMITH

Ben Oil had a hundred niggers. He just raised niggers, on his plantation. His brother-in-law, John Cross, raised niggers, too. He had a hundred and twenty-five niggers. He had a nigger farm. His older brother-in-law, old man English, had a hundred niggers. Dey all jes' had nothin' else but niggers.

—HANNAH JONES

It took a smart nigger to know who his father was, in slavery time. I just can remember my mother.

—ELIAS THOMAS

My mammy am owned by Massa Fred Tate and so am my pappy and all my brudders and sisters. How many brudders and sisters? Lawd A'mighty! I'll tell you, 'cause you asks, and dis nigger gives de facts as 'tis. Let's see; I can't 'lect de number. My pappy have twelve chillun by my mammy and twelve by anudder nigger, name' Mary. You keep de count. Den, dere am Lisa. Him have ten by her. And dere am Mandy. Him have eight by her. And dere am Betty. Him have six by her. Now, let me 'lect some more. I can't bring de names to mind, but dere am two or three others what have jus' one or two chillun by my pappy. Dat am right—close to fifty chillun, 'cause my mammy done told me. It's disaway: my pappy am de breedin' nigger.

—LEWIS JONES

It come to de time Old Marster have so many slaves he don't know what to do wid them all. He give some of them off to his chillun. He give them mostly to his daughters, Mis' Marion, Mis' Nancy, and Mis' Lucretia. I was give to his grandson, Marse John Mobley McCrory, just to wait on him and play wid him. Little Marse John treat me good sometime' and kick me round sometime'. I see now dat I was just a little dog or monkey, in his heart and mind, dat it 'mused him to pet or kick, as it pleased him.

—HENRY GLADNEY

Whenever white folks had a baby born, den all de old niggers had to come th'ough the room, and the master would be over 'hind the bed, and he'd say, "Here's a new little mistress or master you got to work for." You had to say, "Yessuh, Master," and bow real low, or the overseer would crack you. Them was slavery days, dog days.

—HARRIETT ROBINSON

Narratives

———⊃⊦ ⊦⊂———

CALVIN MOYE

ISAAC STIER

CHARLIE MOSES

CALVIN MOYE

I WAS born in Atlanta, Georgia, December 25, 1842. My father's and mother's boss told dem to calls me Calvin, so dat was what dey named me—Calvin Moye.

My father's name was Isom and my mother's name was Mamie Moye. Both of dem was born and brought up by Maser Richmond Ingram's father and later moved to Atlanta, Georgia, when dey was about grown. Dat was before Maser Ingram's father died, and dey married after dey was working for him. Of course, dey didn't marry like we do now, but dey was married anyway, as far as Maser Ingram was concerned, and dey was bound to each other as much as we is now. Some plantations didn't see it dat way, but Maser Ingram did. Maser Richmond Ingram was our maser, and he was the only one I could ever remember. I says right now that he was one of the best men that ever breathed.

I never did know anything about my grandmamas and grandpapas. There wasn't many slaves dat could tells you about dem, either, and plenty of dem didn't knows anything about der mothers and fathers. The plantation owners just sold and traded Negroes in dem days, like de horse and cattle traders do now. A Negro did not know any more about where his mama was den a calf does, now. 'Course, some was lucky. Like cows now, if dey was good workers der masers would generally keeps dem, just like a man keeps a calf, if it looks like it is going to be a good milker. Some was lucky ter be with a good maser, like my mother and father was, and gets to keeps der chilluns and raise dem.

My mother and father has seven chilluns, and dey raised us all ter be grown, under de same maser. I has two brothers older den me.

PLATE 14: Postbellum blacks picking cotton in the old slavery-time way.

Louis was de oldest and Aaron was de next. I had four sisters, Delia, Adalyn, and Mary—the other died when small. We were all born in Georgia and was on a plantation a little way from Atlanta, and it was owned by Maser Ingram's father, who handed it down ter him and another brother, when he died. But dey didn't agrees wid each other, so when I was a big boy, maybe eight or ten years old, Maser Ingram traded his part ter his brother, and we all hits out to Texas. A man out here somewhere writes to Maser Ingram about this rich country, and Maser Ingram sells out and gets some ox wagons fixed up, and buys a lot of food, and puts in all we can dat we has at de plantation, and starts out wid seventy slaves dat is big enough to work and deir chilluns.

Sometimes, we would comes ter creeks and rivers, dat we couldn't cross, and we would travel up or down de stream huntin' a place ter cross, and maybe we couldn't find one, so we would either build a pole bridge or put light logs on de side of de wagons and float dem across like boats.

Every evening before camp time, some of de older men would travel along ahead of us out to the side of the road and kill fresh meat for us to eat. Or if we came to a river or creek, we would stop long enough fer de men folks ter takes a seine and catch some fish.

We always camped close to water, so we could has plenty water for us and de stock. Dem ole oxens would runs ter water when dey begins ter gits thirsty. You just couldn't hold dem back, and dey can smells water a long ways. If we happened ter comes fer a long ways and not run across any water, we could always tell when we was getting close ter water by de way dem oxens acted. Dey was slow, but dey would gits in a hurry when dey was thirsty and was smellin' water. I has had dem drag me, wagon and all, in more dan one hole of water and den tried ter lay down in it or wade in it bettern belly deep.

When we comes ter dese streams and floats de wagons across, we would swim de stock across. Maser Ingram rode a horse, and when we comes ter a warm stream, he would let me hold his horse's tail and swim across, and when we was out on de road I would hold his horse's tail and run along behind him, while de horse was trottin', and sometimes he would kick de horse in a long, fast pace and stand me on my head in de dirt.

De men dat watched at night slept in de wagons in de daytime, when we was all traveling. When we camped fer de night, we would pull all de wagons in a big circle and puts de tongue of one wagon under de back end of another, and puts de stock in dis circle and turns dem loose. At first, we couldn't sleeps fer dem and de varmits' hollerin', but finally we got use ter dem and got ter where we could sleeps as sound as we could back in Georgia in our log cabins.

Maser Ingram wasn't afraid of nothin' but de Indians. One night, after we got out into Texas, we was camped and de moon was shinin' as bright as day. Something comes up pretty close ter camp, and de dogs just barked and barked. Dey woke Maser Ingram up and he shot out dat way a few times, and somethin' begins movin' out, and de dogs would follow it out and then come back. Maser Ingram thought it might be some Indian scouts and dat dey might come back about daylight and attack us, so we made every man gits ter yokin' de oxens ter de wagons, and we hits de trail further west. Maser Ingram leads de way and tells everybody ter keeps a watch out fer de Indians and ter keeps de guns all loaded and, if any of dem saw an Indian and was sure of it, ter gives de alarm and fer all of us ter stays close together. We was always lookin' fer some of dem Indians ter scalp us, but we never did sees any of dem, and we never did know fer sho' what it was dat scared us dat night.

When we got to Navarro County, dar wasn't no kerens, no railroads or nothin' much, in de east end of de county. Dar was a little town dat grows up where we settled, called Rural Shade. Dat is where Maser Ingram stops at and bought about five or six hundred acres of de levelest land dat I ever saw. It was rich and had grass as high as my head on it—some of de best grazin' any of us had ever seen—and dar was plenty timber round everywhere.

Dey got to be lots of cowboys around here, and dey would ride wild bronco horses and run races and has a good time. What people calls a "good time" now, is gettin' half full of booze and gettin' in a good car and startin' out spendin' money and just thinking dey is having a good time.

When we first pulls in and camps, we was camped for three or four days before Maser Ingram found de land he wanted and gets it bought. Den he puts us all to cuttin' logs, building rail fences, building houses, barns, and other outbuildings. We all worked, and we worked hard. De first houses that was finished was Maser Ingram's and de meat house and smokehouse and barn. Den we went to building houses for de slaves. Den we builds a big blacksmith shop opened to de south, wid logs standing straight up and down on de other three sides and boards over de north side. In here, de beds, chairs, tables, and other furniture for all de slaves and Maser Ingram was made. All de blacksmith work was done dar too, such as shapin' plows, makin' beams for plows, tongues for wagons, and spokes, and hubs.

As soon as de shed was finished, Maser Ingram says to me, "Now, Calvin, dis is where I wants you to start to work. Uncle Zeke is gettin' ole, and I's going to needs a new blacksmith before long. You must watch every move he makes and do just what he does and you will make a good blacksmith some day."

Den he told Uncle Zeke, who was an ole slave, dat he wants him to learns me the wood work first, dat I was too young to do much blacksmithing yet. So de next morning, I was down to de shop befo' Uncle Zeke was, 'cause I sho' was glad to gits out of dat field work, and I knows I would like dat blacksmith work.

Uncle Zeke comes walkin' slow to de blacksmith shop, and when he sees me he begins laughing at me and says, "I see de new blacksmith is down early to go to work. Well, son, I hopes you like it and makes a good one, 'cause in de spring you is goin' to have plenty of hard work. We is got plenty to do right now in wood work, making furniture, so roll up your sleeves and let's go to work. We will start to makin' tables and chairs first."

Uncle Zeke starts me out to splitting de oak logs. We splits out several and den we starts to smoothin' out de boards, layin' each part in a separate place for de tables and de same way for de chairs. We gits enough made for everybody befo' we puts any of dem together. Uncle Zeke was watchin' and tellin' me all de time, and befo' we got through he said I was about as good as he was, already, doing this.

We had plenty to eat all de time—most anything we wanted: mutton, beef, pork, deer, fish, squirrel, rabbit, possum, turkey, chicken, vegetables of all kinds, and biscuits every Saturday and Sunday. Maser Ingram kills four sheep a week, and I don't know how many hogs a year. He was killing a beef ever three or four days, and dey would hunt deer, turkey, or other game, so we didn't ever goes hungry. We would all go seining and catch a wagonload of fish and comes back home and splits dem open, cleans dem, cuts de heads off, and salts all dem down what we don't wants to eat. My favorite food was fish, and it is yet.

We had one big garden. It had about ten acres of beans, peas, cabbage, sweet and Irish potatoes, onions, and things like dat, and each family was allowed certain things out of it each day. But we had another big field of sweet and Irish potatoes, onions, peas, and beans, and no one was allowed to bother it till dey was ready to gather.

Maser Ingram wasn't tight on us like some of de other white folks was. He would lets us go huntin' when it was too wet to work or durin' a slack time of de seasons, and we caught lots of possums and rabbits and some wild turkeys. Wild game was plentiful in de timber, and on de prairie we could finds wild prairie chickens.

All de food dat we cooked in dem days was cooked in a bog rock fireplace or stick-and-dirt fireplace. Most people had stick-and-dirt chimneys. De womenfolks done all de cookin', and dey has big cast-iron pots to boil in and big cast-iron skillets to do de bakin' and fryin' in. All de cookin' den was better dan what de womens cooks now, on these oil stoves. You kin taste de oil in some of de cookin' now, and you couldn't taste nothin' like dat in de eats in dem days.

People den had a better time dan dey does now. Nobody goes hungry, like we does now, or half-naked, trying to save enough money to pay de rent. Dar wasn't any rent den.

Dey can talks about slavery times being a bad time if dey wants to, but lots of de things dat was told was lies. Most all de slaves had place to live, clothes to wear, and plenty to eats, and dat is more dan we has now. About half de niggers in dis town goes cold and hungry in de winter. When I was with Maser Ingram we hads good strong clothes to wear all de time. Dey was all made on de plantation by de slaves, but dey was warm. We wore cotton clothes in summer and wool clothes in de winter, and had plenty to keeps us warm, too. But now, we wears summer clothes in winter, with plenty of patches on dem to make dem last six or eight years, and den we can't live like human folks.

Maser Ingram was a man about six feet tall and was about average weight and had brown eyes and brown hair. He was never married, but he was a kind man and was very smart, too. He made lots of money. Nearly every way he turned he made money out of it, and he give lots of advice to my father 'bout makin' money.

Maser Ingram didn't has no overseer. He was his own boss. He always said if a slave couldn't work he couldn't eat, and if he eats he has to work. He would always start de slaves out to work, but den maybe he would go over to de other side of de place to see 'bout somethin', and den he would picks out one of de slaves to lead de others when he was away, and he would picks de fastest one. Maybe he would picks out one dis time, and next time he would picks out another one, to lead de field. Dey all liked to be de leader, and when dey was de leader, dey would works harder dan dey would if dey was following de leader.

I guess Maser Ingram had 'bout seventy slaves. De slaves woke up every mornin' before daylight, and all de chores was done, and de menfolks got in de field before sunup. When de womenfolks got de housework done and de dinner made, dey comes to de field and brought dinner for dem and de men, and dey goes to work little after sunup. Dey would work till 11:30 and den takes time off and eats dinner. Dey goes back to work at one o'clock by Maser Ingram's watch, and works till 'bout an hour by sun. Den de womenfolks and chilluns would quit and goes in and do up de chores, and de womenfolks would cook supper while de chilluns would git in wood and kinlin' at de cabins, and a little after sundown de menfolks would quit and comes in.

Every slave knows what time to git up in de mornin', and he better gits up, too. You better not lays in bed and be late to git to work. Maser Ingram would tells you one time, but he would tells you in a way dat makes you know dat it would be too bad if you lays there de next time.

Every mornin' when de slaves would goes to work, 'specially in de spring and fall of de year, you could hears singin' and hollerin' all aroun' there. Dey would drown out de birds singin' and hammerin' at de blacksmith's shop where I worked, when we has work to do, and dat was most all de time.

Maser Ingram was good to us, and he never did whip any of us unless we needed it. But he had one Negro slave dat was named Charlie, and he was a single man, big and stout. I has seen Maser Ingram whip dat Negro, and I has heard him begs for mercy till it was pitiful. Maser Ingram would tie his hands above his head to a pole, and his feet together, and lay him down and whips him, and sometimes whips him every day, for stealin'. He wouldn't steal from us or Maser Ingram, but he would steal from de neighbors. De patterrollers would try to catch him. Dey would lay and waits for him, but dey never could catch him. Maser Ingram said he hopes dey would catch him and beat him up good, but he always got aroun' dem.

I has seen him bring in a big cotton basket full of meat he stole from somebody's smokehouse. He would bring it home and Maser Ingram would catch him wid it and whips him, and he knowed dat he was goin' to steal something dat night sho' as he was turned loose, and sho' enough, dat night, after everybody had gone to bed and was asleep, he would slips out and steals a set of harness or just anything he could gits home wid, and Maser Ingram would whips him again. He even goes in people's houses and steals money, clothes, and even gits der gun while de people was asleep.

It was just born in dat Negro to steal, and Maser Ingram could not breaks him. Maser got afraid somebody would kill him sometime and he had whole lots of money invested in dat Negro, so he takes him off down close to Houston and sells him. Dat was de only slave dat Maser Ingram ever sold or whipped very hard, and he done de whippin' for dis Negro's own good. But he couldn't breaks him from stealin'. It was just born in him and it couldn't be took out.

I has seen slaves bought and sold. I has seen dem auctioned off, and I has seen dem drove off by de speculators in big long droves, from nursin' babies to old gray-headed men.

De speculators would comes through wid big long droves of slaves dey would buy, sell, or trade, just like de horse traders did a few years ago. Dar was never but one bunch dat stopped by Maser Ingram's, and dis man tried his best to sell Maser some slaves, and he wouldn't buy none. Dis speculator tried to trade some wid Maser, but he wouldn't do dat. Den he begins askin' what he would takes for dis one and dat one, and Maser Ingram said he didn't wants to sell any of us slaves. Den he pointed at me and ask what he would takes for dat boy up dar, and I begins backin' off and went off aroun' de blacksmith shop and says to myself, "I don't believe dat Maser Ingram would sells me, but if dis man just keep on tryin' to do some tradin', he might just do it to gits rid of him."

I was just makin' up my mind to run off de first chance I got, if he did sells me. Dis man just keeps on, and finally Maser Ingram gits mad and tells him to git on down de road and don't stop dar anymore. When I comes round de front side of de shop, dey was goin' off down de road, and I sho' was glad, for I sho' didn't wants to git in any of dem speculator bunches of road slaves. Maser Ingram says, "Calvin, what's de matter wid you? Did you wants to go wid dem? If you does, I'll calls dem back and sells you to him." I tells him right quick, "No sah, I sho' don't wants to go. Let dat man alone, and let him git out of my sight."

Dey was lots of dem speculators coming by de road in front of de plantation, and ever' time I see dem coming, cold chills run over me till I see dem go on by our lane. We all felt like we had a home till we died, and we all worked harder and tried to do our work better for Maser Ingram.

Uncle Zeke and me done all de work dat come into de blacksmith shop, such as repairing and making de furniture, and takin' care of all de farm tools, and making wagons. And I learns how to get a welding heat on any part of steal or iron. In about four years, Maser Ingram and Uncle Zeke says I could beat Uncle Zeke.

De only thing dat went against me in de blacksmith shop was I didn't knows how to figure and write. De white folks didn't even tries to learns me or any of us even how to figure. Maser didn't tries to learn us anything 'long dat line, 'ceptin' to count money. My father could read and write a little, but my mother didn't know how to do either one. Dar wasn't another person on de plantation, 'ceptin' Maser Ingram, dat could beats my father. So, you see, we didn't knows how to do anything but work, and any slave has to know how to do dat, if he didn't wants to git de cat-o'-nine-tails on his back.

I can read now a little in de Bible, and I can write my name if I have plenty of time. Once and awhile, when we was small chilluns, my father would read de Bible to us all, but he read slow like I does now.

We all went to church once and awhile, but not regular. De church was about a mile from de plantation, and my mother went every chance she had. My father never did go unless my mother got after him too hot, and den he would go once or twice to ease her off.

I has seen as many as fifty baptized at one baptizing—both whites and blacks. The time my first wife was baptized dar was about fifty in dat bunch. Dey would baptize de white folks first, and den de slaves would wade out into de tank and dey would be baptized. Dey would sing religious songs when dey was baptizing. 'Course, if anybody joined de church, dey is a worse sinner if dey backslides out of de church den dey was if dey had never joined de church. But de people nowadays dey joins de church one night and goes to a dance and gits drunk de next night and comes to church de next Sunday and prays like a real Disciple of de Lord. Dar is going to be more church folks in dat lake of fire den de Devil can stir.

Dar was a few of de old slaves dat died a few years after we comes to Texas, and when dey died it was mine and Uncle Zeke's job to make a coffin to bury dem in. De coffins was made out of pine or some other soft lumber, and we lined dem wid black cloth dat was made and dyed on de plantation. We had to make de planks and plane dem smooth wid de tools we had in de shop. I lived to make Uncle Zeke's coffin.

When a slave died, Maser Ingram would let us take time off from work to have a funeral. Like de white folks, we got Preacher Prayar or Preacher Simmons to preach de funeral. We would takes dem to de buryin' ground dat was on de plantation in de pasture over in one corner and bury dem. We builds a fence around deir graves every time dey would get growed up.

Maser Ingram would hates to see one of de slaves die, 'cause he had lots of money invested in dem, and every time one died he lost money, and he lost lots of work aroun' de plantation, too.

We worked every day in de week except Saturday, and if we was up wid de crop pretty well, my father would takes off on Friday at dinner. My father sold whiskey when he wasn't working on de plantation. Maser Ingram would give him a pass so's he wouldn't be bothered by de patterrollers, and he goes over to a big still and buys some whiskey, and goes to Corsicana and sells it out, and gits back to de plantation in time to go to work on Monday morning. When de War was over between de North and South, he had over two thousand dollars in Confederate money.

On Saturday nights, all de slaves on de plantation would either has a dance or go to a dance on another plantation, and dey would dance till daylight on Sunday mornings, sometimes, and dey never did start any trouble or gits drunk, like dey do now.

Every Christmas morning, Maser Ingram would come around and gives ever' family a present of twenty-five dollars and tells dem to spend it for things dey needed worst. De single men, such as Uncle Zeke, he gives dem ten dollars. So we all bought Sunday clothes, 'ceptin' Uncle Zeke, and he just wore de clothes dat was made on de plantation. He said we better save all de money dat we can gits our hands on, 'cause we was going to be free some day and would has to hustle for ourselves. Uncle Zeke always said dat de Bible say dat we would be free, and he sho' believed it, too. I guess him and my father was de only slaves on dat plantation dat had any money to amount to anything. Maser Ingram always gives Christmas presents every year till after we was free. He kept his money den. Guess he thought he lost enough money when we was all freed.

De Fourth of July was always a big day for de whites and de colored people, too. Maser Ingram would either has a big dinner or lets us go to a big celebration down there somewhere. Dey generally has horse racing, and de men would rides wild horses and big bulls and things like dat all day, and dey would has ropin', too. And people would takes deir dinner with dem and has a big time. Dey didn't do likes dey do now—buys deir dinner and soda pop and such things.

Dem two days was all de holidays we had. When New Year's Day comes aroun', we worked hard all day. Saturday or not, rain or snow, we worked. Maser Ingram sho' wouldn't lose New Year's Day or a Monday. If it was raining, we shucked corn or cleaned out de barn. If it was snowing, we would cut wood or something like dat. He always had a job for us. He would has us split rails and work de top of de tree up into wood, build a fence, burn brush, clear land, or anything.

When de cotton pickin' time come on, everybody dat was big

enough to pick cotton was put in de field. All de big folks was given two baskets, a big one and a little one. We picks in de little basket till it gits full and empties it in de big one. De littlest chilluns would pick wid deir mamas or papas. When we gits de big basket full, we would hauls it out to de quarters where dar was a gin. Maser Ingram had oxens to haul it out of de field to de gin. Dis gin was like de syrup mills is now: you hook up de oxens and dey goes aroun' and aroun' when you is ginning. De cotton was carried to de gin in baskets and de ginned cotton and seed was carried away. If we got along very well, we could gin three bales of cotton a day.

De boys had to learn to do everything on de plantation, and Maser Ingram had de girls to learn everything dat a woman was supposed to know, so when dey gots married dey wouldn't has to fool aroun' trying to learn how to do things. All de slaves married young—dat is most of dem did—but I didn't marries till I was nearly forty years old. I didn't thinks dar was any of dem women good enough for me.

While Maser Ingram was livin', when any of de slaves got married, he makes dem all gits married by de preacher.

Maser Ingram was pretty good to us. Every time one of de slaves gits married, he would lets dem have a weddin' dance to celebrates de weddin'. Most of de slave owners would have a sham weddin' and lets dem go at dat, when dey wasn't legally married. But nothin' like dat happened at Maser Ingram's place, even if one of de slaves was from another plantation. Maser Ingram never was married, and I guess dat is why I waited so long to gits married myself. Maser Ingram was such a fine man till I wanted to be like him as much as I could.

When any of de white folks about us in dat country got married, dey always had a big supper and dance. Dey would cook for two or three days before de weddin', and de night de weddin' would happen dey would dance all night, de white folks and de slaves, too, and dey would have separate places to dance.

When I was a small boy, we didn't play like chilluns do now'days. We was more like monkeys and was tougher dan dey is now. We would climb up in trees and dare each other. We would has a leader and he would jumps from one limb to another and from one tree to another. We would gits where de trees was thick, and we would goes a long ways dat way, and when we got to a place where some of us couldn't follow de leader, or till de leader out-dared dem all, or till somebody else out-dared de leader, den we would choose another leader and starts over again in another place. Sometimes, some of us would fall, or de leader would gits out on a black jack or a post oak limb a little too far, and it would break, and down it would come. Sometimes, we would cry and sometimes we wouldn't. It is a wonder some of us chilluns didn't git killed. We would have, but de good Lord was just watchin' over us.

Some folks don't believe there is any ghosts, but I knows there is. I has seed some of dem myself. I saw one, one night, a little while after my first wife died. I went to bed and went to sleep, and 'bout de middle of de night, I woke up. I heard my wife callin' me, and when I looks down at de foot of my bed I sees my wife standing dere with her hands on de foot of my bed. I sets up dar lookin' at her, and she said, "Calvin, you is been fooling wid whiskey, and you knows I don't like dat, and you is going to git in trouble soon if you don't quits dat. Now I is warning you." And den she just disappeared right dar in front of my eyes.

I sets dar and just looks where she was standing and calls her several times, but she wouldn't come back. I layed back down, but I didn't sleeps no mo' dat night, and I got up befo' daylight de next morning thinking 'bout dat and went and told de man I was selling whiskey wid dat I was quitting, and I did. I says den, dat if a dead person knows what I was doing, I sho' wanted to do de right thing. So I changed my life and went de honest way and jined de church, and I has had a Bible in my home ever since.

One thing happened dat is funny now, and I tells it to de chilluns round here once and awhile. Back in slavery times, when I was a big boy 'bout sixteen years old, one Sunday I went over to some big pecan trees dat was 'bout a hundred yards off Maser Ingram's land. It was in de early winter and it had been raining and was muddy. When I climbs over de fence, I stops and looks all around for some patter-rollers, and didn't seed none. I had left my pass at de house, and I knows dat I would gits a licking if de patterrollers ketched me off Maser Ingram's land.

I got up in de tree and pulls off de pecans close to me and puts dem in my pocket. I got my pockets about half full and den I begins thrashing de tree. And when I got up in de very top of dis big tree I looked down and dar was eleven men, one on a horse and ten picking up pecans and puttin' dem in a sack. I thought I had been lookin' around all de time and dar I had done gone and let dem patterrollers slip up on me. I stopped and looked at dem and den begins coming down, but de man on de horse says, "Keep on thrashing dat tree, boy, till you gits all de pecans out," and I did, and dey kept picking dem up. I specks they got 'bout three hundred pounds off dat tree.

When I got through, de man on de horse says, "Come on down, boy, and show us your pass." I says I left it at home. He says, "Well, come on down and we will give you a lesson you won't forget, dat will make you remembah to git it de next time." I knew dey was going to whip me, so I waited a little while, and de man on de horse says, "Men, knock dat coon out of dat tree," and dey began throwing mud balls, sticks, and rocks, too, at me. Well, I begins comin' down out dat tree, jumpin' from one limb to another, and when I got 'bout fifteen feet from de ground, I jumps out and hits de ground, and by de time I got up, de man on de horse had his horse's neck over me. I bent over and begins rolling up my pants legs, and he says, "What you rolling dem up for? We going to knock dem down wid dat wet rope." I tole him I wanted to keep de mud off dem, and when I gets both of dem rolled up past my knees, I begins running.

He took after me on his horse, but I outrun his horse to de fence, and when I gets to de fence I dived through it head first and hits in de mud on de other side on my face and stomach. When I got up, I was running again. I had so much mud on my face I couldn't see where I was going, but I was gitting away from de patterrollers. I runs clear to de house as fast as I could go, and it was about one-half mile. I got dar and got cleaned up, and dat evening some of us boys was walking round close to dat road when de same patterrollers come riding by, and one of dem says to de others, "Dar is dat running black devil," and he hollers to me, "Boy, we is going to whip you yet, de first time we ketches you off dat plantation," but I knows dat dey wasn't going to ketch me off widout a pass, 'cause I come too near gitting a whipping.

When any of us slaves got sick, Maser Ingram made us take calomel, blue moss, or aloe, but if we gots too bad he would call out de doctor. He says ever day dat a slave is out of de field it is costing him money, and de longer he is sick de mo' doctor bill he is got to pay, and maybe lose de slave, too, so he wasn't taking no chances. Most things we had was chills and fever and sometimes pneumonia. He would doctor for chills and fever hisself, and for bad colds, but if de cold seemed like it was tighting up a little, he gits a doctor 'bout soon as he could. De chilluns would wear asafoetida on a string around deir necks to keeps off de whooping cough, measles and mumps, and such diseases dat chilluns has, but I don't think it does so much good.

When de War comes on, we all felt de effects of it. We all has to work harder and we has to give to help win de War. Maser Ingram gives money, corn, hogs, and cattle, and had us to make sabers for de soldiers. Uncle Zeke and me made lots of dem things. Maser Ingram had de womenfolks on de plantation to make up lots of clothes for de soldiers. I has seen several wagonloads of clothes hauled off from dar at one time.

Finally, de War was over and Maser Ingram calls us all up in his yard. He says, "You all sits down on de grass. I has something to tells you." We all sets down and looks at him, for we guessed we was all freed and we didn't know what we would do if Maser Ingram made us all leave and rustle for ourselves. Wasn't nobody sayin' a word. We was waitin' fer him to say something, and when he begins he says, "Now you all know dar has been a war goin' on between de North and de South, and we of de South has give and done our part. But de South has lost de War, and you all knows what dat means. De North wanted to free de slaves, and dey is done it. Now you all is free to goes where you wants to, to makes a livin' for yourselves. Now you is got to work, and raise or buy your own feed and clothes and medicine. You don't have a maser anymo'. You is your own maser. My slaves and everybody's slaves is free to go anywhere dey can make a livin'. Now you is free to go, or you can stay here and work fer me if you wants to."

Dar wasn't any of dem dat wants to leave, so Maser Ingram fixed it up fer some of dem to work by de day and some to farm on de halvers. I rented a crop on de halvers and bought de blacksmith shop, and I worked de crop and run de shop, too. I hired some work done in de rush season and done de rest myself.

We all sho' was glad to gits started out fer ourselves wid Maser

Ingram behind us, 'cause we know he wasn't goin' to let us starve. But lots of de slave owners wouldn't help deir old slaves at all. Dey just beat dem out of all dey could. Some of de slaves was worse off dan dey was in slavery times.

But de lid blowed off of everything de next year, fer Maser Ingram took sick and died. We got de best doctors aroun' dar fer him, but dey couldn't saves him, and dey sho' tried hard enough. Dey would comes and stays all night and day, but it didn't do no good. It was just his time to die, I guess, and when it happens dat way you can't do no good.

When Maser Ingram died, people come from ever'where to de funeral. He sho' did have lots of friends. He was buried on his own plantation just like he wanted to be, and we all cried 'bout him dyin' like we would had he been our own daddy.

When de doctors seed he was goin' to die, dey wrote to his brother back East and tole him to come out here. So he comes out here, but he got dere after Maser Ingram died and was buried. He wasn't like Maser Ingram. He was one of dem kind of men dat take your last dime and den gits mad 'cause you didn't have a quarter.

Maser Ingram's brother comes down and took charge. He tole everybody dat had crops on de halves dey could finish up de crop, but de ones dat was workin' by de day, dat dey would either have to git in shape for a halvers crop or go somewhere else to work after dis crop was over. But there wasn't any of dem able to farm, 'cause he wouldn't help dem like Maser Ingram did, and dey had to drift on.

We all thought dat he ought to have divided up Maser Ingram's land and de stock and tools among us ole slaves, and let him take de money, for we had worked for Maser all de time. 'Course, we knew dat Maser had been good to us, but he didn't had no wife and no chilluns, and his brother had mo' land and money and things than Maser did, and he didn't needs it—but we never tole him 'bout dat and he never mentioned it. He thought dat we ought to have made mo' money den we did. He did say dat we was lazy, and us was workin' hard all de time. He was a greedy man, and de mo' he got de mo' he wanted, and he generally got what he wanted, 'specially when a po' man had it. He kicks dis one out and dat one, till dar wasn't many of us left. I stays dar and farms for twenty-two years.

I farms on de halvers till he comes round one day and says, "Calvin, you is got to furnish your own team, tools, and feed, and farm dis place on de third-and-fourth,* if you wants to stay here." He didn't thinks I could buy de team and tools, but I fools him. I says, "Maser Ingram, what you wants fer de team of mares and de tools of yours dat I am farmin' wid?" I knows dat I was going to have to buy dem or hunt me another place, and I wanted to stay, 'cause places was hard to find fer darkies, as de white folks had begun to rent places on de third-and-fourth. I expected Maser Ingram to ask me two prices fer de team and tools, but he didn't, and I paid him cash fer it. And when he took de money he says, "Calvin, you is better off den most of de niggers. How you keep your money? Don't you ever spend any of it?" I says, "Yes sah, I buys what I needs, but I don't spend no money fer foolishness"—and I didn't either, and I never is. I had too many things to think 'bout besides buying foolish things.

Finally, I got to courtin' a little girl dat lived a little way from me. Her name was Georgia Ann Lyon. I was 'bout eighteen years older dan she was, but we married. I had thought dat I was too good fer any women all dis time, but dis girl had some sense. She didn't tries to spend all de money she gits aholds of either, like all de other women-folks. Most all de colored folks just wanted to spend money all de time, like dey does now, just 'cause dey got deir freedom and got to makin' a little money of deir own. Dat is why dey never did have nothing. I had been courtin' dis girl about three or four years. 'Course, we had our little arguments, but all I had to do to make her quit fussing at me 'bout something she thought I ought to do or not to have done was to tell her dat if she didn't hush I would take her back to her pappy's. Den she would hush, 'cause she sho' didn't wants to go back over there.

Me and my first wife had four chilluns—one boy and three girls. My wife died when de last girl was born. We lost de chile, too. After I paid de funeral bills and de doctor bills, it nearly broke me up, and I was left wid de three little chilluns.

I batched and farmed two years and lets my parents keep de chilluns, but my mother and father was gittin' ole and de chilluns was gittin' to where dey was gittin' into lots of meanness and causing dem

* Sharecropping for three-fourths of the crop.

lots of trouble. So I sold out everything I had, 'ceptin' some feed and some hogs and a cow, and moved to Corsicana and bought me a little home on de northeast side and begins to do odd jobs and day labor.

Finally, all de chilluns married off and left me alone at my home. After dey moved away, I got lonesome and I got to going wid a woman dat lived close to me. Her chilluns had married and had moved out, and she has to pay rent, and she didn't makes much money cooking fer de white folks on de west side. So we got married. She was lonesome and I was, too, and she needed somebody to take care of her. We had 'bout de same ideas, so we makes up, and we got along 'bout as good as me and my first wife, and she was a good housekeeper and cook, too.

I is got one boy and one girl living. My boy is still farmin' third-and-fourth, but he ain't went tractor-crazy yet. He still works his mules and he ain't in debt. This is my girl I is livin' wid, and she is doin' housework and washin' and cookin' fer some white folks on de west side. 'Course we all hits it hard fer a while, and it ain't so terrible much better now, but my daughter and her husband ain't on relief now, likes dey was two years ago. Dey gits enough work now to live and pay rent. I is got fifteen grandchilluns and five great-grandchilluns.

You takes dese young people comin' up now'days. Dey is most all in town, and dey ain't work fer dem. All dey do is just wander aroun', both white and black, and fifty percent of dem ain't worth killin'. Dey just ain't no 'count. If dey was out on de farm where dey could work all de time, dey might amount to somethin' some day. Dat is why our jails and penitent'aries are always full. Idle brains is de Devil's workshop.

I is a religious man and has been fer years, and I prays fer our good President* dat de good Lord will spare him and help him to take care of us ole people in de way of a pension de last few days we got to live on dis ole sin-cursed world. I is ready to go when de good Lord calls me and lets my part go to help some other po' man or woman what needs it.

*Franklin D. Roosevelt.

ISAAC STIER

MY NAME is Isaac Stier, but folks calls me Ike. I done passed into my ninety-ninth year, an' if I lives 'bout ten more months I'll be a even hundred.

I was named by my pappy's young marster, an' I ain't never told nobody all of dat name. It's got twenty-two letters in it, an' folks would laugh, but it's wrote out in de fambly Bible. Dat's how I knows I'll be one hundred years old if I lives till de turn of de year. But my heart's mos' wore out. It can't las' long 'cause I's had a heap of e'sposure.

My ma was Ellen Stier an' my pa was Jordan Stier. Dey marster was prominent long time ago. I don't 'member much 'bout 'em, an' I don't recall how we passed from folks to folks. Mebbe us was sole.

My daddy, he was brought to dis country by a slave dealer from Nashville, Tennessee. Dey traveled all de way on foot, makin' de trip through de Injun country. Dey followed dat road called de Trace; 'twan't nothin' but a Injun trail. When dey got to Natchez, de slaves was put in de pen 'tached to de slave market. It stood at de forks of St. Catherine and Liberty roads. Here dey was fed an' washed an' rubbed down lak racehosses. Den dey was dressed up an' put through de paces dat would show off dey muscles. My daddy was sole as a twelve year old, but he always said he was nigher twenty. De firs' man what bought him was a preacher, but he only kep' him a short while. Den he was sole to Mr. Preacher Robinson.

I was born in Jefferson County, between Hamburg and Union Church, Mississippi. De plantation joined de Whitney place an' de Montgomery place, too. I don't rightly 'member how many acres my marster owned, but it was a big plantation wid eighty or ninety head

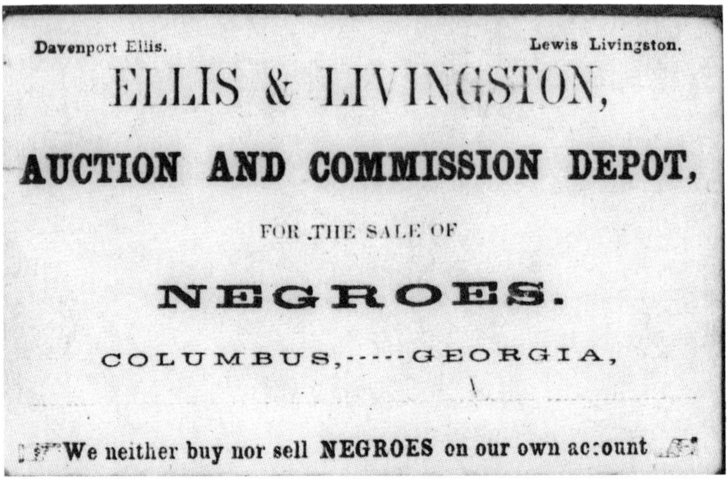

Davenport Ellis. Lewis Livingston.

ELLIS & LIVINGSTON,

AUCTION AND COMMISSION DEPOT,

FOR THE SALE OF

NEGROES.

COLUMBUS,-----GEORGIA,

We neither buy nor sell **NEGROES** on our own account

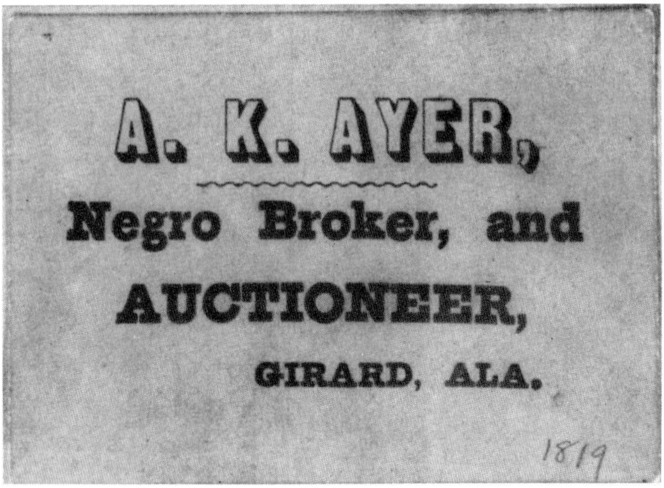

A. K. AYER,

Negro Broker, and

AUCTIONEER,

GIRARD, ALA.

1819

PLATE 15

o' grown folks workin' it. No tellin' how many little black folks dey was.

I b'longed to Marse Jeems Stowers. My mistus was Mis' Sarah Stowers. She teached me how to read, an' she teached me how to be mannerly. On church days, I driv' de carriage. I was proud to take my folks to meetin', an' I allus sat in de back pew an' heard de preachin' de same as dey did.

As a little tyke, I wore long slip-like shirts, but when dey sont me to town I put on breeches an' stuffed de tail of my slip in so hit passed for a shirt. I allus lived in de big house an' played wid de white chillun. I sorta looked aftah 'em. I carried 'em to school an' whilst dey was in school I roamed de woods huntin'. Sometimes I'd git a big bag of game, an' hit was mostly used to feed de slaves.

Us had a overseer on de place, but he warn't mean like I's heard of other folks havin'. He was Mr. William Robinson. He was good to everybody, both white an' cullud. Folks didn't mine workin' for him 'cause he spoke kine. But dey dassen' sass him. He was poor, but my daddy had b'longed to his pa, Mr. John Robinson, a Methodist preacher. Dat was a nice fambly wid sho'-'nuf 'ligion. Whilst dey warn't rich, dey had learnin.'

Us danced plenty. Some of de men clogged an' pigeoned, but when us had dances dey was real cotillions lak de white folks had. Us always had a fiddler, an' on Christmas an' other holidays us'd be 'lowed to invite us sweethearts from other plantations. Old Mis' would let us cook a gran' supper an' Marse would slip us some liquor. Dem suppers was de bes' I ever et. Sometimes us'd have wile turkey, fried fish, hot corn pone, fresh pork ham, baked yams, chitlins, popcorn, apple pie, pound cake, raisins, an' coffee. Law', Miss! De folks nowadays don' know nothin' 'bout good eatin'.

I use' to call out de figgers like "ladies sachet," an' "gents to de lef'; now all swing." Ebberbody like my calls, an' de dancers sho' moved smooth an' pretty. Long after de War was over, de white folks would engage me to come roun' wid de band an' call de figgers at all de big dances. Yes, ma'am, dey always paid me well.

De bes' times I can 'member always come roun' de Fourth of July. Dat was always de beginnin' of de camp meetin's. Ain't nothin' lak 'em in dese days. Ebberbody what had any standin' went. Dey cooked up whole trunks full o' good things an' driv' over to de campgrounds. De preacher had a big pavilion covered wid sweet-gum branches an' carpeted wid sawdust. Folks had wagons wid hay an' quilts whar de menfolks slep'. De ladies slep' in little log houses, an' dey took dey feather beds wid 'em. I always driv' de carriage for my white folks. Whilst dey was worshippin' I'd slip roun' an' tas'e out of dey basket. Ever' day, I'd eat till I was ready to bus'.

One day I got so sick I thought I would. I crawled down to de spring an' wash my face in cole water, but I kept gettin' worse an' worse. When somebody called me, I jist groaned an' groaned. Aftah dat, folks come a-crowdin' to de spring like dey always done when meetin' turned out. Den somebody called out, "Captain Stowers, yo' nigger is dyin'." My marster called de doctor, an' they gib me warm mustard water. In a little bit, here hit all come up: fried chicken, ham, hard-boiled eggs, quince preserves, cucumber pickles, raisin pie, honey, pound cake, an' a lot else I cain't think of now. My marster sho' was 'shamed in public, 'cause he knowed positive I'd been pilferin' in dem baskets. If I hadn' a-been so sick, he mos' likely would a-whipped me good an' proper. If anybody ever needed hit, I did. Dem sho' was good old days, an' I'd love to live 'em over ag'in.

De slaves was well-treated when dey got sick. My marster had a standin' doctor what he paid by de year. Dey was a horspital building near de quarters an' a good old granny woman to nuss de sick. Dey was five or six beds in a room. One room was for de mens an' one for de wimmins. Us doctor was name Richardson, an' he tended us long after de War. He sho' was a gent'men an' a powerful good doctor.

Mr. Abraham Lincoln was a good man, but dey tells me he was poor white an' never cut much figger in his clothes. Dat's why he never un'erstood how us felt toward us white folks. It takes de quality to un'erstand such things.

Mr. Jefferson Davis was pretty good 'bout some things. But if he hadn' a-been mulish, he'd have accepted de proposition Mr. Abe Lincoln made 'im. Den slav'ry would a-lasted always. But he flew into a huff an' swore dat afore he'd let his wife an' daughter dabble dey purty white hands in dishwater an' washtubs, he'd fight till ebery gun an' sword in de country was gone. Aftah dat, he say he'd whip de

Yankees wid cornstalks. Dat made Mr. Lincoln so mad he sot 'bout to free de slaves.

When de big War broke out, I sho' stuck to my marster, an' I fit de Yankees same as he did. I went in de battles 'long side of him, an' us both fit under Marse Robert E. Lee. I reckon you is heard of him, ain't you? I seen mo' folks killt dan anybody could count. Heaps of dem was all tore to pieces an' cryin' to God to let 'em die. I toted water to dem in blue de same as dem in grey. Folks wouldn' b'lieve all de trufe if I was to tell all I knows 'bout dem ungodly times.

'Fore de War, I nevah knowed what hit was to go empty. My marse sho' set a fine table an' fed his people de highest. De hongriest I ever been was at de siege of Vicksburg. Dat was a time I'd like to forgit. De folks et up all de cats an' dogs an' den went to devourin' de mules an' hosses. Even de wimmin an' little chillun was starvin'. Dey stummicks was stickin' to dey backbones. Us niggers was sufferin' so, us took de sweaty hoss blankets an' soaked 'em in mudholes where de hosses had tromped. Den us wrung 'em out in buckets an' drunk dat dirty water for pot-likker. It tasted kinda salty an' was strength'nin', like weak soup.

Dem Yankees tuck us by starvation. Hit wasn' a fair fight. Dey called hit a victory an' bragged 'bout Vicksburg fallin', but hongry folks ain't got no fight lef' in 'em. Our folks was starved into surrenderin'.

De War was over in May 1865, but I was captured at Vicksburg an' hel' in jail till I 'greed to take up arms wid de Nawth. I figgered it was 'bout all I could do 'cause dey warn't but one war at Vicksburg an' dat was over. I was all de time hopin' I could slip off an' work my way back home, but de Yankees didn' turn me loose till 1866.

Den I worked in St. Louis. My job was in a saloon. Dat was 'bout all I know how to do. All de time I was cravin' to come back to Mississippi. It sho' suits my tas'e better 'n anywheres I's ever been.

Aftah de War, me an' my marster come a-trompin' home. De fences was gone, de cattle was gone, de money an' de niggers was gone, too. On top of all dat, de whole country was overrun and plumb tuk over by white trash. It was cautious times.

De slaves 'spected a heap from freedom dey didn't git. Dey was led to think dey would have a easy time, go places widout passes, an' have plenty of spendin' money. But dey sho' got fooled. Mos' of 'em didn' find deyselves no bettah off. Pussonally, I had a harder time after de War dan I did endurin' slav'ry.

De Yankees pass as us frien's. Dey made big promises but dey was poor reliance. Some of 'em meant well towards us, but us was mistole 'bout a heap o' things. Dey promise us a mule an' forty acres o' lan'. Us ain't seen no mule yet. Us got de lan' all right, but twan't no service. Fac' is, it was way over in a territory where nothin' would grow. I didn' know nothin' 'bout farmin' nohow, 'cause I was always a coachman an' a play companion to de white chillun.

All de cullud folks what lived to git back home took to de lan' again. If dey marster was dead dey went to his frien's an' offered to put in a sharecrop. Dey was all plumb sick of war. It sho' is ungodly business. I never will fergit de fearsome sight o' seein' men die 'fore dey time. War sho' is de Debil's own work.

When I landed back home, my white folks welcome me. After a while, I married a gal what was real smart 'bout farmin' an' chicken raisin'. Us sharecropped an' raised a fambly. Somehow us always scraped along. Sometimes it was by de hardes', but us always had plenty t'eat.

De Ku Klux Klan didn't bother me none. 'Course, I was feared of 'em at firs', but I soon learnt dat long as I behaved myself an' 'tended to my business dey warn't after me. Dey sho' disastered dem what meddled wid de white folks, but nobody but a smart-alec would a-done dat. Only niggers huntin' trouble mixed into white folks' affairs. Once or twice I seen Ku Kluxes ridin' by, but dey always traveled fas' an' I kep' my mouf shut.

After a while, robbers an' low-down trash got to wearin' robes an' 'tendin' dey was Ku Kluxes. Folks called dem de "white caps." Dey was vicious an' us was more scared of dem dan us'd ever been of de Klan. When dey got liquored up, de Debil sho' was turn't loose.

I's gittin real feeble, an' I been to de doctor. He says I is got a bad heart. Wait jest a minute, Miss, whilst I set on de curb an' rest myself a spell. I gits kinda windless when I talks 'bout all I's been through. Now I'se got my breath an' am feelin' better. You see, Miss, I rents a place on Providence Plantation, 'bout three miles south of Natchez.

De trip to Natchez in a rickety old wagon is mos' too much in dis hot weather.

Right now, I loves my marster an' his wife in de grave. Dey raised me an' showed me kindness all dey lives. I was proud of dem an' now I's under treatment of young Dr. Kurtze Stowers, my marster's grandchile. I trusts him an' he is good to me.

My wife is been dead 'bout seventeen years an' my chilluns is so scattered dat I don' know where dey is. De folks I stays wid is powerful good to me an' sees after me same as dey was my own. I reckon I don' need nothin' else. Nobody needs more dan dey can use, nohow.

Dis generation ain't got much sense. Dey is tryin' to git somewheres too fas'. None of 'em is sati'fied wid plain livin'. Ebberbody wants de moon wid a fence around hit. Dey wants a car an' fine clothes. Den dey has to git book learnin' an' take vacations an' go travelin'. In dis day an' time, dey ain't no satisfaction wid life. Folks is seekin' what dey cain't find. De thing to find is peace an' simple things. It ain't de thing dat costs money what gibs de mos' happiness. But folks is rushin' too fas' an' dey don't know where. Dey ain't headed fur nothin' in particular.

CHARLIE MOSES

WHEN I gits to thinkin' back on them slavery days I feels like risin' out o' this here bed an' tellin' ever'body 'bout the harsh treatment us colored folks was given when we was owned by poor-quality folks.

My marster was mean an' cruel. I hates him, hates him! The God Almighty has condemned him to eternal fiah. Of that I is certain. Even the cows and horses on his plantation was scared out o' their minds when he come near 'em. Oh, Lordy! I can tell you plenty 'bout the things he done to us poor niggers. We was treated no better than one o' his houn' dogs. Sometimes he didn't treat us as good as he did them. I prays to the Lord not to let me see him when I die. He had the Devil in his heart.

His name was Jim Rankin an' he lived out on a plantation over in Marion County. I was born an' raised on his place. I spec' I was 'bout twelve year old at the time o' the War.

Old man Rankin worked us like animals. He had a right smart plantation an' kep' all his niggers, 'cept one houseboy, out in the fiel' a-workin'. He'd say, "Niggers is meant to work. That's what I paid my good money for 'em to do."

He had two daughters an' two sons. Them an' his poor wife had all the work in the house to do, 'cause he wouldn' waste no nigger to help 'em out. His family was as scared o' him as we was. They lived all their lives under his whip. No, Sir! No, Sir! There warn't no meaner man in the world than old man Jim Rankin.

My pappy was Allen Rankin an' my mammy was Ca'line. There was twelve o' us chillun, nine boys an' three girls. My pa was born in Mississippi an' sole to Marster Rankin when he was a young man. My

PLATE 16: Isaac, a slave carpenter once owned by Thomas Jefferson.

mammy was married in South Carolina an' sole to Marster Rankin over at Columbia. She had to leave her family. But she warn't long in gittin' her another man.

Oh, Lordy! The way us niggers was treated was awful. Marster would beat, knock, kick, kill. He done ever'thing he could 'cept eat us. We was worked to death. We worked all Sunday, all day, all night. He whipped us till some jus' lay down to die. It was a poor life. I knows it ain't right to have hate in the heart, but—God Almighty— it's hard to be forgivin' when I think of old man Rankin.

If one o' his niggers done something to displease him, which was mos' ever' day, he'd whip him till he'd mos' die, an' then he'd kick him roun' in the dust. He'd even take his gun an', before the nigger had time to open his mouf, he'd jus' stan' there an' shoot him down.

We'd git up at dawn to go to the fiel's. We'd take our pails o' grub with us an' hang 'em up in a row by the fence. We had meat an' pork an' beef an' greens to eat. Many a time when noontime come an' we'd go to eat our vittles, the marster would come a-walkin' through the fiel' with ten or twelve o' his houn' dogs. If he looked in the pails an' was displeased with what he seen in 'em, he took 'em an' dumped 'em out before our very eyes an' let the dogs grab it up. We didn't git nothin' to eat then till we come home late in the evenin'. After he left we'd pick up pieces of the grub that the dogs left an' eat 'em. Hongry—hongry—we was so hongry!

We had our separate cabins, an' at sunset all of us would go in an' shut the door an' pray to the Lord that Marster Jim wouldn' call us out.

We never had much clothes, 'ceptin' what was give us by the marster or the mistis. Wintertime, we never had 'nuf to wear nor 'nuf to eat. We wore homespun all the time. The marster didn' think we needed anything, but jus' a little.

We didn't go to church, but Sundays we'd gather roun' an' listen to the mistis read a little out o' the Bible. The marster said we didn't need no religion an' he finally stopped her from readin' to us.

When the War come, Marster was a captain of a regiment. He went away an' stayed a year. When he come back he was even meaner than before.

When he come home from the War he stayed for two weeks. The

night 'fore he was a-fixin' to leave to go back, he come out on his front porch to smoke his pipe. He was a-standin' leanin' up agin' a railin' when somebody sneaked up in the darkness an' shot him three times. Oh, my Lord! He died the nex' mornin'. We never knowed who done it. I was glad they shot him down.

Sometimes the cavalry would come an' stay at the house an' the mistis would have to 'tend to 'em an' see that they got plenty to eat an' fresh horses.

I never seen no fightin'. I stayed on the plantation till the War was over. I didn't see none o' the fightin'.

I don't 'member nothin' 'bout Jefferson Davis. Lincoln was the man that set us free. He was a big general in the War. I 'member a song we sung, then. It went kinda like this:

> Free at las',
> Free at las',
> Thank God Almighty
> I's free at las',
> Mmmmm, mmmmm, mmmmm.

When the mistis tole us we was free—my pappy was already dead then—my mammy packed us chillun up to move. We traveled on a cotton wagon to Covington, Louisiana. We all worked on a farm there 'bout a year. Then all 'cept me moved to Mandeville, Louisiana, an' worked on a farm there. I hired out to Mr. Charlie Duson, a baker. Then we moved to a farm above Baton Rouge, Louisiana, an' worked for Mr. Abe Manning. We jus' traveled all over from one place to another.

Then I got a letter from a frien' o' mine in Gainesville, Mississippi. He had a job for me on a boat, haulin' lumber up the coast to Bay St. Louis, Pass Christian, Long Beach, Gulfport, an' all them coast towns. I worked out o' Gainesville on this boat for 'bout two year. I lost track o' my family then an' never seen 'em no more.

In the year 1870 I got the call from the Lord to go out an' preach. I left Gainesville an' traveled to Summit, Mississippi, where another frien' o' mine lived. I preached the words o' the Lord an' traveled from one place to another.

I only seen the Klu Klux Klan once. They was a-paradin' the streets here in Brookhaven. They had a nigger that they was a-goin' to tar an' feather.

In 1873 I got married an' decided to settle in Brookhaven. I preached an' all my flock believed in me. I bought up this house an' the two on each side of it. Here I raised seven chillun in the way o' the Lord. They is all in different parts o' the country now, but I sees one of 'em ever' now an' then. Las' April the Lord seen fit to put me a-bed an' I been ailin' with misery ever since.

The young folks nowadays are happy an' don't know 'bout war an' slavery times, but I does. They don't know nothin' an' don't make the mark in the worl' that the old folks did. Old people made the first roads in Mississippi. The niggers today wouldn' know how to act on a plantation. But they are happy. We was miserable.

Slavery days was bitter, an' I can't forgit the sufferin'. Oh, God! I hates 'em, hates 'em. God Almighty never meant for human beings to be like animals. Us niggers has a soul an' a heart an' a mine. We ain't like a dog or a horse. If all marsters had been good like some, the slaves would all a-been happy. But marsters like mine ought never been allowed to own niggers.

I didn' spec' nothin' out o' freedom 'ceptin' peace an' happiness an' the right to go my way as I pleased. I prays to the Lord for us to be free, always. That's the way God Almighty wants it.

Voices

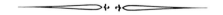

RELIGION AND EDUCATION

NOAH had three sons, and when Noah got drunk on wine, one of his sons laughed at him, and the other two took a sheet and walked backwards and threw it over Noah. Noah told the one who laughed, "You' children will be hewers of wood and drawers of water for the other two's children, and they will be known by their hair and their skin being dark." So, Miss, there we are, and that is the way God meant us to be. We have always had to follow the white folks and do what we saw them do, and that's all there is to it. You just can't get away from what the Lord said.

—GUS ROGERS

We went to the white folks' church, so we sit in the back on the floor. They allowed us to join their church whenever one got ready to join or felt that the Lord had forgiven him of his sins. We told our determination. This is what we said: "I feel that the Lord have forgiven me of my sins. I have prayed and I feel that I am a better girl. I belong to master so-and-so, and I am so old." The white preacher would then ask our mis' and master what they thought about it, and if they could see any change. They would get up and say, "I notice she don't steal, and I notice she don't lie as much, and I notice she works better." Then, they let us join. We served our mistress and master, in slavery time, and not God.

—SARAH DOUGLAS

On Sundays, us would git tergether in de woods an' have worship. Us could go to de white folks' church, but us wanted ter go whar us

PLATE 17: While most slave children were prohibited from learning to read or write, their owners did occasionally read them Bible stories.

could sing all de way through, an' hum 'long, an' shout—yo' all know, jist turn' loose lak.

—EMILY DIXON

On Sundays, us would meet at log cabins ter worship, as us didn't hab no churches. De slaves did like ter git tergether an' praise de Lord. Dey would set fer hours on straight oncomfo'table benches an' planks, while some would be seated on de ground or standing. Dey would hum deep an' low in long mournful tones, swayin' to an' fro. Udders would pray an' sing soft, while de brudder preacher wuz a-deliverin' de humble message. De songs wuz old Negro spirituals sung in de deep, rich voice of our race. We didn't hab no songbooks, nor couldn't read if we had 'em. We sorter made 'em up, as us went 'long.

We loves music. Most any cottage you pass, especially at night, yo' can hear soft music an' singin'. De slave owners uster say, when dey had a bunch wukkin' in de fields, as long as dey could hear 'em singin', dey knowed dem niggers wuz a-wukkin', but when dey got quiet, dey had ter go put 'em back to wuk, fer when dey stopped singin', dey stopped wuk, too.

—STEVE WEATHERSBY

They say us can carry de song better than white folks. Well, maybe us does love de Lord just a little bit better, and what's in our mouth is in our hearts.

—DINAH CUNNINGHAM

De mos' fun we hed was at our meetin's. We hed dem mos' every Sunday, an' dey lasted way inter de night. De preacher I lakked de bes' was name' Matthew Ewing. He was a comely nigger, black as night, an' he sho' cud read outen his han'. He neber larned no real readin' an' writin', but he sho' knowed his Bible, an' wud hole his han' out an' mek lak he wuz readin', an' preach de purt'est preachin's you ever heard. De meetin's last from early in de mawnin' till late at night. When dark come, de men folks wud hang up a wash pot, bottom up'ards, in de little brush chu'ch house us hed, so's it'd catch de noise an' de oberseer wudn' hear us singin' an' shoutin'. Dey didn' mind us meetin' in de daytime, but dey thought if we stayed up half de night, we wudn' work so hard de next day. An' dat was de trufe.

When us hed our big meetin's, dere'd allus be some darkies from de plantations 'round to come. Dey wud hev to slip off, 'cause dey marsters was a-feared dey wud get hitched up wid some other black boy or gal on de other plantation, an' den dey wud either hev to buy or sell a nigger, 'fore dey cud get any work outen dem.

—CLARA YOUNG

Mis' Bessie fixed me up to be baptized at the Limestone Baptist Church. We had to go to the spring pond called Austin's Pond, where all the baptizing took place. The white folks carried on their baptizing there, too. The first warm Sunday in May was when I was baptized.

All Saturday, I prayed, and Mis' Bessie told me what I was going to do, and read to me from the Bible about baptizing and about John the Baptist baptizing Christ. Mis' Bessie was telling my ma how to fix my clothes while she was reading the Bible to me. A crowd was to be baptized at 2:30 o'clock, that afternoon. I went with my folks. Mis' Bessie went, and all the white folks went to see their Negroes go under.

When we got there, the banks of Austin's Pond was lined with Negroes shouting and singing glory and praises. They sang all the songs they could think of, and the preacher lined out more songs to them. The people to be baptized congregated before the preacher, and he told them what to do. Then, we went in and put on the clothes we was to go under in.

I had a long white gown gathered from my shoulders, and it had a big kind of sleeves. On my head, I wore a white cap, and kept on my white stockings, but I pulled off my black shoes. I felt so good that I seemed to walk real light. While we were getting in our baptizing clothes, we shouted praises, as the people on the banks sang. Some of us jumped up. When my time come, I started to the pond, and just before the preacher turned to take my hand, I shouted, "Lord, have mercy," and clapped my hands over my head. Somebody said, "Dat child sho' is gitting a new soul."

Down in the water I went. First, it hit my ankles, and then I felt the hem of my skirts getting wet. I looked down and my gown was floating on top the water. I took my hand and pushed it down. The preacher pulled me to him, and I went in water to my waist. I said, "Oh, Lordy," when that water hit my stomach. The preacher said, "Now, sister, you just hold your breath and shut your mouth. Trust in the Lord and don't act like a grunting pig, but have faith." Then, the singing seemed far off, and the preacher's voice got deep. He put his big hand over my mouth and told me to limber up my back. His other hand was under my back. He pushed me over, and down in the water I went. Then, up I come. The preacher put a towel over my face, and while I was getting water out of my eyes and mouth, he was saying the Lord done reached down from Heaven and created a new soul.

I felt real funny, when I turned to walk up out of the water. I could hardly walk, for I had on so many clothes, and they were so heavy. As soon as I could, I got into the clothes that I wore to the baptizing and put on my black shoes and the pair of white stockings that I had fetched with me. While Aunt Kizie Lockhart was tying the handkerchief around my head that Mis' Bessie give me, I told her about how I felt. She said, "Why, sure, child, ain't you done washed your sins away and got converted?"

Then, she grabbed me by the hand and we went out among the people, shouting praises to the Lord. I ain't never felt the same since. When the preacher had got them all baptized, we went into the church and had services. The white folks went on home, after the baptizing was over. At the church, we shouted till we could not shout no more. Folks don't do like that now. They don't feel good when they join the church no more, either. I ain't had nothing to come against me, since I was baptized. My head loses lots of things, but not my religion.

—EASTER LOCKHART

That religion I got in them way-back days is still with me. And it ain't this piecrust religion, such as the folks are getting these days.

The old-time religion had some filling between the crusts. Wasn't so much empty words, like they is today. The Negroes of today needs another leader like Booker Washington. Get the young folks to working. That's what they need. And get some filling in their piecrust religion, so's when they meet the Lord, their souls won't be empty, like is their pocketbooks, today.

—PRINCE BEE

It been de rule to follow what de Bible say do, in dat day en' time. En' now, it seem like de rule must be, do like you see de other fellow is doin'.

—HESTER HUNTER

Marster neber 'low he slaves to go to chu'ch. Dey hab big holes out in de fiel's dey git down in and pray. Dey done dat way 'cause de white folks didn' want 'em to pray. Dey uster pray for freedom. I dunno how dey larn to pray, 'cause dey warn't no preachers come roun' to teach 'em. I reckon de Lawd jis' mek 'em know how to pray.

—ELLEN BUTLER

I've heard 'em pray for freedom. I thought it was foolishness, then, but the old-time folks always felt they was to be free. It must have been something 'vealed unto 'em. Back then, if they'd catch you writing, they would break you if they had to cut off your finger, but still the old-time folks knew they would be free. It must have been 'vealed unto 'em.

—ANONYMOUS

Our master took his slaves to meetin' with him. There was always something about that I couldn't understand. They treated the colored folks like animals and would not hesitate to sell and separate them, yet they seemed to think they had souls and tried to make Christians of them.

—MALINDA DISCUS

190

On Sundays, we'd just put a old Prince Albert coat on some good nigger and make a preacher out of him. The white folks was mostly Methodists, and sometimes they would listen to our preachin's and sorta keep an eye on us thataway.

—JEPTHA CHOICE

I's been preaching the Gospel and farming, since slavery time. I jined the chu'ch eighty-three years ago, when I was a slave of Master Gaud. Till freedom, I had to preach what they told me to. Master made me preach to the other niggers that the Good Book say that if niggers obey their master, they would go to Heaven. I knew there was something better for them, but I darsen't tell them so, 'lest I done it on the sly. That I did lots. I told the niggers—but not so Master could hear it—that if they keep praying, the Lord would hear their prayers and set them free.

—THE REVEREND ANDERSON EDWARDS

My mother, all de time she'd be prayin' to de Lord. She'd take us chillun to de woods to pick up firewood, and we'd turn around to see her down on her knees behind a stump, a-prayin'. We'd see her wipin' her eyes wid de corner of her apron—first one eye, den de other—as we come along back. Den, back in de house, down on her knees, she'd be a-prayin'.

—REBECCA GRANT

My religion is my life. It is the most important thing that I know now or that I will ever know.

—MARY—

I was a 'ligious chile, in dem days, and I'm 'ligious now, too, but colored folks jes' naturally had more 'ligion back dere, 'fore de War. I kin remember when my ma used to put us chillun outside de cabin in de quarters, and den she would shut de doors, and shut de windows tight, and sit a tub of water in de middle of de floor, and kneel down, and pray dat de yoke of bondage be removed from de nigger's neck. All de niggers done dat. Dey did. Ma allus said de sound of dey voices went down into de tub of water and de white folks couldn't hear dem prayin'.

—RACHEL REED

My marster was a preacher, and I got to seekin' de light when I was a little thing. I used to sleep in de room wid Mistis' chillun, and I would pray all night. One night, de light come frough, and I roused de whole house, shoutin', "Glory, hallelujah!" I was so happy it was lak I was floatin' on de air. I sang, and I prayed, and I shouted. Dey couldn't keep me f'om jinin' de chu'ch den, 'cause dey knowed I'd been save'. So dey tuk me into de white chu'ch to baptize and to jine. We went to de white folks' chu'ch, den. I was so little dey had to put me on a table. A white pusson helt me on one side, and a nigger on de udder. Everybody was happy, and sang, and shouted. I felt like I had got wings, and I knowed I was a child o' God.

—"GRAMMAW"———

When I been converted, I went to Hebben in de sperrit an' see wid de eye ob fait'. I done been dere. Hebben is white as snow. God an' de Holy Ghost, dey is one 'an set at a big table wid de book stretch' out befo' 'em. God's two eyes jes' lak two big suns shining, an' he hair lak lamb's wool. I walk in dere an' look ober he shoulder. He had a long gold pen, an' writ down de name' ob de people down on de ert yet, an' when he call de roll up dere in he own time, he know dem.

Oh, I 'joicing! I 'joicing! Neber de lak befo'. An angel tek me an' show me de stars, how dey hang up dere by a silver chord, an' de moon jes' a ball ob blood, but I ain't know how it hold up, an' de sun on de rim ob all dese, goin' round an' round, an' Christ settin' in a rocking chair ober de sun. Gabriel an' Michael was wid 'im— one on dis side, an' one on de odder—holding de laws. I see eberyt'ing jes' lak I say. Sweet Jesus, I hope I reach dat place I see.

When I was seeking de Lord, befo' I converted, he place me in hell

192

to convince me. I stay down dere mos' a hour. Den I knowed dere a hell.

Hell one turrible place. What de wicked do on dis ert, it jes' lak dat in hell—cussing, shooting, fighting one anodder—but dey, being sperrits, cain't do any hurt. De fire down dere is a big pit ob brimstone a-roaring an' a-roaring. It bigger dan Charleston, seem lak.

I see de souls biling in de pit ob brimstone. Oh! God hab mercy on my soul. I's a hahd believer. Neber did I t'ink dere could be a hell. But I know now, ef you don' pray, hell go' be you' home. It no flower bed ob ease down dere. What you sow in wicked doings you sure reap down dere.

—OPHELIA JEMISON

Everybody ought to b'long to some church, 'cause it's 'spectable, and membership in de church is both a fire and a life insurance. It 'sures you 'ginst hellfire, and gives you, at death, an eternal estate in Hebben. What you laughin' at? It's de Gospel truth I'm givin' you, right now.

—HENRY JENKINS

Dey did 'low us to go to church on Sunday, about two miles down de public road, and dey hired a white preacher to preach to us. He never did tell us nothing but be good servants, pick up Old Marse' and Old Mis' things about de place, and don't steal no chickens or pigs, and don't lie 'bout nothing. Den, dey baptize you and call dat, "You got religion." Never did say nothing 'bout a slave dying and going to Heaven. When we die, dey bury us next day, and you is just like any of de other cattle dying on de place. Dat's all 'tis to it and all 'tis of you. You is jest dead. Dat's all.

—ALICE SEWELL

It seems dat every livin' thing is 'fraid of dat thing called death. I 'spects de reason of dat is 'cause dey ain't never died and don't know 'nuf 'bout it. Most of us just don't like to do new things nohow, and dis gwine-out-business is sho' new to all of us. Dat's right.

—JOE MORRIS

On our place, when a slave died, dey washed de corpse good wid plenty of hot water and soap, and wropt it in a windin' sheet, den laid it out on de coolin' board, and spread a snow-white sheet over de whole business, till de coffin wuz made up. De windin' sheet wuz sorter lak a bed sheet, made extra long. De coolin' board wuz made lak a ironin' board, 'cept it had laigs. White folkses wuz laid out dat way, same as niggers.

De coffins wuz made in a day. Dey tuk de measurin' stick and measured de head, de body, and de footses, and made de coffin to fit dese measurements. If it wuz a man what died, dey put a suit of clothes on him, before dey put him in de coffin. Dey buried de 'omans in de windin' sheets. When de niggers got in from de fields, some of 'em went and dug a grave. Den, dey put de coffin on de oxcart and carried it to de graveyard, whar dey jus' had de burial dat day.

Dey waited 'bout two months, sometimes, before dey preached de fun'ral sermon. For the fun'ral, dey built a brush arbor in front of de white folkses' church, and de white preacher preached de fun'ral sermon, and white folkses would come listen to slave fun'rals. De song most sung at fun'rals wuz "Hark from de Tomb." De reason dey had slave fun'rals so long atter de burial wuz to have 'em on Sunday or some other time when de crops had been laid by, so de other slaves could be on hand.

When white folkses died, deir fun'rals wuz preached before dey wuz buried. Dat wuz de onliest diff'unce in de way dey buried de whites and de niggers. Warn't nobody embalmed, dem days, and de white folkses wuz buried in de graveyard on de farm, same as de niggers wuz, and de same oxcart took 'em all to de graveyard.

—WILLIS COFER

We used to steal off to de woods and have church, like de spirit moved us—sing and pray to our own liking and soul satisfaction—

and we sure did have good meetings, honey—baptize in de river, like God said. We had dem spirit-filled meetings at night on de bank of de river, and God met us dere. We was quiet 'nuf so de white folks didn't know we was dere, and what a glorious time we did have in de Lord.

—SUSAN RHODES

Dey sent us to church reg'lar, and de preacher say to us, "Any you all see anybody stealin' Old Mis' chickens or eggs, go straight to Old Mis' and tell her who 'tis and all about it. Anyone steal Old Marse' hogs or anything belong to Old Marse, go straight to him and tell him all about it." Den, he ask us, "What your daddy bring home to you when he come? And what he feed you chillun, at night?" We scared to death to tell anything, 'cause if we did, de nigger get a killin', and our mammy tie up our feet and hang us upside down by our feet, build a fire under us, and smoke us—scare us plumb to death. We swear Mammy goin' to burn us up. Lord, child, dat was an awful scare. Yes, m'am, it was. De old preacher told us go on work hard, tell Old Mis' and Old Marse de truth, and when we die, God going let us in Heaven's kitchen to sit down and rest from all dis work we doin' down here.

We believe dat, den. We didn't know no better—honest, we didn't, honey. Our old mis' used to tell us, "I want all my niggers to always tell de truth. If dey kill you, die telling de truth." But bless your soul, our mammy done smoked 'nuf of us upside down, to not tell dem white folks nothin', a lie nor de truth. No siree. Who want to get smoked up?—likely to burn up hanging there, as not. No sir, tell dem white folks, dey find out anything, dey jes' find out by themselves. Dat's it.

—DELIA HILL

De missy knows ever'thing dat am gwine on. She have de spies 'mong de cullud folks. She tries to git me to report to her, but she finds Ise not 'pendable fo' sich, den stops. Once, she sends me to de sewin' room to see if de womens am wukkin'. Some of dem am, an' some of dem ain't. When Ise returns, Ise says, "Dey's all wukkin'." Yous see, Ise raised by my mammy to tell nothin' Ise sees. Dat means to mind my own business.

—BETTY POWERS

De olden people was mighty careful of de words dey let slip dey lips.

—LIZZIE DAVIS

The white folks' house must have been tall off the ground, 'cause we would get under it to hear what the white folks was talking about. The white folks would come to our house to eavesdrop, too. It was a habit for us to talk about "white horses" when we meant white folks, so if they heard us they wouldn't know we was talking about them. That's the reason you can't 'pend on nothing colored folks tells you, to this good day—they learned to be so deceiving, when they was young.

—EDWARD JONES

Marse Carter had a house gal by de name uf Frances, an' she had to wait on de white folks all day long, an' when night wud come, he made her slip out 'mongst de slaves an' see what dey wus doin' an' talkin' 'bout.

My mammy wus livin' wid 'nudder man, named Joe, an' one night Joe an' my mammy an' some more slaves wus down on deir knees prayin' fur de good Lord to sot dem free, an' Frances wus slippin' round de corner uf de house an' heard what dey wus sayin'. An' she goes back to de house an' tells de old marse, an' he sont de oberseer down dar an' brung ebery one uf dem to de stake, an' tied dem, an' whupped dem so hard dat blood come from some uf dem's backs.

—JULY HALFEN

Though Marster was a Mef'dis' preacher, he whip his slaves, an' den drap pitch an' tuppentine on dem from a bu'nin' to'ch.

196

Marster preach to de white folks Sunday mo'nin'. Den, at night, all de marsters roun' dat country sen' dey slaves, an' he preach to us. He hab two fav'rit tex'es he uster preach from to de slaves. One was, "Serv'nts, obey your marsters." He didn' say much 'bout de Marster in Hebben, but allus tole us to obey our earthly marsters. De other tex' was, "Thou shalt not steal." He preach dat over an' over, to de niggers. Dey couldn' read deir Bibles, so dey hatter b'liebe jis' what he say.

Since I's got to readin' an' studyin', I see some of de chu'ches is wrong, an' de preachers don' preach jis' like de Bible say.

—JACK WHITE

I's larned to read de Bible, an' my chillun larned to read an' write, but our white folks didn't believe in niggers larnin' anything. Dey thought hit would make de niggers harder to keep slaves, an' to make dem wuk. All de slaves dat I knowed couldn't read nor write.

—SARAH WILSON

My pappy, he had a stolen ejucation. 'At was 'cause his mistress back in South Ca'lina helped him to learn to read an' write, 'fo he lef' there. You see, in dem days, it was ag'inst de law for slaves to read.

—JAMES SINGLETON

Lordy, mist'ess, ain't nobody never told you it was agin' de law to larn a nigger to read and write, in slavery time? White folks would chop your hands off for dat quicker dan dey would for 'most anything else. Dat's jus' a sayin', "Chop your hands off." Why, mist'ess, a nigger widout no hands wouldn't be able to wuk much, and his owner couldn't sell him for nigh as much as he could git for a slave wid good hands. Dey jus' beat 'em up bad when dey cotched 'em studyin', readin', and writin', but folks did tell 'bout some of de owners dat cut off one finger evvy time dey cotch a slave tryin' to git larnin'.

How-some-ever, dere was some niggers dat wanted larnin' so bad dey would slip out at night and meet in a deep gully whar dey would study by de light of lightwood torches. But one thing sho': dey better not let no white folks find out 'bout it, and if dey was lucky nuf' to be able to keep it up till dey larned to read de Bible, dey kept it a close secret.

—WILLIAM MCWHORTER

When Dr. Cannon found out dat his carriage driver had larned to read and write whilst he was takin' de doctor's chillun to and f'om school, he had dat nigger's thumbs cut off, and put another boy to doin' de drivin' in his place.

—TOM HAWKINS

De slaves would run away, sometimes, an' hide out in de big woods. Dey would dig pits an' kivver de spot wid bushes an' vines, an' mebbe lay out fer a whole year. An' dey had pit schools, in slave days, too—way out in de woods. Dey *was* woods den, an' de slaves would slip out o' de quarters at night an' go to dese pits, an' some niggah dat had some learnin' would have a school.

De way de cullud folks would learn to read was from de white chillun. De white chillun thought a heap of de cullud chillun, an' when dey come out o' school wid deir books in deir han's, dey take de cullud chillun, an' slip off somewhere, an' learns de cullud chillun deir lessons, what deir teacher has jus' learned dem.

—MANDY JONES

Dere wuz Uncle George Bull. He could read and write, and, chile, de white folks didn't lak no nigger what could read and write. Old man Carr's wife, Mis' Jane, uster teach us Sunday school, but she did not 'low us to tech a book wid us hands. So dey uster jes' take Uncle George Bull and beat him fur nothin'. Dey would beat him, and take him to de lake, and put him on a log, and shev him in de lake, but he always swimmed out. When dey didn't do dat, dey would beat him till de blood run outen him, and den t'row him in de ditch in de field, and kivver him up wid dirt, head and ears, and den stick a stick up at his haid. I wuz a water toter and have stood and seen 'em do him dat way more'n once, and I stood and looked at 'em till dey went 'way to de other rows, and den I grabbed de dirt offen him, and he'd bresh de dirt off and say, "T'ank yo'," git his hoe, and go on back to work. Dey beat him lak dat, and he didn' do a thin' to git dat sort uf treatment.

—MARGRETT NICKERSON

I's educated, but I ain't educated in de books. I's educated by de licks an' bumps I got.

—SUSAN SNOW

Missy Hogan was de good woman and try her dead level best to teach me to read and write, but my head jes' too thick. I jes' couldn't larn. My uncle, Ben, he could read de Bible, and he allus tell us some day us be free. And Massa Henry laugh, "Haw, haw, haw," and he say, "Hell, no, yous never be free. Yous ain't got sense 'nuf to make de livin', if yous was free." Den, he takes de Bible 'way from Uncle Ben and say it put de bad ideas in he head, but Uncle gits 'nother Bible and hides it, and Massa never finds it out.

—JOHN BATES

If I was caught trying to read or figger, dey would whip me something terrible. After I caught on how to figger, the white kids would ask me to teach them. Master Brown would often say, "My God O'mighty, never do for that nigger to learn to figger."

We weren't allowed to count change. If we borrowed a fifty-cent piece, we would have to pay back a fifty-cent piece, not five dimes, or fifty pennies, or ten nickels.

—HAL HUTSON

No sir, the white people, they did not try to help me learn to read and write; said they did not have time to fool with us, as we were too thick-headed to ever learn anything.

—ANNA LEE

You'll be s'prised at what Mammy told me 'bout how she got her larnin'. She said she kept a schoolbook hid in her bosom all de time, and when de white chillun got home from school, she would axe 'em lots of questions all 'bout what dey had done larned dat day, and 'cause she was proud of evvy little scrap of book larnin' she could pick up, de white chillun larned her how to read, and write, too. All de larnin' she ever had she got from de white chillun at de big house. And she was so smart at gittin' 'em to larn her, dat atter de War was over, she got to be a schoolteacher.

—ALICE GREEN

You know, they lays a heap of stress on edication, these days. But edication is one thing, an' fireside trainin' is another. We had fireside trainin'.

—JOHN JACKSON

No siree, I never did learn how to read and write. I just hold to the end of the pencil so the white man can sign my name.

—ELI DAVISON

Narratives

RACHEL CRUZE

JACOB MANSON

MARTIN JACKSON

JOSH HORN

RACHEL CRUZE

I WAS born on the ninth of March, 1856, on the farm of Major William Holden, at Strawberry Plains, Knox County, Tennessee. There used to be a college there, but the War tore it up and the little place does not amount to much. There were many large farms around it, though. The biggest and most important of these was the Holden, Meeks, and Macabee farms. This was not in the cotton county but up in the farming section northeast of it, where they grow corn, wheat, potatoes, and other vegetables. We were just sixteen miles from Knoxville.

My father was William Holden, Jr., the youngest child of Major Holden. My mother, Eliza Mobley, was the colored cook. Later she married John Meek, a slave, and then went by the name of Meek. She had twelve children. I was the oldest.

When Mis' Melindy, Old Major's daughter, married John Luttrow, my mother and brother Frank were handed over to Mis' Melindy, but John Luttrow, although a Southerner, hated the colored folk and did not want to be bothered with the ownership of any, so he persuaded Mis' Melindy to sell my mother down South.

Mis' Melindy thought heaps of Mamma. She taught her to talk just like the white folks. She would not let her do any "flat" talking. Mamma had ways just like Mis' Melindy.

Mamma was quite dark, but she had a pretty little sharp nose. Her father was a dark man, although my grandmother was very light.

My great-grandmother and her brothers and sisters all had straight black hair. My great-grandmother was over a hundred when she died, and up to the last she was real bright, and so were her brothers.

And the blood kept coming down and coming down to another.

PLATE 18: A former slave.

My mamma always thought Major Holden's refusal to let me go to Mis' Melindy at that time had something to do with old Luttrow's idea of selling her to a nigger trader. When the subject was mentioned to Old Major, he made short work of the suggestion: "What you mean? No, sir! You're not pullin' her off her mistress' lap or keeping her from staying here and waiting on me!"

When Mis' Nancy, the wife of Major Holden, heard of what the Luttrows intended doing she went right over to Mr. Rufus Meeks and asked him to buy Mammy, as she did not believe in breaking up families in this manner. Mr. Meek did this, and from then on Mamma lived with one of his slaves, my stepfather, John Meek. The Meek farm was just two miles from Old Major's place, and I used to visit Mamma whenever I wanted to, and she came to see us often. But at that time I did not think of her as my mother, but called her Eliza.

Until I was about twelve years old I looked upon Mis' Nancy as my mother, when in reality she was my white grandmother. I lived with Old Major's family until I was that age; then I was sent over to the Meeks' place to live with my mother and stepfather. Mis' Nancy felt I should get to know my mother better. Then, too, by that time the Major's oldest son, John, had married a woman who believed in beating the slaves and slapping them around. She slapped me once and I tell you Old Major cussed her out. It was partly because of her that I was sent to Mamma.

I lived in Old Major's house as a member of the family all those years. I was their baby, and my first recollections are of sleeping in a little bed at the foot of the one occupied by the Major and Mis' Nancy. As I look back on those times, I can see that Mis' Nancy took especially good care of me, always looking me up to see what I was doing. She was particularly interested in my clothes, and for years after I left her and was living with Mamma, she clothed me. I always felt particularly close to her, and one time when my stepfather gave me a lick, I ran the two miles to tell Mis' Nancy about it. I had never been whipped, and I thought I was ruined when my stepfather struck me. It was with Mis' Nancy that I went to my first Sunday school and church. My days with her and Old Major were carefree, happy ones, the hardest thing I had to do being a trip to the spring for a glass of water for the Major, or getting his pipe for him.

No, I never received anything from my father's estate. My colored grandmother always used to tell me I would get thirteen acres, a plot of land my father, William, had been given by Old Major—also a cow and horse. But I never got anything.

You see, my father, William, died when I was a little girl, before the War. Drink was possibly the real cause of his death, but it was a fever that took him off. Yes, he always kept hid a quart bottle of whiskey in a hole in an apple tree I knew, and then another quart down in the crusher. Crusher? That was where we ground up the corn for the stock. It was as big as this room and was turned by a horse.

When William was sick with the fever it happened I was the one to give him his last drink of water. Mis' Nancy had said, "Go keep the flies off William," and when I went to him he said, "Baby, go get me a drink of water and don't let anybody see you." You see, people with fever were not to have water, but I did as William told me, and I crept down to the spring and brought him a right big coffee cup of water. He took some of it and I hid the cup under his bed. I was so little, I remember, I had to climb up onto the bed to put the cup to his lips. Well, the minute he took that water it caused a change for the worse. I was frightened and ran to Mis' Nancy for her to come to William. She took one look at him and said, "You have given him water." He asked to be carried over to the fireplace, and he died there shortly after. Mis' Nancy was heartbroken because he was her youngest child, and she said to me, "You have killed Will with that drink."

Old Major's farm was on right level ground, but there were hills all around. The house was white and lay right along the road, with a porch running its full length both at the front and back. The front porch was a real fine one, with broad steps and nice-turned spindles, and at the end where Old Major used to sit there was a tea rose growing right up to the top of the porch. The other was the dirt porch, and the women in the kitchen used to sit there when they would be preparing vegetables for dinner.

The creek over which the spring house was built came to us from high up over the hill, and before it struck the lower level of the farm the water passed through two caves, one much higher than the other, so that the water, being shielded from sun and dust, was cold and sparkling. Sometimes in summer, when some big doings meant the killing of sheep or hogs, the fresh meat would be placed in the upper cave and covered with walnut leaves, and it would keep there just as though it were in a refrigerator. All the neighbors round about used it at times.

My colored grandmother cooked for the hands down at the quarters. When she wanted vegetables she just sent someone up into the master's garden for them, and if she wanted meat or lard she went over to the smokehouse where, every fall, Old Major stored a hundred to a hundred and twenty hogs. There never was no stint in the food given Old Major's people.

There are heaps of pleasant things to look back on. The week before Christmas was always a lively one, what with dances and corn-huskin's in the neighborhood. I've seen many a corn-huskin' at Old Major's farm when the corn would be piled as high as the house. Two sets of men would start huskin' from opposite sides of the heap. It would keep one man busy just getting the husks out of the way, and the corn would be thrown over the huskers' heads and would fill the air like birds. The women usually had a quilting at those times, so they were pert and happy.

About midnight, the huskin' would be over and plenty of food would make its appearance—roast sheep and roast hogs and many other things—and after they had their fill, they would dance till morning. Things would continue lively in the neighborhood till New Year's Day, and then they got down to work, as it was that time the yearly cleaning and repairing of the farm took place.

The material for the cotton clothes worn on the farm in summer was woven right in our own kitchen. We bought the raw cotton, usually, but sometimes we would grow a small patch. Then we would card it, spin it, and weave it on the big loom in the kitchen. I have spun many a broach. They take it off and wind it on a reel, and make a great hank of thread—there would be four cuts in a hank. They would first size the thread by dipping it in some solution, and then, when it was dry, they would dye it. Dyestuffs would be gotten from the barks and roots of different trees, and with these we would be able to make red, brown, and black dyes. We would then weave the thread into jeans—a heavy cotton for men's coats and pants—or the lighter linsey for women's clothes.

Counterpanes and coverlids were made of wool. Yes, we raised sheep by the hundreds. The raw wool was first sent to the mill to be carded, then we would spin it into a thread, to be dyed just as the cotton was. The wool, too, would be woven into jeans for the heavier winter clothing for the men, and into linsey-woolsey for the women's warmer dresses.

I can still hear the "lam-lam-lamlam, lam-lam-lamlam" of the big loom.

Many slaves had a wife on a neighboring farm, and Mis' Nancy was always good about seeing that the men quit work at twelve o'clock on Saturday; then they'd get their selves cleaned up and go to visit their wives until Sunday night. She always sent along with each man, as a present to his wife, food of some kind. Sometimes it would be meat, or butter, or sweet potatoes, or maybe grapes—but something was always sent with the man for his wife. Mis' Nancy said she didn't want anyone feeding her niggers. If any of the men had truck patches, they were welcome to work these on Saturday afternoons.

Saturday afternoons and Sunday nights were the times the young fellows looked about for likely mates. Gainan Macabee, who owned a large farm across the river, had a great number of lively-looking girl slaves, and all the young men in the neighborhood would make it their business to get over there if possible. Gainan, he watched his girls closely—used to sit on a chair between his two houses where he could see everything—and if a skinny, reedy sort of nigger made his appearance among the young people, Gainan would call him over and say, "Whose nigger are you?" The boy would tell him. Gainan would look him over and say, "Well, that's all right, but I don't want you comin' over to see my gals. You ain't of good stock." And it would just be too bad for that nigger if Gainan caught him there again.

But when he saw a well-built, tall, husky man in the crowd, Gainan would call him and say, "Whose nigger are you?" And when he was told, he'd say, "Well, that's all right. You can come over and see my gals anytime you want. You're of good stock."

Do you know, the pore white folks of the South mostly had a harder time than the colored folks, under slavery, because the other white folks did not want them around. Many pore white folks would have starved if it had not been for slaves who stole food from their masters to feed the white folks.

Fanny Oldsby was one of the pore whites who lived near Mis' Nancy, and Mis' Nancy would sometimes give her sewing to do, but she had to take it home to do it. Mis' Nancy wouldn't have her around the place. I used to get pretty lonesome sometimes because there wasn't a child of my age to play with. Fanny Oldsby had a little girl who came with her sometimes, but do you think Mis' Nancy would let me play with her? No, ma'am. I'd no more than sit down close to the little girl than I'd hear, "Rachel, you come here this minute." And, when I would go to her, Mis' Nancy would say, "Don't you sit near her. Why, she'll bite you and she'll get your head full of lice." The pore child would look at me and I'd look at her, but I didn't want her to bite me, so I didn't get close to her.

Everybody leaving the farm had to have a pass. If they didn't, the old paddyrollers "worked on" them. Yes, those paddyrollers were poor white trash. Nobody who amounted to anything would go about the country like they did—just like dogs hunting rabbits.

Uncle Ben, one of the boys on the farm, was the only one of Major Holden's people who had any trouble with them, and then it wasn't his fault, really. Mis' Melindy, she was going over to see the daughter of a neighbor and she told Ben he could go with her, that he didn't need a pass as she would explain to Pappy. When they arrived at the neighbor's farm, as Ben was about to leave her for the quarters, Mis' Melindy says, "You just call me if anybody says anything."

Well, sure enough, one of those paddyrollers came snooping around and he sees Ben and he says, "Where's your pass?" And Ben says, "Mis' Melindy will explain." But the paddyrollers grabbed him and said, "We'll Mis' Melindy you." They dragged him off towards the woods to whip him, but as they passed the big house, Ben called Mis' Melindy and told her, and didn't she bless them out! She just dared them to touch Ben; and she went right home and told Old Major. And he immediately notified them that they were never to touch a nigger of his under any circumstances, that if his niggers did anything that wasn't right, the paddyrollers might come and tell him, but he would do his own whipping.

Old Major said he'd do his own whipping right bravelike, but he really wasn't very successful at it. First time he tried to whip a slave was before I was born. Mamma told me the story. The slave was an old one who belonged to Mis' Nancy, but instead of Old Major punishing him, he whipped Old Major, and that was the end of that.

Some years after that, a young boy named Sico needed punishment, and Old Major set out to hold him by sticking Sico's hand between his knees and hitting him with a cornstalk. Sico howled and leaned over and bit him. Then Old Major, he howled and called to Mis' Nancy, "Take dis rascal away. He done bit me."

The third and last time for Old Major was when he set out to lick Uncle Henry. I called all the men on the farm "Uncle." Uncle Henry was a good-looking young fellow—carried himself straight as a stick. He had grown up with my father, William, and he was forever getting into trouble with William for stealing William's horse out of the barn at night and riding him all around the country till the pore horse would be nearly dead. William had complained and complained to Old Major, and Old Major had threatened to tear open Henry's back, but nothing had happened. Finally, Henry brought the matter to white heat by riding the horse so hard one long night that it died as it reached its stall, next morning.

The whole house then decided Henry must be whipped. William was furious, and he saw to it himself that the big piece of perforated leather was fastened to the paddle. When anybody asked him what he was doing, he'd mutter, "Pappy's going to lick Henry." After the leather was securely fastened on the paddle, William went over to the pump and wet the leather good. Then he filled a pan with water into which had been poured salt and pepper.

This is the way a whipping like this was done: first, the back was beaten with the perforated leather thong, the perforations raising blisters which were smartly broken open with a well-handled buggy whip. Then the salt and pepper water was poured into the cuts to keep the man in lively suffering.

Well, Old Major came out to the barn, and Henry was tied up to a branch, having first been stripped to the waist. William sat by on his hunkers, whittling a piece of wood—he was always whittling. Old Major raised the paddle and the leather thong came swishing down upon the back of the groaning Henry. A second time it cracked through the air, mingling with the age-old cry of the slave, "Pray, master." This was too much for William, who jumped up and with one slash of his sharp knife cut Henry down.

Henry just lay where he fell and groaned as he held his side. William and Old Major were beside themselves, and between them they got Henry up to the house and laid him on a bed in the dining room. Mis' Nancy was horrified. "Now I suppose you are satisfied since you've killed him. William, run and get Dr. Sneed."

Henry's mother, Julia, had come up from the quarters, and she was frantic. Henry had never ceased groaning and holding his side, and Old Major, he'd say, "Now, Henry, you mustn't die."

Dr. Sneed finally arrived and examined Henry thoroughly. Then he gravely ordered some medicine to be given regularly, with complete rest. Julia followed the doctor to the door, asking him, "Doctor, is he goin' ter die?" The doctor leaned over and whispered, "Julia, there is not a damn thing the matter with Henry." And, do you know that Henry laid up there for two weeks, right in the Major's dining room.

Henry had high ideas. Sometimes he'd walk off with Old Major's gold-headed cane and strut around the neighborhood with it, putting it back the next morning before the Major was up. He had even been known to steal out with Old Major's overcoat. These, however, were easily forgiven; but, when he stole the preacher's shoes, Old Major solemnly told Mis' Nancy, "I'll just have to kill that Henry, after all."

The preacher was staying overnight and, as usual, he left his shoes outside his door at bedtime, to be shined. Well, Henry came along and saw the boots and proceeded to put them on for his nightly strut. His feet were much larger than those of the preacher and, by the time morning came, Henry's feet were so swollen he couldn't get the boots off. He tried and tried and, finally giving up, he threw himself on Mamma's bed in the kitchen and fell asleep.

Those boots were the first things Mis' Nancy saw when she came into the kitchen. Everybody tried to get the boots off but they could not be budged. So Old Major was called. That is when he told Mis' Nancy, "I'll just have to kill that Henry."

Mis' Nancy started to giggle, " 'Pears to us de preacher needs a new pair of shoes, anyhow. Just look at 'em." Old Major looked at the shoes and agreed and sent a servant down to his store for a pair. The preacher was more than delighted, and it was decided to let Henry have the old ones.

But all the people we knew were not so lenient to their slaves. There was a rich farmer by the name of MacMillan who lived not far from us who was so stingy and mean to his colored people, he did not allow them to eat sweet potatoes—said they were too good for 'em. And the mean old man would go round about ten o'clock, searching through their cabins to see if they had stowed any away.

Well, it happened that Mr. MacMillan's brother had borrowed Jim, one of his slaves, to help him hoe yams one day, and as Jim finished the work, the brother picked up a nice big yam and told him to have that for his supper. "Oh, no, thank you," said Jim, "the Marster, he don' 'low us ter have yams nohow." But the brother insisted. So Jim took the yam to his cabin, made up a good fire in his fireplace, and put the yam in the hot ashes to bake. It was Jim's intention to hide the yam till after his master had made his nightly round, and then enjoy his feast. He baked the yam to a beautiful golden brown and set it out to cool. But, as Jim sat there, in the cool of the evening, watching his yam and thinking how good it was going to be, he fell asleep, and the next thing he knew he was lying on the ground with a cracked head. His master had come up while he was sleeping and, seeing the yam, decided Jim had stolen it. So, after cracking Jim over the head with his heavy stick, he picked up the yam and took it home and ate it for his breakfast.

Jim always laughed fit to kill himself when he told about that yam. I have noticed so many times that when a colored person is telling of some real cruel treatment he has had at the hands of his master, he seems to think it funny and laugh and laugh. I can't understand it.

I used to love to have stories told me. Once I heard my colored grandmother and grandfather tell a story of something that happened some years before the War, probably before I was born. A nigger trader had been around the neighorhood buying up tall husky men for the cotton fields down South, and as he bought each one he put handcuffs on him and shackled him to the others. They accompanied him on foot day after day, as he traveled on horseback through that section. He had with him several wagons in which they could lie at night, but during the day they had to walk.

As they walked together, they talked about their future, and they all agreed that death would be preferable to the living death of the cotton fields. And they decided that the first time they had to ferry across a river with the nigger trader, they would walk onto the ferryboat and keep right on walking till they had walked off the other end. At the end of Dr. Sneed's farm was a ferry to carry people over to the Macabee farm on the other side, and when the nigger trader drove those slaves onto the ferry, that is exactly what they did: they all walked off into the deep of the river at the other end. If there was any among them who was lukewarm he was shoved in by the ones behind him.

That nigger trader was nearly crazy because of the money loss. He had not bought all the men outright, but had paid some down on every one of them, with a signed contract to complete payment when he received his money from the cotton raisers. Now he had to make good those notes.

Some years after the War had ended, some boys in the neighborhood were fording the river about a mile downstream from Dr. Sneed's place, and they found fifteen handcuffs, bright and shining and all fastened together. When the father of one of the boys saw them, he recalled the drowning up at Dr. Sneed's place.

The wife of Jim Johnson—that was Mis' Nancy's brother—was mean to her slaves, too. She brought down Mis' Nancy's anger when Mis' Nancy went over there one time and found that she had the colored folks wearing clothing made of hemp, which was coarse and scratchy. Her men were in the fields wearing long garments like nightshirts, made of this hemp. No, nothing else on them but those long-tailed shirts, no trousers or anything. She made dresses of the same coarse, scratchy material for the house girls.

Mis' Nancy, she just blew up when she found how that hempen material had scratched and bruised their skin. "You ought to be ashamed of yourself," she cried. "Why, their skin is all scratched up from that coarse hemp." Jim's wife claimed, "Niggers are just too lazy, and I find this makes them right smart." But Mis' Nancy

wouldn't listen. She went out in the field and blest out Jim about it.
He was a lot like Mis' Nancy about things concerning his people, and
when she told him about that scratched, bleeding skin, he went into
the house and raised such a fuss about it his wife went and bought a
bolt of domestic, or muslin, or something of that sort, and made up
dresses out of that. She was that mad at Mis' Nancy. "Just getting all
the slaves to like her; that's what she wants," she told Uncle Jim. "I
don't care what she had in mind," he said. "I'm not having any
nigger of mine working in tow clothes."

Mis' Nancy walked the line with them all. Whatever she said
went. Her black hair turned white later on, but she was peppery right
to the last—always seeing that everybody was being taken care of.
Lots of nights, when a person would be thinking she was in bed, she
was slipping around to see what her colored people were doing. Both
she and Old Major looked upon all their people as their children.

Old Major did most of his overseeing with his horse and buggy. I
always sat on the seat beside him, and if he got down to walk around a
little he handed me the lines—just as though I could have done
anything with that horse if he had a mind to act up.

When war came, all the men left the plantation but one colored
man whom I called Uncle Reeves—a young man of twenty. Well,
Old Major knew that when the War was over the others would come
back freemen and that he'd never get any money out of them again, so
he undertook to sell Uncle Reeves to a farmer there who had been
teasing him for some time to sell Uncle Reeves to him. Old Major
never believed in selling his people, but he finally agreed to sell
Uncle Reeves for twelve hundred dollars. A contract was drawn up
between the two men, the agreement calling for the payment of the
twelve hundred dollars at the end of the War, in the currency of the
one who whipt [won].

Old Major put the contract away in his big iron safe and then he
took Uncle Reeves over to his new master. But before Uncle Reeves
left, Mis' Nancy called him aside and told him not to sleep in the
quarters that night but to sleep in the barn, and then, when the
others were sleeping, to return to the farm. Uncle Reeves did this,
and when he returned about midnight he was put into a Union
uniform. Old Major was waiting for him in the horse and buggy, and

out came Mis' Nancy and a servant with a carpetbag filled with clothes and food. That night Old Major drove him down to Fort Sanders, at Knoxville, Tennessee.

Four years later, when the War was over, all Old Major's people returned to him, and among them was Uncle Reeves, and about the first thing he said to Old Major was, "Did you ever git dat money fo' me?" And Old Major replied, "No, but I'm going to get it right now." And he did, although it meant that the other man had to sell his farm to pay the note.

Don't understand by this that Old Major was Union. No, he was a Rebel. But Mis' Nancy was Union, and whatever she said was the thing done. You see, most of the slaves belonged to Mis' Nancy from her first marriage, and of course she had the full say over them. All her people loved Mis' Nancy. Even after they were free and many of them had gone to work on other farms, they would come back regularly to the Holden place to see Mis' Nancy. Not a week went past without some of them being there. And if they got sick they would send at once for Mis' Nancy, and she'd get on her old horse and go to them.

Old Major played safe with both sides during the War, and, in fact, he and Mis' Nancy were kind to both of them.

Old Major had both a Rebel and a Union suit, and he wore whichever seemed to be most fitting at the time. Sometimes a spy would come along in advance of an army, and I'd call to Old Major, who was sitting on the porch, "Major, here comes a spy." And Old Major he'd start up from his chair and bawl, "Who-o-w-a-at?" If I said, "It's Johnny," and he was in a Rebel suit, he'd throw out his chest and prepare to greet them. But if I said, "Union," he'd sneak to his room, change into the blue uniform with its red-lined cape, and come back out on the porch. As he sat down, he'd throw back the corner of his blue cape to show its red lining.

The house was here, and there below was the brook, and up there on a high hill was a field—Ridge Field, we called it. Both the Union boys and the Johnnies [Confederates] camped there at times, and trained new recruits there.

If the Rebels had won the War, Old Major would have been wealthy. At the beginning of the War he had put the bulk of his money into a seegar box, and he took out a couple of small stones from the foundation of the house and said, "Now, Baby, look sharp and dig a hole inside there large enough to hide this box, and never tell anybody about this money." I was rather afraid to crawl into the darkness under the house, but I did as I was told, and nobody ever knew anything about that money but Old Major and me. When the soldiers would say, "Where's the Major's money?" I'd always point to the big iron safe and say, "All the Johnny money is in there." Well, they were not looking for Johnny money, so they never bothered to open it. After the War was over, Old Major had me crawl under the house again and bring out the seegar box filled with money, but it wasn't worth anything. I used to play "house" with it.

Uncle Henry, the young fellow who figured in the whipping by Old Major, came back to the farm once at the head of a dozen soldiers. He had become a recruiting officer—now, I think they call it "drafting." Old Major was sitting in his favorite chair on the porch when he saw Henry coming with those soldiers, and he almost fell, he was that scairt. You see, so many times the slaves had returned to kill their masters, and poor Old Major thought Henry remembered that whipping.

But Henry drew the men up in front of Old Major and he said, "This is my master, Major Holden. Honor him, men." And the men took off their caps and cheered Old Major. And he nearly fell again— such a great big burden was off his shoulders, then.

When Henry commanded his men to stack arms, they all stacked their guns together in front of Old Major, except one soldier who was the lookout. The others then went into the house to see Mis' Nancy; and Mis' Nancy sent out to have some chickens killed, and in no time at all those men were all seated around the dining room table having a regular feast—that is, all but the one who had to watch the guns, and he was fed later.

The first funeral I ever saw was that of Gran'pap Holden. I must have been quite young, as I do not remember him being around the home alive. It must have been the coffin that so impressed me. They put the coffin in the spring wagon and took the long way round, by road, up to the burying ground on the hill. A young girl, Melindy Leaper, walked behind the wagon singing:

We're travelin' to the grave,
We're travelin' to the grave,
We're travelin' to the grave,
To lay this pore body down.

That same girl was the first person I ever remember to hear shoutin'. The preacher was holding evening service in his home. I was sitting close up to Mis' Nancy, as usual, when all of a sudden, that girl, who had been sitting in the corner, jumped up and began shoutin' and clappin' her hands. I nudged Mis' Nancy, "What's bit her?" Mis' Nancy frowned and said, "Hush, child, she's happy!" But I didn't know what "happy" meant, and I was horror-struck that a young girl should speak right out like that when the preacher was talking. Those were the days when children were not heard.

I was about thirteen years old before I went to school. That was about a year after the War ended, and the Freedmen's Bureau of Philadelphia, sponsored by the Presbyterians, sent two colored teachers down to the new box-like affair they built on Dr. Sneed's land for a school. One of those teachers was meaner than the other. They treated the colored students more as if they were dogs than humans. Mr. Jones and Mr. Luck were their names. Mr. Jones, who had been a blacksmith in the North, was finally given a good whipping by the boy students, and the community sent both of them packing, and brought other teachers from Knoxville.

I was lucky if I got to school two days in a week, but I learned to read and write. At that time I had gone to live with Mammy, and I found it much harder to live with my colored stepfather than I ever did with my white master. The day after Mis' Nancy sent me to Mamma, my stepfather sent me into the field to drop corn. Sometimes, in the early morning, it would be snowing so hard I could not see the checks in which to plant the corn.

Yes, I dropped corn, hoed corn, thinned corn, and in the fall I pulled corn. I was so little I had to pull the stalks down to me to reach the ears.

My mamma and stepfather stayed a long time on the Meek place after the War, renting a small acreage from their former master. Then, they began to move about from place to place, depending on day work to see them through, as so many of the colored people did when they were freed. When they were renting from the Meek farm, they paid for their acreage by giving to the owner two-thirds of their crop.

I don't know the year I was married—I have the certificate upstairs—but it was on the second day of January, and I would have been twenty on the ninth of March coming. I married William Cruze, of North Carolina. At that time he was doing day work on the farm of Captain Parrot, where he was paid ten dollars a month and was furnished with a house and garden. If one had a cow, pasture was furnished for it, and the family could raise hogs and chickens, or whatever was wanted.

I had six children—four boys and two girls. They were Walter, Sylvester, Harry, Max, Edna, and Roberta. Then there were two grandchildren—Walter Junior and William—that I raised. All of them are gone but Harry, and I have lost track of him. I do not know whether he is living or not. He was William Junior's father. William is here in the city somewhere, but I never see him.

I came north in 1910. Walter, my son, was living here in Cleveland and wanted I should come for a visit. I came and liked it, so I stayed.

And now I think you've got all I have. Take good keer of yourself.

JACOB MANSON

I T HAS been a long time since I wus born. 'Bout all my people am dead, 'cept my wife an' one son an' two daughters.

I belonged to Colonel Bun Eden. His plantation wus in Warren County, an' he owned 'bout fifty slaves or more. Dere wus so many of 'em dere he did not know all his own slaves. We got mighty bad treatment, an' I jest wants to tell you a nigger didn't stan' as much show dere as a dog did. Dey whupped fur mos' any little trifle. Dey whupped me—so dey said—jes' to help me git a quicker gait. De patterollers come sneakin' round often an' whupped niggers on Marster's place. Dey nearly killed my uncle. Dey broke his collarbone when dey wus beatin' him, an' Marster made 'em pay for it, 'cause Uncle never did git over it.

Marster would not have any white overseers. He had nigger foremen. Ha, ha—he liked some of de nigger women too good to have any udder white man playin' aroun' wid 'em.

We worked all day an' some of de night, an' a slave who make a week, even atter doin' dat, wus lucky if he got off widout gettin' a beatin'. We had poor food, an' de young slaves wus fed outen troughs. De food wus put in a trough an' de little niggers gathered round an' et. Our cabins wus built of poles an' had stick-an'-dirt chimneys, one door, an' one little winder at de back end of de cabin. Some of de houses had dirt floors. Our clothin' was poor an' homemade.

Many of de slaves went bareheaded and barefooted. Some wore rags roun' deir heads and some wore bonnets. Marster lived in de greathouse. He did not do any work but drank a lot of whiskey, went dressed up all de time, an' had niggers to wash his feet an' comb his hair. He made me scratch his head when he lay down, so he could go to sleep. When he got to sleep I would slip out. If he waked up when I started to leave, I would have to go back an' scratch his head till he went to sleep agin. Sometimes I had to fan de flies 'way from him while he slept.

No prayer meetings wus allowed, but we sometimes went to de white folks church. Dey tole us to obey our marsters an' be obedient at all times.

When bad storms come, dey let us rest, but dey kept us in de fields so long sometimes dat de storm caught us 'fore we could git to de cabins. Niggers watched de wedder in slavery time, an' de ole ones wus good a' prophesyin' de wedder.

Marster had no chilluns by white women. He had his sweethearts 'mong his slave women. I ain't no man for tellin' false stories. I tells de truth, an' dat is de truth. At dat time it wus a hard job to find a marster dat didn't have women 'mong his slaves. Dat wus a ginerel thing 'mong de slave owners.

One of de slave girls on a plantation near us went to her missus and tole her 'bout her marster forcing her to let him have somethin' to do wid her, and her missus tole her, "Well, go on. You belong to him."

Another marster named Jimmie Shaw owned a purty slave gal, nearly white, an' he kept her. His wife caught 'im in a cabin bed wid her. His wife said somethin' to him 'bout it, an' he cussed his wife. She tole him she had caught 'im in de act. She went back to de greathouse an' got a gun. When de marster come in de greathouse, she tole 'im he must let de slave girls alone, dat he belonged to her. He cussed her agin an' said she would have to tend to her own damn business an' he would tend to his. Dey had a big fuss an' den Marster Shaw started towards her. She grabbed de gun an' let him have it. She shot 'im dead in de hall. Dey had three chillun—two sons an' one married daughter. Missus Shaw took her two sons an' left. De married daughter an' her husband took charge of de place. Missus an' her sons never come back as I knows of.

A lot of de slave owners had certain strong, healthy slave men to serve de slave women. Ginerally, dey give one man four women, an' dat man better not have nothin' to do wid de udder women, an' de women better not have nothin' to do wid udder men. De chillun wus

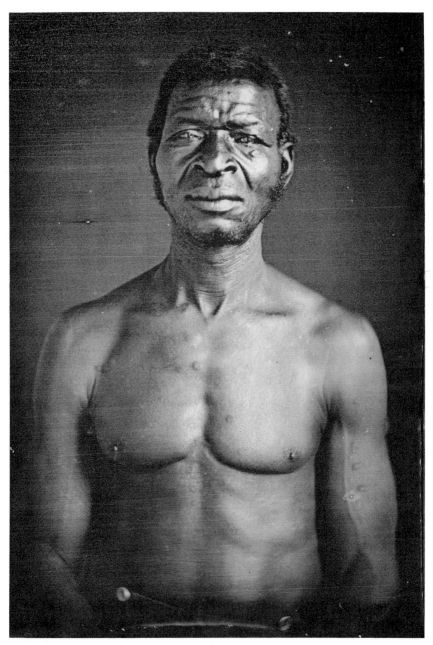

PLATE 19: Overlooker, or driver, of other slaves on a Carolina plantation.

looked after by de ole slave women who were unable to work in de fields, while de mothers of de babies worked. De women plowed an done udder work as de men did. No books or larnin' of any kind wus allowed.

One mornin', de dogs begun to bark, an' in a few minutes the plantation wus kivvered wid Yankees. Dey tole us we wus free. Dey axed me whar Marster's things wus hid. I tole 'em I could not give up Marster's things. Dey tole me I had no marster, dat dey had fighted four years to free us, an' dat Marster would not whup me no more. Marster sent to de fields an' had all de slaves come home. He told me to tell 'em not to run but to fly to de house at once. All plow hands an' women come running home. De Yankees told all of 'em dey wus free.

Marster offered some of de Yankees somethin' to eat in his house, but dey would not eat cooked food; dey said dey wanted to cook deir own food.

I married Roberta Edwards fifty-one years ago. We had six sons and three daughters. After the War, I farmed around from one plantation to another. I have never owned a home of my own. When I got too ole to work, I come an' lived wid my married daughter, in Raleigh. I been here four years. I think slavery wus a mighty bad thing. It's been no bed of roses since, but den no one can whup me no mo'.

MARTIN JACKSON

I HAVE about eighty-five years of good memory to call upon. I am ninety, and so I am not counting my first five years of life. I'll try to give you as clear a picture as I can. If you want to give me a copy of what you are going to write I will appreciate it. Maybe some of my children would like to have it.

I was here in Texas when the Civil War was first talked about. I was here when the War started, and followed my master into it with the First Texas Cavalry. I was here during the European World War, and the second week after the United States declared war on Germany I enlisted as cook at Camp Leon Springs.

This sounds as if I liked the war racket. But, as a matter of fact, I never wore a uniform—grey coat or khaki coat—or carried a gun unless it happened to be one worth saving after some Confederate soldier got shot. I was the official lugger-in of men that had got wounded, and might have been called a Red Cross worker if we had had such a corps connected with our company. My father was head cook for the battalion, and between times I helped him out with the mess. There was some difference in the food served to soldiers in 1861 and 1917.

Just what my feelings were about the War, I have never been able to figure out myself. I knew the Yanks were going to win from the beginning. I wanted them to win and lick us, but I hoped they were going to do it without wiping out our company. I'll come back to this in a minute. As I said, our company was the First Texas Cavalry. Colonel Buchell was our commander. He was a full-blooded German and as fine a man and a soldier as you ever saw. He was killed at the Battle of Marshall and died in my arms. You may also be interested to

Plate 20: A former slave.

know that my old master, Alvy Fitzpatrick, was the grandfather of Governor Jim Ferguson.

My earliest recollection is the day that my old boss presented me to his son as his own property. I was about five years old, and my new master was only two.

The master's name was usually adopted by the slave after he was set free. This was done more because it was the logical thing to do and the easiest way to be identified than it was through affection for the master. Also, the government seemed to be in a almighty hurry to have us get names. We had to register as someone so we would be citizens. Well, I got to thinking about all us slaves that was going to take the name Fitzpatrick. I made up my mind I'd find me a different one. One of my grandfathers in Africa was called Jeaceo, and so I decided to be Jackson.

Lots of old slaves close the door before they tell the truth about their days of slavery. When the door is open, they tell how kind their masters were and how rosy it all was. You can't blame them for this, because they had plenty of early discipline, making them cautious about saying anything uncomplimentary about their masters. I myself was in a little different position than most slaves and, as a consequence, have no grudge or resentment. However, I can tell you that the life of the average slave was far from rosy. They were dealt out plenty of cruel suffering. But slavery, I believe, had a more degrading influence upon slave owners than it had upon the slaves.

Even with my good treatment, I spent most of my time planning and thinking of running away. I could have done it easy, but my old father used to say, "No use running from bad to worse, hunting better." Lots of colored boys did escape and joined the Union army, and there are plenty of them today still drawing a pension for deserting the Confederacy.

My father was always counseling me. He said, "Every man has to serve God under his own vine and fig tree." He kept pointing out that the War wasn't going to last forever, but that our forever was going to be spent living among the Southerners after they got licked. He would cite examples of how the whites would stand flat-footed and fight for the blacks the same as they would for members of their own family. I knew that all that was true; but still, from inside me, I rebelled. I think I really was afraid to run away, because I thought my own conscience would haunt me. My father knew I felt this way, and he would rub my fears in deeper. One of his remarks still rings in my ears: "A clear conscience opens bowels, and when you have a guilty soul it ties you up and death will not for long desert you."

No, sir. I haven't had any education. I should have had one, though. My old missus was sorry, after the War, that she didn't teach me. Her name, before she married my old master, was Mrs. Long. She lived in New York City and had three sons. When my old master's wife died, he wrote up to a friend of his in New York, a very prominent merchant named C. C. Stewart. He told this friend he wanted a wife and gave him specifications for one. Well, Mrs. Long, whose husband had died, fitted the bill, and she was sent down to Texas. She became Mrs. Fitzpatrick. She was not the grandmother of Governor Ferguson, however. Old Fitzpatrick had two wives that preceded Mrs. Long. One of the wives had a daughter named Fanny Fitzpatrick, and it was her that was the Texas governor's mother.

I seem to have the complicated family tree of my old master more clear than I have got my own, although mine can be put in a nutshell: I married only once and was blessed in it with forty-five years of devotion. I had thirteen children and a big crop of grandchildren.

It was in the Battle of Marshall in Louisiana that Colonel Buchell got shot. I was about three miles from the front, where I had pitched up a kind of first-aid station. I was all alone there. I watched the whole thing. I could hear the shooting and see the firing. I remember standing there and thinking that the South didn't have a chance. All of a sudden I heard someone call. It was a soldier, who was half carrying Colonel Buchell in. I didn't do nothing for the Colonel. He was too far gone. I just held him comfortable, and that was the position he was in when he stopped breathing. That was the worst hurt I got, when anybody died. He was a friend of mine. He had a lot of soldiering before and fought in the Indian Wars.

Well, the Battle of Marshall broke the back of the Texas Cavalry. We began straggling back towards New Orleans, and by that time the War was over. The soldiers then began to scatter. They was a sorry-lookin' bunch of lost sheep. They didn't know where to go, but most of 'em ended up pretty close to the towns they started from.

They were like homing pigeons with only the instinct to go home, and yet most of them had no homes to go to.

If you don't mind, I'd like to tell you some ideas I have on American slavery. I believe that slavery in this country, taking everything into consideration, was a Godsend for the slaves. The twenty million Negroes are descended from four million sent over from Africa. If it had not been for the slave traffic, we would still be living in Africa. I would be a heathen and my children would be heathens. Out of bad comes good and out of good, I am afraid, is going to come bad. The colored man is going to lose his strength and natural cunning, and he is going to slide downhill faster than the American white man, and that's fast enough. The white man can't stand up anymore without a helping crutch—some kind of help from the government. People look to education to save them. That's a lot of damn rot. Education don't modify fools, it increases fools.

No, sir, I never went into books. I used to handle a big dictionary three times a day, but it was only to put it on a chair so my young master could sit up higher at the table. I never went to school. I learned to talk pretty good by associating with my masters in their big house. We lived on a ranch of about a thousand acres, close to the Jackson County line, in Victoria County, about a hundred and twenty miles from San Antonio. Just before the War ended they sold the ranch, slaves and all, and the members of the family that weren't away fighting moved to Galveston. Of course, my father and me was not sold with the other blacks because we was away at war.

My mother was drowned years before, when I was a little boy about so high. I only remember her after she was dead. I can take you to the spot in the river today just where she was drowned. She drowned herself. I never knew the reason behind it, but it was said that she started to lose her mind and preferred death to that.

JOSH HORN

All right, Miss, I's glad to tell you what I knows, and it ain't gonna be a lot of fibbin', but jes' lak everything was.

De fust thing I 'members 'bout slav'ry time, I wan't nothing but a boy, 'bout fifteen, I reckon. Us belonged to Marse Ike Horn, right here on dis place whar us is now. But dis here place didn't belong to me den; dis here was all Marse Ike's place.

'Twixt daylight and sunup, us was all standing dar at de gate and us heard a little fine horn up de road. Us didn't know what dat meant was coming to de house. Den, by-'m-by, Mr. Beesley, what live not fur from Marse Ike, he rode up and he had five dogs—"nigger dogs" is what dey called 'em—and soon as he come, Marse Ike's hoss was saddled up and Marse Ike and him rode off down de road and de dogs wid 'em, 'head of us. Us followed 'long behind 'em—stayed as close as dey 'lowed us—to see what dey was up to.

When dey got close to de gin house—it was right 'side de road— dey stop us and Mr. Beesley told Old Brown to go ahead. Old Brown was de lead dog and had a bell on him, and dem dogs was fasten' togedder wid a rod, jes' lak steers. Mr. Beesley turn 'em loose, and den he popped de whip and hollered at Old Brown and told him, "Nigger!" Old Brown hollered lak he was hit. He want to go, but dey was a fence on bofe sides of de road dat made it a lane, so he put Old Brown over de fence on de gin house side and told him, "Go ahead!" Old Brown run all aroun' de gin house, and dey let him in de gin room, and he grabbled in de cotton seed, in a hole.

Den somebody holler, "Guinea Jim!" I looks and I didn't see him. Didn't nobody see him, but dey knowed dat's whar he been hiding. Mr. Beesley told Old Brown he jes' fooling him, but Old Brown

PLATE 21: Daguerreotype of a field hand during slavery.

holler agin, lak he killing him. Mr. Beesley say, "Go git dat nigger!"
Old Brown started 'way from dar lak he hadn't been hunting nothing. He went aroun' and aroun' dat gin till Mr. Beesley told him he
hadder do better dan dat or he'd kill him, 'cause he hadn't come dar
for nothing.

Old Brown made a circle aroun' dat gin, 'way down to de rail fence,
but he was so fat he couldn't git through it. He stop and bark for help.
Dey put him on top de fence and he jump way out in de road. He run
up and down in de road but couldn't find no scent of Jim.

Well, Old Brown come back dar, and dis is de trufe, so help me
God: he bark and look lak for dem to lift him back on de fence, and
bless God if dat dog didn't walk dat rail fence lak he walking a log, as
fur as from here to dat gate yonder, and track Jim jes' lak he was on de
groun'. He fell off once, and dey put him back, and he run Jim's track
right to whar Jim jumped off de fence way out into de road. Old
Brown run right 'cross de road to de other fence and treed agin on
t'other side de road, toward Konkabia [Creek]. He walk de fence on
dat side of de road a good piece, jes' lak he done on de other side.

When Old Brown jump off dat fence, he jump jes' as fur as he can
on de field side, lak he gwine ketch Jim lak a gnat or somepin', and
he never stop barking no more—jes' lak he jumping a rabbit. Den,
Mr. Beesley turn dem other dogs loose, 'cause he say Old Brown done
got the thing straight. And he had it straight. Dem dogs run dat
track right on down to Konkabia and crossed over to de Blacksher
side. Dey was a big old straw field dar den, and dey crossed it and
come on through dat field wid all dem dogs barkin' jes' lak dey was
looking at Jim. Direc'ly, dey come up on Jim running wid some pine
bresh tied behind him to drag his scent away. But dat didn't bother
Old Brown.

When dem dogs begin to push him, Jim drap de bresh and runned
back toward Konkabia. Now on Konkabia dere used to be beavers
worse den on Sucarnatchee now. Dere was a big beaver dam twixt de
bridge and de Hale place, and Jim run to dat beaver dam. You know,
when beavers build dey dam, dey cut down trees and let 'em fall in de
creek and den pull in bresh and trash, same as folks does, to dam de
water up dar till it's knee deep.

De dogs seen Jim. Old Brown was looking at him jes' 'fore he jump in 'bove de dam, right 'mongst de bresh and things dem beavers had drug in dar. Old Brown seed him, and he jump in right behind him. Jim jes' dive down under de bresh and let he nose stick outer de water. Every once in a while, Jim, he put he head down under—he holding onto a pole down dar—and once Mr. Beesley seed him, he jes' let him stay dar.

Old Brown would swim 'bout 'mongst de bresh, back'erds and for'erds, and direc'ly Mr. Beesley told him, "Go get Jim." Den all de men got poles and dug 'bout in de water hunting him. Dey knowed he was dar, and Marse Ike had a pole and was giggin' aroun' trying to find him, too. Den, he told Mr. Beesley to give him de hatchet and let him fix he pole. He sharpen de pole right sharp. Den, Marse Ike start to gig aroun' wid de pole, and he kinder laugh to hisse'f, 'cause he knowed he done found Jim.

'Bout dat time, Jim poke he head up and say, "Dis here me," and everybody holler. Den, he ax 'em, please, for Gawd's sake, don't let dem dogs git him. Dey told him to come on out.

You see, Jim belonged to Mis' Mary Lee, Mr. John Lee's ma, and her husband was kilt in de War, so Mr. Beesley was looking out for her.

Well, dey took Jim outer dar, and Mr. Beesley whipped him a little and told him, "Jim, you put up a pretty good fight and I's gwine to give you a head start for a run wid de dogs." Jim took out towards Mis' Mary's, and Mr. Beesley held de dogs as long as he could. Dey caught him and bit him right smart. You see, dey had to let 'em bite him a little to satisfy de dogs. Jim could have made it, 'cept he was all hot and wore out.

Now, 'bout how us is getting along, I's telling you de trufe: if I was took 'fore God, I'd say jes' lak I's saying now: if my chillun ever et a moufful dat wasn't honest, dey et it somewhar else, 'cause I ain't never stole a moufful of somepin'-t'-eat for 'em in all my life. It's honest vittles dey et, and varmits I's killed in de woods, 'cause us raised chillun fast, and us had a heap of em'—sixteen, if I 'members right—and soon's I found out dat I could help feed 'em dat way, I done a heap of hunting. And everybody knows I's a good hunter. Alice used to make me go every Friday night; den us always had a possum or two for Sunday.

Alice is a good Christian woman, and she knowed I'd hunt mighty nigh all night, and she didn't want nobody to see me coming in Sunday morning wid a gun and dogs. So I went every Friday night and went in de week, too, and dat help a lot to feed de chillun. I don't owe nobody, not a nickel.

I's getting on all right now, and so is my chillun. Us is got fourteen living, and dey's all been to school. Ain't but one been to Booker Washington's school, but dey kin all read and write, and some of 'em is teaching school out here in de country.

Last night, Alice was back dere wid me in de kitchen, and I got through eating and I come out and set down in de swinger to git some air. De moon was shining, and Alice come out, saying loud as she could, "Who is you? Who is you?" De chillun run to her wid a lamp and I run, and 'twan't nobody dere. Well, Alice said 'twas a big man standing right 'side her dressed in black, and she called him Death. Us couldn't do nothing wid her, and she didn't know nobody, me nor de chillun, so I went to Livingston atter Dr. McCain, and he come and set wid her 'bout a hour. He said 'twas de 'cute 'digestion or somepin' lak dat.

We's having a barbeque on de Fo'th of July, and us wants you to come down to it, if Alice gits along well, and I's gwine to tell you some sho'-'nuf tales. You sort of caught me when my min' wan't zackly on it. I ain't had no sleep, jes' settin' side de bed by Alice, ketching a nod now and den. I's too sleepy to sing you a song, but one I laks is dis. It suits me now in my age:

> My lates' sun is sinking fas',
> My race is nearly run,
> My stronges' trial now is pas',
> My triump' jes' begun.

You come back and I'll sing de res'. I's got to see 'bout things now.

Voices

―――――❧ ❧❦❦――――――

BULLWHIP DAYS

ONE time, one of the slaves was helping Mistress there in the yard, and he passed too close to her, as he was hurrying fast as he could, and sort of bumped into her. She never paid him no attention, but Maser saw him. He let him go on ahead and finish what he was doing, then he called that poor Negro to him and took him out in the pasture, tied his hands together, throwed the other end of the rope over a limb on a tree, and pulled that Negro's hands up in the air to where that Negro had to stand on his tiptoes. And Maser, he took all that Negro's clothes off and whipped him with that rawhide whip until that Negro was plumb bloody all over. Then, he left that poor Negro tied there all the rest of the day and night.

When Maser did let that Negro down, he could not stand up or get his hands down from over his head. But that did not keep Maser from giving him another whipping, as he thought the Negro was putting on, but he found out he was not. Then, Maser called an old Negro mama that he had there on the plantation to rub and work on that poor Negro until she finally got him limbered up, so he could move around some. Son, that was one of the sickest Negroes you ever saw, after that. Maser thought for more than a week he was going to die, but the old Negro mama just kept working on him until she pulled him through. Maser did have to kill him after that, as it had made an outlaw out of him. He got to where he would not work, and Maser was whipping him all the time, and he would sass Maser, right out.

Then, Maser sold that Negro to another man, and his new maser carried him to the field and thought he would work, but no sir, he just lay his hoe down and walked right off from his new maser and right back to his old maser; said if he ever got a chance, he was going to kill his old maser. Maser had to give that man his money back. Then, he sold that Negro to another man that lived in another state, and just as soon as he turned him loose, why he just walked off from that new maser and come right back home. Maser had to give that man's money back, too, as he could not keep that Negro; he had had to come and get him three or four times.

That Negro's old maser done got scared of him and put him in chains. Of course, he would have to unfasten his hands in the daytime so he could work, but he never took the chains off his legs. At night, he was locked in his quarters. We was all locked in at night, for that matter.

Then, one day, Maser had that Negro working, and he was not watching him and went to show some of the other slaves something, and turned his back. And that Negro thought that was his chance, so he jumped right on Maser's back and pinned him to the ground, and was trying to choke him and keep him from getting his gun, all at the same time. But with his feet chained, he could not do it. Some of us run in and started to pull him off Maser, but he made us get away, 'cause he did not want to shoot some of us when he did get his gun, which he finally did, and shot that Negro off of him. He sure hated to kill one of his slaves, 'cause they were a valuable piece of property, in them days, but he had to kill that one. He just drug that Negro off and throwed him in a brush pile. Never even buried him. No sir, he said he was not worth burying.

—WILLIAM COLEMAN

My mother, she didn't work in the field. She worked at a loom. She worked so long and so often that once she went to sleep at the loom. Her master's boy saw her and told his mother. His mother told him to take a whip and wear her out. He took a stick and went out to beat her awake. He beat my mother till she woke up. When she woke up, she took a pole out of the loom and beat him nearly to death with it. He hollered, "Don't beat me no more, and I won't let 'em whip you." She said, "I'm goin' to kill you. These black titties sucked you, and then you come out here to beat me." And when she left him, he wasn't able to walk.

PLATE 22: Slave pens in Alexandria, Virginia.

And that was the last I seen of her until after Freedom. She went out and got an old cow that she used to milk—Dolly, she called it. She rode away from the plantation, because she knew they would kill her, if she stayed.

—ELLEN CRAGIN

Befo' I's a field hand, dis nigger never gits whupped, 'cept for dis: Massa use me for huntin', and use me for de gun rest. When him have de long shot, I bends over and puts de hands on de knees, and Massa puts his gun on my back for to git de good aim. What him kills I runs and fotches, and I carries de game for him.

All dat not so bad, but when Massa shoots de duck in de water and I has to fotch it out, dat give me de worriment. De fust time he tells me to go in de pond, I's skeert, powe'ful skeert. I takes off de shirt and pants, but dere I stands. I steps in de water, den back 'gain, and 'gain. Massa am gittin' mad. He say, "Swim in dere and git dat duck." I says, "Yes, sar, Massa," but I won't go in dat water till Massa hit me some licks. I couldn't never git use' to bein' de water dog for de ducks.

—JOHN FINNELY

My mammy wukked in de big house, a-spinnin' an' a-nussin' de white chillun. All of dem called her "Mammy." Ah 'members one thing jes' lak it was yestiddy. Mis' Sarah went to 'Mospolis [Demopolis] to visit wid her sister, an' whilst she were gone, de oberseer, what go by de name of Allen, whupped my mammy 'crost her back till de blood runned out.

When Mis' Sarah comed back an' foun' it out, she was de maddes' white lady I eber seed. She sont for de oberseer, an' she say, "Allen, what you mean by whupping Mammy? You know I don't allow you to tech my house servants." She jerk her dress down an' stan' dere lookin' like a sojer, wid her white shoulders shinin' lak a snowbank, an' she say, "I druther see dem marks on my own shoulders dan to see 'em on Mammy's. Dey wouldn't hurt me no wuss." Den, she say, "Allen, tek your fambly an' git offen my place. Don't you let sundown

238

ketch you here." So he lef'. He wasn't nothin' but white trash, nohow.

—KATHERINE EPPES

Master Teed Sharpe, Jr., had said he was going to make my brother Peter do as much work as my sister did. She was a young girl, but grown, and stout, and strong. Peter couldn't keep up with her. He wasn't old enough nor strong enough, then. He would have been later, but he hadn't reached his growth and my sister had. Every time that Peter would fall behind my sister, Teed would take him out and buckle him down to a log with a leather strap, and stand way back, and then he would lay that long cowhide down, up and down his back. He would split it open with every stroke, and the blood would run down. The last time he turned Peter loose, Peter went to my sister and asked her for a rag. She thought he just wanted to wipe the blood out of his face and eyes, but when she gave it to him, he fell down dead across the potato ridges.

—ROBERT FARMER

Marse John sho' was de good marse, and we had plenty to eat and wear, and no one ever got whipped. Marse John say iffen he have a nigger what oughta be whipped, he'd git rid of him quick, 'cause a bad nigger jes' like a rotten tater in a sack of good ones—it spoil de others.

—LUCINDA ELDER

The rule was if a nigger wouldn't work, he would be sold. Another rule on that place was that if a man got dissatisfied, he was to go to Old Master and ask him to "put him in his pocket." That meant he wanted to be sold, and the money he brought to be put in the [master's] pocket. I ain't never known of but two asking to be put in the pocket, and both of them was put in.

—PRINCE JOHNSON

I never knew of a slave being guilty of any crime more serious than taking something or violating plantation rules. And the only punishment that I ever heard or knew of being administered to slaves was whipping. I have personally known a few slaves that were beaten to death for one or more of the following offenses: leaving home without a pass, talking back to—"sassing"—a white person, hitting another Negro, fussing, fighting, and ruckussing in the quarters, lying, loitering on their work, taking things—the whites called it stealing.

The plantation rules forbade a slave to: own a firearm, leave home without a pass, sell or buy anything without his master's consent, have a light in his cabin after a certain hour at night, attend any secret meeting, harbor or in any manner assist a runaway slave, abuse a farm animal, mistreat a member of his family, and do a great many other things.

—THE REVEREND W. B. ALLEN

My husband said there was a family named Gullendin which was mighty hard on their niggers. He said ole Missis Gullendin, she'd take a needle and stick it through one of their nigger women's lower lip and pin it to the bosom of her dress, and the woman would go roun' all day with her haid drew down thataway, and slobberin'. Ole Missis Gullendin done her that-away lots of times. There was knots on her lip where the needle had been stuck in it. Me, I don't b'lieve I coulda stood that no time, without goin' crazy.

—MRS. THOMAS JOHNS

I have heard a heap of people say they wouldn't take the treatment what the slaves took, but they woulda took it or death. If they had been there, they woulda took the very same treatment.

—ANONYMOUS

I never knowed 'bout no slave uprisin's. They'd had to uprose wid rocks an' red clods. The black man couldn't shoot. He had no guns.

The slaves had so much work they didn't know how to have a uprisin'. The better you be to your master, the better he treat you. The white preachers teach that in the church.

—CAL WOODS

A nigger uprising? What is a nigger uprising? Why the niggers couldn't do without the white folks, and the white folks couldn't do without the niggers.

—CALLIE GRAY

Yas sar, de marster an' de missy am de best folks dat de Lawd could make. Dey am good wid de wuk, de feed, de clothes, an' de play. Dere am no whuppin', an' sich.

Now sometimes, a nigger fails to 'tend to his wuk jus' lak de marster says, or violate de o'dahs in some way. Well, wid de marster, 'twarn't de whup an' de bawlin', lak 'twas on some ob de tudder places. De marster takes sich nigger an' talks to him, an' 'splains de hahm dat him am causin'. Him 'splains de diff'ence 'twix him an' tudder marsters, an' how 'twould be if him use de whup.

We-uns all lak de marster 'cause of him's way. Yas sar, 'twas mo' dan lak him; we-uns think mo' ob him dan anyone in de world, an' de missy, too. 'Twas yeahs aftah dat, dat de missy an' Ise talk 'bout de marster's treatment, an' she told me dat de marster always says, "If de nigger won't follow de o'dahs by de kind treatment, den sich nigger am wrong in de head an' am not worth keepin'."

—GILES SMITH

My moster would put slaves in a calaboose at night to be whipped de next morning. He always limited de lashes to five hundred. After whipping dem, he would rub pepper and salt on deir backs, where whipped, and lay dem before de fire until blistered, and den take a cat, and hold de cat, and make him claw de blisters, to burst dem.

—ROBERT BURNS

Some masters was kind to deir slaves, and some was cruel, jes' lak some folks treat deir horses and mules—some like 'em and is good to 'em, and some ain't.

—FOSTER WEATHERSBY

I never had no white folks that was good to me. We all worked jest like dogs, and had about half enough to eat, and got whupped for everything. Our days was a constant misery to us. I know lots of niggers that was slaves and had a good time, but we never did. Seems hard that I can't say anything good for any of my white folks, but I sho' can't.

Old Master stayed drunk all the time. I reckon that is the reason he was so fetched mean. My, how we hated him! He finally killed hisself drinking, and I remember Old Mistress called us in to look at him in his coffin. We all marched by him slow-like, and I jest happened to look up and caught my sister's eye, and we both jest natchelly laughed. Why shouldn't we? We was glad he was dead. It's a good thing we had our laugh, fer Old Mistress took us out and whupped us with a broomstick. She didn't make us sorry, though.

—ANNIE HAWKINS

We had one slave there on the plantation that Maser could not do anything with in the way of keeping him at home. When night come, he had him a girl that lived over on another plantation joining ours, and that Negro would go over there, when Maser told him to go to bed in his quarters. Just as soon as Maser got to bed, he would get up and slip off over to see his girl, and he would not come back to his quarters until just before daylight. Then, he would not be any account at all, that day. So Maser, he tried ever' way to get along with that Negro, without putting him in chains. He whipped him, and the patterrollers, they got hold of him several times, but that did not do any good.

So Maser, he finally got him some chains and put them around that Negro's legs. But then, he would get him a pole to hop around on, and he would get over there some way to see his girl. They got to where they could get them chains off that Negro, but Maser, he would not be outdone, so he fixed that Negro a shed and bed close to a tree, there on the plantation, and chained his hands and feet to that tree, so he could not slip off to see his girl.

Maser finally did put a stop to that Negro man running around at night, but then his girl started. She would come over there to his shed and bed, and they would lay around there, talk and go on all night, so that Negro, he would lose so much sleep that he still was not any account.

Still, they could not outdo Maser. He put that Negro up for sale, and no one that lived there close by would offer to buy him, as they knew how he was. But there was a man that came in there from another state and offered to buy him from Maser, and he sold him.

And when that Negro found out that his maser had sold him, he began to beg him not to. He promised Maser that if he would not sell him and take him away from his girl and would let him go to see his girl once a week, he would stay at home and be a real good Negro, as him and his girl had one child, by now. But Maser would not listen to that Negro, as he done had too much trouble with that Negro already, so he let the man have him.

The man told that Negro he could not go see any girl there where he was carrying him, as there was not any girls there for him to slip off to see.

—POLLY SHINE

Mr. Henry, Mr. Jake's brudder, and his uncle, Moses, uster come a-visitin' ter de house fer de day. Mr. Henry wus little wid a short leg an' a long one, an' he had de wust temper dat eber wus in de worl'. He loved ter see slaves suffer, near 'bout as much as he loved his brandy. We knowed when we seed him comin' dat dar wus gwine ter be a "whuppin' frolic," 'fore de day wus gone.

Dar wus three niggers, John Lane, Ananias Ruffin, an' Dick Rogers, what got de blame fer eber'thing what happens on de place. Fer instance, Mr. Henry 'ud look in de hawg pen an' 'low dat hit 'peared dat he brudder's stock wus growin' less all de time. Den, Mr. Jake says dat dey done been stold.

"Why don' you punish dem thievin' niggers, Jake?"

Jake gits mad an' has dese three niggers brung out. Deir shirts am pulled off, an' dey am staked down on deir stomichs, an' de oberseer gits wored out, an' leavin' de niggers tied dar in de sun, dey goes ter de house ter git some brandy.

De more dey drinks from de white crock, de better humor dey gits in. Dey laughs an' talks, an' atter a while dey think o' de niggers, an' back dey goes an' beats 'em some more. Dis usually lasts all de day, 'case hit am fun ter dem.

—ESSEX HENRY

Folks a mile away could hear dem awful whippings. Dey wuz a turrible part of livin'.

—DELIA GARLIC

I have seen slaves whipped. Dey took 'em into the barn and corncrib an' whipped 'em wid a leather strap called de cat-o'-nine-tails. Dey hit 'em ninety-nine licks, sometimes. Dey wouldn't allow 'em to call on de Lord when dey were whippin' 'em, but dey let 'em say, "Oh, pray! Oh, pray, Marster!" Dey would say, "Are you goin' to work? Are you goin' visitin' widout a pass? Are you goin' to run away?" Dese is de things dey would ax him, when dey wus whippin' him.

—ALEX WOODS

The last whipping Old Mis' give me she tied me to a tree and—oh, my Lord!—she whipped me that day. That was the wors' whipping I ever got in my life. I cried and bucked and hollered, until I couldn't. I give up for dead, and she wouldn't stop. I stop crying and said to her, "Old Mis', if I were you and you were me, I wouldn't beat you this way." That struck Old Mis's heart, and she let me go, and she did not have the heart to beat me anymore.

—SARAH DOUGLAS

Old Mistress got sick, and I would fan her with a brush, to keep the flies off her. I would hit her all in the face. Sometimes, I would make out I was 'sleep and beat her in the face. She was so sick she couldn't sleep much, and couldn't talk, and when Old Master come in the house, she would try to tell him on me, but he thought she just meant I would go to sleep. Then, he would tell me to go out in the yard and wake up. She couldn't tell him that I had been hitting her all in the face. I done that woman bad. She was so mean to me.

Well, she died, and all the slaves come in the house just a-hollering and crying and holding their hands over their eyes—just hollering for all they could. Soon as they got outside of the house, they would say, "Old goddamn son of a bitch, she gone on down to hell."

—ANONYMOUS

Father come from Dallas, Texas, when a young man, before he married. Him and two other men was shipped in a box to Indian Bay. I've heard him and Ike Jimmerson laugh how they got bumped and bruised, hungry and thirsty, in the box. They was sent on a boat, and changed boats where they got tumbled up so bad. It was in slavery or war times, one. White folks nailed them up and opened them up, too, I think.

—WILLIAM GUESS

Well, the way we traveled as slaves was just about like you have seen people drive cattle to market. Our maser would put us in the road ahead of him, and he would be on a horse behind us as we traveled, and he would follow, and we had to travel pert—no laggin' on behind. If we lagged, he always had a whip that he would tap us up with. Boy!—when he hit us across the legs, we could step real lively, and I don't mean maybe, either.

—POLLY SHINE

Ole Mis' had a nigger oberseer, an' dat was de meanest debil dat eber libbed on de Lawd's green earth. I promise myself when I growed up dat I was a-goin' to kill dat nigger, iffen it was de las' thing I eber done. Lots of times, I's seen him beat my mammy, an' one day I seen him beat my auntie who was big wid a chile, an' dat man dug a roun' hole in de groun' an' put her stummick in it, an' beat an' beat her for a half hour straight, till de baby come out right dere in de hole.

—HENRY CHEATAM

That whipping machine was a funny thing. Old Master just had it to set around so the slaves could see it, I think. He loaned it out to a man one time, though, and the man used it. It was a big wooden wheel with a treadle to it, and when you tromp the treadle, the big wheel go round. On that wheel was four or five big leather straps with holes cut in them to make blisters, and you lay the Negro down on his face on a bench, and tie him to it, and set the machine close to him. Then, when you tromp the treadle, the wheel go round and flop them straps across his bare back and raise the skin. Getting a Negro strapped down on that bench had him cured long before you had to tromp that treadle.

—HENRY CLAY

Old Marster had an overseer that went round and whipped the niggers every morning, and they hadn't done a thing. He went to my father one morning and said, "Bob, I'm gonna whip you this morning." Daddy said, "I ain't done nothing." And he said, "I know it. I'm gonna whip you to keep you from doing nothing," and he hit him with that cowhide—you know, it would cut the blood out of you with every lick, if they hit you hard. And Daddy was chopping cotton, so he just took up his hoe and chopped right down on that man's head and knocked his brains out. Yes'm, it killed him. But they didn't put colored folks in jail then, so when old Charlie Merrill, the nigger trader, come along, they sold my daddy to him, and he carried him way down in Mississippi. Old Merrill would buy all the time—buy and sell niggers just like hogs.

—ANONYMOUS

I ain't never seen no jail till after peace was declared. In slavery times, jails was all built for the white folks. There warn't never nobody of my color put in none of them. No time for them to stay in jail. They had to work. When they done wrong, they was whipped and let go.

—SQUIRE IRVIN

If a good nigger killed a white overseer, they wouldn't do nothin' to him. If he was a bad nigger, they'd sell him. They raised niggers to sell; they didn't want to lose them. It was just like a mule killing a man.

—HENRY BANNER

De las' overseer dat come down befo' de War start, he like to kilt us. He'd strip us down to de wais', tie men to trees, and drink and beat 'em jus' to be whipping. I 'member dere wuz two old women; dey couldn't work much. De overseer so mean, he tie 'em to a buggy, stark mother nekked, put a belly band on 'em, and driv 'em down de road, like dey wuz mules, whippin' 'em till dey drap down in de road. Dere wuz some white ladies what see it, and dey reported him and prosecuted him, and he got run out of de county.

—MATILDA MUMFORD

My marster had a barrel, with nails drove in it, that he would put you in when he couldn't think of nothin' else mean enough to do. He would put you in this barrel and roll it down a hill. When you got out you would be in a bad fix, but he didn't care. Sometimes he rolled the barrel in the river and drowned his slaves.

—ANONYMOUS

Alex Hunter had come over from the Hunter plantation and got into a fight with Noah Billamy. Alex cut Noah in the belly so bad that his insides came out. Then, John Savage, the overseer, came

247

running up and whipped Alex until they quit fighting. They tied Alex up, and sent word to Alex's massa, old Hunter, and he sent word back to pretty near kill Alex, but not quite.

So they whipped him and then turned the dogs loose on him. They tore him pretty near to pieces, and I don't know but what the dogs ate some of what they pulled off. Then, they took the dogs off Alex and poured raw alcohol on him. He had been screaming all the time the dogs were tearing him, but it was worse than ever when they put the alcohol onto him. I tried to get away from it, but old Savage told me if I didn't stay and see it, he would give me some of the same thing. So, I had to stay and see poor Alex try to get away from the dogs. He finally died, and old Hunter lost a thousand dollars on account of his death.

—SPEAR PITMAN

If one slave kilt another, Marse Billy made de overseer tie dat dead nigger to de one what kilt him, and de killer had to drag de corpse round till he died, too. De murderers never lived long a-draggin' dem dead ones round. Dat jus' piorely skeered 'em to death.

—CALLIE ELDER

De nigger fights am mo' fo' de white folks' 'joyment, but all us niggers am 'lowed to see dem. De marsters ob de diffe'nt plantations match deir niggers 'cordin' to size, an' den bet on dem.

Marster Finnely has one nigger dat weighed 'bout a hundred an' fifty pounds, an' him was awful good fightah. Dat nigger am quick lak a cat, an' powe'ful fo' his size, an' he lak to fight. Dat nigger win de battle quick. None last long wid him. Well, aftah a while, dere am a new nigger come to de neighbahood, an' den dere was a vicious fight. Ise see dat one.

De fight am held at night by de pine torch light. A ring am made by de folks standin' roun' in de circle, an' de niggers git in dat circle. Dey fight widout a rest till one give up or can't git up. Dey's 'lowed to do anything wid dey hands, head, and teeth. Sho', dat's it—nothin' barred, 'cept de knife an' clubs.

Well sar, dem two niggers gits into de ring. Tom—dat am de marster's nigger—him stahts quick, lak him always do, but de udder nigger stahts jus' as quick, an' dat 'sprise Tom. It am de fust time a nigger's jus' as quick as him. When dey come togedder, it am lak two bulls. Kersmash!, it sounds, when dey hits. Den, it am hit, kick, bite, an' butt, anywhar, anyplace, anyway fo' to best de udder. Fust, one down an' de udder on top a-poundin'; den, 'tis de udder one on top. De one on de bottom bites, knees, or anything dat him can do. Dat's de way it goes fo' half an houah. Both am awful tired an' gittin' slow, but am still fightin'. 'Tain't much 'vantage fo' either one.

Finally, dat udder nigger gits Tom in de stomach wid his knee an' a lick 'side de jaw, at de same time. Down goes Tom, an' de udder nigger jumps on him wid both feet, den straddles him, an' hits wid right, left, right, left, right, 'side Tom's head. Dere Tom layed, makin' no 'sistence. Ever'body am sayin', "Tom have met his match. Him am done." Both am bleedin' an' am awful sight. Well, dat nigger relaxes fo' to git his wind or something, an' den Tom, quick lak a flash, flips him off an' jumps to his feet. Befo' dat nigger could git to his feet, Tom kicks him in de stomach, 'gain an' 'gain. Dat nigger's body stahts to quiver, an' his marster says, " 'Nuf." Dat am de clostest dat Tom ever came to gittin' whupped dat Ise know ob. Dey m'ybe found someone, aftah dat. If dey did, Ise don't know 'bout it, 'cause Ise become a runaway nigger a sho't time aftah de fight.

—JOHN FINNELY

In slavery days, I b'longed to Mr. Armstrong Flowers. I was a yard boy, an' de Flowers was rich an' had a heap o' slaves. But Marse Flowers died wid de whiskey fits. He was a powerful fine man, till one of dem fits come on. Den, he was turrible. He'd jus' run us niggers nearly to death, an' he'd grab Old Mistus by de hair of her head an' drag her up an' down de long front gallery.

Us niggers was so scared we didn' have good sense. Sometimes, he'd think he seen de Debil an' he'd make us try to cetch him. He'd holler, "Dig a deep hole for de Debil!" When us seen Old Marse wasn' lookin', us niggers would yell, "Yon' he go, Marse. Yon' he go! De

Debil done jump out an' jus' a-runnin'." An' we'd p'int 'way off, so as he would turn loose of pore Mistus' hair an' jump off de gallery. Den, he'd say, skeered like, "He'p me cetch him, boys. He'p me cetch him!" Den, we'd all start a-runnin' after a debil what warn't dere, an' round an' round de place we'd go.

Sometimes, he'd fall out, like he was clean wore out, an' one day he died in one of dem whiskey fits.

—LEWIS WALLACE

Old Marster like fiddlin' and dancin', an dat was one thing he 'lowed de niggers on his place to do. We'd have a big time, till he'd go and get drunk and tell de overseer to whip everybody.

—JAKE DAWKINS

Narratives

GEORGE FLEMING

ARNOLD GRAGSON

CATO CARTER

ELMO STEELE

GEORGE FLEMING

I WAS born in 1854 in de month of August. I disremembers what dat pension lady said was de day. She de one dat found out all about it.

I 'clare dat was de biggest plantation, whar I was born, dat I is ever seed or heard tell of. Lawd-a-mercy! Ain't no telling how many acres in dat place, but dar was jes' miles and miles of it. It was in Laurens County, not fur [far] frum de town of Laurens. I 'longed to Marse Sam Fleming. Lawd, chile, dat's de best white man what ever breathed de good air. I still goes to see whar he buried every time I gits a chance to venture t'wards Laurens. As old as I is, I still draps a tear when I sees his grave, fer he sho' was good to me and all his other niggers.

Marse Sam's boys, Lyntt and Frank, sho' was tigers, but co'se [course], dey wasn't mean tigers. Dey had real long beards. Marse Lyntt was my young marster, and he de bestest man I ever know'd, 'cepting his daddy. He allus doing something to have fun outen us li'l niggers, but us didn't mind, 'cause we got fun outen it, too. I 'member how he used to sot us in de hog pens, but we wasn't as scared as we 'lowed we was.

My pa named Bill. He was stole frum Virginia. I don't know how Marse got him. Sometimes dey would buy 'em and agin dey would steal 'em—sort of like stealing a dog. Ma, her name Hannah. Dey got married on de plantation. I only has one whole sister living, and she name' Jennie.

Mercy on us, dem was de happy days. Dey was heavenly days, 'sides what we 'speriences now. Us li'l kids played lots of games den, some of dem like what dey plays now, but we had a better time. Befo' we was big enough to work, 'cept tote water and de like of dat, we

PLATE 23: A former slave.

played sech things as marbles. We had purty red and blue marbles dat Marse Lyntt brung frum de store. Sometimes we wrestle, too, and Old Marse laugh till his fat belly shake all over when he see de li'l niggers head buried in de white sand. Sometimes we play "warm jacket." Dat was worked by each one gitting a brush from a tree or bush and flailing de other'un till it got too hot fer him.

De older boys and gals had big frolics, 'specially in de fall of de year. Sometimes dey be on our plantation, and agin dey be on neighboring ones. When dey have 'em close home, some of us li'l niggers would slip off and git in de corner or up in de loft of de house and spy on 'em. Dey cotch us sometimes and thrash us out. One game dey played was "please and displease." When de gal say, "What it take to please you?" de boy say, "A kiss frum dat purty gal over dar."

Yes, dey played "hack back," too. Dat's when dey faced each other and trotted back and forth. Lawd, dey sho' had some awful times dancing and cutting jigs. Twan't much drinking, 'cepting on de side.

White ladies didn't go to de frolics, but some of de white men did. De patrollers was allus around to see dat everybody had passes, and if dey didn't have 'em dey was run back home. Sometimes de overseer was dar, too. Lawd, dey sho' did kick up de dust at dem frolics. De music was mostly made by fiddles, and sometimes dey had quill blowers. De quills was made from cane, same as de spindles was, but dey was cut longer and was different sizes. All de quills was put in a rack and you could blow any note you wanted to off of dem. Boy, I sho' could blow you out of dar wid a rack of quills. I was de best quill blower dat ever put one in a man's mouth. I could make a man put his fiddle up, and I could hit you so hard wid "Dixieland" dat I knock you off de seat. Gals wouldn't look at nobody else when I start blowing de quills.

Dar was also heaps and lots of other big affairs, 'sides de frolics. De corn-shuckings—Lawd-a-mercy, you ain't seen nothing. Niggers frum all over de place shucking corn, and somebody setting on one of de big piles calling de corn-shucking song, jes' like dey do in de square dance. Dat kept 'em happy. Everybody jine in de chorus. A jug of liquor sot at de bottom of de pile; everybody try to be de first to get to de liquor. Lawd, dey holler and take on something awful when dey get to de bottom. White folks have big supper ready—liquor, brandy, and everything. Dem was de times; pick up somebody and kivver 'em up wid de shucks. Had cotton pickings, too. Dat work not so fast, but we had good times. Sometimes dey be on our plantation; den we sometimes go to other places.

Didn't need no passes when a bunch of slaves went to other plantations to dem big gatherings. 'Rangements was already made so de patrollers wouldn't bother nobody. Dat policy didn't hold fer de frolics, though. Sho' had to have a pass frum de marse if you went.

On de plantation we lived jes' like a great big family, wid Marse de daddy of 'em all. Co'se, he had overseers to watch atter de work and keep things straight. He allus kept more dan two hundred head of slaves. De quarters was made up of lots of cabins, some wid one room, some wid two or three. Dat's 'cording to how big de family was. Dey wasn't built in rows, but scattered about over de plantation. Some of de cabins was made of logs and some wid planks, but all was warm and comfortable. Dey had all kinds of chimneys, too—some brick, some rock, and some de old stick-and-mud kind. Dey all had big fireplaces. Dat was whar us done de cooking. Hitches [hooks] was on de sides of de fireplace whar big iron pots hung to bile and cook in. We had pans and leads [lids] and things to bake in, too. Yes Lawd, dem was de days, fer we sho' had plenty to eat—everything we wanted.

All de things we had in de house was homemade, but we sho' had good beds. Dey was made wid boards, and, 'stead of slats, ropes was stretched twixt de sides real tight by slipping dem through holes and making knots in de ends. Over dese we laid bags, den feather or straw ticks. We had plenty kivvers to keep us warm. We had shelves and hooks to put our clothes on. We had benches and tables made wid smooth boards. Missus Harriet—dat Marse Sam's wife—she gives us a looking glass so we could see how to fix up. Lawd-a-mercy, Missus Harriet was one fine woman. She allus looked after us to see dat we didn't suffer fer nothing.

Some of de women dat didn't have a passel of li'l brats was 'signed to de job of cooking fer de field hands. Some of 'em come home to eat, but mostly dey stayed in de fields. De dinner horn blowed 'zactly at twelve o'clock and dey knowed it was time fer grub. Everybody drapped what dey was doing and compiled demselves in groups. Dey could see de buckets coming over de hill. Dar was more dan one group, fer de fields was so big dat dey couldn't all come to one place. Co'se, all dat was planned out by de overseers. Had lots of overseers and dey had certain groups to look out fer.

Most of de food was brung to de fields in buckets, but sometimes de beans and de like of dat come in de same pots dey was cooked in. It took two big niggers to tote de big pots. Dar was no want of food fer de hands. Marse knowed if dey worked dey had to eat. Dey had collards, turnips, and other good vegetables, wid corn bread. Chunks of meat was wid de greens, too, and us had lots of buttermilk.

Women worked in de field same as de men. Some of dem plowed jes' like de men and boys. Couldn't tell 'em apart in de field, as dey wore pantelets or breeches. Dey tied strips round de bottom of de legs, so de loose dirt wouldn't git in deir shoes.

De horn blowed to start work and to quit. In de morning, when de signal blowed, dey all tried to see who could git to de field first. Dey had a good time and dey liked to do deir work. Us didn't pay much mind to de clock. Us worked from sun to sun. All de slaves had to keep on de job, but dey didn't have to work so hard. Marse allus said dey could do better and last longer by keeping 'em steady and not overworking 'em.

Dar was all kinds of work 'sides de field work dat went on all de time. Everybody had de work dat he could do de best. My daddy worked wid leather. He was de best harness maker on de place, and he could make shoes. Dey had a place whar dey tanned cowhides. Dat was called de tanner's.

Dey didn't do much spinning and weaving in de home quarters; most of it was done in one special place Marse had made for dat purpose. Some of de slaves didn't do nothing but spin and weave, and dey sho' was good at it, too. Dey was trained up jes' fer dat particular work. Dey picked de seeds out of de cotton; den put de cotton in piles and carded it. Dey kept brushing it over and over on de cards till it was in li'l rolls. It was den ready fer de spinning wheels whar it was spun in thread. Dis was called de filling.

Dem spinning wheels sho' did go on de fly. Dey connected up wid de spindle, and it go lots faster dan de wheel. Dey hold one end of de cotton roll wid de hand and 'tach de other to de spindle. It keep drawing and twisting de roll till it make a small thread. Sometimes dey would run de thread frum de spindle to a corn shuck or anything dat would serve de purpose. Dat was called de broach. Some of dem didn't go any further dan dat; dey had to make sech and sech number of broaches a day. Dis was deir task. Dat's de reason some of dem had to work atter dark—dat is, if dey didn't git de task done befo' dat.

Overseers lived on de plantation. No, dey wasn't poor whites. All Marse Sam's overseers was good men. Dey lived wid deir families, and Marse's folks 'sociated wid dem, too. Dey had good houses to live in; dey was built better dan ours was. Marse didn't 'low dem to whip de slaves, but dey made us keep straight. If any whipping had to be done, Marse done it, but he didn't have to do much. He didn't hurt 'em bad, den, jes' git a big hick'ry and lay on a few. He would say, if dat nigger didn't walk de chalk, he would put him on de block and sell him. Dat was usually enough, 'cause Marse meant dat and all de niggers knowed it.

Jes' one or two of Marse Sam's slaves ever run away, but lots of other niggers did. Some of dem try to go to de North, but mostly dey come polling back by demselves when dey git hungry. If dey didn't come back purty soon, deir marse sent out to look fer 'em. Lawd, I heard de nigger hounds yelping befo' day, many times. Dat was de blood-hounds dey sicked on de runaway niggers, and dey sho' run 'em back home. When dey hear de hounds dey was glad to git home.

De patrollers would go out and look fer de niggers. Dey almost skin 'em alive if dey cotch 'em befo' dey git home. Patrollers was made up of jes' anybody dat wanted to jine 'em, poor white trash and all. One thing dey sho' couldn't do, and dat was tech a nigger atter he done got on his marse's grounds. Dey almost got pa one time, but he saved his hide by falling over a rail fence jes' befo' dey cotched him. All de plantation owners, dey pay so much to de patrollers to be on de lookout fer de slaves, and dat's de way dey kept so many frum running away.

Some men, like old Joe Crews, was reg'lar nigger traders. Dey bought niggers, stole 'em frum Virginia and places, and drove 'em through de country like a bunch of hogs. Dey come in great gangs. In town dey have big nigger sellings, and all de marsters frum all over de countryside be dar to bid on 'em. Dey put 'em up on de block and holler 'bout dis and dat dey could do and how strong dey was. "Six hundred—yip, yip, make it six fifty," I heard 'em call many times when I be dar wid Marse. Some of dem throw a thousand dollars quick as dey would ten at a purty gal. Some traders stop a drove of niggers at de plantation and swap or sell some.

Slaves started to work by de time dey was old enough to tote water and pick up chips to start fires wid. Some of dem started to work in de fields when dey about ten, but most of 'em was older. Lawd, Marse Sam must have had more dan a dozen house niggers. It took a lot of work to keep things in and round de house in good shape. Co'se, most of de slaves was jes' field hands, but some of dem was picked out fer special duties. Slaves didn't get any pay in money fer work, but Marse give 'em li'l change sometimes.

Everybody have plenty to eat. Lots of times we had fish, rabbits, possums, and stuff like dat; lots of fishing and hunting in dem days. Some slaves have li'l gardens of deir own, but most de vegetables come from de big garden. Missus was in charge of de big garden, but co'se she didn't have to do no work. She sho' seed atter us, too. Even de poor white trash had plenty to eat back in dem times. Marse have a hundred head of hogs in de smokehouse at one time. Never seen so much pork in my life. We sho' lived in fine fashion in hog-killing time, 'cause de meats was cured and us had some all de year. Yes sir, Marse ration out everybody some every week. Watermelons grow awful big; some of 'em weigh a hundred pounds. Dey was big striped ones, called "rattlesnakes," so big you can't tote one no piece.

Didn't wear much clothes in summer 'cause we didn't need much, but all de grown niggers had shoes. Lawd, I wore many pair of Marse Lyntt's boots—I means sho' 'nuf good boots. Marse had his own shoemakers, so twan't no use us gwine widout. Had better clothes fer Sunday. Most de washing was done on Saturday afternoons, and we be all setting purty fer Sunday. In cold weather we was dressed warm, and we had plenty bed kivvers, too. Co'se, all slaves didn't have it as good as Marse Sam's did. Lawd, I is seed li'l naked niggers setting on a rail fence like a pa'cel of buzzards, but Marse Sam's niggers never had to go dat way.

Slaves didn't have no church or schools. Lots of dem went to de white folks' church, but Marse Sam didn't make his slaves go if dey didn't want to. Deir benches was on de sides and in de back of de church. All preachers was white men. Old preacher Moore sho' was a humdinger, and a good one. He pizen deir minds wid Salvation, soak 'em in de oil of de Holy Ghost, and set 'em on fire. Lawd-a-me! When he got lit up all over till his eyes shine and sparkle, he sho' could bring down de house. Twan't no seats in school fer de slaves, though. Some of de slick ones slipped around and larn't de letters.

When de slaves come from de field, deir day's work was done. Fact is, everybody's work was done, 'cept maybe some of de spinners or weavers dat didn't quite finish deir task. Dey was de onliest ones dat had to ever work atter dark, and dat not often. Sometimes on Saturdays we didn't have to work atall—dat is in de fields—and sometimes we had to work till twelve o'clock. Lots of de men went fishing and hunting, and mostly de women washed. Saturday nights some groups would git together and sing. I can still hear dem old songs in my mind, but I doesn't recall de words.

Christmas sho' was a handsome time. Christmas and New Year's we had a good time. Marse jes' sort of turned 'em loose. We got a li'l extra liquor and brandy on de holidays, but co'se, we had some all along enduring de whole entire year. Marse had three stills on de place and dar was plenty liquor, but he didn't let anybody git drunk. He call de li'l niggers, too, sometimes, and give 'em a drink, and he give 'em jelly biscuits. He call everybody up to de big house on Christmas and make a speech; den he give everybody some good brandy.

I doesn't recall nothing 'bout no ghosts. Ain't nothing in dem things. Co'se, if you goes round de graveyards atter dark, you might see sech things, but I ain't gwine dar. Nigger come in once a-telling something 'bout a witch making a knot in his horse's tail, but I don't think dar was nothing to it.

When any of de slaves got sick, Marse took good care of 'em till dey got well. If dey was bad sick he sont fer de doctor. Some of de women knowed how to bile up herbs and roots and make tea for colds and fevers, but I don't know what kind dey used. When de chilluns was born, Marse seed to it dat de mammy was rightly took care of. He kept a old granny woman wid dem till dey got up and well.

De slaves mostly got married in Marse Sam's backyard, and he sho' fixed up fine fer 'em. Dat's de way Ma and Pa got married. I got married twice on Dr. Wright's place. He fixed up fer de 'casion like Marse did. Had twelve waiters both times. We had supper in de kitchen and den had dancing and music. Dem dat got married back den sho' did have it in high fashion. Man would have a good striped suit, and de woman have silk and satin clothes. Dey was married by a white preacher same as de white folks. A dinner was fixed in deir honor, too. Co'se, as I say, Marse Sam's slaves was treated better dan most any I ever knowed of, and all of dem loved him, too.

Dar was a burying ground jes' fer de slaves and de funeral was sort of like dat of de white folks. Niggers was baptized jes' like de white people, too, and by de same preacher. I saw thirty niggers baptized at one time in de river. Dat's whar everybody was baptized, den. Now dey has a basin in de church, wid glass all round de top, but I 'spects it do 'bout as much good.

During de War, food got kind of scarce, but didn't nobody suffer none on our place. Lawd yes, we carried de farming right on while de War was gwine on. Marse Sam's boys went to de War, but dey come back all right. Dey sho' had a homecoming time fer 'em when dey got back. I heard 'bout de Yankees coming through and 'stroying things, but I never seed none. Our place stood jes' like it was, all enduring de War. I didn't see no Ku Klux, neither.

When Freedom come, Marse called all de slaves up to de big house and say, "I wants to know what you all is gwine to do now, fer you is free to go if you wants to." Everybody spoke alike, "We wants to stay wid Marse." Every one of de slaves stayed right on wid Marse Sam till dey could git a place to go to. Lots of 'em stayed till dey died. He divided de land up in patches and give each one a third of what was made.

Soon atter de War, dar was a lot of trouble 'bout voting for de governor. Some folks, like old Joe Crews, tried to put it in de niggers' heads to vote fer de Republicans, but I knowed better. I voted fer Hampton, like Marse did. Fact is, I voted twice for him. Joe Crews and other scalawags like him had done made all de money dey could off selling niggers, so dey thought dey could make some more by making 'greements wid de Republicans. My daddy, Bill, was bullheaded. He done got dem ideas in his head and he said he gwine to vote fer de Republicans in spite of hell.

De Democrats done got scared 'cause so many niggers gwine to vote fer de other side, so dey formed a s'ciety called de Red Shirts. Dat was jes' to scare de niggers from coming to de polls. I was young, but I jined right up wid dem and wore a red shirt, too.

Dey had a reg'lar battle in Laurens when de voting started. All de Republican niggers had deir guns stored in Tin Pot Alley, fer Joe Crews told 'em dey couldn't bring 'em to de polls. He thought de Yankees would protect de niggers, but fact is, de Yankees done been paid off by de Democrats and left town. Us Democrats broke in de storehouse in Tin Pot Alley and got every one of dem guns. De niggers' names was on de stocks of de guns. We sho' had a hot time when dem niggers come up dar trying to vote. Dat's when my daddy got kilt. He had already been shot in de leg befo' dat, and dey called him "Cripple Bill." Dem was de purtiest guns I ever seed. Dey click three times when de trigger [hammer] was pulled back. Old Joe Crews was kilt, too, at dat time. Wash Hill was de one dat got him. He was shot at Crew's Branch. 'Twan't long atter dat till things begin to settle down, fer de Democrats sho' did lick up dem Republicans.

I been married three times. First time, I married Sarah Peterson. I 'clare to goodness, I sho' can't 'member dat second one. Let me see, let me see—Lonie, Lonie, oh yes, Lonie Golding. Us married in Laurens County on Dr. Wright's place whar I married de first one. She didn't live long and we didn't have no chilluns. My last wife name Elizabeth McKantz. She frum Abbeville. She cooked fer Mr. Jones. Her daddy was a white man, and she look jes' like a Indian. I jes' had one chile by de first wife, but he dead. I got two chilluns by de last wife dat be living: dat's Mattie, de oldest, and Hugh, de third one. I doesn't know whar neither one lives now.

Some folks didn't like slavery, but I sho' did. Mercy, Lawd, we had a good time den—heap better dan now. I been a long time gitting dis pension, and it ain't much when you gits it. Back in slavery times we didn't have no worries 'bout rent or something-to-eat. We had a job long as we lived, dat is if Freedom hadn't come.

ARNOLD GRAGSON

MOST of the slaves didn't know when they was born, but I did. You see, I was born on a Christmas mornin'—it was in 1840. I was a full-grown man when I finally got my freedom.

Before I got it, though, I helped a lot of others get theirs—Lawd only knows how many; might have been as much as two, three hundred. It was way more than a hundred, I know. But that all came after I was a young man—"grown" enough to know a pretty girl when I saw one, and to go chasing after her, too.

I was born on a plantation that b'longed to Mr. Jack Tabb, in Mason County, just across the river, in Kentucky. Mr. Tabb was a pretty good man. He used to beat us, sure, but not nearly so much as others did, some of his own kin people, even. But he was kinda funny sometimes; he used to have a special slave who didn't have nothin' to do but teach the rest of us how to read and write and figger. Mr. Tabb liked us to know how to figger. But sometimes, when he would send for us and we would be a long time comin', he would ask us where we had been. If we told him we had been learnin' to read, he would near beat the daylights out of us—after gettin' somebody to teach us. I think he did some of that so that the other owners wouldn't say he was spoilin' his slaves.

He was funny about us marryin', too. He would let us go a-courtin' on the other plantations near anytime we liked, if we were good. And if we found somebody we wanted to marry, and she was on a plantation that b'longed to one of his kinfolks or to a friend, he would swap a slave so that the husband and wife could be together. Sometimes, when he couldn't do this, he would let a slave work all day on his plantation, and live with his wife at night on her plantation. Some of the other owners was always talking about his spoilin' us.

He wasn't a Dimmacrat like the rest of 'em in the county. He belonged to the Know Nothin' Party, and he was a real leader in it. He used to always be makin' speeches, and sometimes his best friends wouldn't be speaking to him for days at a time.

Mr. Tabb was always specially good to me. He used to let me go all about—I guess he had to; couldn't get too much work out of me, even when he kept me right under his eyes. I learned fast, too, and I think he kinda liked that. He used to call Sandy Davis, the slave who taught me, "the smartest nigger in Kentucky."

It was 'cause he used to let me go around in the day and night so much that I came to be the one who carried the runnin'-away slaves over the river. It was funny the way I started it, too.

I didn't have no idea of ever gettin' mixed up in any sort of business like that, until one special night. I hadn't even thought of rowing across the river myself.

But one night I had gone on another plantation courtin', and the old woman whose house I went to told me she had a real pretty girl there who wanted to go across the river, and would I take her? I was scared and backed out in a hurry. But then I saw the girl, and she was such a pretty little thing—brown-skinned and kinda rosy, and looking as scared as I was feelin'—so it wasn't long before I was listenin' to the old woman tell me when to take her and where to leave her on the other side.

I didn't have nerve enough to do it that night, though, and I told them to wait for me until tomorrow night. All the next day I kept seeing Mr. Tabb laying a rawhide across my back or shooting me, and kept seeing that scared little brown girl back at the house, looking at me with her big eyes and asking me if I wouldn't just row her across to Ripley, Ohio. Me and Mr. Tabb lost, and soon as dusk settled that night, I was at the old lady's house.

I don't know how I ever rowed that boat across the river. The current was strong and I was trembling. I couldn't see a thing there in the dark, but I felt that girl's eyes. We didn't dare to whisper, so I couldn't tell her how sure I was that Mr. Tabb or some of the other

$100
REWARD.

Ran away from my farm, near Buena Vista P. O., Prince George's County, Maryland, on the first day of April, 1855, my servant MATHEW TURNER.

He is about five feet six or eight inches high; weighs from one hundred and sixty to one hundred and eighty pounds; he is very black, and has a remarkably thick upper lip and neck; looks as if his eyes are half closed; walks slow, and talks and laughs loud.

I will give One Hundred Dollars reward to whoever will secure him in jail, so that I get him again, no matter where taken.

MARCUS DU VAL.

BUENA VISTA P. O., MD.,
   MAY 10, 1855.

PLATE 24

owners would "tear me up" when they found out what I had done. I just knew they would find out.

I was worried, too, about where to put her out of the boat. I couldn't ride her across the river all night, and I didn't know a thing about the other side. I had heard a lot about it from other slaves, but I thought it was just about like Mason County, with slaves and masters, overseers and rawhides; and so, I just knew that if I pulled the boat up and went to asking people where to take her I would get a beating or get killed.

I don't know whether it seemed like a long time or a short time, now—it's so long ago. I know it was a long time rowing there in the cold and worryin', but it was short, too, 'cause as soon as I did get on the other side the big-eyed, brown-skinned girl would be gone. Well, pretty soon I saw a tall light and I remembered what the old lady had told me about looking for that light and rowing to it. I did, and when I got up to it, two men reached down and grabbed her. I started tremblin' all over again, and prayin'. Then, one of the men took my arm and I just felt down inside of me that the Lord had got ready for me. "You hungry, boy?" is what he asked me, and if he hadn't been holdin' me I think I would have fell backward into the river.

That was my first trip. It took me a long time to get over my scared feelin', but I finally did, and I soon found myself goin' back across the river with two or three people, and sometimes a whole boatload. I got so I used to make three and four trips a month.

What did my passengers look like? I can't tell you any more about it than you can, and you wasn't there. After that first girl—I never did see her again—I never saw my passengers. It would have to be the "black nights" of the moon when I would carry them, and I would meet them out in the open or in a house without a single light. The only way I knew who they were was to ask them, "What you say?" And they would answer, "Menare." I don't know what that word meant—it came from the Bible. I only know that that was the password I used, and all of them that I took over told it to me before I took them.

I guess you wonder what I did with them after I got them over the river. Well, there in Ripley was a man named Mr. Rankins. I think

266

the rest of his name was John. He had a regular station there on his place for escaping slaves. You see, Ohio was a free state, and once they got over the river from Kentucky or Virginia, Mr. Rankins could strut them all around town, and nobody would bother them. The only reason we used to land them quietly at night was so that whoever brought them could go back for more, and because we had to be careful that none of the owners had followed us. Every once in a while they would follow a boat and catch their slaves back. Sometimes they would shoot at whoever was trying to save the poor devils.

Mr. Rankins had a regular "station" for the slaves. He had a big lighthouse in his yard about thirty feet high, and he kept it burnin' all night. It always meant freedom for a slave if he could get to this light.

Sometimes Mr. Rankins would have twenty or thirty slaves that had run away on his place at a time. It must have cost him a whole lot to keep them and feed them, but I think some of his friends helped him.

Those who wanted to stay around that part of Ohio could stay, but didn't many of them do it, because there was too much danger that you would be walking along free one night, feel a hand over your mouth, and be back across the river and in slavery again in the morning. And nobody in the world ever got a chance to know as much misery as a slave that had escaped and been caught.

So a whole lot of them went on North to other parts of Ohio, or to New York, Chicago, or Canada. Canada was popular then because all of the slaves thought it was the last gate before you got all the way inside of Heaven. I don't think there was much chance for a slave to make a living in Canada, but didn't many of them come back. It seem like they rather starve up there in the cold than to be back in slavery.

The Army soon started taking a lot of them, too. They could enlist in the Union Army and get good wages, more food than they ever had, and have all the little gals wavin' at them when they passed. Them blue uniforms was a nice change, too.

I never got anything from a single one of the people I carried over the river to freedom. I didn't want anything. After I had made a few trips I got to like it, and even though I could have been free any night myself, I figgered I wasn't gettin' along so bad, so I would stay on Mr. Tabb's place and help the others get free. I did it for four years.

I don't know to this day how he never knew what I was doing. I used to take some awful chances, and he knew I must have been up to something; I wouldn't do much work in the day, would never be in my house at night, and when he would happen to visit the plantation where I had said I was goin', I wouldn't be there. Sometimes I think he did know and wanted me to get the slaves away that way so he wouldn't have to cause hard feelin's by freein' them.

I think Mr. Tabb used to talk a lot to Mr. John Fee. Mr. Fee was a man who lived in Kentucky, but Lord how that man hated slavery! He used to always tell us—we never let our owners see us listenin' to him, though—that God didn't intend for some men to be free and some men to be in slavery. He used to talk to the owners, too, when they would listen to him, but mostly they hated the sight of John Fee.

In the night, though, he was a different man. For every slave who came through his place going across the river he had a good word, something to eat, and some kind of rags, too, if it was cold. He always knew just what to tell you to do if anything went wrong, and sometimes I think he kept slaves there on his place till they could be rowed across the river. Helped us a lot.

I almost ran the business in the ground after I had been carrying the slaves across for nearly four years. It was in 1863, and one night I carried across about twelve on the same night. Somebody must have seen us, because they set out after me as soon as I stepped out of the boat back on the Kentucky side. From that time on they were after me. Sometimes they would almost catch me. I had to run away from Mr. Tabb's plantation and live in the fields and in the woods. I didn't know what a bed was from one week to another. I would sleep in a cornfield tonight, up in the branches of a tree tomorrow night, and buried in a haypile the next night. The river, where I had carried so many across myself, was no good to me; it was watched too close.

Finally, I saw that I could never do any more good in Mason County, so I decided to take my freedom, too. I had a wife by this time, and one night we quietly slipped across and headed for Mr. Rankins' bell and light. It looked like we had to go almost to China to get across that river. I could hear the bell and see the light on Mr. Rankins' place, but the harder I rowed the farther away it got, and I knew if I didn't make it I'd get killed. But finally, I pulled up by the lighthouse, and went on to my freedom—just a few months before all of the slaves got theirs. I didn't stay in Ripley, though. I wasn't taking no chances. I went on to Detroit and still live there with most of my ten children and thirty-one grandchildren.

The bigger ones don't care so much about hearin' it now, but the little ones never get tired of hearin' how their grandpa brought Emancipation to loads of slaves he could touch and feel, but never could see.

CATO CARTER

I'M HOME today, 'cause my little old dog is lost and I had to stay around to hunt for him. But he ain't come back and I ain't found him. I been going every day on the truck to the cotton patches. I don't pick no more on account of my hands get too tired and begin to cramp on me. But I go and set in the field and watch the lunches for the other hands.

I am a hundred and one years old, 'cause I was twenty-eight, going on twenty-nine, a man growned, when the breaking-up came. I'm pretty old, but my folks live that way. My old black mammy, Zenie Carter, lived to be a hundred and twenty-five years old. And Ol Carter, my white marster, who was the brother of my daddy, lived to be a hundred and four. He ain't been so long died. Al Carter, my daddy, lived to be very ageable, but I don't know when he died.

Back in Alabama, Mis' Adeline Carter took me, when I was past my creepin' days, to live in the big house with the white folks. I had a room built on the house where I stayed, and they were always good to me, 'cause I was one of their blood. They never hit me a lick nor slapped me once, and they told me that they would never sell me away from them. They were the best quality white folks, and they lived in a big two-story house with a big hall that ran all the way through it. They wasn't as rough as some white folks was on their niggers.

My mammy lived in a hewn-oak log cabin, in the quarters. There was a long row of cabins, some bigger than tothers on account of family size, 'cause my marster had over eighty head of slaves. Those little old cabins was cozy, 'cause we chinked them with mud, and they had stick chimneys daubed with mud mixed with hog hair.

The fixings in the cabins were just plain things. The beds were draw beds—wooden bedstids held together with ropes drawn tight to hold them and to put the mattresses on. We scalded moss and buried it for a while and stuffed it into ticking to make mattresses. Them beds slept good—better than the ones nowadays.

There was a good fireplace for cooking, and on Sundays the mistress would give the niggers a pint of flour and a chicken, for to cook a mess of vittles for themselves. Then, there was plenty of game for the niggers to find for themselves. Many is the time when I killed seventy-five or eighty squirrels out of one big beech. There was a lot of deer and bears and quails and every other kind of game, but when they run the Indians out of the country, the game just followed the Indians. Wherever the Indians left, the game all left with them, for some reason I dunno.

Talking about vittles, the eating on our place was good. Can't say the same for all places. Some of the plantations would half starve their niggers and 'lowance out their eating, until they wasn't fittin' for work. They has to slip about to niggers on other places to piece out their meals.

Our place was fifteen hundred acres in one block, and besides the crops of cotton, corn, and the home rice and the ribbon cane we raised in the bottoms, we raised vegetables and sheep and beef. I couldn't hardly eat fresh beef, but mostly we dried beef on scaffolds we built. I used to tend the beef as we were drying it out. But best of anything to eat I liked a big fat coon, and I always liked honey. Some of the niggers had little garden patches they tended for their own use.

Everything I tell you is the truth, but they is plenty that I can't tell you. I heard plenty of things from my mammy, too, and from my grandpappy and my grandmammy. My grandpappy was a fine diver. He used to dive in the Alabama River for the things that was wrecked out of boats, and the white folks would get him to go down for things that they wanted in the river. They would let him down by a rope to find things on the bottom of the riverbed. He used to get a piece of money from the whitefolks for doing it.

My grandmammy was a "juksie," because her mammy was a nigger and her daddy was a Choctaw Indian. That's what makes me so mixed up with Indian, African, and white blood. Sometimes it

PLATE 25

mattered to me, sometimes it didn't. It don't no more, 'cause I'm not too far from the end of my days.

I had one brother and one sister that I helped raise. I helped to tend them, and I whupped them. But they was mostly nigger. The Carters told me never to worry about them, though, 'cause my mammy was of their blood, too, and that all of us in our family would never be sold, and that sometime they would make free men and women of us. My brother and sister lived with the niggers, though.

I was trained as a houseboy and to tend the cows. The bears was so bad that a 'sponsible person who could carry a gun had to look after them.

My marster used to give me a little money to buy me what I wanted. I always bought fine clothes. In the summer, when I was a little one, I wore lowerings, like the rest of the niggers. That was the things made from cotton sacking. Most of the boys wore shirttails until they were big yearling boys. When they bought me red russels shoes from the town, I cried and cried. I didn't want to wear no rawhide shoes. So they would take them back. They had a weakness for my crying. I did have plenty of fine clothes—good woolen suits they would spin on the place, and doeskins and fine linens. I drove in the carriage with the white folks, and I was about the most dudish nigger in those parts.

I used to tend to the nursling thread. When the slave women were confined with the babies having to suck and they were too little to take to the fields, the mammies had to spin. I would take them thread and bring it back to the house when it was spun. If they didn't spin seven or eight cuts a day, they would get a whuppin'. It was considerable hard on a woman, when she had a fretting baby, but every morning, those babies had to be taken to the big house so that the white folks could see if they were dressed right. They was money tied up in little nigger young-uns.

They whupped the womens, and they whupped the mens. I used to work some in the tannery on the place, and we made their whips. They used to tie them down, or to a stob, and give them the whuppin's. Some niggers, it would take four men to whup them, but they got it. The overseer used to whup, and sometimes the nigger driver did it. The nigger driver used to be meaner than the white folks. Better not leave a blade of grass in the crops. I have seem them beat a nigger for half a day. That was usually to make them 'fess up to stealing a sheep or a goat. Or they would whup them for running away. It wasn't so hard on them, if they come back of their own accordance when they got hungry and sick in the swamps, but when they had to run them down with the nigger dogs, they would get in bad trouble.

The Carters never did have any real 'corrigible niggers. But I heard of them plenty, on other places. When they was real 'corrigible, the white folks said they was like mad dogs, and they didn't mind to kill them so much as killing a sheep. They would take them to the graveyard and shoot them down and bury them face downward with their shoes on. I never did have to go and see it done, but they used to make some of the niggers go as a lesson to them that they could get the same.

I didn't even have to carry a pass to leave my own place like other niggers. I had a cap with a sign on it: "Don't bother this nigger or there will be hell to pay." I went after the mail in the town all the time. The mail came in coaches, and they put on fresh horses at Pineapple. The coachman would run the horses into Pineapple with a big to-do and a-blowing the bugle to get the fresh horses ready. I got the mail. I was a trusty all my days and never been arrested by the law to this day.

I never had any complaints for my treatment, but some of the niggers hated the syrup-making time, 'cause when they have to work till midnight making syrup, it's four o'clock up, just the same. Sunup-to-sundown was for the field niggers.

Christmas was the big day at the Carters'. Presents for everybody, and the baking and preparin', that went on for days. The little ones and the big ones were glad—'specially the nigger mens, on account of plenty of good whiskey. Mr. Ol Carter got the best whiskey for his niggers.

Used to have frolics, too. Some of the niggers had fiddles, and they played the reels. Niggers love to dance and sing and eat.

Course, niggers had their serious side, too. They loved to go to church, and we had a little log chapel on the place for worship. I never went so much, on account of I went with the white folks to their church. But I have went there, and some of the nigger mens would preach from the Bible that couldn't read a line any more than a sheep could. But I heard them preach about the coming of the automobile and airplanes, and about the big wars, and they told of many wondrous things to come that I have lived to see. They used to sing "Amazing Grace" and other songs I don't recall just now.

The Carters didn't mind their niggers singing hymns and praying, but I heard all the time that some of the other places wouldn't let their niggers worship atall. The niggers had to put their heads in pots to sing or pray.

Most of the niggers I know who had their marriage put in the Book did it after the breaking-up. Plenty I know had it put in the Book after they had grown chillun. When they got married on the places, mostly they just jumped over a broom, and that made them married. Sometimes, one of the white folks would read a little out of the Scriptures to them, and they felt more married.

I was never one for sickness. I had pneumonia once when I was working on the Selma Gulf Railroad laying the tracks. That was the first railroad around there, and that was after the breaking-up, and I was a man some thirty-odd years old. But the niggers in slavery used to get sick. There was jaundice in the bottoms. First off, they would give a sick nigger some castor oil, and if that didn't cure him, they gave him blue moss. Then, if he was still sick, they had a doctor, which they paid to look after the slaves, to come out to see him.

They used to cry the niggers off, just like so much cattle, and we didn't think no different of it. I seen them put them on the block and brag on them something big. Everybody liked to hear them cry off niggers. The crier was a clown, and made funny talk, and kept everybody laughing.

When my marster and the other mens on the place went off to the War, he called me and said, "Cato, you is always been a 'sponsible man, and I leave you to look after the womens and the place. If I don't come back, I want you to always stay by Mis' Adeline." I said, "Befo' God, I will, Mr. Ol." He said, "Then I can go away peaceable."

We thought, for a long time, the sojers had the Federals whupped to pieces, but they was plenty bad times to go through. I carried a gun and guarded the place at nighttime. The paddyrollers was bad. I captured them and took them to the house more times than one. They wore black caps and put black rags over their faces, and was always skullduggerying around at night. We didn't use torches anymore when we went around at night, 'cause we were afeared. We put out all the fires around the house at nighttime.

The young mens in the grey uniforms used to pass so gay and singing in the big road. Their clothes was good, and they looked so fine, and we used to feed them the best we had on the place. Mis' Adeline would say, "Cato, they is our boys, and give them the best this place 'fords." We took out the hams and the wine, and we killed chickens for them. That was at first.

Then, the boys and mens in blue got to coming that way, and they was fine-looking mens, too, and Mis' Adeline would cry, and she would say, "Cato, they is just mens and boys, and we got to feed them." We had a pavilion built in the yard, like they had at picnics, and we fed the Federals on that. Three times, the Federals said to me, "We is going to take you with us." Mis' Adeline let into crying and say to the Yankee gentlemen, "Don't take Cato. Many of my niggers has run away to the North, and Cato is the only man I got by me now. If you take Cato, I just don't know what I will do." I tell them that so long as I live I got to stay by Mis' Adeline, and that unless somebody forces me away, I ain't gwine to leave. I say, "I got no complaints to make. I want to stay by Old Mis' till one of us die." The Yankee mens say to Mis' Adeline, "Don't 'sturb yourself, Miss. We ain't gwine to take him nor harm nothing of yours."

The reason they was all right by us was 'cause we prepared for them. But with some of the folks they was rough something terrible. They took off all their horses and their corn.

I have seen the trees bend low and shake all over and heard the roar and the popping of cannonballs. There was springs round and about, not too far from our place, and the sojers used to camp there at one of the springs and build a fire to cook a mule, 'cause they got down to starvation. And when some of the other gorillas [guerrillas] would see the fire, they would aim to the fire, and many is the time they spilled the dinner for the sojers. The Yankees did it, and our boys did it, too. There was killing going on so terrible, like people was dogs, and some of the old ones said it was near to the end of time, 'cause of folks being so wicked.

Mr. Ol came back, and all the others did, too, but he came back first. He was all wore out and ragged. He stood on the front porch and called all the niggers to the front yard. He said, "Mens and womens, you are today as free as I am. You is free to do as you like, 'cause the damned Yankees done 'creed that you are. But they ain't a nigger on my place that was born here or ever lived here that can't stay here and work and eat to the end of his days, as long as this old place will raise peas and goobers. Go if you wants or stay if you wants."

Some of the niggers stayed and some went. And some that had run away to the North came back. They always called real humble-like at the back gate to Mis' Adeline, and she always fixed it up with Mr. Ol that they could have a place.

Near to the close of the War, I seen some of the folks leaving for Texas. They said if the Federals win the War, you have to live in Texas to keep the slaves. So plenty of them started driftin' their slaves to the West. They would pass with the womens riding in the wagons and the mens on foot. When some of them came back, they said that it took three weeks to walk the way. Some of them took slaves to Texas, even after the Federals done 'creed a breaking-up.

Long as I lived, I minded what my white folks told me, but once. They was a nigger working in the fields, and he kept jerking the mules, and Mr. Ol got mad, and he gimme a gun, and he told me to go out there and kill that man. I said, "Mr. Ol, please don't tell me to do that. I ain't never killed anybody, and I don't want to." He said, "Cato, you do what I tell you." And he meant it. I went out to the nigger and I said, "You has got to leave this minute, and I is, too, 'cause I is s'pose to kill you, only I ain't, and Mr. Ol will kill me." He dropped the lines, and we ran and crawled through the fence, and ran away.

I hated to go, 'cause things was so bad. Flour sold for twenty-five dollars a barrel, and pickled pork for fifteen dollars a barrel. You couldn't buy nothing 'lessn you had gold. I had plenty of Confederate money, only it don't buy nothing. But today, I am a old man, and my hands ain't stained with no blood, and I is always been glad that I didn't kill that man.

Mules run to a turrible price. A right puny pair of mules sold for five hundred dollars. But the Yankees give me a mule, and I farmed that year for a white man, and I had a job all the time to watch a herd of mules. I stayed with those mules until four o'clock on Sundays, for just a little time off. So many scoundrels were going about stealing mules that you had to watch all the time. That year, I was bound out by agreement with a white man, and I made three hundred and sixty dollars. The Bureau [Freedmen's Bureau] came by that year looking at the contracts with the niggers to see they don't get skunt out of their rightful wages from the white folks. Mis' Adeline and Mr. Ol didn't stay mad at me, and every Sunday they come by to see me and bring me little delicate things to eat.

The Carters said they were regretful a hundred times that they never learned me to read or write, and they said my dada had put up five hundred dollars for me to go to the New Allison School for colored people. I started in, and Miss Benson, a Yankee lady, was my teacher. I was twenty-nine years old and just starting in the blue-back speller. I was there a little while, when one morning at ten o'clock my pore old mammy came by and called me out. She tells me that the niggers she was living with and working with done put her out of the place, 'cause she wasn't a good hand. I told her not to worry, that I was the family man now, and she didn't never need to get three-quarter hand wages anymore.

For years, I turned my hand to anything I could find to do, and I never had trouble finding work, 'cause the white folks know Cato was a good white folks' nigger. I didn't have no trouble. They was hanging niggers like they was sheep.

I left my mammy with some fine white folks, and she raised a whole family of they chillun for them. Their name was Bryan, and they lived on a little bayou. Them young-uns was crazy about her, and they used to send me word not to worry about my little black mammy, 'cause she would have the best of care, and when she died, they was 'tendin' to her buryin'.

I came to Texas, 'cause I thought there was money for the taking, out here. I got a job splitting rails for two years, and from then on have farmed, mainly. I married a woman and lived with her forty-seven years, rain and shine. We had thirteen chillun, but only eight of them are living today.

Enduring the big war,* I got worried about my little black mammy and I wanted to go back to see her and the old places. I went, and she was shriveled up to not much of anything. That was the last time I saw her. But, for forty-four years, I didn't forget to send her things I thought she would want. I saw Ol Marster. He had married after I went away, and raised a family of chillun. I saw Mis' Adeline, and she was a old woman. We went out and looked at the tombstones and the rock markers in the graveyard on the place, and some of them had nearly melted away. I looked good at lots of things, 'cause I knew I wouldn't be that way again. So many had gone on, since I had been there before.

I married again, after my wife died. My wife is a good woman, but she is old, and has lost her voice, and has to be in Terrell most of the time. But I get along all right, 'cept my hands cramp some.

You going to take my picture? I lived through plenty and I lived a long time, but this is the first time I ever had a picture taken. If I had knowed you wanted to do that, I would have tidied up and put on my best.

*World War I.

ELMO STEELE

As I sits here before de fire waitin' till de las', I thinks ob de days an' things I's told 'bout here. I thinks way back on de things my grandparents an' great-grandpas tole me. I wish I had writ it all down, fer it tires me to tell it, now. I's had to ask de ones I's givin' dis story to, to let me rest, when I wanted to talk an' tell mo'. But I wants my race to know deir story.

My great-grandfather came from Africa to be made a slave, but by some way my grandpa wuz set free, an' I have oftentimes heard him tell the followin' story:

Back in Africa, he says, dey didn't wear no clothes atall an' de hair growed several inches long all over deir body. Dey lived in thatched cabins wid dirt floors. Dey didn't know what a bed of any kind wuz—jes' lay down on de ground of de cabins, an' was jes' lak pigs. Dey all had big families, an' sometimes would cultivate not more dan two acres, an' never raised anything but corn an' taters. 'Bout de biggest part ob deir eatin' wuz meats cooked 'bout half-done in ovens made of clay. De meat wuz laid on de hot clay an' let to cook a few minutes an' wuz turnt over wid sticks. De grease would drip down, an' dey would ketch dat an' eat dat wid de meat. Dey hardly ever eat any bread atall. Deir knives an' forks wuz cut out from hickory.

Now de way dey kotched de wild animals, dey run 'em down an' killed 'em wid sticks. Dey wuz swift on foot an' could run lak a deer, an' wuz long-winded an' strong. Sometimes a wild animal would kill one ob 'em, but dey didn't pay no mo' attention to one ob 'em gittin' kilt dan if it had been de animal dey wuz after. Dey jes' run off an' left 'em.

It wuz somethin' rare fer one ob 'em to git sick, an' when dey did

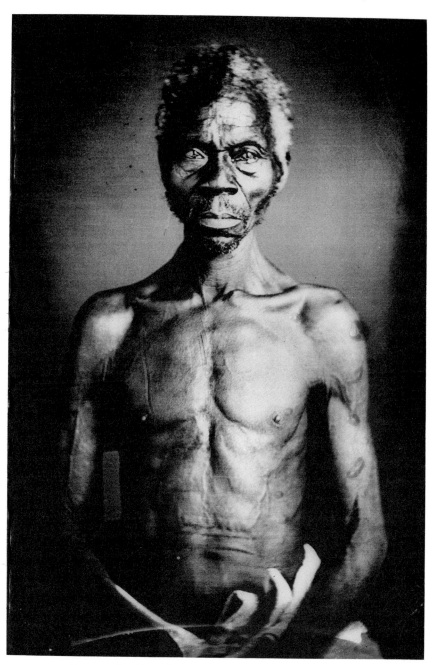

PLATE 26: Slave field hand on a Carolina plantation.

dey wuz usually ole an' jes' died, an' dey took 'em way off an' throw 'em down, an' dat wuz all dey wuz to it.

When dey got ready to wuk a ox, dey jes' went out to de praire and fotch a wild one an' brung him in an' wukked him till dey wuz through wid 'em, den turn't 'em loose. De way dis wuz done, a bunch went after deir wild ox, an' dey had strong ropes made by skinnin' de bark from trees an' plaitin' it. Dey had kind of a yoke made from hickory with two holes through it. When the ox wuz kotched, dis yoke wuz slipped over de horns an' he wuz tied an' led by de ropes. De ox wuz made to do all de pullin' by de head. Of course, dey bucked an' cut up powerfully, but de savages did, too, an' dey keep up wid 'em. If dey wuz plowin', it didn't make no difference which way de ox went, as dey jes' wanted de dirt broke up, an' dey done de res' wid a stick. Dey sho' did use sticks a lot. Dey eat wid 'em, cultivated wid 'em, kilt de wild animals wid 'em, an' fought wid 'em. Deir bare hands an' sticks wuz all dey had to fight wid.

Now dey walked everywhere dey went. Dey had trails dey followed an' fordin' places at de streams, lak cattle do over here. When a civilized man went dere, dey toted him whar he wanted to go, an' when dey got tired dey sot him down right whar dey happened to be at. Dey didn't understand dat it could make any difference. If dey happened to be out in de middle ob a lake dat dey had to cross an' got tired, down de man went. Dey had never wore clothes, an' didn't know what it meant to git wet an' messed up. Yet dey lakked de looks ob dressed-up folks. A civilized man could go dere an' dey would be so proud ob him dat dey would tote him round fer days, an' if another tribe tried to take him dey would fight 'em.

Matches wuz unknown. Dey got what dey called spunk from trees an' struck rocks against it an' kindled fires. De fire coals wuz kept covered an' kindled when dey needed 'em.

These folks didn't know nothin' ob churches or God, but dey had a feelin' dat some kind ob worship ought to be done, fer they would git together an' carry on somethin' lak preachin'. Dey would git up an' try to say somethin', an' dey wouldn't even know what dey meant deirselves; an' dey would sing an' dance an' knock bones together fer time.

Dey had a queer way ob gittin' married. If two boys wuz in love wid de same girl an' dey couldn't decide who would git her, she would run an' de two boys would run after her, an' de one dat kotched her would marry her. De marriage ceremony was simple. Dey used branches from bushes for brooms, an' one ob dese brooms wuz laid across de floor, an' de boy an' gal run an' jumped over it an' dey wuz married.

Voices

SLAVE AUCTIONS,

FORCED BREEDING,

RAPE,

AND RUNAWAYS

I SAW slaves sold. I can see that old block now. My cousin Eliza was a pretty girl, really good-looking. Her master was her father. When the girls in the big house had beaus coming to see 'em, they'd ask, "Who is that pretty gal?" So they decided to git rid of her right away.

The day they sold her will always be remembered. They stripped her to be bid off and looked at. I wasn't allowed to stand in the crowd. I was laying down under a fig bush. The man that bought Eliza was from New York. The Negroes had made up 'nuf money to buy her off theyself, but the white folks wouldn't let that happen. There was a man bidding for her that was a Swedeland. He allus bid for the good-looking cullud gals and bought 'em for his own use. He ask the man from New York, "What you gonna do with 'er when you git 'er?" The man from New York said, "None of your damn business, but you ain't got money 'nuf to buy 'er."

When the man from New York had done bought her, he said, "Eliza, you are free from now on." She left and went to New York with him. Mama and Eliza both cried when she was being showed off, and Master told 'em to shet up, before he knocked they brains out.

—DANIEL DOWDY

At dem sales, dey would put a nigger on de scales and weigh him, and den de biddin' would start. If he wuz young and strong, de biddin' would start round a hundred and fifty dollars, and de highest bidder got de nigger. A good young breedin' 'oman brung two thousand dollars easy, 'cause all de marsters wanted to see plenty of strong healthy chillun comin' on, all de time. Cyarpenters and bricklayers and blacksmiths brung fancy prices, from three thousand to five thousand dollars, sometimes. A nigger what warn't no more'n jes' a good field hand brung 'bout two hundred dollars.

—WILLIS COFER

Early one morning, when we was crossing the Sabine River, one of Master Bullard's brother-in-laws killed him. They had been fussing a couple of days. All of Bullard's darkies was separated by the killing. One of his brother-in-laws took my mother and father and brothers and sisters on to the West, but I fell into the hands of lawyer Wilson, first. He kep' me a while and sold me to one of Master's brother-in-laws, Tom Dwyer. I think he was connected with the killing, some way. He give lawyer Wilson five hundred dollars for me and hid me out on a cotton farm, in Louisiana. I don't 'member how long I stayed with Dwyer. I know when the sheriff came and told him that he would have to give me up, Dwyer said, "I give five hundred dollars for this nigger, and got to have me money back." John Womack was sheriff, then. He took me to the courthouse, and I was sold for a thousand dollars in gold.

Old "Whispering Joe" Taylor cried me off. He was a big man, and they say you could hear him holler five miles. He put me on the courthouse steps and say to me, "Boy, can you count?" I say, "Yes, Sah," and counted, "One, two, three, four, five, six, seven, eight, nine, ten." He say, "That's far enough. Can you tend to a hoss?" I told him I could catch a hoss and saddle and unsaddle him. Then, "Whispering Joe" say to the crowd, "Folks, look what a fine, smart, strong boy. If I was buying niggers, I would give ten dollars a pound for him." Senator Greer, of Marshall, bought me for his boy to play with, and was my master till the niggers was freed.

—ALLEN WILLIAMS

We ain't been in New Orleans very long till Mr. Abram took sick and die, and we is taken to the trader yard to be sold. I reckon I musta been 'bout six or mebbe seven year old, at the time.

Major Long was the one who owned the trader yard where we was

CREDIT SALE OF A CHOICE GANG OF 41

SLAVES!

COMPRISING MECHANICS, LABORERS, ETC.

FOR THE SETTLEMENT OF A CO-PARTNERSHIP OF RAILROAD CONTRACTORS.

BY J. A. BEARD & MAY, J. A. BEARD, AUCT'R.

WILL BE SOLD AT AUCTION, AT BANKS' ARCADE, MAGAZINE STREET,

ON TUESDAY, FEBRUARY 5th, 1856,

AT 12 O'CLOCK,

A VERY VALUABLE GANG OF SLAVES,

Belonging to a co-partnership, and sold to close the same. The said slaves comprise a gang of 41 choice Negroes. On the list will be found a good Blacksmith, one superior Bricklayer, Field Hands, Laborers, one Tanner, one Cooper, and a first rate woman Cook.

Name		Age	Description
LEWIS, a black man, aged		32	good field hand and laborer.
SHELLY,	do	26	do do
PHILIP,	do	30	fair bricklayer.
HENRY,	do	24	fair cooper.
JACOB BATES,	do	22	good field hand and laborer.
BOB STAKELEY	do	35	do do
COLUMBUS,	do	21	do do
MARTIN,	do	25	do do
GEORGE,	do	30	No. 1 blacksmith.
WESTLY, a griff,		24	a fine tanner and bricklayer.
NELSON, a black man,		30	a good field hand and laborer.
DOCK,	do	28	do do
BIG FRED,	do	24	do do
LITTLE SOL,	do	22	do do
ALFRED, a griff,		28	do do
SIMON, a black man,		21	do do
WATT,	do	30	do do
JIM LEAVY,	do	24	do do
JIM ALLEN,	do	26	do do
FRANK GETTYS, a griff,		26	do do
JERRY GETTYS, a black,		23	do do
BILL GETTYS,	do	23	do do
GRANDERSON,	do	24	do do
LITTLE FED,	do	23	do do
FRANK HENRY, a griff,		23	do do
EDMOND,	do	21	do do
ANDERSON, a black man,		24	a No. 1 bricklayer and mason.
BOB SPRIGS, a griff,		25	a good field hand and laborer.
ELIJAH, a black man,		35	do do
JACK,	do	30	do do
REUBEN,	do	28	unsound.
STEPHEN,	do	22	a good field hand and laborer.
YELLOW JERRY, a griff,		28	a good teamster.
BIG SOL, a black man,		26	a good field hand and laborer.
BILL COLLINS,	do	28	do do
JESS,	do	26	do do
JUDGE,	do	30	do do
JERRY CARTER,	do	28	do do

LOUISA, a griff, 38 years, a good Cook and seamstress, and an excellent servant.
ROBERT, 13 years old, defect in one toe.
JASPAR, 24 years old, an extra No. 1 laborer, driver and coachman.
The slaves can be seen four days previous to the day of sale. They are fully guarantied against the vices and maladies prescribed by law, and are all selected slaves.

TERMS OF SALE—One year's credit for approved city accept-
ances or endorsed paper, with interest at 7 per cent. from date, and mortgage on the slaves if required
ACTS OF SALE BEFORE WM. SHANNON, NOTARY PUBLIC, AT THE EXPENSE OF THE PURCHASERS.

After the sale of the above list of Slaves, will be sold Another lot of Ne-
groes, comprising Field Hands, House servants and Mechanics. A full description of the same will be given at the sale. The slaves can be seen two days previous to the sale.

PLATE 27

put, and I guess we was kept there 'bout a week, 'fore my sister Mary was sold away from us.

One morning, our family is all kinda huddled up together in a corner of the yard away from the rest, and 'long comes Major Long, carrying his bullwhip in his hand, with another man. He makes Mary stand up and says to the man with him, "Here's jes' the girl you want for a nurse girl."

Mama begs Major Long not to separate us folks, and hugged Mary and Jane and me to her. The major and the man with him talks a while, and then the major come over to where we are and pulled Mary away from Mama, and he and the man took her off. 'Twan't till after Freedom that we ever saw her again.

Man, man, folks what didn't go through slavery ain't got no idea what it was. I reckon there musta been a hundred colored folks in that trader yard, and the dirt and smell was terrible, terrible. I was jes' a little chap, like I've told you, but I can remember that place like it happened yesterday—husbands sold away from wives, and children taken away from mothers. A trader, them days, didn't think no more of selling a baby or little child away from its mother than taking a little calf away from a cow.

I rec'lec', the night after Mary is sold away from us, the colored folks in the trader yard hold prayer meeting. Mama was very religious—very religious—and if ever a soul went to Heaven, hers did. Seems like Major Long was gone that evening, and Mama and some more of the folks in the yard got together for a praying time. Didn't do no singing, 'cause that would have 'tracted attention, and the major didn't 'low no meetings. But someone saw the folks praying and told him the next morning, and he come out in the yard with a cat-o'-nine-tails and rounds everybody up. Then, he said, "You niggers what was praying last night, step out here."

None come out, though, 'cept Mama, 'cause they was 'fraid they was going to get whipped. Major said to Mama, "Well, you are the only truthful one in the yard, and I won't whip you, 'cause you have been truthful. I'll see if I can keep you and your man and your other children together and not see you separate." Mama jes' fell on her knees and thanked the good Lord right in front of the major, and he never touched her with his whip.

'Twan't but a little while till he comes back and says for us to get our bundles and come with him. We didn't know where we was going, but any place was better'n that trader yard. Jes' to get away from that place was a blessing from the good Lord.

The major kept his word to Mama and sell us to Mr. Dan Sullivan, and he takes us up to Alexandria in a wagon.

—STEPHEN WILLIAMS

The slaves are put in stalls like the pens they use for cattle—a man and his wife with a child on each arm. And there's a curtain, sometimes just a sheet over the front of the stall, so the bidders can't see the "stock" too soon. The overseer's standin' just outside with a big blacksnake whip and a pepperbox pistol in his belt. Across the square a little piece, there's a big platform with steps leadin' to it.

Then, they pulls up the curtain, and the bidders is crowdin' around. Them in back can't see, so the overseer drives the slaves out to the platform, and he tells the ages of the slaves and what they can do. They have white gloves there, and one of the bidders takes a pair of gloves and rubs his fingers over a man's teeth, and he says to the overseer, "You call this buck twenty years old? Why there's cup worms in his teeth. He's forty years old, if he's a day." So they knock this buck down for a thousand dollars. They calls the men "bucks" and the women "wenches."

When the slaves is on the platform—what they calls the "block"—the overseer yells, "Tom or Jason, show the bidders how you walk." Then, the slaves step across the platform, and the biddin' starts.

At these slave auctions, the overseer yells, "Say, you bucks and wenches, get in your hole. Come out here." Then, he makes 'em hop, he makes 'em trot, he makes 'em jump. "How much," he yells, "for this buck? A thousand? Eleven hundred? Twelve hundred dollars?" Then, the bidders makes offers accordin' to size and build.

—JAMES MARTIN

I 'members when they put me on the auction block. They pulled my dress down over my back to my waist, to show I ain't gashed and slashed up. That's to show you ain't a mean nigger.

—LU PERKINS

I had a brother, Jim, who wuz sold ter dress young Missus fer her weddin'. De tree am still standin' whar I set under an' watch 'em sell Jim. I set dar an' I cry an' cry, specially when dey puts de chains on him an' carries him off. An' I ain't neber felt so lonesome in my whole life. I ain't neber hyar from Jim since, an' I wonder now, sometimes, iffen he's still livin'.

—BEN JOHNSON

My mother was sole and took from my father when I was jes' a few months old. I never seed him till I was six. I had to be tole who he was. He saw my mother for de first time in six years in de fiel's where we was a-working. Dey didn't know how to ac' or what to say. Dey seemed kinda let down, lak. You see, he had married ag'in, an' my mother had, too.

—FOSTER WEATHERSBY

Oh, dat wah a te'ble time! All de slaves be in de field, plowin', hoein', singin' in de boilin' sun. Ole Marse, he come t'rough de field wif a man call' de specalater. Dey walk round, jes' lookin', jes' lookin'. All de da'kies know what dis mean. Dey didn' dare look up, jes' wuk right on. Den, de specalater, he see who he want. He talk to Ole Marse; den, dey slaps de han'cuffs on dat slave an' take him away to de cotton country. Oh, dem wah awful times! When de specalater wah ready to go wif de slaves, effen dey wah any what didn' wanta go, he thrash 'em, den tie 'em 'hind de waggin an' mek 'em run till dey fall on de groun'. Den, he thrash 'em till dey say dey go 'thout no trouble. Sometime', some o' dem run 'way an' come back t' de plantation. Den, it wah hahdah on dem den befoah.

When de da'kies went t' dinnah, de ole niggah mammy, she say whar am sich-an'-sich? None o' de othahs wanna tell huh. But when she see dem look down to de groun', she jes' say, "De specalater, de specalater." Den, de teahs roll down huh cheeks, 'cause mebbe it huh son o' husban', an' she know she nebah see 'em agin. Mebbe dey leaves babies t' home, mebbe jes' pappy an' mammy.

—MARJORIE JONES

'Bout de middle of de evenin', up rid my young marster on his hoss, an' up driv' two strange white mens in a buggy. Dey hitch deir hosses an' come in de house, which skeered me. Den, one o' de strangers said, "Git yo' clothers, Mary. We has bought yo' from Mr. Shorter." I c'menced cryin' an' beggin' Mr. Shorter not to let 'em take me away. But he said, "Yes, Mary, I has sole yer, an' yer must go wid 'em."

Den, dose strange mens, whose names I ain't never knowed, tuk me an' put me in de buggy an' driv' off wid me, me hollerin' at de top o' my voice an' callin' my ma. Den, dem speculataws begin to sing loud, jes' to drown out my hollerin'.

Us passed de very fiel' whar Paw an' all my folks wuz wukkin', an' I calt out as loud as I could an' as long as I could see 'em, "Good-bye, Ma! Good-bye, Ma!" But she never heard me. Naw sah, dem white mens wuz singin' so loud, Ma couldn' hear me. An' she couldn' see me, 'cause dey had me pushed down out o' sight on de flo' o' de buggy.

I ain't never seed nor heard tell o' my ma an' paw, an' brothers, an' sisters, from dat day to dis.

—MARY FERGUSON

I wuz too little to have any sense. When dat man bought me—dat Mr. Henry—he put me up in de buggy to take me off. I kin see it all right now, and I say to Mama and Papa, "Good-bye, I'll be back in de mawnin'." And dey feel sorry fer me and say, "She don' know what happenin'."

—JANIE SATTERWHITE

293

After I was sold, they let me go visit my mother once a year, on Sunday morning, and took me back at night.

—PIERCE HARPER

I was raised right here in Tennessee till I was eleven year old; then Major Ellison bought me and carried me to Mississippi. I didn't want to go. They 'zamine you just like they do a horse: they look at your teeth, and pull your eyelids back and look at your eyes, and feel you just like you was a horse. Major Ellison 'zamined me and said, "Where's your mother?" And I said, "I don't know where my mammy is." He said, "Would you know your mammy if you saw her?" And I said, "Yes, Sir, I would know her." They had done sold her, then. He said, "Do you want us to buy you?" And I said, "No, I don't want you to buy me. I want to stay here." He said, "We'll be nice to you and give you plenty to eat." I said, "No, you won't have much to eat. What do you have to eat?" And he said, "Lots of peas and cotton seed and things like that." But I said, "No, I'd rather stay here, because I get plenty of pot-licker and bread and buttermilk, and I don't want to go; I get plenty."

I was staying with some half-strainers,* and I didn't know that that wasn't lots to eat. He said, "Well, I have married your mistress, and she wants me to buy you." But I still said, "I don't want to go." They had done sold my mother to Mr. Armstrong, then. So he kept talking to me, and he said, "Don't you want to see your sister?" I said, "Yes, but I don't want to go there to see her." They had sold her to Mississippi before that, and I knowed she was there, but I didn't want to go.

I went on back home, and the next day the old white women whipped me, and I said to myself, "I wish that old white man had bought me." I didn't know he had bought me anyhow, but soon they took my cotton dresses and put 'em in a box, and they combed my hair, and I heard them tell me that Major Ellison had done come after me, and he was in a buggy. I wanted to ride in the buggy, but I didn't want to go with him. So, when I saw him, I had a bucket of water on my head, and I set it on the shelf and ran just as fast as I could for the

* Young slaves who were required to do only half a normal day's work.

294

woods. They caught me, and Aunt Bet said, "Honey, don't do that. Major Ellison done bought you, and you must go with him."

She tied my clothes up in a bundle, and he had me sitting up in the buggy with him, and we started to his house, here. I had to get down to open the gate, and when I got back up, I got behind in the little seat for servants. He told me to come back and get inside, but I said I could ride behind up to the house; and he let me stay there, but he kept watching me. He was scared I would run away, because I had done run away that morning, but I wasn't going to run away then, because I wouldn't know which way to go, after I got that far away.

When we got to the house, my mistress came out with a baby in her arms and said, "Well, here's my little nigger. Shake hands with me." Then, Major Ellison come up and said, "Speak to your young mistress." And I said, "Where she at?" He said, "Right there," and pointed to the baby in my mistress' arms. I said, "No, I don't see no young mistress; that's a baby."

—ANONYMOUS

One day, Marster Young comes to buy we-uns. We-uns don't know a thing 'bout it till he comes. Marster Atkinson calls all us to de yard, an' Marster Young looks we-uns over lak 'twas mules him was gwine to buy. He am mo' pa'ticular 'bout Mammy. He looks on her fo' marks, feels her muscles to see if dey am hard, an' looks all over her. Den, dey dickers back an' fo'th. Atkinson says, "Ise take a thousand dollars fo' de two," meanin' me, too.

"Ise gives you seven hundred," says Marster Young.

"No, Sar! Dey's worth fifteen hundred," Marster Atkinson says.

"M'ybe so, if 'twarn't fo' de Wah, but dey's m'ybe worth nothin' next yeah," Marster Young told him.

"Dat's why Ise offer dem fo' a thousand. Dat am five hundred less dan dey's worth. You's takin' dem to Texas, whar dey's sho' to have slaves," de marster comes back at him.

"Ise gives you nine hundred, an' not a cent mo'," says Marster Young.

"Look at dat boy—wide shoulders, big muscles—when he am eighteen yeahs old, he will be worth a thousand dollars. An' de womens am strong as de ox. Ise can't 'cept nine hundred. If 'twarn't fo' de Wah, Ise not sell at any price," de marster says.

"Well, 'tain't no chance fo' a trade, so Ise gwine," says Marster Young. Gosh, Mammy an' my hearts stop beatin', we-uns am so dis'pointed. Den de marster says, "Tell you what Ise do. Ise splits de diff'nce."

" 'Tis a trade," says Marster Young, an' we-uns goes wid him, right den. Dat am in 1861, an' in de fall of de yeah. We-uns starts fo' Texas a few days after we-uns am bought.

—LOUIS YOUNG

More slaves was gettin' born dan dies. Old Moster would see to dat, himself. He breeds de niggers as quick as he can—like cattle—'cause dat means money for him. He chooses de wife for every man on de place. No one had no say as to who he was goin' to get for a wife. All de weddin' ceremony we had was with Moster's finger pointin' out who was whose wife. If a woman weren't a good breeder, she had to do work with de men. But Moster tried to get rid of a woman who didn't have chillun. He would sell her and tell de man who bought her dat she was all right to own.

But de nigger husbands weren't de only ones dat keeps up havin' chillun. De mosters and de drivers takes all de nigger girls dey want. One slave had four chillun right after de other, with a white moster. Deir chillun was brown, but one of 'em was white as you is. Just de same, dey was all slaves, and de nigger dat had chillun with de white men didn't get treated no better. She got no more away from work dan de rest of 'em.

—JAMES GREEN

Sometime', nigger folks git so mixed up about who kin to who, they marry their own sister or brother. Sometime', when a nigger marry his sister, they find out this way. One night, they gits to talking. She say, "One time, my brother had a fight and he git a awful scar over his left ear. It long and slick, and no hair grow there." He say, "See this scar over my left ear? It long and slick, and no sign of a

296

hair." Then, she say, "Lawd God, help us po' niggers. You is my brother." It happen like that. Many a time I see it, and that the gospel truth.

—RICHARD CARRUTHERS

One boy was traded off from his mother when he was young, an' after he was grown, he was sold back to de same marster an' married to his own mother.

—WESLEY BURRELL

My mother's mistress had three boys—one twenty-one, one nineteen, and one seventeen. One day, Old Mistress had gone away to spend the day. Mother always worked in the house; she didn't work on the farm, in Missouri. While she was alone, the boys came in and threw her down on the floor and tied her down so she couldn't struggle, and one after the other used her as long as they wanted, for the whole afternoon. Mother was sick when her mistress came home. When Old Mistress wanted to know what was the matter with her, she told her what the boys had done. She whipped them, and that's the way I came to be here.

—MARY PETERS

I ain't sayin' nothin' 'bout my white folkses, but sometimes I does wonder why I's red-headed, when my pappy an' mammy wuz black as tar. Maybe I is part white, but I ain't sayin' nothin' 'bout my white folkses, as I done tole yo'.

—TEMPE PITTS

You have no idea de worry and de pain a mulatto have to carry all his eighty-four years. Forced to 'sociate wid one side, proud to be related to de other side. Neither side lak de color of your skin.

I jine' de Methodist church here, and 'tend often as I can, and as I

hear my preacher preach dat dere will be no sex in Hebben, I hopes
and prays dat dere'll be no sich thing as a color line, in Hebben.

—CHARLIE ROBINSON

My uncle, Romaine Vidrine, was a lan'holder and a slaveholder.
Dey was a number of Negroes in Lou'siana what owned slaves.
Romaine, he have 'bout thirty-eight slaves to wuk de big plantation.
Dey was a big diff'rence mek between de slave niggers and de owner
niggers. Dey was as much diff'rence between dem as between de
white folks and de cullud folks. My uncle, he wouldn' 'low de slave
niggers to eat at de same table wid him or wid any of de freebo'n
niggers.

Folks uster come down from de No'th, and dey come roun' and
mistook de slave for de owner or de owner for de slave, an' dat was
lookin' odd. My uncle was sich a purty bright man. He muster been a
quadroon. He have long sideburns and wo' a long-tailed coat, all de
time. He was very dignified. He was good to all de slaves on de place,
but he mean for dem to wuk when he say wuk. He ain' never 'low
none of dem to be famil'ar wid him. He would allus say dat de darkes'
one dem darkies was de meanes' one what he have on de place.

—SYLVESTER WICKLIFFE

Then, one day, along comes a Friday. Friday is my unlucky star day,
and it is my lucky star day, too. I was playin' around de house, and
Mr. Williams comes up and says:

"Delia, will you let Jim walk down the street with me?"

"All right, Master," says my mother, "and Jim, you be a good boy."

Dat was de last time I ever heard my mother speak, or ever see her.
We walks down where de houses grows close together, and pretty
soon we comes to de slave market. I ain't never seed one before and
didn't know what it was. Mr. Williams says to me to get up on de
block. I gets up, like I was told. As soon as I stood straight, I got a
funny feelin'. I knows somehow what was happenin'. But I just stood
there. In a few minutes, they told me to get down, and turned me
over to a man named John Pinchback.

Pinchback was my new master. He had Saint Vitus dance. It seems he likes to make niggers suffer to make up for his own squirmin' and twistin'. He was de biggest devil on earth.

We starts to leave right away for Texas. My master lives there on a ranch, in Columbus. I was put to work when we got there, without eating. I was told to carry de water for de stock.

Dat night, I makes up my mind to run away. But de next day, they drives me and some other new slaves over to look at de dogs. De dogs lived in a fine house with a fence around it. Den, they chooses me to train de dogs with. I was told I had to play de part of a runnin'-away slave. Before I start, they tells me to run any direction I want, and after I had run five miles, to climb up a tree. I didn't know what it meant, but one of the nigger drivers tells me kind of nice, to climb up as high in de tree as I could, if I didn't want my body to be tore off my legs. So I runs a good five miles and climbs up in a tree where the branches was gettin' small.

I sits there a long time. Den, I sees de dogs comin'. They had their heads down, not lookin' where they was runnin'. When they gets under my tree, they stops and runs around. Den, they looks up and sees me and starts to bark. After dat, I never got thinkin' of runnin' away, and I don't believe no slave ever escaped from Texas, in spite of all de stories de niggers tells.

—JAMES GREEN

I 'member once when I tole 'bout seein' a nigger runnin' away, boss got his hymn book, set down, put me 'cross his knees, an' as he'd sing de hymns, he'd whup me to de tune of 'em. Believe me, when he got through, I didn' set down for a week, an' I ain' never seed no more niggers runnin' away, neither!

—ANDERSON WILLIAMS

They'd send for a man that had hounds to track you, if you run away. They'd run you and bay you, and a white man would ride up there and say, "If you hit one of them hounds, I'll blow your brains out." He'd say "your damn brains." Them hounds would worry you and bite you and have you bloody as a beef, but you dassen't to hit one of them. They would tell you to stand still and put your hands over your privates. I don't guess they'd have killed you, but you believed they would. They wouldn't try to keep the hounds off of you; they would set them on you to see them bite you. Five or six or seven hounds bitin' you on every side, and a man settin' on a horse holding a doubled shotgun on you.

—HENRY WALDON

My mother was smart and apt, and Old Mis' took her for a house servant. One day, she got mad about something what happened at the big house, so she runned off. When she couldn't be found, they hunted her with dogs. Them dogs went right straight to the ditch where my mother was hid, and before the men could get to them, they had torn most of her clothes off her and had bitten her all over. When they brought her in, she was a sight to see—all covered with blood and dirt. Old Mis' flew into a rage, and she told those men not to never again hunt nobody on her place with dogs.

—EVIE HERRIN

De fiel' hands, dey sho' had a time of it wid dat man Duncan. He was de overseer man out on de plantation, an' he hev' dem poor niggers to where dey don't know iffen dey was gwine in circles or what dey was doin'. One day, I was out in de quarters when he brung back old Joe from runnin' away. Old Joe was always a-runnin' away, an' dat man, Duncan, an' his dawgs always brung him back in. Dis day I's speakin' of, Duncan put his han' on old Joe's shoulder an' look him sorrowful in de eye. "Joe," he say, "I is sho' pow'ful tired o' huntin' for you. I spec's I's gwine have to git de marster to sell you somewheres else. 'Cause if you gits sole to some other marster, he might git to whippin' you all over de groun', if he cotch you runnin' away lak dis. I's sho' sad for you, if you gits sole away. We miss you lots roun' dis nice plantation." After dat, old Joe stay close in, an' dey warn't no mo' trouble out o' him.

—GABE EMMANUEL

My master wuz good to us sometimes, and sometimes he wuz mean to us. He didn't whip us much. He started to sell me once, but I cried and my mother cried, and I didn't want to be took away from my mother, so he decided not to sell me. He'd spoil us and then beat us. My father would run off and hide in the swamps, and my master would hire a man what had bloodhounds, and dey would find my father, maybe hid up in a tree, in de moss on de tree. My master would tell my father to come down or he would shoot him out. My father would say, "Go ahead and shoot. You be de loser." My master would coax him, and say he wouldn' whip him.

Finally, my father would come down, and de man wid de dogs, he would go to whip my father, and my master would say, "Don' you whip my nigger. I don' 'low nobody to whip my niggers. If dey do, I will whip dem." If de dogs ac' like dey wuz goin' to jump on my father, my master would tell de man wid de dogs, "Don' you let your damn dogs hurt my nigger, or I'll kill your dogs." Ole houn's would go, "Owoo, ow, ow."

—RICHARD JOHNSON

Ho, ho! Lawsy, I is recallin' one time when de big old houn' dog what fin' de runaway niggers done die wid fits. The overseer, he say us was gwine hol' de fun'ral rites over dat dog, an' us niggers might bes' be powerful sad, when us come to dat fun'ral.

An' was dem niggers sad over de pitiful death o' dat po' old dog what had chased 'em all over de country? Dey all stan' roun' a-weepin' an' a-mournin', an' ever' now an' den dey'd put water on dey eyes an' play lak dey was a-weepin' bitter, bitter tears.

"Po' old dog, she done died down dead an' can't cotch us no more. Po', po' old dog. Amen! Amen! De Lawd have mercy!"

—GABE EMMANUEL

When the white folks would die, the slaves would all stand around and 'tend like they was crying, but after they would get outside, they would say, "They going on to hell like a damn barrel full of nails."

I remember once when one of the white folks died, old Uncle

301

Albert keeled over on the floor and was just a-crying, but when he saw nobody was looking, he was just dying a-laughing.

— ANONYMOUS

I met many runaway slaves. Some was trying to get north and fight for de freeing of they people. Others was jes' runnin' 'way 'cause dey could. Many of dem didn't had no idea where dey was goin', and told of havin' good marsters. But, one and all, dey had a good strong notion to see what it was like to own your own body.

— EDWARD LYCURGAS

Narratives

———⫸⫷———

JOHN CRAWFORD

LULU WILSON

WILLIAM MOORE

JOHN CRAWFORD

I WAS born in the days of the double-j'inted folks down on Grandpappy Jake Crawford's plantation in Mississippi. I come up in his backyard and I served him past eighteen years. And I tell some of these folks who are tighter across the breast than a baked field lark that I was a white folks' nigger of old-time slavery days that served them and served them faithful, and my old master Grandpappy Jake left his dying word with me and the whitefolks that I was to be keered for till I die. Don't mean nothing to them, 'cause they don't know the things I know and they didn't come up in old Grandpappy's yard like I did.

Grandpappy Jake and my pappy and his pappy was born and bred in old Virginia state, in Charlotte County. They knowed how to live and how to behave like gentlemens, and no niggerin' 'bout it. When Grandpappy Jake Crawford, my master, come to Mississippi he bought the land, so my pappy tell me, at fourteen cents a acre, and he bought it by the miles. He was the richest man I ever heared tell of. He was the bestest man, too, that ever put a shoe on.

My pappy was named Henry Crawford for Grandpappy Jake Crawford's pappy. My pappy and Grandpappy Jake used to say we is all Crawfords and we got to stick together, and they is always been fools 'bout each other.

My mammy's name was Jane, and it looks lak she and Old Mistus—her name Mis' Christina—just run a race to see how many babies they going have. They have them like shelling peas out a pod. Seems like they was plumb scared they wasn't going have no company in they old age. My mammy brought fifteen chilluns.

Old Mistus mighty fine, portly looking woman, but she was a

305

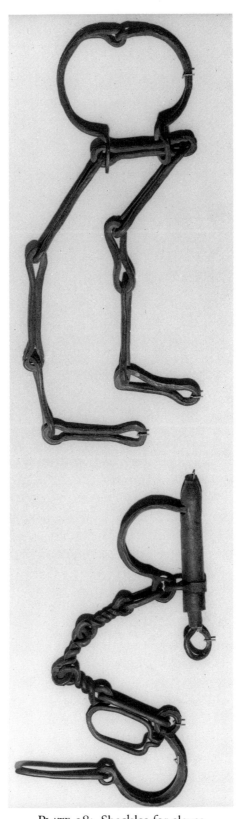

PLATE 28: Shackles for slaves.

mighty sperrited woman. I ain't saying she wasn't a good woman, but she don't love her little niggers like Grandpappy Jake, and the niggers don't love her like they do Grandpappy. I is heared the niggers muttering against her. But 'course they never backtalk her or loudtalk her where she hear them. I seen her once cut a young buck across the face with her riding whip that laid the skin back, 'cause he girthed her horse too tight. She always put store by her horse and she layed it on the niggers if they don't take keer of him.

Now Grandpappy Jake set all the time on his porch, maybe in the front, maybe in the back, with his rifle, and a-readin' out of a book. Many-a-time I seen white men come riding up and throw they reins over the hitching post and ask him could he use a overlooker [overseer]. Grandpappy always say, "Traveler, I is the overlooker on my lands. I can take keer of my niggers. Nobody bosses them or whups them but me, and I ain't having nobody knock my niggers round. I wouldn't give four bits a month for a overlooker. If I tell a nigger to do something once and he don't do it, then I whups him and then he know better next time. I feels right pleasant to bed you and vittleize you here for a resting spell, but if you is looking to be a overlooker you is on the wrong place."

When I was a little bitty boy I 'members that Grandpappy used to call all the little niggers up round him on the porch and show us how to make shuck dolls and tell us to feel in his pockets for stick candy, rock candy, and marbles. He used to rub his hand over our head and say, "Grandpappy wouldn't take nothing for his little burr-head niggers."

They jest ain't no tellin' how much land Grandpappy had. But he worked twenty-seven yoke of oxes, and mules and horses besides. Enduring the Civil War he sent his mules to work on the government breastworks. He had fifty-two hundred beehives, nine hundred head of sheeps, three hundred head of hogs, and lots of cows. He said he wanted 'nuf milk on his place that if he want to swim in it he could.

He had nine hundred slaves and more sometimes. They went to breakfast at sunup and then to the fields till 'leven thirty, when they come back to the house at the ringing of a bell for dinner, and then back to the fields at one o'clock and work till 'bout five. I always remember seeing the slaves come trooping up to the house for dinner in sech a long line. And it 'pears to me plumb unreasonable for one man to own that many people and keep what they make and sell them off or keep them just as he notions.

My pappy told me that when he was a young man Grandpappy sold him off to some folks who took him off to a place called Denver. He said he slipped away from them and was three years getting back to old Grandpappy. He said he walked it barefoot for hundreds of miles, and when he come home old Grandpappy cried and swore a swear that he won't sell no more niggers that don't want to go. He said Grandpappy counted out eighteen hundred dollars to send the folks, to buy him back.

Grandpappy was mighty good to the niggers. He told them plenty times, "I ain't a man that cares for wealth. Everything I got you niggers made it out'n you' sweat. And I want you to take time to set and enjoy it. I got more things that I want to do than set and count money." He never worked us in bad weather or in the cold, and when it was hot we didn't work in the middle of the day.

There is only one thing I could say agin' Grandpappy, and I hates to say that, but he taught me hisself, "Don't tell a lie for credit when you can tell the truth for cash." Grandpappy don't want the niggers to have learnin' out of books and don't want them to pray. He is scared they will pray for freedom, and he b'lieves they will git it, if they pray. Better not let Grandpappy ketch you prayin'. He reads us out'n the Bible every morning and night. He was a powerful godly man. Sometimes we little niggers plumb thought he *was* God. Leastways, Old Master was so purty—tall, with shiny black eyes and a face like a woman's face—that we thought God look jest like Grandpappy.

But at night in our little log cabin in the quarters, Mammy bring the wash pot out of the yard and set it in the middle of the floor and she laugh and cry and sing a little, then she puts her head down in the pot clear to her shoulders and mumbles. We chilluns say, "What you sayin', Mammy?" She say, "Shh, I'm prayin'." We say, "What you prayin' 'bout?" She say, "I'm prayin' for the freedom, but if Grandpappy hear you tell it he will birchbark you." Strangest thing is that, while Mammy was in her spell of prayin', a little boy was eight year old up North, who grew up and set the niggers free.

But Pappy say to Mammy, "I'm right happy and my face is glad when I gets up in the morning and know I got Grandpappy to keer for me. I love Grandpappy 'cause he sets sech store by me."

Now, Grandpappy's chilluns was angel chilluns, and his grand-chilluns was sweet as they could be. Mr. Bill was the one that thought so much of me. He was a real gentleman, and when he was a young man they called him Mr. Tipsy Bill 'cause he looked too long down the whiskey glass. But the chilluns and grandchilluns of Grandpappy went to school in a carriage all dressed fine. Mammy always have to button Mis' Fannie, Mis' Gladyce, and Mis' Phelia's shoes for them. She said it outdone her, 'cause her chilluns had to go barefoot and crack they heels open and have the ground itch in they feet. Grandpappy wore a special-made boot, and he was always glad when he boys say they want boots like his'n, so he can measure off they feet, making 'lowances for growing, and get the boots in New Orleans, when he went down the river.

Well, all the Crawford chilluns is book smart, and they want to teach the little niggers how to say they letters out of a book. They set in the pine grove and spell out the letters to us.

One day Old Mistus saw us with a book and she come outside with stick candy held out in her hand, and she say, "I give you all of this you want if you tell me where you got the book and learned the letters." I spoke up smart as you please and told her. They was 'bout six of us little niggers, and she took us in the house and she held our heads between her legs and she whipped our back ends with a big wooden paddle. Then she stuck us up the chimney where it was dark and kept us there forty minutes. We was scared fit to die. When she took us out, we didn't have as much sense as a wild hog.

That's the only time Old Mistus whup me. Grandpappy whup me more than once, but he jest pick up little piece of shuck or sech-like and whup us. Then he always shuck hands with us and tell us, "Course, I am not your father, but I got to be your father to see that you get chastising, or you will grow up wild as a steer and not fit for killin'." He was known in them parts for kind advisements.

We went to doing light work when we was seven or eight years old—picking up brush and chunks—but we didn't work long and had plenty playtime.

There is so many things I can't get over, and things I can't forget. One thing is the kitchen in Grandpappy's house. It was bigger'n a barn. There was four eight-foot fireplaces with ovens and four pot racks in each one. There was three womens and one man to do the cooking. There was a big hall with great long tables in it where the slaves et. We et with tin plates and cups, and wooden spoons, knives, and forks that the niggers made.

There was more than a-plenty to eat and folks et three times as much then as they do now. Everything was raised on the place, and the only thing folks have now that we didn't have then is ice cream. Plenty of corn was grown and ground for bread in Grandpappy's grist mill. We et greens, hominy, boiled beef, punkins, taters, whipper-will peas, cabbage, boiled peanuts, pork, rabbit, chicken, milk, drip cheese, cakes, custards, molasses, and honey in the comb. We drank meal bran and peanut coffee and cottonseed tea. There wan't no Sunday vittles; every day was Sunday the way we et. But on Christmas we had biscuits.

Grandpappy Jake had biscuits at his table every morning, but flour cost sixty-eight dollars a barrel in New Orleans, and Old Mistus always say, "Don't know where I'm going get any more flour when this give out." But Grandpappy say, "I ain't going cheat my table none." He had so much money he didn't have to. In his counting room he had stacks of gold money that he let the grandbabies play with, and he had little hogsheads holding dollars in silver, and little dimes that they called five-cent pieces. When the Civil War come, my real grandpappy was one that went with Grandpappy Jake and measured three-quarters of a mile from the house to bury the gold and silver. I seen after the War, when he had Confederate money bailed like cotton in the counting room.

You couldn't hardly move round that place 'thout stepping on a little nigger, and if Grandpappy see you hanging in the door, he call you in an' give you a cup of coffee. He drank Arbuckle coffee he got in New Orleans, and he put white sugar in it. Most of the time niggers had brown sugar. He say, "Little niggers need a little sweetnin'; coffee plum good for black and white."

There was a big smokehouse full of hams and sausage and middlin' meat and dried beef. Grandpappy and the boys and some of the niggers would go on big hunting trips and fishing trips. They used to come back with wagons loaded with deer and wild hogs and turkeys and possums and coons, for the table. I have seen them in the kitchen puttin' in four or six big middlin's from hogs, for the niggers. The pots in the kitchen held forty gallons.

Old Grandpappy used to send mens and the dogs to hunt panthers. They liked to run at night, and you could hear the dogs a-bayin' up and down the creeks.

Billy Buck was a old nigger man didn't do nothing but keep Grandpappy's still. They made whiskey out of corn and made whiskey out of peaches. Then they made apple cider and grape wine and dandelion wine and alder [elderberry] wine. The alder was for the niggers. At the parties and at Christmas, the niggers got plenty of whiskey.

The Christmas I was fourteen, I got drunk. Grandpappy caught my head in his arm and drubbed my head a-laughin' fit to kill, and said, "Little nigger, you is drunker than a coot; but a little whiskey is good for white and black."

There was big doings at Christmas. Christmas morning there was a big tree in Grandpappy's best parlor, and he would set in the parlor and wait while all the niggers try to slip in and get him to say, "Christmas gift." Each one try to say it first, before Grandpappy say it. At Christmas, everybody gets new clothes and tobacco and some special thing. The chilluns get toys and oranges and candy. Then one of Grandpappy's girls play on the organ and one on the harp and everybody sings "Hark a Savior is Born." Then we have breakfast with fried chicken and biscuit and real coffee. For dinner we always have roasted wild turkeys and walnut and fruitcake. We drank and ate so much it takes us a day or two to get over it.

If we get sick though, old Grandpappy liked to come and measure out the medicine. He give us copperas, blue mass, ipecac, rhubarb, and walnut tea. Every spring he doses the little niggers with Jerusalem oak and sorghum syrup for worms. Niggers would sho' git wormy.

When I think of what the 'calcitrant niggers did and what Grandpappy did, I feel like laughin' all over agin. There was some niggers wouldn't work, and they went off in the swamplands, down in the bottoms on the place, and they would sleep in the bresh all day, and at night slip up to the potato kiln, where they baked the potatoes in ashes, and take out potatoes and go to the smokehouse and get the meat, and they cook and eat in the swamps. Grandpappy finally ketched them with the dogs, and brought them up to the house, and then sent for a smithy. He had thought up a way to keep them where they b'longed. He had a iron band put round they leg and one round they waist, and a iron pole that went straight up in the air fastened on the side of they leg through the iron bands. And five feet over they heads he hung a brass bell on the top where they can't reach it. Then he turned them loose and told them, "Don't you let me hear that bell leavin' this place, or God have mercy on your black hides."

Well, those niggers would get down in the bottom land, where the mud was, and lay down and scoot 'long in the mud till they fill the bell up with mud. Then they lay in the sun or by a fire, till it bakes the mud and the clapper don't move, and then they slips off and gets somebody to cut it loose. Grandpappy got outdone buying bells.

Those niggers told me a sure way to keep the dogs from ketching you. They said if you put red pepper and turpentine in your shoes they can't run you, 'cause they can't scent you. Another way was, when you go through a fence, if you take the fence pole up and turn it upside down and stick the top in the posthole, then the dogs will stop and bay at the pole. But they said the bestes' way was to go straight to a young hickory sapling, take a knife and split it up and down, and then tie the top together and crawl through the slip, and no dog can follow you then.

Grandpappy always ketch them someway or tother. I was with him once hunting the niggers, and we was riding horseback, and we heard the dogs baying down in the brakes. When we got there, they was four niggers in the tallest, slimmest pines. I don't see how they got there. Grandpappy said them just be half ape-monkeys. Said he knew he had some half-devil niggers, but didn't know they was half ape-monkeys.

One time we was passing a place and we seen some niggers they had put in yokes. It was plumb bad. They lifted the second rail on the fence and sot it down over the neck of the nigger and held it betwixt the bottom rail and the second rail. The white men had a leather strap one inch thick, two inches wide, and 'bout a yard long, with a wooden handle. They whupped the niggers over the head and they called it the "red heifer." Heared tell that they break some of them's necks.

Seems like niggers had hard time on lots of farms, but at Grandpappy's we never wanted for work and something to eat and a place to sleep, and we know we git buried right.

In the cabins we had good lowering mattresses, and Mammy and Pappy had a bed. We made the ticking out of good strong lowering cloth that they wove in the weaving house, and we fill it up with moss and it slep' right well. And we have plenty of fire in the fireplace with good lighter [pine] knots to make a big light and fire.

We had to light fires from a big flint rock what look like a Indian arrowhead. We hold a piece of cotton to ketch the spark when you knock the rocks together downways.

Master sent off to buy candles. But one day there was a man named Dr. Goodloe came a-visiting and said it was foolishment, and he showed how to make the candles at home. They got some brass molds and they melt out the mutton and beef suet, and they put a twisted thread in the mold with a loop tied in the end, and they pour the hot suet in the mold over the thread. Then they take and run a stick through the loops in the thread all in a line of molds, and when it sets they just lift the stick and the candles come out. They used to make hundreds of them at one setting. They used to make fat ones big as your arm. Then they put them in the lamps a-hanging down from the ceilings in the big house and light it up big as day. In the cabins, we put fried meat grease in a tin cup and hang a wicker of wool over the side and light it up, and it give a pretty fair light.

Grandpappy had 'leven parlors and bedrooms, 'cause he had so many folks to bed down, and the company come in wagons and carriage loads. He put powerful store by the house. He had big tall beds laced together with ropes, with posts that went nearly to the ceiling, and satin-lined teasters. The ticking was filled with feathers, and you could nearly smother to death in them feather beds; they just fill up round the folks. All the furniture in the house was made out'n wood.

I 'members when they got a pianny [piano]. Didn't look like the ones they got now. Look more like a table. All the niggers come up to the house to see it, and folks came in admiring it. Some of the niggers say the organ was a-plenty good for them.

Windows was different in them days, too. They all got wooden side shetters on the outside, so they can close them up tight.

Used to have parties in the big house with dancing and music, and the womens and the mens dressing fine, and the niggers playing fiddles for them. I told Grandpappy I want to fiddle and he gets me a fiddle, and I used to be one of the finest fiddlers round in them parts.

The niggers have the patting parties on Saturday nights. They call them patting parties 'cause the ones that don't dance set round and pat they hands. We danced the reels, and twenty-five or thirty niggers was playin' the fiddles. One of the best songs went like this:

> Chicken crow at midnight,
> It's almost day.
> Go and get your Georgia Lover,
> 'Cause it's almost day.
> Go and get your Georgia Lover,
> We danced the night away.

And 'nuther one was:

> Two barrels pickled pork,
> Two barrels meal,
> Going tell my Jesus
> Got religion in my heel.

Now, sometimes, some of the niggers think you ought not dance. We had a nigger preacher named "Hi Bill" Phil Anderson, what Grandpappy bought off'n a man come by with a drove of slaves. He was a shoutin' Baptist preacher what talked out of the Bible. He held the prayer meetings in the bresh arbor and the niggers set there on Sundays from 'leven in the morning till past dark at night. My mammy got converted to the song:

> Way down yonder by myself,
> Couldn't hear nobody pray.

Way down yonder in the valley,
Couldn't hear nobody pray.
Had to pray myself,
Jest had to pray myself.

Then:

Father I stretch my hand to thee,
No other help I know.

Most pretty song was:

I am going to preach my gospel,
Said the Lord,
Said the Lord.
Going to preach my gospel,
And lead my great commission on.
Don't be damned by wronging,
And let my Gospel go on,
And I'm going to be with my father,
In that holy land.

There was lots of jest make-up songs. Niggers like to sing and make up songs. In the fields, when they pick cotton, a bunch a-going one side lift up they head and roll out, "uhm-m-m-m-m, yo-o-o-o," and then those on tuther side pick it up and go the same way and jest put some make-up words to it.

I seen some niggers chained in a line that was a-driftin' to the west. They swing they ankle chains and it clinks to make music, and they champs a song, "Yo-o-o-o--o, Yo-ho-ho-ho-ho--, Swing 'long, my bullies, swing, swin-n-ng 'long, my bullies." They didn't have no hair on they heads.

One morning 'fore sunup, when my mammy is on the way to the big house, she hears a horse a-running. She goes back and gets my pappy and he comes and helps the man off his horse, and he is a nigger offen Grandpappy's olderest daughter's place, over in 'nuther county. They wakes Grandpappy and Old Mistus up and tells her the little gal baby done died from a choking spasm she got, and they wants them to come to the funeral. Grandpappy and Old Mistus cry like they done broke they heart, but Grandpappy says, "Wake everybody on this place up," and he has his boy Joe blow the horn. All the niggers come to the house. He tells them no work on the place, and he is raging mad at Young Mistus' husband, 'cause he 'lows to bury the little gal over there. Grandpappy says, "Hitch up the carriage and the biggest wagon; we going go fetch the little baby home. None of my blood going to be stored away in strange country, all by itself." So they starts off a-running the horses, and my pappy goes a-driving the coffin wagon.

They comes back in mournful procession, and folks from that county come. All the womens cry and the mens jest hold they hats in they hands. And they puts the little gal baby in a high green pretty piece of ground and plants the place round with cape jessamine [jasmine]. Pore Grandpappy is a grievin' man and his eyes don't shine no more.

He was always one with a fondering for the little babies. He goes out to the nursing house every day and looks at the little niggers and pokes them in they bellies and fusses if they not fat and full. He heists them up in the air and says, "This is a fine young-un." Sometimes he shout out, "Change they swaddlin's, plenty hippins. Ain't no good for white or black to lay in muck."

Sometimes niggers die, but not much; folks was so much healthier in them days. There was a burying ground down by the creek on a knoll. When they die, Grandpappy tell all the niggers they can have work time off to mourn and go to the funeral. He makes the other niggers go to the family that has the dying and wash up they house and clothes for them so they can wail. They didn't have no coffins in them days; they morticed out a pine log with a food adze and lined it with curzey cloth, and put the dead in that. Then they hauled it down to the burying ground and Grandpappy read out of the Book. He always say, "The Lord giveth and the Lord taketh away. Blessed be the name of the Lord." And, "I know he was good, and the Master up there going to look kind on his chilluns jest like old Grandpappy look kind on you down here; and Grandpappy going jine with him up yonder some day."

When the weather's so bad they can't have much of a burying, he lets the niggers take 'nuther day off, later on in good weather, for mournin'.

One night the bell rings, and all the niggers come up to the place, and Grandpappy stand on the porch and tell them that the Yankees done fire cannon guns on the folks and that Mr. Tom and Mr. Phil and Mr. Tipsey Bill got to go fight the Yankees.

My pappy and my grandpappy say they got to go look after the young masters, and I want to go with Mr. Tipsy Bill, but Grandpappy says I'm just a little nigger. But Mr. Tipsy Bill says he will bring me a Yankee sword. They jined with the Ninth and Tenth Cavalry. I seen them when they rid away. Grandpappy laugh and slap the horses on the rump, and the gals a-laughing and Old Mistus a-laughing and a-crying too. That was in 1861.

Them was the baddest days. "They runs the old coons over the fence and the young ones through the cracks." I spent them four years on my knees in the weaving house. I threw the shickle [shuttle] for Old Mistus to weave. Some of the nigger womens spin, some card, and some weave. I 'members we made a cloth with three stran's cotton and two of wool. Mistus had a fine spinning machine that, every time it spin a hundred and fifty yards of thread, it go double click. We measured cloth by the hanks. A hank and a half was a yard. I got the whirring noise in my ears now from the spinning wheels. The first machinery I ever seen was a sewing machine that Grandpappy brought up the river from New Orleans. It worked by winding a wheel on the side by hand.

Course, they made all our clothes in the weaving house, and the clothes were good. But shoes were miserable. They soaked a beef hide in the creek and got it soft and all the hair come off, and then they make shoes out of that; and we called it the "everlasting leather."

The folks in them parts start coming into the big house a-crying and saying the bushwhackers what was deserters from the army is coming and taking they things and having no mercy on the womens. The bushwhackers was hiding in the hills and swooping down when menfolks was gone. They ain't never bother Grandpappy's place, 'cause he sets all the time with that rifle gun. But he sends word all 'bout them parts for the women and chilluns to come to his house and he will keer for them, and ain't no bushwhacker going bother them 'cause of the rifle gun. That's what they do; the womens come and bring the chilluns and we beds them and feeds they horses.

One night, the mens what ain't at the War come and tell Grandpappy to ride with them to hang the bushwhackers. He goes on his horse with them. Later, me and Mammy is setting in the cook house, and we hears a lot of horses, and Mammy sends me running to tell the womens to get to the loft 'cause mens is coming. I comes back with Mammy. 'Bout twenty-five or thirty bushwhackers come in, and they is the worserest looking mens I ever seen. They tell Mammy get them something to eat. She starts slicing ham, and they say, "Where is the white womens?" She tells them they all gone fur away, and they ain't nobody 'bout. Then a baby cries up in the loft. Mammy puts her apron over her head and say, "I pray to God to die." The bushwhackers stay up there two or three hours, and then they come down and grab something to eat and ride away. They is swinging old muzzleloaders 'bout all the time.

The womens come down and they swear life ain't worth the living in them days. Old Mistus say, "If the mens don't kill them, I will kill them myself." All the womens was mooded to die.

Then the mens come riding home with Grandpappy and they horses is lathered. They come in, and the womens tell them that they ain't seen no mercy. Grandpappy nearly tear his hair out. They go and get on they horses. That day the womens set on the chairs not moving nor talking a word. Old Mistus sets on the doorsteps with a gun crost her knees. That night the mens come home and they say the bushwhackers is buzzard bait; they is hanging up in the air off'n a limb. Grandpappy's horse is blowed and he lay down and never get up.

Lord God there was sorrowin' in them days and in that house. Grandpappy gets mighty enfeeblin', and the sperrit all gone out of Old Mistus.

Well, the time come when Grandpappy call me and 'nuther boy and tell us we got to go in the wagon to Mansfield, Louisiana. Grandpappy goes on the horse. When we got there we find Grandpappy with Pappy and my real grandpappy, and the place is a terrible sight. It was so long ago, but it 'pears to me it's Mr. Tom is dead. Grandpappy done cry till his beard is wet. A few mens is moving around, but the most of the folks ain't moving, 'cause they is lying scattered around dead. Folks is moving around looking at them.

Well, we helps to dig a big trench three-quarters of a mile long, six feet deep, and six feet wide, and we puts the mens in there and kivver them with dirt. But we puts Mr. Tom in the waggin and takes him home. Afore we left, Pappy, Phil, Bill, and me picked up 'nuf lead that when we moulded it into bullets we had 'nuf to last us eight years. I heared guns and shootin' poppin' way off somewheres. Grandpappy tells my pappy and grandpappy to come home to stay. When we got home I runs to the cabin 'cause I say I ain't going to see Old Mistus when she sees Mr. Tom. But I seen her come runnin' out'n the house with her hands throwed to the sky.

Well, pretty soon things sort of settle down, and then the Yankees come. They come down there with fine uniforms and they stay a week, and Grandpappy says, "You ain't 'vinced me none." But one day he calls all the niggers up to the house and he stands on the porch with his best coat on and says, "Abraham Lincoln, a Yankee gentleman, done sent these blue-coated gentlemen down here to tell me that I don't own my niggers no more and that you got to be 'constructed.* You is good mens and womens and I is been a good master, and I ain't going to let you starve and go wandering round 'mongst strange folks. I got uncut land. You got axes. I'm going to send you down in the woods and you going to clear you out a little piece of land for yourself and for your chilluns. But anybody want to work on my land for me and live in they little cabins can have part of what they make." 'Pears like that was in June.

Some of the niggers went in the woods and start clearing land, and they get vittles from Grandpappy. They put up little houses. They put pine poles in the ground, 'bout two foot apart and 'cross from each other in a line, and made a square out of them. And then they started filling these pine poles with long logs and notched the ends together. Shortly after they build they houses was the first time I ever seen any nails. Grandpappy gave the little pieces of land to the niggers that cleared them. Then he made my pappy the overlooker on his place for the niggers who work for him.

Grandpappy Jake got more and more enfeeblin', 'cause he was a

* Reconstructed.

very old man. For a year he lingered round not able to do anything but to set in the sun and grieve. He stayed in his bedroom most of the time, and he talked to my pappy there 'bout the land and the planting.

Then one time he said to my pappy, "Henry, I'm going to get me a new suit and some new boots. Measure me off for them. And don't you never take my boots off'n me till I'm ready for the new ones." Pappy said it was a new black suit that cost seventy-five dollars.

One afternoon Grandpappy sent for Pappy and tells him not to works the niggers the next day and to send word to those in the new-cut ground to come up to the house the next day, 'cause that is the day he is going to die. Well, I helped move his bed out in the great hall, and all day long the niggers came by his bed, and he shuck they hands and give them all kind advisements, and they cry and say, "Please, Grandpappy, don't go 'way and leave us." But he done have some of the mens morticing out his coffin from a big pine. They done cry all the time they worked.

All day the niggers stand in the yard and wait to hear what Grandpappy got to say after he done tell them goodbye. Later, he says to Pappy, "Henry, I got the most confidence in you. Don't know but when all is said and done if you ain't been the best frien' I ever had in this world. 'Cause I love you and you loves me, I done put a burthen on you. Hold this place together. Every nigger gets a piece of land of his own and a little piece of money. Don't let them go wild. See they mind your old mistus. You knows my mind; see things go on jest like I was here. I'm sorrowin' I can't stay with you all the time, but I done hear the call to my other home."

Well, I have never seen such wailing and mourning as when Old Master die that night. My pappy stayed by his side and he come and told the niggers in the yard. They mourned and wailed all night. The womens cry they aprons limp. Some say, "Sweet Jesus, take me where Old Grandpappy gone."

I ain't never forget that Old Grandpappy shuck me by the hand on his dyin' bed and said, "John, mind what Old Grandpappy tell you and walk honestly afore your God. Be faithful to Old Mistus and all the Crawford blood, and I'm going to shake your hand on Judgment Day." Sometimes when I dozes off and I'm hongry and cold, it 'most seems I can see Old Grandpappy standing in the door a-laughing out of his black eyes down on me.

Grandpappy left us all some land, but all of us didn't get land. Least I didn't. But my pappy stayed on the place for 'leven years and made and saved a piece of money.

But short to the time Grandpappy died, some Mexicans come on horses by our place and put up there and talked me into going with them to get rich. They was named Peter Babbo, John Babbo, Felicita Babbo, and Dolly Warren. Pappy don't want me to go, but he give me a good horse and we start off. We go through Louis'ana and Texas. I passes through Hord's Ridge, by Dallas, and there wasn't but thirty-two houses there, but that was seventy-two years ago and I was 'bout twenty year old. I went down into Mexico but I didn't get rich. I wandered round for a while and I never got in any trouble. But plenty times I wished I had one of them passes Grandpappy wrote out for me that said, "This is a Crawford nigger, and anybody that bothers him got to answer to Grandpappy Jake Crawford."

In Nachodoches [Texas], I met a girl, pretty as a chocolate chiny doll. I married with her. I lived with her thirty-seven years and I never called her a fool once. We had six chilluns, all named Crawford names, but three of them died. When my wife died, she left us the little baby gal to raise, and I never married again.

I seen my pappy back in Mississippi once afore he died, after I left, and he had grown so old and gray, and the changing had set in over that country.

I lived in Joplin, Missouri, and I lived other places. I tried to work hard and do right and bring the chilluns up right. But I had the sorrowin' of two wars. Two of my boys were in the world civil war for eighteen months. John Henry was a sojer—he is my youngest boy— and Arthur was a surgeon doctor. He is my fine educated boy, but I can't hardly b'lieve he is a pretty old man hisse'f. He lives in Detroit, Michigan, and he got eight chilluns.

When I went for my pension, the white folks say, "You don't look old," and I say, "Shah, you don't know nothing. I could tell you plenty. I seen plenty. I was born in the days of the double-j'inted folks."

LULU WILSON

COURSE I's born in slavery, ageable as I am. I's a old-time slavery woman, and the way I been through the hackles, I got plenty to say 'bout slavery. Lulu Wilson says she knows they ain't no good in it, and they better not bring it back.

My paw wasn't no slave. He was a freeman, 'cause his mammy was a full-blood Creek Indian. But my maw was born in slavery, down on Wash Hodges' paw's place, and he give her to Wash when he married. That was the only woman slave what he had, and one man slave, a young buck. My maw say she took with my paw and I's born, but a long time passed and didn't no more young-uns come. So they say my paw am too old and wore out for breedin', and they wants her to take with this here young buck. So the Hodges sot the nigger hounds on my paw and run him away from the place, and maw allus say he went to the free states. So she took up with my step-paw, and they must of pleased the white folks what wanted niggers to breed like livestock, 'cause she birthed nineteen chillun.

When I's li'l, I used to play in that big cave they calls Mammoth Cave, and I's so used to that cave it didn't seem like nothin' to me. But I was real li'l then, for soon as they could they put me to spinnin' cloth. I 'members plain, when I was li'l there was talk of war in them parts, and they put me to spinnin', and I heard 'em say it was for the sojers. They marched round in a li'l small drove and practices shootin'.

Now, when I was li'l, they was the hardes' times. They'd nearly beat us to death. They taken me from my mammy, out the li'l house built onto they house, and I had to sleep in a bed by Missus Hodges. I

322

PLATE 29

cried for my maw, but I had to work and wash and iron and clean and milk cows when I was most too li'l to do it.

The Hodges had three chilluns, and the olderes' one they was mean to, 'cause she so thickheaded. She couldn't larn nothin' out a book, but was kinder and more friendly-like than the rest of the lot. Wash Hodges was jes' mean, pore trash, and he was a bad actor and a bad manager. He never could make any money, and he starved it outen the niggers. For years, all I could git was one li'l slice of sowbelly and a puny li'l piece of bread and a tater. I never had 'nuf to stave the hongriness outen my belly.

My maw was cookin' in the house and she was a "clink"—that am the bes' of its kind. She could cuss and she warn't 'fraid. Wash Hodges tried to whop her with a cowhide, and she'd knock him down and bloody him up. Then he'd go down to some his neighbor kin and try to git them to come holp him whop her. But they'd say, "I don't want to go up there and let Chloe Ann beat me up." I heard Wash tell 'is wife they said that.

When my maw was in a tantrum, my step-paw wouldn't partialize with her. But she was a 'ligious woman and 'lieved time was comin' when niggers wouldn't be slaves. She told me to pray for it. She seed a old man what the nigger dogs chased and et the legs near off him. She said she was chased by them bloody hounds, and she jus' picked up a club and laid they skull open. She say they hired her out and sold her twic't but allus brung her back to Wash Hodges.

Now, Missus Hodges studied 'bout meanness more'n Wash done. She was mean to anybody she could lay her hands to, but special mean to me. She beat me and used to tie my hands and make me lay flat on the floor, and she put snuff in my eyes. I ain't lyin' 'fore Gawd when I say I knows that's why I went blind. I did see white folks sometimes what spoke right friendly and kindly to me.

I gits to thinkin' now how Wash Hodges sold off Maw's chillun. He'd sell 'em and have the folks come for 'em when my maw was in the fields. When she'd come back, she'd raise a ruckus. Then, many's the time I seed her plop right down to a-settin' and cry 'bout it. But she 'lowed they warn't nothin' could be done, 'cause it's the slavery law. She said, "O, Lawd, let me see the end of it 'fore I die and I'll quit my cussin' and fightin' and rarin'." My maw say she's part Indian, and that 'count for her ways.

One day they truckled us all down in a covered wagon and started out with the fam'ly and my maw and step-paw and five of us chillun. I know I's past twelve year old. We come a long way and passed through a free state. Some places we druv for miles in the woods 'stead of the big road, and when we come to folks they hid us down in the bed of the wagon. We passed through a li'l place, and my maw say to look, and I seed a man gwine up some steps, totin' a bucket of water. She say, "Lulu, that man's your paw." I ain't never think she's as consid'ble [considerate] of my step-paw as of my paw, and she give me to think as much. My step-paw never did like me, but he was a fool for his own young-uns, 'cause at the end of the wars, when they sot the niggers free, he tramped over half the country, gatherin' up them young-uns they done sold 'way.

We went to a place called Wadefield, in Texas, and settled for some short passin' of time. They was a Baptist church next to our house, and they let us go twic't. I was fancified with the singin' and preachin'. Then we goes on to Chatfield Point, and Wash Hodges built a log house and covered it with weather boarding and built my maw and paw quarters to live in. They turned into raisin' corn and taters and hawgs. I had to work like a dog. I hoed and milked ten cows a day.

Missus told me I had ought to marry. She said if I'd marry she'd togger me up in a white dress and give me a weddin' supper. She made the dress and Wash Hodges married me outen the Bible to a nigger 'longin' to a nephew of his'n. I was 'bout thirteen or fourteen. I know it warn't long after that when Missus Hodges got a doctor to me. The doctor told me less'n I had a baby, old as I was and married, I'd start in on spasms. So it warn't long till I had a baby.

In 'twixt that time, Wash Hodges starts layin' out in the woods and swamps all the time. I heared he was hidin' out from the War and was sposed to go, 'cause he done been a volunteer in the first war and they didn't have no luck in Kentucky.*

*The narrator thinks of battles and campaigns as whole wars.

One night, when we was all asleep, some folks whopped and woke us up. Two sojers come in and they left more outside. They found Wash Hodges and said it was midnight and to git 'em something to eat. They et and some more come in and et. They tied Wash's hands and made me hold a lamp in the door for them to see by. They had some more men in the wagon, with they hands tied. They druv away and, in a minute, I heared the reports of they guns three or four times. Nex' day I heared they was sojers and done shot some conscripts in the bottoms back of our place.

Wash Hodges was gone away four years, and Missus Hodges was meaner'n the Devil, all the time. Seems like she jus' hated us worser than ever. She said blobber-mouth niggers done cause a War.

Well, now, things jus' kind of drifts along for a spell and then Wash Hodges come back, and he said, "Well, now, we done shot the hell out them blue bellies, and that'll larn 'em a lesson to leave us alone."

Then my step-paw seed some Fed'ral sojers. I seed them, too. They drifted by in droves of fifty and a hundred. My step-paw 'lowed as how the Feds done told him they ain't no more slavery, and he tried to p'int it out to Wash Hodges. Wash says they's a new ruling, and it am that growed-up niggers is free, but chillun has to stay with they masters till they's of age.

My maw was in her cabin with a week-old baby, and one night twelve Ku Kluxes done come to the place. They come in by ones and she whopped 'em one at a time.

I don't never recall just like [exactly] the passin' of time. I know I had my little boy young-un and he growed up, but right after he was born I left the Hodges and felt it's a fine, good riddance. My boy died, but he left me a grandson. He growed up and went to 'nother war, and they done somethin' to him and he ain't got but one lung. He ain't peart no more. He's got four chillun and he makes fifty dollars a month. I'm crazy 'bout that boy and he comes to see me, but he can't holp me none in a money way. So I'm grateful to the President* for gittin' me my li'l pension. I done study it out in my mind for three years. And tell him Lulu says if he will see they ain't no more slavery,

*Franklin D. Roosevelt.

326

and if they'll pay folks liveable wages, they'll be less stealin' and slummerin' and goin's on.

I worked so hard. For more'n fifty years I waited as a nurse on sick folks. I been through the hackles if any mortal soul has, but it seems like the President thinks right kindly of me, and I want him to know Lulu Wilson thinks right kindly of him.

WILLIAM MOORE

M Y MAMMY told me that the reason why her and my paw's name was Moore is because afore to the time they b'longed to Marse Tom Waller, they b'longed to Mr. Moore. But Mr. Moore sold them off to Marse Tom Waller.

Marse Tom heared they was going to 'mancipate the slaves in Selma, Alabama, so he got his things and niggers together and come to Limestone County, Texas. My mammy said they come in kivvered wagons and just plain wagons into this country. I don't 'member nothing 'bout it, 'cause maybe I wan't even born then. The first ricollections I got is down in Limestone County.

Marse Tom had a fine, big house painted white and he had a big prairie field in front of his house, and two or three farms and some orchards. He had four, five hunnerd head of sheeps. And I spent most my time in slavery being a shepherd boy. George was a half-idiot boy that was the first shepherd boy, but he couldn't keep no count of the sheeps and he would lose two or three of them. Marse Tom seen beating him done no good, so he started sending Mandy, my sister, to hope [help] him out. But Mandy and George didn't hit if off so good to keep count of the sheeps. So Marse Tom says he wants me to learn to be the shepherd boy. I starts out when I'm little boy and learns fast to keep good count of the sheeps.

My mammy's name was Jane and my paw's name was Ray Moore Waller. I had one brother named Ed and four sisters: Rachel, Mandy, Harriet, and Ellen. And the names of the other slaves I can remember is Uncle Peter, the overseer, Aunt Mary, and Billy, and Sam, and George. There was some others, but at my age your mem'ry slips a little.

PLATE 30

We had pretty hard time to make out. We was hongry plenty times. Marse Tom didn't feel called on to feed his hands any too much. I 'members I had a craving for vittles all the time. My mammy used to say, "My belly craves something, and it craves meat." I used to take the lunches to the fields for the hands and they would say, "Lord God, it ain't 'nuf to stop the gripe in your belly." We would make out on things we take from the fields, and rabbits we cooked in little fires.

We had little biddy cabins made out'n logs with a puncheon bed and a bench and fireplace in them. We chilluns made out by sleeping on little pallets on the floor.

Now, some Sundays we went to church at one of the other farms or someplace. Marse Tom make us hitch up a yoke of oxen and go. We always like to go anyplace. There was a white preacher preached to us. He always told us to obey our masters and work hard and to sing at our work, and when we die we go to Heaven. Marse Tom didn't mind us singing in the cabins at night, but we better not let him ketch us prayin'.

In the cabins at night after supper, the slaves would sing some songs. I 'members some of them. One we used to sing was "Am I Born to Die?"

> Am I born to die and lay this body down,
> And must my trembling spirit fly
> Into a world unknown.
> Oh am I born to die, to die-e-e.

The prettiest song of all was "Hark From the Tomb."

> Princes, this clay must be your bed,
> In spite of all your towers,
> The tall, the wise, the reverent head
> Must lie as low as ours.

Some, like niggers, just got to pray; half their life is in prayin'. Some nigger take turn with 'nuther nigger to watch to see if Marse Tom anywheres 'bout, and then they circle themselves 'bout on the floor in the cabins and pray. They they get to moanin' low and gentle, "Someday, someday, someday this yoke going to be lifted off'n our shoulders, someday, someday, someday."

Some farms had parties for their slaves, but I never been to none. Marse Tom used to give some the growed niggers passes on Saturday night and let them go. They said they had fine times and big eatin'.

Marse Tom been dead long time now. I guess he is in hell. Seems like that is where he b'longs. He was a turrible mean man and he had a indifferent mean wife. But he had the finest, sweetest chilluns that the Lord ever let live and breathe on this earth. They was so kind and sorrowing over us slaves.

There was Mr. Lewis, Mr. Tom, Mr. Abby, Mr. Joe, and Miss Liza and Miss Mary. Miss Mary was so plump and pretty and good. When I'm little boy, she married Mr. Sam McClendon and moved three miles from her paw's house. She was up to her folks' house a lot of the time.

All the chilluns was fine good folks, and some of them favored the slaves having book learning and they used to read us little things out'n papers and books. We used to look at books and papers like there was something mighty curious 'bout them, but we better not let Marse Tom or his wife know it.

Marse Tom was a fitty man for meanness. He just 'bout had to beat somebody every day to satisfy his craving. He had a big whip called a bullwhip. He get mad at a nigger and stake him on the groun' and make 'nuther nigger hold his head down with his mouf in the dirt, and he would whip the nigger till the blood would run out and red up the groun'. We little niggers would stan' roun' and see it done. Then he would say to one of us, "Run to the kitchen and get some salt from Jane"—Mammy was the cook. Then he would sprinkle the salt in the cut open places, and the skin would jerk and quiver and the man would slobber and puke. Then their shirts stick to their backs for a week or more.

My mammy had a back that was turrible bad once. I seen her trying to get her clothes off her back and I heared a woman say, "Why, Mama, what is the matter with your back? It is raw and bloody." And she says Marse Tom done beat her with a handsaw with the teeth to her back. She died with the marks on her, with the teeth holes going crosswise her back. I axed her 'bout it, and she said she would tell me 'bout it sometime, but to hesh up then. When I was growed up, I axed her 'bout it. She said she forgot just 'zactly how it come to be, but that Marse Tom got mad 'bout the cookin' and grabbed her by the hair and drug her out the house and grabbed the saw off the tool bench and whupped her.

One day, I am down in the hog pen riling the hogs and teasing them like any yearling boy will do, when I hear a loud agony screaming up to the house. I can't make out who 'tis. I'm curious and I start up to the house and I hear, "Pray, Marse Tom. Pray, Marse Tom." But still I can't tell who 'tis. When I get up close I see Marse Tom got my mammy tied to a tree with her clothes pulled down and he is laying it on her with a bullwhip and the blood is running down her eyes and off her back.

I goes crazy. I say, "Stop, Marse Tom," and he swings the whip and it don't reach me good, but it cuts just the same. I sees Miss Mary standing in the cook house door. I run around crazy like, and I see a big rock and I take it and I throw it and it ketches Marse Tom in the skull and he goes down like a poled ox.

Miss Mary comes out and lifts her paw and helps him git into the house, and then she comes and helps me undo Mammy. And Mammy and me takes to the woods for two or three months, I guess. My sisters would meet us and grease Mammy's back and bring us vittles. Pretty soon they said it was safe for us to come into the cabins to eat at night, and they watch for Marse Tom. I'd come up 'bout the house, but I stayed clear of Marse Tom.

One day Marse Tom's wife is in the yard, and she calls me to come there, and she says she has got something for me. She keeps her hand under her apron. She keeps begging me to come to her. She says, "Gimme your hand." I reaches out my hand and she grabs it and slips a slipknot rope over it. I sees then, that was what she had under her apron and that the other end is tied to a little bush. I tries to get loose and run around, and I trip her up and she falls and breaks her arm. I get the rope off my arm and run.

We see Sam and Billy, and they tell us that there is a war and there is going to be fighting over the niggers. Then they told us they done 'clared to Marse Tom that there ain't going to be no more beatings, and they would work when they wanted to, and then when they didn't feel called they was just going to hunt and fish. They said we could come up and stay in our cabins all the time, and they would see Marse Tom didn't do nothing. And that is what Mammy and me did.

Billy and Sam told Marse Tom they is taking charge of the niggers themselves and they ain't goin' stand for any more beatings. They got the shotguns out of the house someway or tother. Then, one day, all the niggers is doing nothing, and Billy and Sam is by the house with the guns, and Marse Tom is setting in a rocker on the porch, and they sees a drove of mens coming toward the house. I'm leaning 'ginst the side of the house 'bout that time, and I see mens coming on horseback. And there is five of them. And when they gets near, Sam say to Marse Tom, "The first white man sets hisself inside the rail fence gets it from the gun." The mens come near and Marse Tom waves with his hand to go back, but they keep coming. He waves and waves them back. They gallop right up to the fence and throw the reins over the post and swings off their horses.

Marse Tom say, "Stay outside, gentlemen—please do—I done changed my mind." They say, "What's the matter here? We come to whip the niggers like you done hired us to." Marse Tom say, "I changed my mind, but if you will stay outside I will bring you your money." They argue to come in, but Marse Tom outtalk them and they say they will go away if he bring them their three dollars apiece. He takes them the money and they goes away.

Marse Tom cuss and rave, but the niggers just stay in the woods and fool away their time. They say ain't no use to work for nothing all their days.

One day I'm in a 'simmon [persimmon] tree in the middle of a little pond gathering 'simmons and eating them, when my sister Mandy comes running. I know it's funny she outside 'cause it's the time of day for the churning. She calls me to come down out'n the tree. "What for?" says I. She says, "The niggers is free." I didn't b'lieve nor think nothing much 'bout it. She say, "Mammy free, you free, all us niggers free. Don't have to work for Marse Tom no more." I looked over to the house and I seen the niggers piling their little bunch of clothes and things outside their cabins and then fixing them in bundles and setting them on top of their heads.

Mammy and some other niggers came running down there, and

Mammy was the head runner. I clumb down out of the tree and come to meet her. She told me that Marse Tom done told her that he going to keep me for a shepherd boy and he is going to pay her for it. She is a-scared that I will stay if I want to or not, and so she runs to beg me not to stay.

We get up to the house, and all the niggers are standing there with their little bundles on their head and they all say, "Where we going?" Mammy said, "I don't know where you going, but me myself is going to Miss Mary." So all the niggers get in with Mammy and we start to Miss Mary's. She sees us coming in a drove and meets us outside the back door. She said to Mammy, "Come in, Jane, and all your chilluns and all the rest of you. You kin see my door is open, and the smokehouse door is open to you, and I'll bed you down till we figures a way for you niggers to make your way."

I 'members plain that we all cried and sang and prayed, and we was so 'cited that we didn't eat no supper, though Mammy stirred up some vittles.

'Twarn't long till Mr. McClendon found places to work for the niggers. He found us a place with a fine white man and told him we had had a rough time, but we was honest and good. We worked there on sharance,* then we drifted round to some other place. We lived in Corsicana for a while, and we bought Mammy a house and she died there.

I got married and I had three chilluns—cute, fetching little chilluns—and they went to school. Wasn't no trouble when my chilluns went to school, but I 'members there was some trouble 'bout the schools when the 'Mancipation came. My brother Ed was in school then and the Ku Klux came and driv' the Yankee lady and gentleman out and closed the school.

My chilluns growed up and my wife died, and I tuk 'nuther one, and I spent most my days working hard on farms, and doing first one thing and then tuther.

Now I'm old and throwed away. But I'm thankful to God and praiseful for the pension that lets my wife and me have a little something to eat and a place to stay.

*As sharecroppers.

Voices

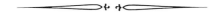

THE CIVIL WAR

AND

STATUTORY FREEDOM

Now everything wuz stirred up fer a long spell, fo' de war to free us come on. It wuz talked an' threatened, an' all kinds o' bad signs p'inted to war, till at las' dey jes' knowed it wuz bound to come on. De slaves wan't allowed to read a thing writ on a piece o' paper. Of course, dey wan't much danger o' dat, as sich a few could read, nohow. Dey wan't allowed to talk to strangers for fear dey would be tole things by de Yankees. De white folks wuz upsot over de fear o' losing all deir slaves. In spite o' everything, it got floated round dat de slaves wuz to be freed, an' sometimes dey hear dat dey would git a home, or land, or mules, an' de lak. But, as things always go during wartimes, nobody knows jes' what to expect. De niggers wuz afraid o' de Yankees, an' after de War broke, us would run when us seed a troop ob 'em a-marchin' through.

—TEMPLE WILSON

During de War and befo' Mawster Bouldin come back, some of de men on de plantation would slip up to a open winder at de big house at night and try to hear what was goin' on. Some would be layin' outside de winder and listen to what was read f'om a letter. Den, de talk would be lak dis':

"Sh-h-h, good news, good news!" one ob de boys would whisper.

"What's in de lettah?"

"It says dat de Yankees ain't against de niggers."

"I'll bet it says dat one Southerner was enough fo' six Yankees."

"No, dat one Yankee was enough fo' a dozen Southerners."

"I don't believe it."

"Sh-h-h."

PLATE 31: One of the hundreds of thousands of former slaves who fought for their freedom in the Civil War.

De next day, dat's what de folks would talk about in de fields. Some ob de pickers and workers would say, "I don't believe it. If we is to be freed, it's a long time a-gittin' here."

—J. W. KING

Mr. Joe Walton said, when he went to war, dat dey could eat breakfast at home, go and whup the North, and be back for dinner. He went away, and it wuz four long years before he come back to dinner. De table wuz shore set a long time for him.

I wuz afraid of the Yankees, because Missus had told us the Yankees were going to kill every nigger in the South. I hung to my mammy, when dey come through.

—HANNAH CRASSON

Us was skeered of dem Yankees, 'cause us chillun didn' know what dey was, and de oberseer, Jim Lynch, done tole us little-uns dat a Yankee was somepin' what had one great big horn on he haid and just one eye, and dat right in de middle of he breast. And boss, I sure was s'prised when I seen a sure 'nuf Yankee, and seen he was a man, just like any of de res' of de folks.

—JAMES GILL

When I went to the War, I was turning seventeen. I was in the Battle of Nashville, when we whipped old [General] Hood. I went to see my mistress on my furlough, and she was glad to see me. She said, "You remember when you were sick and I had to bring you to the house and nurse you?" And I told her, "Yes'm, I remember." And she said, "And now, you are fighting me!" I said, "No'm, I ain't fighting you. I'm fighting to get free."

—ANONYMOUS

De Yankees come to our place an' runned Massa Jim away, an' tuk de house for a horsepittil. Dey tuk all of Massa Jim's clothes an' gived dem to some of deir frien's. Dey burned up all de cotton, hay, peas, an' ever'thing dat was in de barns. Dey made de white folks cook for de colored, an' den serve 'em while dey et. De Yankees made 'em do for us lak we done for dem. Dey showed de white folks what it was to work for somebody else. Dey stayed on our place for de longes'. When dey did leave, dere warn't a mouthful to eat in de house.

—MARY GRANDBERRY

Slave Song

Has anybody seen my massa,
Wid de mustache on he face,
Go 'long de road some time dis mornin',
Like he gwine to leabe de place?

De massa run, ha, ha!
De darkie stay, ho, ho!
It must be now dat de Kingdom am a-comin',
An' de year ob jubalo.

He seed a smoke way up de riber,
Where de Lincoln gunboats lay;
He pick up he hat an' he lef' real sudden,
An' I 'spect dat he runned away.

He six feet one way, three feet tudder,
And he weigh three hundred pound;
He coat so big dat he can't pay de tailor,
An' it won't go half way round.

De oberseer, he gib us trubble,
An' he dribe us round a spell;
Den we lock him up in de smokehouse cellar,
Wid de key done throwed in de well.

De whip am lost an' de han'cuff broken,
An' Massa'll get he pay;
He big enough, old enough, orter known better,
But he gone an' runned away.

De massa run, ha, ha!
De darkie stay, ho, ho!
It must be now dat de Kingdom am a-comin',
An' de year ob jubalo.

I remember when the Yankees come to this town. My old boss hit me that mornin' and he didn't know the Yankees were in town, and when he found it out, he come back beggin' me to stay with him, and said he was sorry.

—ANONYMOUS

One time, some Yankee soldiers stopped and started talking to me. One asked me what my name was. I say, "Liza," and he say, "Liza who?" I thought a minute and I shook my head, "Jest Liza. I ain't got no other name."

He say, "Who live up yonder in dat big house?" I say, "Mr. John Mixon." He say, "You are Liza Mixon." Den he say, "Do anybody ever call you 'nigger'?" And I say, "Yes, Sir." He say, "Next time anybody call you 'nigger,' you tell 'em dat you is a Negro and your name is Miss Liza Mixon." The more I thought of that, the more I liked it, and I made up my mind to do jest what he told me to.

My job was minding the calves, while the cows was being milked. One evening, I was minding the calves and Old Master come along. He say, "What you doin', nigger?" I say real pert-like, "I ain't no nigger, I's a Negro, and I'm Miss Liza Mixon." Old Master sho' was surprised, and he picks up a switch and starts at me.

Law', but I was skeered! I hadn't never had no whipping, so I run fast as I can to Grandma Gracie. I hid behind her, and she say, "What's the matter wid you, child?" And I say, "Master John gwine whip me." And she say, "What you done?" And I say, "Nothing." She say she know better, and 'bout that time Master John got there. He say, "Gracie, dat little nigger sassed me." She say, "Lawsie, child, what does ail you?" I told them what the Yankee soldier told me to say, and Grandma Gracie took my dress and lifted it over my head and pins my hands inside, and Lawsie, how she whipped me, and I dassen't holler loud, either. I jest said dat to de wrong person, didn't I?

—ELIZA EVENS

A Yankee took my father down to a beautiful piece of plantation property that lay on the east side of the forks of a road, near

Summerville, and said, "Nigger, the government is going to give every ex-slave forty acres of land and a mule, but it will cost twenty dollars to make out the papers. Meet me here with twenty dollars next Monday morning, and I'll make over forty acres of this fine land to you, and give you the mule later."

Well, my father got up the twenty dollars and met the man and gave it to him, and received a paper from him. But Father couldn't read, so just to be on the safe side, before taking possession of what he had been given, he took his deed to a local white man to read. And this is the wording of that Yankee's deed: "This is to certify that this Negro has been able to secure a piece of paper called a deed to forty acres and a mule, and I hope that he gets both, someday." Of course, my daddy never forgave that Yankee for cheating him.

—THE REVEREND W. B. ALLEN

While Master Jim is out fighting the Yanks, the mistress is fiddling round with a neighbor man, Mr. Headsmith. I is young then, but I knows well enough that Master Jim's going be mighty mad when he hears about it.

The mistress didn't know I knows her secret, and that I'm fixing to even up for some of them whippings she put on me. That's why I tell Master Jim, next time he come home:

"See that crack in the wall?" Master Jim say yes, and I say, "It's just like the open door, when the eyes are close to the wall." He peek and see into the bedroom.

"That's how I find out about the mistress and Mr. Headsmith," I tells him, and I see he's getting mad.

"What you mean?" And Master Jim grabs me hard by the arm, like I was trying to get away.

"I see them in the bed."

That's all I say. The demon's got him, and Master Jim tears out of the room, looking for the mistress.

Then, I hears loud talking, and pretty soon the mistress is screaming and calling for help, and if old Master Ben hadn't drop in just then and stop the fight, why I guess she be beat almost to death—that how mad the master was.

—ESTHER EASTER

We neber had no trouble till de Yankees come, en dey skeered us nearly to death. Dey was mad 'cause Ole Mistis done hid all de meat, en all de flour, en all de meal, down in de swamp, en hid de silver summuz—I dunno whar. Dey cussed right 'fore Ole Mistis en ride dey hosses all ober her flower yard. Dey tied Unker Luke, Old Mistis' head nigger, to er tree en whipped him wid er bridle, 'cause he wudden't tell whar Ole Mistis hid t'ings. But Unker Luke didn't open he mout'—jes' let 'em whip. Ole Mistis en all of us cried whilst de Yankees wuz whippin' Unker Luke, and she sho' did bless 'em out. Dey wuz so mad dey sot de barn erfire, en dey sot de crib erfire, en burnt hit up wid evvyt'ing Ole Mistis had in de world. When she fotch anyt'ing outen de house, dey flung hit back—even her little chillun's pictures, what wuz dead. Us chillun wuz skeered so, we runned clear off, en I got lost all night en didn't get back till next day, en dere wan't nobody dar, en I wuz hongry. Dem Yankees done burnt up all de cabins, en all de niggers wuz gone.

— HATTIE CLAYTON

I's seed dem Yankees cut de hams offen a live pig or ox an' go off leavin' de animal groanin'. De massa had 'em kilt den, but it wuz awful.

— ELBERT HUNTER

One day, a Yankee soldier climbed in the back window and took some of the quilts. He rolled 'em up and was walking out of the yard, when Mother saw him and said, "Why you nasty, stinkin' rascal. You say you come down here to fight for the niggers, and now you're stealin' from 'em." He say, "You're a g—— d—— liar. I'm fightin' for fourteen dollars a month and the Union."

— SAM WARD

When the Yankees come, what they do? They did them things they ought not to have done, and they left undone de things they ought to have done. Yes, dat just 'bout tells it.

One thing you might like to hear. Mistress got all de money, de silver, de gold, and de jewels, and got de well-digger to hide them in de bottom of de well. Them Yankees smart. When they got dere, they asked for de ve'y things at de bottom of de well. Mistress wouldn't tell. They held a court of 'quiry in de yard, called slaves up one by one, good many. Must have been a Judas 'mongst us. Soon, a Yankee was let down in de well, and all dat money, silver, gold, jewelry, watches, rings, brooches, knives and forks, butter dishes, goblets, and cups was took and carried 'way by a army dat seemed more concerned 'bout stealin' than they was 'bout de holy war for de liberation of de poor African slave people. They took off all de hosses, sheeps, cows, chickens, and geese, took de seine and de fishes they caught, corn in crib, meat in smokehouse, and everything. Marse General Sherman said war was hell. It sho' was. And mebbe it was hell for some of them Yankees, when they come to die and give account of de deeds they done in Sumter and Richland counties.

—HENRY JENKINS

The end of the War came like that—like you snap your fingers.

Abe Lincoln freed the nigger
With the gun and the trigger,
And I ain't a-goin' to get whipped anymore.
I got my ticket
Leavin' the thicket,
And I'm a-headin' for the Golden Shore!

Soldiers, all of a sudden, wuz everywha'—comin' in bunches, crossin', and walkin', and ridin'. Everyone wuz singin'. We wuz all walkin' on golden clouds. Hallelujah!

Union forever,
Hurrah, boys, hurrah.
Although I may be pore,
I'll never be a slave,
Shoutin' the battle cry of freedom.

Everybody went wild. We didn't feel like anybody had done anythin' for us. We all felt like heroes, and like nobody had made us that way but ourselves. We wuz free! Just like that, we wuz free. It didn't seem to make the whites mad, either. They went right on giving us food, just the same. Nobody took our homes away. But, right off, colored folks started on the move. They seemed to want to get closer to freedom, so they'd know what it wuz—like it wuz a place or city. Me and my father stuck close as a lean tick to a sick kitten.

—FELIX HAYWOOD

When the Yankee soldiers came, the niggers run and hid under the beds, and the soldiers came and poked their bayonets under the beds and shouted, "Come on out from under there. You're free."

—DICEY THOMAS

Glory! Glory! Yes, child, de Negroes are free, an' when dey knew dat dey were free—oh, baby!—dey began to sing:

> Mammy, don't yo' cook no mo',
> Yo' are free, yo' are free!
> Rooster, don't yo' crow no mo',
> Yo' are free, yo' are free!
> Ole hen, don't yo' lay no mo',
> Yo' free, yo' free!

—FANNIE BERRY

One Wednesday mawnin', I think it was, I was layin' out in de sagebrush, herdin' my sheep, when I heard someone blowin' de bugle, at de big house. I knowed it wasn't time to go to dinnah. At fus', it was a big blowin', den dah was a "toot, toot" two times, and dat meant fo' us to hurry to de big house. I called to my lead sheep, and we hurried home. Mawster Wills met me at de bawn, and said, "Put dem sheep up, and den come to de house."

When I come to de house, I seen five white men sittin' dah, wid lahge brass buttons on dey uniforms. One of de white men said to me, "Hello, little tap."

I jes' pulled off my hat and scratched my head. I looked over at Mawster Wills, and he was grinnin'.

"Is yo' hongry, little tap?" de white man in de uniform asked me.

"Naw, suh," I tole him, "I ain't hongry."

"Don't you wanta go wid me?"

"Naw, suh. I wanta stay here wid my mawster."

"Aw, he'd jes' beat yo' up and run yo' to death."

I had de bes' mawster in de world, so I said, "Naw, suh, Mawster Wills don't do dat. I wanta stay here wid him."

"But yo' don't have no mo' mawster. Yo' is free!"

I pointed to Mawster Wills and said, "Yonder is my mawster!"

I jes' as well tell de truth and say dat I didn't know what he meant. When I went aroun' to de kitchen ob de big house, Mothaw tole me, "Well, we jes' ain't no slaves no mo'."

I didn't understand her, even den. She tole me den dat we could pick up and leave, and dat we didn't have no mo' mawsters. I finally understood.

—J. C. ALEXANDER

After the War, many soldiers came to my mistress, Mrs. Blakely, trying to make her free me. I told them I was free, but I did not want to go anywhere—that I wanted to stay in the only home that I had ever known. In a way, that placed me in a wrong attitude. I was pointed out as different. Sometimes, I was threatened for not leaving, but I stayed on.

—AUNT ADELINE

When freedom come, Marster tells us all to come to front of de house. He am standin' on de porch. He 'splains 'bout freedom and says, "You is now free and can go whar you pleases." Den, he tells us he have larned us not to steal and to be good, and we-uns should 'member dat, and if we-uns gets in trouble, to come to him and he will help us. He sho' do dat, too, 'cause de niggers goes to him lots of times, and he always helps.

Marster says dat he needs help on de place, and sich dat stays, he'd pay 'em for de work. Lots of dem stayed, but some left. To dem dat leaves, Marster gives a mule or cow, and sich, for de start. To my folks, Marster gives some land. He doesn't give us de deed, but de right to stay till he dies.

—BETTY BORMER

You ought to been behind a tree the day young Master George told me I was free. You would have laughed fit to kill. I was down on the farm plowing, and Master George rid up on a hoss and say, "Morning, Allen." I say, "Morning, Master George." "Laying by the crap [crop]?" he say. "Yes, Sah," I told him. Then, he say, "Allen, you is free." I say, "What you mean, 'free'?" "The damn Yankees is freed you," he say.

I got off the plow, and he grabbed me by the arm, and pushed my sleeve up, and p'inted to my skin, and say, "Allen, my daddy give a thousand dollars in gold for that, didn't he?" "He sho' did," I told him. Then, he say, "Didn't my daddy give you to me? And didn't I put them clothes on you?" "Sho' 'nuf, you did," I say to him. Then, Master George say, "Yes, and the damn Yankees took you away from me. But them is my clothes." Then, he made like he was gonna take my clothes away from me, and we scuffled all round the field.

Then, Master George begin to laugh, and say, "Allen, I ain't gonna take your clothes. I's gonna put some better ones on you. You is free, but I want you to stay right on and tend to your mistress, like you been doing." I lived with them till after I was grown. I was in and out five or six years, 'fore I married. When I couldn't get work, I went back to them and et Old Mistress' meat and bread.

—ALLEN WILLIAMS

We went right on workin', after freedom. Old Buck Adams wouldn't let us go till dey have a man select' to go out through de country an' tell de slaves dat dey was free, now. Dat was way after de

War was over. De freedom man come to our place an' read a paper what de Pres'dent had writ what said we was now free, an' he talk to us 'bout freedom an' tole us not to work no more, 'less we got paid for it.

When he had finished an' gone, old Buck Adams' wife, old Mary Adams, come out an' spoke to us. I rec'lec' what she say jes' as well as if I jes' hear her say it. She say, "Ten years from today, I'll have you all back 'gain." Yes, sir. "Ten years from today, I'll have you all back 'gain." Dat ten years been over a mighty long time, an' she ain' got us back yet, an' she is dead an' gone.

Us ain' had no time for no celebration, for dey make us git right off de place—jes' like you take an old horse an' turn it loose. You see a lot of cattle in de field eating de grass wit' a fence round dem, an' den somebody open de gate an' say, "Git!" Dat's how we was. No money, no nothin'—jes' turn' loose wit'out nothin'.

—WILLIAM MATTHEWS

I remember well how the roads was full of folks walking and walking along, when the niggers were freed. Didn't know where they was going. Just going to see about something else, somewhere else. Meet a body in the road and they ask, "Where you going?" "Don't know." "What you going to do?" "Don't know." And then sometimes we would meet a white man, and he would say, "How you like to come work on my farm?" And we say, "I don't know." And then maybe he say, "If you come work for me on my farm, when the crops is in, I give you five bushels of corn, five gallons of molasses, some ham meat, and all your clothes and vittles while you works for me." "All right! That's what I do." And then, something begins to work up here and I begins to think and to know things. And I knowed then I could make a living for my own self, and I never had to be a slave no more.

—ROBERT FALLS

348

The master, he says we is all free, but dat it don't mean we is white, and it don't mean we is equal—just equal for to work and earn our own living and not depend on him for no more eats and clothes.

—GEORGE KING

We b'longs to Papa Day. His name Isaiah, but us all call him Papa Day, 'cause he won't 'low none he cullud folks to call him master. He say us is born free as he is, only de other white folks won't tell us so, and our souls is jes' as white, and de reason us am darker on de outside is 'cause us is sunburnt. I don't reckon dere am anybody as good to deir cullud folks as he was.

One mornin', Papa Day calls all us to de house and reads de freedom papers and say, "De gov'ment don't need to tell you you is free, 'cause you been free all you' days. If you wants to stay, you can, and if you wants to go, you can. But if you go, lots of white folks ain't gwine treat you like I does."

For de longest time, maybe two years, dey wasn't none of Papa Day's cullud folks what left. But den, first one fam'ly den 'nother gits some land to make a crop on, and den Daddy gits some land and us leaves, too. Maybe he gits de land from Papa Day, 'cause it ain't far from his plantation. Us sho' work hard on dat place, but I heared Mama say lots of times she wishes we stay on Papa Day's place.

—LAURA CORNISH

After de War ended and Tom Williams had come home, he called everybody togedder and tell dem dey was free, but dat he want to hire dem till Christmas—dat was in May—to help lay de crop by. He said he'd pay good wages, too. Everybody stayed, but de next spring my daddy say he gwine ter leave.

Now, I guess he was one of de bigges' niggers anywhere round, and he was right smart, too. He could run a gin, and was a right peart carpenter.

Tom Williams wanted him to stay, but my daddy didn' have much use for him, and so he say he gwine ter leave, anyhow. Den, Tom

Williams got mad, and grabbed my daddy's hands, and tied dem over his head to a branch on a oak tree, and holler to me, "By de Lawd God who made Moses, go get my whip, you Frank!" He tuk de whip, what was made outen a gin belt, and lashed my daddy till de blood come. He say, "Now you change yo' mind and give up?" And my daddy say no.

He left him dere three or four days, but all de time he made me stay wid him and bring him water and bread. Den, he thought he might die, so he say, "Henry, I's gwine ter let you down and give you a nice soft bed on de porch, till you makes up your mind." But 'fore he unties his hands, he put a chain on his legs.

Den, he carries him over to de porch and chains him to one of de posts. He say, "Henry, I'm gwine ter let you have one of Mis' Martha's soft beds, and I'm gwine ter feed you fried chicken. Now, is you gwine ter stay?" He kept him dere for about a week, but my daddy never did say he would stay.

So, finally, Tom Williams go out and tell everybody for miles around dat my daddy is a bad nigger and dat he wouldn't work, and for none of dem to hire him. Den, he come home and tell Daddy what he done, and turn him loose, and say, "Now go get a job, iffen you can." He thought all de time my daddy would have to come back to him, so's his family wouldn't starve to death.

We sot out and come to Aberdeen, and all of us worked hard at fust one thing and den another. I was a houseboy in two or three places, and my daddy worked a little farm and made horse collars to sell. We finally saved up enough to buy dat little farm.

—FRANK WILLIAMS

One day, aftah de War am fightin' fo' mo' dan two yeahs, de marster gits a letter f'om Marster Billy. Dat letter says de nigger sho' am gwine to be free, de Wah am 'bout over, dat him will be home soon, an' dat John am killed. When de missy heahs dat letter read, she stahts a-cryin' an' says, "My poor boy, my poor boy, my Johnny. Ise not see him any mo'." She keeps dat up till she am 'zausted. Den, she lay down an' was a-moanin'. De marster says nothin', jus' sits an' stares. Den, suddenly, him jumps up an' stahts cussin' de War, de nigger, Abe Lincoln, an' ever'body. He goes to de fiahplace, picks up a hot pokah, an' says, "Free de nigger, will dey? Ise free dem." Den, he hits my mammy on de neck. Dat lick bu'ns a scah dat Mammy carries to her grave. My mammy stahts moanin' an' screamin' an' draps on de floah. Dere 'twas, de missy a-moanin', my mammy a-moanin', an' de marster am a-cussin' loud as him can. He was a-sayin', "Ise free de nigger f'om slavery." Den, him takes his gun off de rack an' stahts fo' de field whar de niggers am a-wukkin'. My sistah an' Ise in de house, an' when we-uns see dat, we-uns stahts runnin' an' screamin', 'cause we-uns have sistahs an' brudders in de field, an' we-uns don' wants 'em shoot. Lawd-a-massie! Dat was a crazy place, an' nobody knows what to do. It looks lak dem niggers in de field sho' will be killed.

De good Lawd took a han' in dat mess, den. De marster ain' gone far in de field, when he draps, all of a sudden. When de niggers in de field sees him drap, dey come a-runnin' to him. Dey fine dat de marster can' talk nor move. De niggers picks him up an' totes him in de house. Den, my brudder rides fo' de doctah. When de doctah comes, he 'zamines de marster an' says, "Well, 'tis a question if he lives." Befo' de doctah leaves, him fix my mammy's neck. De nex' day, de marster dies.

When dey have de marster' fune'al, 'twarn't any sorry niggers. 'Bout de only mo'nah am de missy. Aftah de fune'al, 'twarn't long till Marster Billy comes home, an' de break-up took place, wid freedom fo' de niggers. Mos' ob de cullud folks lef' soon's dey could. Dey sho' wants to git f'om dat place.

Aftah we-uns moved, 'twarn't long till de missy had some mo' sorrow. She foun' Marster Billy in de shed, dead, wid his throat cut an' de razor 'side him. Dere was a piece ob paper dat him wrote on. He said dat him not care fo' to live, 'cause de nigger am free, an' dey's all broke up.

—ANNIE ROW

When de War was over, de Yankees was all roun' de place tellin' de niggers what to do. Dey tole dem dey was free, dat dey didn' have to slave for de white folks no more.

One day, my mammy come to de big house after me. I didn' want to go. I wanted to stay wid Mis' Polly. I 'gun to cry, an' Mammy caught hold of me. I grabbed Mis' Polly an' held so tight dat I tore her skirt bindin' loose, an' her skirt fell down 'bout her feets.

"Let her stay wid me," Mis' Polly said to Mammy. But Mammy shook her head.

"You took her away from me an' didn' pay no mind to my cryin', so now I's takin' her back home. We's free now, Mis' Polly. We ain' gwine be slaves no more to nobody." She dragged me away. I can see how Mis' Polly looked, now. She didn' say nothin', but she looked hard at Mammy, an' her face was white.

—SARAH DEBRO

My mother and daddy was free niggers, 'cause they bought they freedom from John Williams, in Mississippi. When they was through with they work in the fields, they did work on they own and bought themselves free. My mother spinned, and knitted galluses [suspenders], and did tufting on counterpanes to make a little something extra. My daddy sold bodark [bois d'arc] seeds and set out hedges for folks. They saved up the money and bought they freedom. My growed-up brother worked and bought his freedom, and I heared later on how he give fifty dollars to the missus of me to buy my freedom. I don't know what come of the money, but I know that I was supposin' to be free when I get eighteen years old. Only, the War come first and set me free.

—LU PERKINS

When we wuz freed, de slaves dat wuz married all had to git license an' be married over again. My pa quit my ma when he found dis out, an' wouldn't marry her over again. A heap ob 'em quit dat way. I reckon dey felt free sho' 'nuf, as dey wuz freed from slavery an' from marriage. I wonders, sometime', what would happen in dis day an' time, if everybody wuz tole dey wuz free from deir marriages. Dere would be some stirrin' 'bout. A few ob 'em would do jest lak my pa done.

—PRIMOUS MAGEE

When the War was over, Master told us, "You are free now, jest like I am, and as you have no places to go, you can stay on and work on halvers." We stayed on three years, after slavery. We got little money, but we got room and board and didn't have to work too hard. It was 'nuf difference to tell you was no slaves anymore.

—LEWIS BONNER

I guess we musta celebrated 'Mancipation about twelve times, in Hornett County. Every time a bunch of No'thern sojers would come through, they would tell us we was free, and we'd begin celebratin'. Before we would get through, somebody else would tell us to go back to work, and we would go. Some of us wanted to jine up with the army, but didn't know who was goin' to win and didn't take no chances.

—AMBROSE DOUGLASS

After peace was made, Old Master called us all to him and told us that we was free now—jest as free as he was—and that he had some things that he wanted to tell us. He talked to us jest like we was his own children, wid tears running down his cheeks. He said, "Cindy, I've raised you from a baby, and you, Henry, since you was a young man. I've tried to be good to you and take good care of you in return for the good work you have always done for me. I want you to go out in the world now and make good citizens. Be honest and respectable, and don't turn against the good raisin' you have had, and remember, me and my wife loves you all.

—EVA STRAYHORN

I was old enough to know what de passin' 'way of Old Marster and Missus meant to me. De very stream of lifeblood in me was dryin' up, it 'peared lak. When Marster died, dat was my fust real sorrow. Three years later, Missus passed 'way. Dat was de time of my second sorrow. Then, I 'minded myself of a little tree out dere in de woods, in November. Wid every sharp and cold wind of trouble dat blowed, more leaves of dat tree turnt loose and went to de ground, just lak they was tryin' to follow her. It seem lak, when she was gone, I was just lak dat tree wid all de leaves gone, naked and friendless. It took me a long time to git over all dat. Same way wid de little tree: it had to pass through winter and wait on spring to see life again.

—EZRA ADAMS

Young Marse got killed in de Civil War. Old Marse live on. I went to see him, in his last days, and I set by him and kept de flies off while dere. I see de lines of sorrow plowed on dat old face, and I 'membered he'd been a captain on hossback in dat war. It come into my 'membrance de song of Moses, "De Lord has triumphed glorily and de hoss and his rider have been throwed into de sea."

—SAVILLA BURRELL

I wuz pow'ful glad when I wuz freed. One thing they did wuz to whitewash de bullwhip and hang it on de side of de house.

—HESTER NORTON

Narratives

———◦—————

NEAL UPSON

CHARLIE DAVENPORT

ELLEN BETTS

NEAL UPSON

GOOD mornin', Miss. How is you? Won't you come in? I would ax you to have a cheer [chair] on the porch, but I has to stay in de house 'cause de light hurts my eyes.

Miss, I's mighty glad you come today, 'cause I does git so lonesome here by myself. My old 'oman wuks up to de court'ouse, cookin' for de folkses in jail, and it's allus late when she gits home. 'Scuse me for puttin' my old hat back on, but dese old eyes jus' can't stand de light even in de hall, 'less I shades 'em.

Lawsy, Missy, does you mean dat you is willin' to set and listen to old Neal talk? 'Tain't many folkses what wants to hear us old niggers talk no more. I jus' loves to think back on dem days, 'cause dem was happy times—so much better'n times now. Folkses was better den. Dey was allus ready to help one another, but jus' look how dey is now!

I was borned on Marster Frank Upson's place down in Oglethorpe County, nigh Lexin'ton, Georgy. Marster had a plantation, but us never lived dar, for us stayed at de home place what never had more'n 'bout eighty acres of land round it. Us never had to be trottin' to de sto' evvy time us started to cook, 'cause what warn't raised on de home place, Marster had 'em raise out on de big plantation. Evvything us needed t'eat and wear was growed on Marse Frank's land.

Harold and Jane Upson was my daddy and mammy; only folkses jus' called Daddy "Hal." Both of 'em was raised right dar on de Upson place whar dey played together whilst dey was chillun. Mammy said she had washed and sewed for Daddy ever since she was big enough, and when dey got grown dey jus' up and got married. I was deir only boy and I was de baby chile, but dey had four gals older'n me. Dey was: Cordelia, Anne, Perthene, and Ella. Ella was

357

named for Marse Frank's onliest chile, little Mis' Ellen, and our little mis' was sho' a good little chile.

Daddy made de shoes for all de slaves on de plantation and Mammy was called de house 'oman. She done de cookin' up at de big 'ouse and made de cloth for her own fambly's clothes, and she was so smart us allus had plenty t'eat and wear. I was little and stayed wid Mammy up at de big 'ouse and jus' played all over it, and all de folkses up dar petted me.

Aunt Tama was a old slave too old to wuk. She was all de time cookin' gingerbread and hidin' it in a little trunk what sot by de fireplace in her room. When us chillun was good, Aunt Tama give us gingerbread, but if us didn't mind what she said, us didn't git none. Aunt Tama had de rheumatiz and walked wid a stick, and I could git in dat trunk jus' 'bout anytime I wanted to. I sho' did git 'bout evvything dem other chillun had, swappin' Aunt Tama's gingerbread. When our white folkses went off, Aunt Tama toted de keys, and she evermore did make dem niggers stand round. Marse Frank jus' laughed when dey made complaints 'bout her.

In summertime dey cooked peas and other veg'tables for us chillun in a washpot out in de yard in de shade, and us et out of de pot wid our wooden spoons. Dey jes' give us wooden bowls full of bread and milk for supper.

Marse Frank said he wanted 'em to learn me how to wait on de white folkses' table up at de big 'ouse, and dey started me off wid de job of fannin' de flies away. Mist'ess Serena, Marse Frank's wife, made me a white coat to wear in de dinin' room. Missy, dat little old white coat made me git de onliest whuppin' Marse Frank ever did give me. Us had comp'ny for dinner dat day and I felt so big showin' off 'fore 'em in dat white coat dat I jus' couldn't make dat turkey wing fan do right. Dem turkey wings was fastened on long handles, and atter Marster had done warned me a time or two to mind what I was 'bout, the old turkey wing went down in de gravy bowl, and when I jerked it out it splattered all over de preacher's best Sunday suit. Marse Frank get up and tuk me right out to de kitchen, and when he got through brushin' me off I never did have no more trouble wid dem turkey wings.

Evvybody cooked on open fireplaces, dem days. Dey had swingin'

PLATE 32: Slaves cooked for their owners at kitchen fireplaces like this one.

racks what dey called cranes to hang de pots on for b'ilin'. Dere was ovens fer bakin', and de heavy iron skillets had long handles. One of dem old skillets was so big dat Mammy could cook thirty biscuits in it at one time. I allus did love biscuits, and I would go out in de yard and trade Aunt Tama's gingerbread to de other chilluns for deir sheer of biscuits. Den dey would be skeered to eat de gingerbread, 'cause I told 'em I'd tell on 'em. Aunt Tama thought dey was sick and told Marse Frank de chilluns warn't eatin' nothin'. He axed 'em what was de matter and dey told him dey had done traded all deir bread to me. Marse Frank den axed me if I warn't gittin' enough t'eat, 'cause he 'lowed dere was enough dar for all. Den Aunt Tama had to go and tell on me. She said I was wuss den a hog atter biscuits, so our good marster ordered her to see dat li'l Neal had enough t'eat.

I ain't never gwine to forgit dat whuppin' my own daddy give me. He had jus' sharpened up a fine new ax for hisself, and I traded it off to a white boy named Roar what lived nigh us when I seed him out tryin' to cut wood wid a sorry old dull ax. I sold him my daddy's fine new ax for five biscuits. When my daddy found out 'bout dat, he 'lowed he was gwine to give me somepin' to make me think 'fore I done any more tradin' of his things. Mist'ess, let me tell you, dat beetin' he give me evermore was a-layin' on of de rod.

I used to cry and holler evvy time Mis' Serena went off and left me. Whenever I seed 'em gittin' out de carriage to hitch it up, I started beggin' to go. Sometimes she laughed and said, "All right, Neal." But when she said, "No, Neal," I snuck out and hid under de high-up carriage seat and went along jus' de same. Mist'ess allus found me 'fore us got back home, but she jus' laughed and said, "Well, Neal's my little nigger, anyhow."

Dem old cord beds was a sight to look at, but dey slept good. Us cyarded [carded] lint cotton into bats for mattresses and put 'em in a tick what us tacked so it wouldn't git lumpy. Us never seed no iron springs, dem days. Dem cords, crisscrossed from one side of de bed to de other, was our springs, and us had keys to tighten 'em wid. If us didn't tighten 'em evvy few days, dem beds was apt to fall down wid us. De cheers was homemade, too, and de easiest-settin' ones had bottoms made out of rye splits. Dem oak-split cheers was all right, and sometimes us used cane to bottom de cheers, but evvybody lakked to set in dem cheers what had bottoms wove out of rye splits.

Marster had one of dem old cotton gins what didn't have no engine. It was wukked by mules. Dem old mules was hitched to a long pole what dey pulled round and round, to make de gin do its wuk. Dey had some gins in dem days what had treadmills for de mules to walk in. Dem old treadmills looked sorter lak stairs. But most of dem gins was turned by long poles what de mules pulled. You had to feed de cotton by hand to dem old gins, and you sho' had to be keerful or you was gwine to lose a hand and maybe a arm. You had to jump in dem old cotton presses and tread de cotton down by hand. It tuk most all day long to gin two bales of cotton, and if dere was three bales to be ginned, us had to wuk most all night to finish up.

Dey mixed wool wid de lint cotton to spin thread to make cloth for our winter clothes. Mammy wove a lot of dat cloth and de clothes made out of it sho' would keep out de cold. Most of our stockin's and socks was knit at home, but now and den somebody would git hold of a sto'-bought pair for Sunday-go-to-meetin' wear.

Colored folkses went to church wid deir own white folkses and set in de gallery. One Sunday, us was all settin' in dat church listenin' to de white preacher, Mr. Mansford, tellin' how de old Debil was gwine to git dem what didn't do right.

Missy, I jus' got to tell you 'bout dat day in de meetin'ouse. A nigger had done run off from his marster and was hidin' out from one place to another. At night he would go steal his somepin'-t'-eat. He had done stole some chickens and had 'em wid him up in de church steeple whar he was hidin' dat day. When daytime come, he went off to sleep lak niggers will do when dey ain't got to hustle, and when he woke up, Preacher Mansford was tellin' 'em 'bout how de Debil was gwine to git de sinners.

Right den a old rooster, what he had stole, up and crowed so loud it seemed lak Gabriel's trumpet on Judgment Day. Dat runaway nigger was skeered, 'cause he knowed dey was gwine to find him sho', but he warn't skeered nuffin' compared to dem niggers settin' in de gallery. Dey jus' knowed dat was de voice of de Debil what had done come atter 'em. Dem niggers never stopped prayin' and testifyin' to de Lord, till de white folkses had done got dat runaway slave and de rooster out of de steeple. His marster was dar and tuk him home and give him a good, sound thrashin'.

Slaves was 'lowed to have prayer meetin' on Tuesday and Friday round at de diffunt plantations whar deir marsters didn't keer, and dere warn't many what objected. De good marsters all give deir slaves prayer meetin' passes on dem nights so de patterollers wouldn't git 'em and beat 'em up for bein' off deir marster's lands. Dey most nigh kilt some slaves what dey cotch out, when dey didn't have no pass.

White preachers done de talkin' at de meetin'ouses, but at dem Tuesday and Friday night prayer meetin's, it was all done by niggers. I was too little to 'member much 'bout dem meetin's, but my older sisters used to talk lots 'bout 'em, long atter de War had brung our freedom. Dere warn't many slaves what could read, so dey jus' talked 'bout what dey had done heared de white preachers say on Sunday. One of de fav'rite texties was de third chapter of John, and most of 'em jus' 'membered a line or two from dat.

Missy, from what folkses said 'bout dem meetin's, dere sho' was a lot of good prayin' and testifyin', 'cause so many sinners repented and was saved. Sometimes at dem Sunday meetin's at de white folkses' church, dey would have two or three preachers de same day. De fust one would give de text and preach for at least a hour, den another one would give a text and do his preachin', and 'bout dat time another one would rise up and say dat dem fust two brudders had done preached enough to save three thousand souls, but dat he was gwine to try to double dat number. Den he would do his preachin', and atter dat one of dem others would git up and say, "Brudders and sisters, us is all here for de same and only purpose—dat of savin' souls. Dese other good brudders is done preached, talked, and prayed, and let the gap down. Now I'm gwine to raise it. Us is gwine to git 'ligion enough to take us straight through dem pearly gates. Now, let us sing whilst us gives de new brudders and sisters de right hand of fellowship." One of dem old songs went sort of lak dis:

> Must I be born to die
> And lay dis body down?

When dey had done finished all de verses and choruses of dat dey started:

Amazin' grace, how sweet de sound
Dat saved a wretch lak me.

'Fore dey stopped dey usually got round to singin':

On Jordan's stormy banks I stand,
And cast a wishful eye,
To Canaan's fair and happy land,
Whar my possessions lie.

Dey could keep dat up for hours, and it was sho' good singin', for dat's one thing niggers was born to do—to sing when dey gits 'ligion.

When old Aunt Flora come up and wanted to jine de church, she told 'bout how she had done seed de hebbenly light and changed her way of livin'. Folkses testified den 'bout de goodness of de Lord and His many blessin's what He give to saints and sinners, but dey is done stopped givin' him much thanks anymore. Dem days, dey 'zamined folkses 'fore dey let 'em jine up wid de church. When dey started 'zaminin' Aunt Flora, de preacher axed her, "Is you done been borned again, and does you believe dat Jesus Christ done died to save sinners?" Aunt Flora, she started to cry, and she said, "Lordy, is He daid? Us didn't know dat. If my old man had done 'scribed for de paper lak I told him to, us would have knowed when Jesus died." Missy, ain't dat jus' lak one of dem old-time niggers? Dey jus' tuk dat for ign'ance and let her come on into de church.

Dem days, it was de custom for marsters to hire out what slaves dey had dat warn't needed to wuk on deir own land, so our marster hired out two of my sisters. Sis' Anna was hired to a fambly 'bout sixteen miles from our place. She didn't lak it dar, so she run away and I found her hid out in our tater 'ouse. One day when us was playin', she called to me right low and soft lak and told me she was hongry and for me to git her somepin'-t'-eat, but not to tell nobody she was dar. She said she had been dar widout nothin' t'eat for several days. She was skeered Marster might whup her. She looked so thin and bad I thought she was gwine to die, so I told Mammy. Her and Marster went and brung Anna to de 'ouse and fed her. Dat pore chile was starved most to death.

Marster kept her at home for three weeks and fed her up good. Den he carried her back and told dem folkses what had hired her dat dey had better treat Anna good and see dat she had plenty t'eat. Marster was drivin' a fast hoss dat day, but bless your heart, Anna beat him back home. She cried and tuk on so, beggin' him not to take her back dar no more, dat he told her she could stay home. My other sister stayed on whar she was hired out till de War was over and dey give us our freedom.

Daddy had done hid all Old Marster's hosses when de Yankees got to our plantation. Two of de ridin' hosses was in de smokehouse and another good trotter was in de hen'ouse. Old Jake was a slave what warn't right bright. He slep' in de kitchen and he knowed whar Daddy had hid dem hosses, but dat was all he knowed. Marster had give Daddy his money to hide, too, and he tuk some of de plasterin' off de wall in Marster's room and put de box of money inside de wall. Den he fixed dat plasterin' back so nice you couldn't tell it had ever been tore off.

De night dem Yankees come, Daddy had gone out to de wuk 'ouse to git some pegs to fix somepin'—us didn't have no nails, dem days—when de Yankees rid up to de kitchen door and found Old Jake by hisself. Dat pore old fool was skeered so bad he jus' started right off babblin' 'bout two hosses in de smoke'ouse and one in de hen'ouse, but he was tremblin', so he couldn't talk plain. Old Marster heared de fuss dey made and he come down to de kitchen to see what was de matter. De Yankees den ordered Marster to git dem his hosses. Marster called Daddy and told him to git dem his hosses, but Daddy, he played foolish lak and stalled round lak he didn't have good sense. Dem sojers raved and fussed all night long 'bout dem hosses, but dey never thought about lookin' in de smoke'ouse and hen'ouse for 'em, and 'bout daybreak dey left widout takin' nothin'. Marster said he was sho' proud of my Daddy for savin' dem good hosses for him.

Marster had a long pocketbook what fastened at one end wid a ring. One day, when he went to git out some money, he dropped a roll of bills dat he never seed, but Daddy picked it up and handed it back to him right away. Now, my Daddy could have kept dat money jus' as easy, but he was a 'ceptional man and believed evvybody ought to do right.

One time Marster missed some of his money and he didn't want to 'cuse nobody, so he 'cided he would find out who had done de debbilment. He put a big rooster in a coop wid his haid stickin' out. Den he called all de niggers up to de yard and told 'em somebody had been stealin' his money, and dat evvybody must git in line and march round dat coop and tetch it. He said dat when de guilty ones tetched it, de old rooster would crow. Evvybody tetched it 'cept one old man and his wife; dey jus' wouldn't come nigh dat coop whar dat rooster was a-lookin' at evvybody out of his little red eyes. Marster had dat old man and 'oman sarched and found all de money what had been stole.

Mammy died 'bout a year atter de War, and I never will forget how Mist'ess cried and said, "Neal, your mammy is done gone, and I don't know what I'll do widout her." Not long atter dat, Daddy bid for de contract to carry de mail, and he got de place, but dat made de white folkses mighty mad, 'cause some white folkses had put in bids for dat contract. Dey 'lowed dat Daddy better not never start out wid dat mail, 'cause if he did he was gwine to be sorry. Marster begged Daddy not to risk it, and told him if he would stay dar wid him he would let him have a plantation for as long as he lived, and so us stayed on dar till Daddy died, and a long time atter dat us kept on wukkin' for Old Marster.

White folkses owned us back in de days 'fore de War, but our own white folkses was might good to deir slaves. Dey had to larn us 'bedience fust—how to live right, and how to treat evvybody else right—but de best thing dey larned us was how to do useful wuk.

Folkses warn't sick much in dem days lak dey is now, but now us don't eat strong vittles no more. Us raked out hot ashes den and cooked good old ashcakes what was a heap better for us dan dis bread us buys from de stores now. Marster fed us plenty of ashcake, fresh meat, and ash-roasted taters, and dere warn't nobody what could outwuk us.

A death was somepin' what didn't happen often on our plantation, but when somebody did die folkses would go from miles and miles around to set up and pray all night to comfort de fambly of the daid. Dey never made up de coffins till atter somebody died. Den dey measured de corpse and made de coffin to fit de body. Dem coffins was lined wid black calico and painted wid lampblack on de outside. Sometimes dey kivvered de outside wid black calico lak de linin'. Coffins for white folkses was jus' lak what dey had made up for deir slaves, and dey was all buried in de same graveyard on deir own plantation.

De fust school I went to was in a little one-room 'ouse in our white folkses' backyard. Us had a white teacher and all he larnt slave chillun was jus' plain readin' and writin'. When de War was over, dey closed de little one-room school what our good Marster had left in his backyard for his slaves, but our young Mis' Ellen larnt my sister right on till she got whar she could teach school. Daddy fixed up a room onto our house for her school, and she soon had it full of chillun. Dey made me study, too, and I sho' did hate to have to go to school to my own sister, for she evermore did take evvy chance to lay dat stick on me, but I s'pects she had a right tough time wid me. When time come round to celebrate school commencement, I was one proud little nigger, 'cause I never had been so dressed up in my life before. I had on a red waist, white pants, and a good pair of shoes; but de grandest thing of all 'bout dat outfit was dat Daddy let me wear his watch.

Evvybody come for dat celebration. Dere was over three hundred folkses at dat big dinner, and us had lots of barbecue and all sorts of good things t'eat. Old Marster was dar, and when I stood up 'fore all dem folkses and said my little speech widout missin' a word, Marster sho' did laugh and clap his hands. He called me over to whar he was settin' and said, "I knowed you could larn if you wanted to." Best of all, he give me a whole dollar. I was rich den, plumb rich. One of my sisters couldn't larn nothin'. De only letters she could ever say was G-O-D. No matter what you axed her to spell, she allus said G-O-D. She was a good field hand, though, and a good 'oman, and she lived to be more dan ninety years old.

Now, talkin' 'bout frolickin', us really used to dance. What I means is sho'-'nuf, old-time "break-downs." Sometimes us didn't have no music 'cept jus' beatin' time on tin pans and buckets, but most times old Elice Hudson played his fiddle for us, and it had to be tuned again atter evvy set us danced. He never knowed but one tune, and he played dat over and over. Sometimes dere was ten or fifteen couples on de floor at de same time, and us didn't think nothin' of dancin' all night long. Us had plenty of old corn juice for refreshment, and atter Elice had two or three cups of dat juice, he could git "Turkey in de Straw" out of dat fiddle lak nobody's business.

One time a houseboy from another plantation wanted to come to one of our Sad'dy night dances, so his marster told him to shine his boots fer Sunday and fix his hoss fer de night, and den he could git off for de frolic. Abraham shine his marster's boots till he could see hisself in 'em, and dey looked so grand he was tempted to try 'em on. Dey was a little tight, but he thought he could wear 'em, and he wanted to show hisself off in 'em at de dance. Dey warn't so easy to walk in, and he was 'fraid he might git 'em scratched up walkin' through de fields, so he snuck his marster's hoss out and rode to de dance.

When Abraham rid up der in dem shiny boots, he got all de gals' 'tention. None of dem wanted to dance wid de other niggers. Dat Abraham was sho' struttin' till somebody run in and told him his hoss had done broke its neck. He had tied it to a limb and, sho'-'nuf, some way, dat hoss had done got tangled up and hung his own self.

Abraham begged de other nigger boys to help him take de daid hoss home, but he had done tuk deir gals and he didn't git no help. He had to walk twelve long miles home in dem tight shoes. De sun had done riz up when he got dar, and it warn't long 'fore his marster was callin': "Abraham, bring me my boots." Dat nigger would holler out, "Yes, suh! I's a-comin'." But dem boots wouldn't come off 'cause his foots had done swelled up in 'em. His marster kept on callin', and when Abraham seed he couldn't put it off no longer, he jus' cut dem boots off his foots and went in and told what he had done.

Abraham's marster was awful mad and said he had a good mind to take de hide off Abraham's back. "Go git my hoss quick, nigger, 'fore I most kills you," he yelled. Den Abraham told him, "Marster, I knows you is gwine to kill me now, but your hoss is done daid." Den pore Abraham had to tell de whole story, and his marster got to laughin' so 'bout how he tuk all de gals away from de other boys and how dem boots hurt him, dat it looked lak he never would stop. When he finally did stop laughin' and shakin' his sides he said, "Dat's all right, Abraham. Don't never let nobody beat your time wid de gals." And dat's all he ever said to Abraham 'bout it.

When my sister got married, us sho' did have a grand time. Us cooked a pig whole wid a shiny red apple in its mouth and set it right in de middle of de long table what us had built out in de yard. Us had evvything good to go wid dat pig, and atter dat supper, us danced all night long. My sister never had seed dat man but one time 'fore she married him.

My daddy and his cousin Jim swore wid one another dat if one died 'fore de other, dat de one what was left would look atter de daid one's fambly and see dat none of de chillun was bound out to wuk for nobody. It warn't long atter dis dat Daddy died. I was jus' fourteen, and was wukkin' fer a brick mason larnin' dat trade. Daddy had done been sick a while, and one night de fambly woke me up and said he was dyin'. I run fast as I could for a doctor, but Daddy was done daid when I got back. Us buried him right side of Mammy in de old graveyard.

It was 'most a year atter dat 'fore us had de funeral sermon preached. Dat was de way folkses done den. Now Mammy and Daddy was both gone, but Old Marster said us chillun could live dar long as us wanted to. I went on back to wuk, 'cause I was crazy to be as good a mason as my daddy was. In Lexin'ton dere is a rock wall still standin' round a whole square what Daddy built in slavery time. Long as he lived, he blowed his bugle evvy mornin' to wake up all de folkses on Marse Frank's plantation. He never failed to blow dat bugle at break of day, 'cep on Sundays, and evvybody on dat place 'pended on him to wake 'em up.

I was jus' a-wukkin' away one day when Cousin Jim sent for me to go to town wid him. Missy, dat man brung me right here to Athens to de old courthouse and bound me out to a white man. He done dat very thing atter swearin' to my daddy he wouldn't never let dat happen. I didn't want to wuk dat way, so I run away and went back home to wuk. De sheriff come and got me and said I had to go back whar I was bound out or go to jail. Pretty soon I runned away again and went to Atlanta, and dey never bothered me 'bout dat no more.

De onliest time I ever got 'rested was once when I come to town to see 'bout gittin' somebody to pick cotton for me, and jus' as I got to a certain nigger's house de police come in and caught 'em in a crap game. Mr. McCune, de policeman, said I would have to go 'long wid de others to jail, but he would help me atter us got dar, and he did. He 'ranged it so I could hurry back home.

'Bout de best times us had in de plantation days was de corn-shuckin's, log-rollin's, and syrup-cookin's. Us allus finished up dem syrup-cookin's wid a candy-pullin'.

Atter he had all his corn gathered and put in big long piles, Marster 'vited de folkses from all round dem parts. Dat was de way it was done; evvybody holped de others git de corn shucked. Nobody thought of hirin' folkses and payin' out cash money for extra wuk lak dat. Dey 'lected a "gen'ral" to lead off de singin', and atter he got 'em to keepin' time wid de singin', de little brown jug was passed round. When it had gone de rounds a time or two, it was a sight to see how fast dem niggers could keep time to dat singin'. Dey could do all sorts of double time den, when dey had swigged enough liquor. When de corn was all shucked, dey feasted, and den drunk more liquor and danced as long as dey could stand up. De log-rollin's and candy-pullin's ended de same way. Dey was sho' grand good times.

I farmed wid de white folkses for thirty-two years and never had no trouble wid nobody. Us allus settled up fair and square, and in crop time dey never bothered to come round to see what Neal was doin', 'cause dey knowed dis nigger was wukkin' all right. Dey was all mighty good to me. Atter I got so old I couldn't run a farm no more, I wukked in de white folkses' gardens and tended deir flowers. I had done been wukkin' on Mrs. Steve Upson's flowers, and when she come to pay, she axed what my name was. When I told her it was Neal Upson, she wanted to know how I got de Upson name. I told her Mr. Frank Upson had done give it to me when I was his slave. She called to Mr. Steve and dey lak to have talked me to death, for my Marse Frank and Mr. Steve's daddy was close kinfolkses. Atter dat I wukked deir flowers long as I was able to walk way off up to deir place, but old Neal can't wuk no more. Mr. Steve and his folkses comes to see me sometimes and I's allus powerful glad to see 'em.

I used to wuk some for Miss Mary Bacon. She is a mighty good 'oman, and she knowed my daddy and our good old marster. Miss

Mary would talk to me 'bout dem old days, and she allus said, "Neal, let's pray," 'fore I left. Miss Mary never did git married. She's one of dem solitary ladies.

Now, Missy, how come you wants to know 'bout my weddin'? I done been married two times, but it was de fust time dat was de sho'-'nuf 'citin' one. I courted dat gal for a long, long time while I was too skeered to ax her daddy for her. I went to see her evvy Sunday jus' 'termined to ax him for her 'fore I left, and I would stay late atter supper, but jus' couldn't git up nerve enough to do it. One Sunday I promised myself I would ax him if it kilt me, so I went over to his house early dat mornin' and told Lida—dat was my sweetheart's name—I says to her, "I sho' is gwine to ax him today." Well, dinnertime come, suppertime come, and I was gittin' shaky in my j'ints when her daddy went to feed his hogs, and I went along wid him. Missy, dis is de way I finally did ax him for his gal. He said he was goin' to have some fine meat come winter. I axed him if it would be enough for all of his fambly, and he said, "How come you ax dat, boy?" Den I jus' got a tight hold on dat old hog pen and said, "Well, Sir, I jus' thought if you didn't have enough for all of 'em, I could take Lida." I felt myself goin' down. He started laughin' fit to kill. "Boy," he says, "is you tryin' to ax for Lida? If so, I don't keer, 'cause she's got to git married sometime." I was so happy I left him right den and run back to tell Lida dat he said it was all right.

Us didn't have no big weddin'. Lida had on a new calico dress and I wore new jeans pants. Marster heared us was gittin' married dat day and he sont his new buggy wid a message for us to come right dar to him. I told Lida us better go, so us got in dat buggy and driv off, and de rest of de folkses followed in de wagon. Marster met us in front of old Salem Church. He had de church open and Preacher John Gibson waitin' dar to marry us. Us warn't 'spectin' no church weddin', but Marster said dat Neal had to git married right. He never did forgit his niggers. Lida, she's done been daid a long time, and I's married again, but dat warn't lak de fust time.

Missy, I wish dere was somebody for me to talk to evvy day, for I's had sich a good time today. I don't s'pect it's gwine to be long 'fore old Neal goes to be wid dem I done been tellin' you 'bout, so don't wait too long to come back to see me again.

CHARLIE DAVENPORT

I WAS named Charlie Davenport an', encordin' to de way I figgers, I ought to be nearly a hund'ed years old. Nobody knows my birthday, 'cause all my white folks is gone.

I was born one night an' de very nex' mornin' my po' little mammy died. Her name was Lucindy. My pa was William Davenport.

When I was a little mite dey turnt me over to de granny nurse on de plantation. She was de one dat 'tended to de little pickaninnies. She got a woman to nurse me what had a young baby, so I didn't know no diff'ence. Any woman what had a baby 'bout my age would wet-nurse me, so I growed up in de quarters an' was as well an' as happy as any other chile.

When I could tote taters, dey'd let me pick 'em up in de fiel'. Us always hid a pile away where us could git 'em an' roast 'em, at night. Old Granny nearly always made a heap o' dewberry an' 'simmon wine. Us little tykes would gather black walnuts in de woods an' store 'em under de cabins to dry.

At night, when de work was all done an' de can'les was out, us'd set roun' de fire an' eat cracked nuts an' taters. Us picked out de nuts wid horseshoe nails an' baked de taters in ashes. Den Granny would pour herse'f an' her old man a cup o' wine. Us never got none o' dat 'less'n us be's sick. Den she'd mess it up wid wild cherry bark. It was bad den, but us gulped it down anyhow.

Old Granny used to sing a song to us what went lak dis:

Kinky-head, ware-fore you skeered?
Old snake crawled off, 'cause he's a-feared.

Pappy will smite 'im on de back
Wid a great big club—ker-whack! Ker-whack!

Aventine, where I was born an' bred, was acrost Secon' Creek. It
was a big plantation wid 'bout a hund'ed head o' folks a-livin' on it. It
was only one o' de marster's places, 'cause he was one o' de riches' an'
highes' quality gent'men in de whole country. I's tellin' you de trufe.
Us didn' b'long to no white trash. De marster was de Honorable
Mister Gabriel Shields hisse'f. Ever'body knowed 'bout him. He
married a Surget.

Dem Surgets was pretty devilish. For all, dey was de riches' fam'ly
in de lan'. Dey was de out-fightin'es', out-cussin'es', fastes'-ridin',
hardes'-drinkin', out-spendin'es' folks I ever seen. But, Lawd!
Lawd!—dey was gent'men, even in dey cups. De ladies was beautiful, wid big black eyes an' sof' white han's, but dey was high-
strung, too.

De marster had a town mansion what's pictured in a lot o' books. It
was called "Montebella." De big columns still stan' at de end o'
Shields Lane. It burnt 'bout thirty years ago.

I's part Injun. I ain't got no nigger nose, an' my hair is so long I has
to keep it wropped. I's often heard my mammy was reddish-lookin',
wid long, straight black hair. Her pa was a full-blooded Choctaw an'
mighty nigh as young as she was. I's been tole dat nobody dast
meddle wid her. She didn' do much talkin', but she sho' was a good
worker. My pappy had Injun blood, too, but his hair was kinky.

De Choctaws lived all roun' Secon' Creek. Some of 'em had cabins
lak settled folks. I can 'member dey las' chief. He was a tall pow'ful-
built man named Big Sam. What he said was de law, 'cause he was de
boss o' de whole tribe. One rainy night he was kilt in a saloon down
in Natchez Under de Hill. De Injuns went wild wid rage an' grief.
Dey sung an' wailed an' done a heap o' low mutterin'. De sheriff kep'
a steady watch on 'em, 'cause he was a-feared dey would do somethin'
rash. After a long time he kinda let up in his vig'lance. Den one night
some o' de Choctaw mens slipped in town an' stobbed de man dey
b'lieved had kilt Big Sam. I 'members dat well.

As I said before, I growed up in de quarters. De houses was clean
an' snug. Us was better fed den dan I is now, an' warmer, too. Us had

PLATE 33: Daguerreotype of a slave in the 1850s.

blankets an' quilts filled wid home-raised wool, an' I jus' loved layin'
in de big fat feather bed a-hearin' de rain patter on de roof.

All de little darkies he'ped bring in wood. Den us swept de yards
wid brush brooms. Den sometimes us played together in de street
what run de length o' de quarters. Us th'owed horseshoes, jumped
poles, walked on stilts, an' played marbles. Sometimes us made bows
an' arrows. Us could shoot 'em, too, jus' lak de little Injuns.

A heap o' times, Old Granny would brush us hide wid a peach tree
limb, but us need it. Us stole aigs [eggs] an' roasted 'em. She sho'
wouldn' stan' for no stealin' if she knowed it.

Us wore lowell cloth shirts. It was a coarse tow-sackin'. In winter
us had linsey-woolsey pants an' heavy cowhide shoes. Dey was made
in three sizes—big, little, an' mejum. 'Twan't no right or lef'. Dey
was sorta club-shaped, so us could wear 'em on either foot.

I was a teasin', miss-chee-vious chile an' de overseer's little gal got
it in for me. He was a big, hard-fisted Dutchman bent on gittin'
riches. He trained his pasty-faced gal to tattle on us niggers. She got a
heap o' folks whipped. I knowed it, but I was hasty. One day she hit
me wid a stick, an' I th'owed it back at her. 'Bout dat time up walked
her pa. He seen what I done, but he didn't see what she done to me.
But it wouldn' a-made no diff'ence if he had.

He snatched me in de air an' toted me to a stump an' laid me 'crost
it. I didn't have but one thickness 'twixt me an' daylight. Gent'men!
He laid it on me wid dat stick. I thought I'd die. All de time his
mean little gal was a-gloatin' in my misery. I yelled an' prayed to de
Lawd till he quit.

Den he say to me, "From now on you works in de fiel'. I ain't gwine
a-have no vicious boy lak you roun' de lady folks." I was too little for
fiel' work, but de nex' mornin' I went to choppin' cotton. After dat, I
made a reg'lar fiel' han'. When I growed up, I was a ploughman. I
could sho' lay off a pretty cotton row, too.

Us slaves was fed good plain grub. 'Fore us went to de fiel', us had
a big breakfas' o' hot bread, 'lasses, fried salt meat dipped in cornmeal, an' fried taters. Sometimes us had fish an' rabbit meat. When
us was in de fiel', two women 'ud come at dinnertime wid baskets
filled wid hot pone, baked taters, corn roasted in de shucks, onion,
fried squash, an' b'iled pork. Sometimes dey brought buckets o' cold

buttermilk. It sho' was good to a hongry man. At suppertime us had hoecake an' cold vittles. Sometimes dey was sweet milk an' collards.

Mos' ever' slave had his own little garden patch an' was 'lowed to cook out o' it.

Mos' ever' plantation kep' a man busy huntin' an' fishin' all de time. If he shot a big buck, us had deer meat roasted on a spit.

On Sundays us always had meat pie or fish or fresh game, an' roasted taters an' coffee. On Christmas, de marster 'ud give us chicken an' barrels o' apples an' oranges. 'Course, ever' marster warn't as freehanded as our'n was. He was sho'-'nuf quality. I's heared dat a heap o' cullud people never had nothin' good t'eat.

I warn't learnt nothin' in no book. Don't think I'd a-took to it, nohow. Dey learnt de house servants to read. Us fiel' han's never knowed nothin' 'cept weather an' dirt an' to weigh cotton. Us was learnt to figger a little, but dat's all.

I reckon I was 'bout fifteen when Hones' Abe Lincoln, what called hisse'f a rail-splitter, come here to talk wid us.* He went all th'ough de country jus' a-rantin' an' a-preachin' 'bout us bein' his black brothers. De marster didn' know nothin' 'bout it, 'cause it was sorta secret-lak. It sho' riled de niggers up, an' lots of 'em run away. I sho' heared 'im, but I didn' pay 'im no min'.

When de War broke out, dat old Yankee Dutch overseer o' our'n went back up North, where he b'longed. Us was pow'ful glad, an' hoped he'd git his neck broke.

After dat de Yankees come a-swoopin' down on us. My own pappy took off wid 'em. He jined a comp'ny what fit at Vicksburg. I was plenty big 'nuf to fight, but I didn' hanker to tote no gun. I stayed on de plantation an' put in a crop.

It was pow'ful oneasy times after dat. But what I care 'bout freedom? Folks what was free was in misery firs' one way an' den de other.

I was on de plantation close to town, den. It was called Fish Pond Plantation. De white folks come an' tole us we mus' burn all de cotton so de enemy couldn' git it.

Us piled it high in de fiel's, lak great mountains. It made my

---

*The narrator is confusing someone else with Lincoln, who visited Mississippi twice, but only before the narrator was born.

innards hurt to see fire 'teched to somethin' dat had cost us niggers so much labor an' hones' sweat. If I could a-hid some o' it in de barn I'd a-done it, but de boss searched ever'where.

De little niggers thought it was fun. Dey laughed an' brung out big armfuls from de cotton house. One little black gal clapped her han's an' jumped in a big heap. She sunk down an' down till she was buried deep. Den de wind picked up de flame an' spread it lak lightenin'. It spread so fas' dat 'fore us could bat de eye, she was in a mountain o' fiah. She struggled up all covered wid flames, a-screamin', "Lawdy, he'p me!" Us snatched her out an' rolled her on de groun', but 'twan't no use. She died in a few minutes.

De marster's sons went to war. De one what us loved bes' never come back no more. Us mourned him a-plenty, 'cause he was so jolly an' happy-lak, an' free wid his change. Us all felt cheered when he come roun'.

Us niggers didn' know nothin' 'bout what was gwine on in de outside worl'. All us knowed was dat a war was bein' fit. Pussonally, I b'lieve in what Marse Jefferson Davis done. He done de only thing a gent'man could a-done. He tole Marse Abe Lincoln to 'tend to his own bus'ness an' he'd 'tend to his'n. But Marse Lincoln was a fightin' man an' he come down here an' tried to run other folks' plantations. Dat made Marse Davis so all-fired mad dat he spit hard 'twixt his teeth an' say, "I'll whip de socks off dem damn Yankees." Dat's how it all come 'bout.

My white folks los' money, cattle, slaves, an' cotton in de War, but dey was still better off dan mos' folks.

Lak all de fool niggers o' dat time, I was right smart bit by de freedom bug for awhile. It sounded pow'ful nice to be tole, "You don't have to chop cotton no more. You can th'ow dat hoe down an' go fishin' whensoever de notion strikes you. An' you can roam roun' at night an' court gals jus' as late as you please. Ain't no marster gwine a-say to you, 'Charlie, you's got to be back when de clock strikes nine.' "

I was fool 'nuf to b'lieve all dat kin' o' stuff. But to tell de hones' trufe, mos' o' us didn' fin' ourse'fs no better off. Freedom meant us could leave where us'd been born an' bred, but it meant, too, dat us had to scratch for us own se'fs. Dem what lef' de old plantation seemed so all-fired glad to git back dat I made up my min' to stay put. I stayed right wid my white folks as long as I could.

My white folks talked plain to me. Dey say real sad-lak, "Charlie, you's been a dependence, but now you can go if you is so desirous. But if you wants to stay wid us you can sharecrop. Dey's a house for you an' wood to keep you warm an' a mule to work. We ain't got much cash, but dey's de lan' an' you can count on havin' plenty o' vittles. Do jus' as you please." When I looked at my marster an' knowed he needed me, I's pleased to stay. My marster never forced me to do nary a thing. Didn' nobody make me work after de War, but dem Yankees sho' made my daddy work. Dey put a pick in his han' 'stid o' a gun. Dey made 'im dig a big ditch in front o' Vicksburg. He worked a heap harder for his Uncle Sam dan he'd ever done for de marster.

I heared tell 'bout some nigger sojers a-plunderin' some houses. Out at Pine Ridge dey kilt a white man named Rogillio. But de head Yankee sojers in Natchez tried 'em for somethin' or 'nother an' hung 'em on a tree out near de Charity Horspital. Dey strung up de ones dat went to Mr. Sargent's door one night an' shot him down, too. All dat hangin' seemed to squelch a heap o' lousy goin's-on.

Lawd! Lawd! I knows 'bout de Kloo Kluxes. I knows a-plenty. Dey was sho'-'nuf devils a-walkin' de earth, a-seekin' what dey could devour. Dey larruped de hide off'n de uppity niggers an' driv de white trash back where dey b'longed.

Us niggers didn't have no secret meetin's. All us had was church meetin's in arbors out in de woods. De preachers 'ud exhort us dat us was de chillun o' Israel in de wilderness an' de Lawd done sont us to take dis lan' o' milk an' honey. But how us gwine a-take lan' what's already been took?

I sho' ain't never heared 'bout no plantations bein' 'vided up, neither. I heared a lot o' yaller niggers spoutin' off how dey was gwine a-take over de white folks' lan' for back wages. Dem bucks jus' took all dey wages out in talk, 'cause I ain't never seen no lan' 'vided up yet.

In dem days, nobody but niggers an' shawl-strop folks* voted. Quality folks didn't have nothin' to do wid such truck. If dey had

*Carpetbaggers.

a-wanted to, de Yankees wouldn' a-let 'em. My old marster didn' vote, an' if anybody knowed what was what, he did. Sense didn' count in dem days. It was pow'ful ticklish times, an' I let votin' alone.

De shawl-strop folks what come in to take over de country tole us dat us had a right to go to all de balls, church meetin's, an' 'tainments de white folks give. But one night a bunch o' uppity niggers went to a 'tainment in Memorial Hall. Dey dressed deyse'fs fit to kill, an' walked down de aisle, an' took seats in de very front. But jus' 'bout time dey set down, de curtin drapped an' de white folks riz up widout a-sayin' 'ary a word. Dey marched out de buildin' wid dey chins up an' lef' dem niggers a-settin' in a empty hall.

Dat's de way it happen ever' time a nigger tried to git too uppity. Dat night, after de breakin'-up o' dat 'tainment, de Kloo Kluxes rid th'ough de lan'. I heared dey grabbed ever' nigger what walked down dat aisle, but I ain't heared yet what dey done wid 'em. Dat same thing happened ever' time a nigger tried to act lak he was white.

A heap o' niggers voted for a little while. Dey was a black man what had office. He was named Lynch. He cut a big figger up in Washington. Us had a sheriff named Winston. He was a ginger-cake nigger an' pow'ful mean when he got riled. Sheriff Winston was a slave an', if my mem'ry ain't failed me, so was Lynch.

My granny tole me 'bout a slave uprisin' what took place when I was a little boy. None o' de marster's niggers 'ud have nothin' to do wid it. A nigger tried to git 'em to kill dey white folks an' take dey lan'. But what us want to kill Old Marster for an' take de lan' when he was de bes' frien' us had? Dey caught de nigger an' hung 'im to a limb.

Plenty folks b'lieved in charms, but I didn't take no stock in such truck. I don't lak for de moon to shine on me when I's a-sleepin'.

De young niggers is headed straight for hell. All dey think 'bout is drinkin' hard likker, goin' to dance halls, an' a-ridin' in a old rattletrap car. It beats all how dey brags an' wastes things. Dey ain't one whit happier dan folks was in my day. I was as proud to git a apple as dey is to git a pint o' likker. Course, schools he'p some, but looks lak all mos' o' de young-uns is studyin' 'bout is how to git out o' hones' labor. I's seen a heap o' fools what thinks 'cause they is wise in books, they is wise in all things.

Mos' all my white folks is gone, now. Marse Randolph Shields is a doctor 'way off in China. I wish I could git word to him, 'cause I know he'd look after me if he knowed I was on charity. I prays de Lawd to see 'em all when I die.

ELLEN BETTS

I GOT borned on de Bayou Teche, close to Opelousas. Dat was in St. Mary's Parish, in Louisiana. I belonged to Tolas Parsons what had 'bout five hundred slaves, countin' de little ones, big ones, dog and cats and Lawd God knows what else. When my eyes was jest barely fresh open, Marse Tolas die and will de hull lot of us to his brother, William. And I tell you dat Marse William was de greates' man what ever walk dis earth. Dat's de truth. I can't lie on him when de po' man's in his grave.

When a whuppin' got to be done, Old Marse do it hisself. He don't 'low no overseer to throw his gals down and pull up deir dress and whup on deir bottoms lak I hear tell dat some of 'em do. When dat have to be done, he do it hisself. Was he still livin', I s'pec' one part of his hands would be with him to dis day. I know I would.

When us niggers go down de road, folks'd say, "Dem's Parsons' niggers. Don't hit one of dem niggers of Parsons for God's sake, or Parsons sho' eat your jacket up."

Aunt Rachel, what cook in de big house for Mis' Cornelia, had four young-uns, and dem chillun was fat and slick as I ever seen. All de niggers have to stoop to Aunt Rachel jes' lak dey curtsy to Missy. I mind de time her husband, Uncle Jim, git mad and hit her over de head with a poker. A big knot raise up on Aunt Rachel's head, and when Marse 'quire 'bout it she say she done bump her head on de door. She dassn't tell on Uncle Jim or Marse sho' beat dat nigger to death. Marse sho' proud of dem black, slick chillun of Rachel's. You couldn't find a yaller chile on Marse's place. He sho' got no use fer mixin' black and white.

Marse William have de pretties' place up and down dat bayou, with a fine house and fine trees and sech. From whar we live, it was five miles to Centerville one way, and five miles to Patterson t'other. Dey haul de lumber from one place or t'other to make wood houses for de slaves. Sometime, Marse buy de fu'niture and sometime de carpenter make it for de slaves.

Mis' Sidney was my marster's fust wife and he had six boys by her. Den he marry de widder Cornelia and she give him four boys. With ten chillun springin' up quick lak dat and all de cullud chillun comin' along fast as pig litters, I don't do nothin' all my days but nuss, nuss, nuss.

I nuss so many chillun it done went and stunted my growth, and dat's why I ain't got nothin' but bones to dis day. When de cullud women have to cut sugarcane all day till midnight and after, I has to nuss de babies for 'em and tend to de white chillun, too. Some of dem babies was so big and fat I had to tote de feet while anudder gal tote de head. I was sech a little one—'bout seven or eight year old. De big folks would leave some toddy for colic and cryin' and sech, and I done drink toddy and let de chillun have de milk. I don't know no better. Lawsy me, it's a wonder I ain't de bigges' drunker in dis here country, countin' all 'de toddy I done put in my young belly.

When late of night come, iffen de babies wake up and bawl, I set up a screech and out-screech 'em till dey shut deir mouth. De louder dey bawl de louder I bawl. Next day somebody from de big house say, "Who dat screechin' to de top of deir voice, last night?" And I say, "Dat must be a old owl or sumpin'." Sometime, when Marster hear de babies cry, he come down and say, "Why de chillun cry lak dat, Ellen?" And I say, "Marse, I git so hungry and tired I done drink de milk up, 'stid of givin' it to de baby."

When I talk sassy, Old Marse jes' shake his finger at me, 'cause he knowed I was a good-un and don't let no little mite starve plumb up. I done drink de milk some from de babies, but I was so little I don't know no better.

One time, anudder gal name Hetty, what nussed lak I did, was mean sho' 'nuf to de babies. One night a baby howl lak sumpin' hurtin' sho' 'nuf, and dis gal won't move a inch to do nothin' 'bout it. Some of de white folks come along and raise de blanket offen de baby whar he lay on de floor by de hearth. A big log done bus' open in de

PLATE 34: A slave nurse.

fire and a chip sprung out on dat po' baby's foot and burn de big toe right off. When Marse find out 'bout dat, he run dat gal off as fast as wind and water could carry her, and we don't never hear nothin' more 'bout her.

Nobody never hit me a lick. Marse don't even let my own pa whup me. Sometime I see him whup a grown un dat would make a li'l chile tote water. Marse allus say dat bein' mean to de young-uns made dem mean when dey grow up, and nobody gwine ter buy a mean nigger. Marse don't even let us chillun go to de big cane patch. He used to plant little bitty patches close to de house, and each little nigger have a patch, and he work dat cane till it got growed. And when de chillun work deir cane and do small chores, Marse used to make de house gals pop co'n for 'em and make candy.

I nussed de sick folk too—white and black. Sometime I dose with blue mass pills, and den sometime Doc Fatchit [Fawcett] come along and leave rhubarb and epicac and calomel and castor oil and sech. Two year after de War, I git marry and git chillun of my own. Den I turn into a wet nuss. I wet nuss de white chillun and black chillun lak dey all de same color. Sometime I have a white un pullin' on de one side and a black one on t'other, and dat de truth. I wish my sister was here to testify for me. I knowed as much 'bout midwifin' as some of dem touty ones, but I git scare de law git on me, do I go ahead and bring de chillun.

I wanted to git de papers for midwifin', or whichever dey make you git, but Law', I don't never have no time for larnin' in slave time. Nohow, if Marse cotch a paper in your hand he sho' whup you. Marse don't 'low no bright niggers round. If dey act bright he sho' sell 'em quick. He allus say, "Book larnin' don't raise no good sugarcane." De only larnin' he 'low was in de church when dey larn de cullud chillun de Mefodis' catechism, and den we git whup', do we tetch dat li'l blue-back book.* De only writin' a nigger ever git was when he git bo'n, or marry, or die; den Marse put de name in de big Book.

Law', I sho' recollec' de time Marse marry Mis' Cornelia. He went on de mailboat and brung her from New Orleans. She was de pretties' woman in de world almost, 'ceptin' she have de bigges' mouth I nearly ever seen. He brung her up to de house and all de niggers and

*The blue-backed speller.

boys and girls and cats and dogs and sech come and salute her. Dere she stand on de gallery with a pretty white dress on, with red stripes runnin' up and down. Marse say to her, "Honey, see all de black folk? Dey belong to you now." She was so tickle' she almost cry, and she wave to us and smile on us. Next day she give her wedding dress to my ma. Dat was de fines' dress I ever seen. It was purple and green silk and we ain't never seen nothin' lak dat dress. All de nigger gals wear dat dress when dey git marry. My sister Sidney wo' it, and Sary and Mary. I don't know 'bout Polly and 'Melia.

Mis' Cornelia was de fines' woman in de world. Come Sunday mo'nin', she done put a bucket of dimes on de front gallery, and she stand dere and throw dimes out to de nigger chillun jes' lak feedin' chickens. And if you don't believe me, honey, I sho' is right here to testify for myself, 'cause I was right dere helpin' to grab. Sometime she done put a washtub of buttermilk on de back gallery and us chillun bring our gourds and dip up dat good old buttermilk until it all git drunk up. Sometime she fetch bread and butter to de back gallery and pass it out, when it don't even come mealtime.

Mis' Cornelia set my ma to cuttin' patterns and sewin' right away. Missy give all de women a bolt of linsey to make clothes, and ma would cut de pattern. We all had fine drawers down to de ankle, buttoned with pretty white buttons on de bottom. Lawsy, Ma sho' cut a mite of drawers, with sewin' for her eleven gals and four boys, too. Wash and Sonny and Charlie git drawers cut for 'em, too. In de summertime we all git a bolt of blue cloth and white tape for trimmin', to make Sunday dresses. For de field, all de niggers git homespun, what you make jumpers out of. I recollec' how Marse used to say, "Don't go into de field dirty Monday morning. Scrub yo'self and put on a clean jumper."

Marse was sho' good to dem gals and bucks what work cuttin' de cane. When dey git done makin' sugar, Marse give a drink dey call "peach 'n' honey" to de womenfolk, and whiskey and brandy to de men, and all de dancin' and caperin' you ever did see. My pa was a fiddler, and we would cut de "pigeon wing" and cut de "buck" and dance and dance. Sometime, Pa git so tired he say he ain't goin' play no mo', and us gals git busy and pop him co'n and make candy so to 'tice him to play mo'.

Po' Marse sho' turn over in his grave, did he know 'bout some of dat molasses. Dem black boys don't care. I seen 'em pull rats out from de sugar barrel, and dey would taste de sugar and say, "Ain't nothin' wrong with dat sugar. It still sweet." One day a pert one pull a dead scorpion out from de syrup kettle. He jus' laugh and say, "Marse don't want waste none of dis syrup." And he stuck out his tongue and lick de syrup right off from dat scorpion's body and legs.

Law' me, I seen thousands and thousands of sugar barrels and kettles of syrup in my day. Lawd knows how much sugarcane my old marse had. To dem dat work cuttin' de cane, it don't seem lak much, but to dem dat work hour in, hour out, dem sugarcane fields sho' stretch from one end of de earth to de other. Marse ship hogs [hogsheads] and hogs of sugar down de bayou. Many a time I seen de ribberboats go down with big signs what say, "Buy dis here molasses," on de side. And Marse raise a worl' of rice and taters and co'n and peanuts, too.

When de work was slight, us black folks sho' used to have de balls and dinners and suppers and sech. We git all day to barbecue meat down on de bayou, and de white folks come right down and eat 'long side de cullud. And when a black gal marry, Marse marry her hisself right in de big house. He let de gal marry on Saturday so dey git Sunday off, too. One time a ribberboat come bearin' licenses for de niggers to git marry with. Marse chase 'em off and say, "Don't you come truckin' no no-'count papers roun' my niggers. When I marry 'em, dey's married as good as if de Lawd God hisself marry 'em, and it don't take no paper to bind de tie." Marse don't stand no messin' round, neither. A gal have to be of age, and she have to ask her ma and pa and marse and missy, and if dey agree, dey go ahead and git married. Marse have a marry book to put de name down.

One time Marse write up to Virginny to buy some fresh hands. When de folks git haul' down to Centerville, Marse take me 'long to help tote de small chillun. Dey was a old man from Virginny dat hobble 'long side de road with us chillun. De chillun start to throw rocks and sech, and one little squirt 'bout nine year old sock dat old man right in de face. Den de dogs start barkin' after him. I keep tellin' de chillun, "Don't you sock dat old man. He ain't done nothin' to you." Den de old man turn roun' to dat prissy one and point his finger at him and say, "Go on, young-un, and you'll be whar de dogs can't bark at you, tomorrow!" Dat pointin' finger scare all de other chillun. But dat little boy don't stop; he jes' pester de old man right into de plantation.

When we git home, de sun done gone down and us chillun all crawl off to bed. Next mornin', we was busy in de kitchen cookin' rice and fryin' up meat when all of a sudden dat li'l boy jes' crumple up dead on de floor. Law', we was scared. Nobody ever bother dat old man after dat, for he sho' lay de evil finger on you.

One day a li'l man come ridin' by on a li'l dun hoss what was runnin' so fast you couldn't see his tail a-switchin'. He was whoopin' and hollerin'. Us niggers don't know no better, and we whoop and holler, too. Den, fust thing you know de Yanks and de Democrats* begun to fit [fight] right dere. Dey was a high old mountain in front of Marse's house, most as tall as a pole, and de Yanks begun to pepper cannonballs down from de top of dat hill. Yes ma'am, de War met right dere, and dem Yanks and Democrats fit for twenty-four hours straight runnin'.

When de bullets start rainin' down, Marse call us and slip us way back into de woods whar it was so black and deep we couldn't see each other. Next day, when de fit was over, Marse came out in de woods with great big wagons. Dem wagons was piled up with barrels of messpoke for de slaves to eat. Dat's what dey call hog meat. He was so glad to see us and sho' glad we 'scape from de Yanks.

When we driv back to de plantation, sech a sight I never seen. Law', chile, de things I can tell. Dem Yanks have kill single men and women. I seen 'em pick up dead babies from de road with deir brains bus' right out. One old man was drawin' a bucket of water and a cannonball had shot him right in de well. Dey has to draw him up with a fishin' line. Dey was a old sugar boat out on de bayou with blood and sugar runnin' longside de busted barrels. Molasses run in de bayou and blood run in de ditches. Marse had a great big orchard right on de road, and it was wipe clean as a whistle. Nary a tree. Nary a plum or peach or orange. Bullets wipe up everything and bus' dat

*Confederates.

sugarcane all to pieces. De house sot far back and 'scape de bullets, but Law', de time dey had.

Dey was awful, awful times after dat. Why, a old cotton dress like dis here I got on cost five dollars. A pound of coffee cost five dollars. Co'se dey was plenty of sugar, but a pint cup of flour cost six bits.

When de Yanks come roun', dey hide in de sugarcane. Dey would dirty up de patch till Marse git so mad he 'bout die. I'm tellin' you de truth. I sho' ain't lyin'.

One day de Yanks come right in de house whar Mis' Cornelia was eatin' her dinner. Marse was out in de field somewhar, and de sojers march all roun' de table jes' scoopin' up de meat and taters and grabbin' co'n pone right and left. Mis' Cornelia don't say a word—jes' smile sweet as honeycake. I reckon dem sojers might a took de silver and sech, only Mis' Cornelia charm 'em by bein' so quiet and ladylike. Dey 'spec' her to storm out, and I reckon it kinder dumb dem, 'cause she act so sweet. Fust thing you know dem sojers curtsy to missy and take deir self right out de door and don't come back.

After de War, dem Ku Kluxers what wear de false faces try to tinker with Marse's niggers. One day old Uncle Dave start to town and one of dem Kluxers meet him on de road and say, "Whar your pass?" Uncle Dave don't know nothin' 'bout no pass and he done keep right on goin'. Dat Kluxer clout him on de back, but Uncle Dave outrun him in de cane and go on back and tell Marse. Marse grab a hoss and go 'rest dat man. Marse was a jedge and he make dat man pay a fine for hittin' Uncle Dave. After dat, dem old pokey faces was sho' scared of Marse, and dey git out from Opelousas and dey stay out. Marse tell 'em he don't want none of his black folks beat up and knock up, 'cause dey was taking keer of his chillun.

When me and my husband, John, come to Texas, de folks say dat Louisiana marsters was de meanes' in de world. And I say right back at 'em dat dey is good and mean in every spot of de earth, and what is mo', de Louisiana marsters free deir niggers a year before any Texas nigger git free.

When 'Mancipation come, Marse git on a big block and say, "You all is as free as I is standin' right here." He say, "Does you want to stay on with me, you can, and I'll pay you for de work." All de niggers cheer and say dey want to stay. But Marse die not long after de War, and all us niggers scatter.

I sho' recollec' dat day pore old Marse die. He won't die till Ma gits thar. All de time he keep sayin', "Whar's Charity? Tell Charity to come." Dey run and fetch Ma from de cane patch, and she hold Marse's hand till he die. Us niggers went to de graveyard, and we sho' cry after Old Marse.

Marse's brother, Goldham, carried all his hands back to de free country to turn 'em loose. He say de free country folks was de ones what was yellin' 'bout slave times, so dey could jes' take keer of de niggers. Marse Goldham was so big dat when he stand in a door you couldn't git by him 'thout he stan' sideways.

Law', de times ain't like dey was in slave days. All my ten chillun dead and my old man gone, and now I reckon my time 'bout arrive. All I got to do now is pray de Lawd to keep me straight. Den, when de great day comes I can march de road to Glory.

Voices

———◁+ +▷———

THE RECONSTRUCTION ERA,

SHARECROPPING,

VOTING,

AND THE KU KLUX KLAN

RIGHT atter de Freedom War, us wuz sharecroppers. Now, I's gwine ter try ter tell you how us did, in sharecroppin'.

'Long 'tween November an' February, de Negro man go ter de planter dat he want ter wuk fer, an' he mos' en general find de white man at de plantation sto'e. White man gwine ask de nigger whar he been livin' 'fo'e, an' how many chillun he got, an' effen he hab any mules er any plows, hoes, an' things ter wuk de place wid. Mos' en general, de nigger, he jes' hab er few clothes, some beddin', some furnichure, an' a dog ter cotch de rabbit wid.

De white man gotta gib de nigger a cabin ter lib in, an' see dat he hab groceries, an' some clothes, an' a doctor an' medicine, f'om de time he starts wuk fer de white man till de cotton git picked, 'long in August, an' dey starts sellin' cotton. De nigger, he don't pay no rent on de cabin, lak dese town niggers had ter, an' de white man gotta see dat dar is a well ob water on de place an' a place fer de nigger ter water he stock, an' a place whar de nigger can cut him some wood ter cook wid an' ter keep warm by. Dey don't charge de nigger fer de wood an' water. Dar is a patch fer de garden furnished, too, an' de seed ter plant de crop wid, an' mos' en general, de mules an' tools ter wuk de land.

De white man say he gwine see dat de sharecropper git somefin' ter eat an' some clothes ter wear, up to a specified 'mount. An' de cropper, he promise ter wuk de land lak de white man want hit done. An' when de crop am gaddered, de sharecropper, he gotta pay half ob de corn and de cotton dat he make on de land as rent; an' he gotta pay fer all de groceries, clothes, an' medicine an' doctor bills dat he had while he makin' de crop.

PLATE 35: A family of free sharecroppers after the Civil War.

No ma'am, de white man, he don't gib de nigger no sho' 'nuf money. He jes' gib him a doodlum book, an' in dis here book dar's little pieces ob paper all printed an' fixed up, an' de sharecropper, he trades dese here little scraps ob paper down at de plantation sto'e fer what he gwine git. But he can't go no whar else ter trade, only jes' on de plantation whar he makin' de crop. Dat er way, de nigger man, he can't go git drunk an' sech, an' de ole woman an' de kids, dey git somefin' dey needs. I lak dat. Co'se, dar wuz some ob de sto'es on some ob de big plantations, whar dey did hab de whiskey.

—SARAH WILSON

Niggers didn' have no lan' at all fo' demselves, even after freedom come. Dey go t' de ole marsters an' rent lan' t' farm. De marster take a lien on de lan'. When he go t' take his part, he choose de sorriest row of co'n fo' de nigger. De marster mos' times furnish groceries, an' clothes, an' shoes, an' take a lien on de crop fo' de payback. If de doctor have to come, he take a lien on de crop, too.

When de crop was harvest' dat way, lots of times de lan'lord had all de crop an' de nigger had nothin'. Iffen dere was a dispute an' dey had t' go t' de Bu'ro [Freedmen's Bureau], de Bu'ro make de arres' all right, but dat night, nigger, don' you stay in dat camp, 'cause de Klu Klux goin' ter git you an' beat you up.

One time, dey got after us an' we tuk t' de woods. We sleep out in de woods, an' dey was plenty of panther an' rattlesnakes. We was terrible scare', but we was more scare' of de Klu Klux. I'd sho' like t' see de soil dat brought me up, but I don' want t' spen' another night in Tyler County.

—JOHN MCDONALD

Seems lak dar warn't no trouble 'mongst de whites an' blacks till atter de Wah. Den, some white mens come down from de Norf an' mess up wid de niggers. I was a mighty little shaver, but I 'members one night atter supper my daddy an' mammy an' us chillun was settin' under a big tree by our cabin in de quarters, when all at wunst, lickety split, heah come gallopin' down de road what look lak a whole army of ghos'es. Mus' hab been 'bout a hundert, an' dey was men ridin' hosses, wid de men an' hosses bofe robed in white.

Cap'n, dem mens look lak dey ten feet high, an' dey hosses big as elephan's. Dey didn't bodder nobody at de quarters, but de leader of de crowd ride right in de front gate an' up to de big dug well, back of our cabin, an' holler to my daddy, "Come heah, nigguh! Ho-oh!" Co'se we skeered. Yassah, look lak our time done come.

My daddy went ober to whar de leader settin' on his hoss at de well. Den, de leader say, "Nigguh, git a bucket an' draw me some cool water." Daddy got a bucket, fill it up, an' han' it to him. Cap'n, would you b'lieve it, dat man jes' lif' dat bucket to his mouf an' neber stop till it empty. Did he hab 'nuf? He jes' smack his mouf an' call for mo'. Jes' lak dat, he didn't stop till he drunk three buckets full. Den, he jes' wipe his mouf an' say, "Lawdy, dat sho' was good. It was de fust drink of water I's had sence I was killed at de Battle of Shiloh."

Was we good? Cap'n, from den on, dar wasn't a nigger dare stick his head out de do' for a week. But next day, we fine out dey was Ku Kluxes, an' dey foun' de body of a white man hangin' to a post oak tree, ober by Gran' Prairie. His name was Billings, an' he come from de Norf. He been ober roun' Livingston messin' up de niggers, tellin' 'em dey had been promised forty acres and a mule, an' dey ought to go 'head an' take 'em from de white folks.

—HENRY GARRY

One time, the Ku Klux come aroun'. They knock on the doah, then they say, "Please give me a drink. Ah ain't had a drink since the Battle of Shiloh." What fo' they say that? Why, you see, they wants us tuh think they's the spirits o' the sojers killed at Shiloh, an' that they been in hell so long, they drinks all the water they kin git. This one man make us carry him five buckets o' water, an' it look like he drink 'em, but nex' mahnin', they's a big mud puddle, 'side the doah.

—FREDERICK ROSS

Baby, them Ku Klux was a pain. The paddyrollers was bad enough, but them Ku Klux done lots of devilment. I worked for a

white man once, who was a Ku Klux, but I didn't know it for a long
time. One time, he said, "Now, when you're foolin' around in my
closet cleanin' up, I want you to be partickler." I seed them rubber
pants what they filled with water. I reckon he had enough things for a
hundred men. His wife say, "Now, Talitha, don't let on you know
what them things is."

—TALITHA LEWIS

The onlies' 'sperience I had myself wid the Ku Klux was one night
'fo' Grandma and Auntie left. Somebody raps on our cabin door.
They opened it. We got scared when we seed 'em. They had the
horses wrapped up. They had on white long dresses and caps. Every
one of 'em had a horse whoop [whip]. They called me out. Grandma
and Auntie was so scared they hid. They tole me to git 'em water.
They poured it somewhah it did not spill on the ground. Kept me
totin' water. Then, they say, "You been a good boy?" They still
drinkin'. One say, "Just from hell. Pretty dry." Then, they tole me to
stand on my head. I turned summersets a few times. They tickled me
round wid the ends of the whoops. I had on a long shirt. They laugh
when I stand on my head. Old Marse White laugh. I knowed his
laugh. Then, I got over my scare.

They say, "Who live next down the road?" I tole 'em Nells Christian. They say, "What he do?" I said, "Works in the field." They all
grunt "m-m-m-m." Then, they say, "Show us the way." I nearly run
to death 'cross the field to keep outer the way of the white horses. The
moon was shining bright as day. They say, "Nells, come out here." He
say, "Holy Moses." He come out. They say, "Nells, what you do?" "I
farms." They say, "What you raise?" He say, "Cotton and corn." They
say, "Take us to see yo' cotton. We jes' from hell. We ain't got no
cotton there."

He took 'em out there, where it was clear. They got down and felt
round. Then, they say, "What is that?" feelin' the grass. Nells say,
"That is grass." They say, "You raise grass, too?" He say, "No. It come
up." They say, "Let us see yo' corn." He showed 'em the corn. They
felt it. They say, "What is this?" Nells say, "It is grass." They say,
"You raise grass here?" They all grunt "m-m-m-m" at everything

Nells say. They give him one bad whoopin' and tell him they be back soon to see if he raisin' grass. They said, "You raise cotton and corn, but not grass, on this farm." Then, they moan "m-m-m-m."

I heard 'em say his whole family, and him, too, was out by daylight wid their hoes, cuttin' grass out their crop.

—HAMMETT DELL

I was pretty good when I was a boy, so I never had any trouble, then. I was right smart size, when I saw the Ku Klux. They would whip men and women that weren't married and were living together. On the first day of January, they would whip men and boys that didn't have a job. They kept the Negroes from voting. They would whip them. They put up notices: "No niggers to come out to the polls tomorrow." They would run them off of government land, which they had homesteaded. Sometimes, they would just persuade them not to vote. A Negro like my father, they would say to him, "Now, Brown, you are too good to get messed up. Them other niggers round here ain't worth nothing, but you are, and we don't want to see you get hurt. So you stay 'way from the polls tomorrow." And, tomorrow, my father would stay away, under the circumstances.

—F. H. BROWN

Well, we voted if our white man said vote and for who he said vote for, as we did not know anything then about voting or who to vote for, unless Maser told us. The way we voted was to go touch the pencil as he voted. We never did know who we voted for or what good we was doing in voting. All we knew was what our white people told us to do, and that we better do it. As I told you, we was not a free people, and still are not.

—MARY GAFFNEY

The only time I voted was when they was voting against whiskey. I voted for it. Some of the white folks said they would whip me, if I voted for it, but Mr. Joe Strickland told me they was just trying to scare me, and to go ahead and vote for it.

—GUS BRADSHAW

I've generally kept out of trouble by keepin' my mouf shet and doin' what I thought was right. Take votin', fer instance. De boss man on de different farms where I worked would tell me, around election time, to vote Democratic. But I knew de Republican Party was on de side of de cullud man. So I nevah say nothin' when de boss man told me how to vote. I nevah promised anything at all. I just went to de polls on election day and put my cross under de eagle.

—MORGAN RAY

I vote de 'Publican ticket, as I try to show my 'preciation, and dat gits me in bad wid de Klu Klux. They scare me, but no touch me. De Red Shirts* try to 'suade me to vote their way. Some of de best white folks was in dat movement, but I 'members old Tom True beating me, often for little or nothing. I sticks out to de end wid de party dat freed me.

—BILL MCNEIL

After freedom, we worked on shares a while. Then, we rented. When we worked on shares, we couldn't make nothing—just over-alls and something to eat. Half went to the white man, and you would destroy your half, if you weren't careful. A man that didn't know how to count would always lose. He might lose anyhow. The white folks didn't give no itemized statement. No, you just had to take their word. They never give you no details. They just say you owe so much. No matter how good account you kept, you had to go by their account, and—now, brother, I'm telling you the truth about this—it's been that way for a long time. You had to take the white

*South Carolina Democrats, in the epochal election of 1878.

man's word on notes and everything. Anything you wanted you could get, if you were a good hand. If you didn't make no money, that's all right; they would advance you more. But you better not try to leave and get caught. They'd keep you in debt. They were sharp. Christmas come, you could take up twenty dollars in somethin'-to-eat and much as you wanted in whiskey. You could buy a gallon of whiskey—anything that kept you a slave. Because he was always right and you were always wrong, if there was difference. If there was an argument, he would get mad and there would be a shooting take place.

—HENRY BLAKE

The worst part of it was we could not read or write, or hold any kind of a job, except farm work. If we left our white people and tried to get work, the KKKs said no. They would not let us prowl around and hunt anything to do, to try and better ourselves. If we went to the little town on Saturday evening, the KKKs were there to make us go home and work. Son, I am telling you, them KKKs was terrible on the Negro, but I guess it was for the best, as some of them would not have tried to work or do anything—just roam around the country and steal everything they could get their hands on.

—PARILEE DANIELS

In them days, the Negroes could not get out and get jobs, like they can now. If we went to another white man and asked him for a job, he asked us, "Aren't you livin' with so-an'-so?" We say, "Yes, sir." Then, he would say to us, "You will have to go to him with your trouble. He is your boss." And that was exactly what we had to do.

—ROSA POLLARD

My father-in-law heard of an opening for a young couple, near Louisville, Kentucky, on the Bardstown Road, with a Widow Ross. My wife and I arrived one cold rainy night and were assigned to a terrible old brick building for the night. The next morning, about 4

A.M., I heard a bell jangling and got up to investigate. As soon as I poked my head out, Mrs. Ross called, "That's for you, nigger!" Well, I complained about the poor quarters, only to be told that anything was good enough for "niggers." This was a terrible woman who kept pistols, guns, and other firearms around, in all rooms.

One night, she ordered me to go about a block and a half to the post office. There was shooting and carousing going on. I was afraid to venture out, but the widow told me those were only "niggers" shooting, and that's all *I* was.

There was a small round house in the yard. I had never seen anything like this, so I looked into it. The widow saw me and called, "That's a whipping house for the likes of you!"

My wife and I put up with this sort of treatment for a week, and couldn't stand it any longer. Mrs. Ross wouldn't furnish any conveyance for our trunk, which was all we had taken with us. I gathered one end and my wife the other, and away we trudged with all our worldly goods. The widow refused to pay us anything, if we left, but all we wanted was to get away before we were shot to death. I guess we made a record in staying an entire week at the widow's.

—PETE JOHNSON

After de colored people was considered free an' turned loose, de Klu Klux broke out. Some of de colored people commenced to farming, like I tole you, an' all de ole stock dey could pick up after de Yankees left, dey took an' took care of. If you got so you made good money an' had a good farm, de Klu Klux'd come an' murder you. De gov'ment built de colored people schoolhouses, an' de Klu Klux went to work an' burn 'em down. Dey'd go to de jails an' take de colored men out, an' knock deir brains out, an' break deir necks, an' throw 'em in de river.

After de Klu Kluxes got so strong, de colored men got together an' made a complaint before de law. De Gov'nor told de law to give 'em de ole guns in de commissary, what de Southern soldiers had use', so dey issued de colored men old muskets an' told 'em to protect deirselves.

De colored men got together an' organized de malicy [militia].

Dey had leaders like regular soldiers, men dat led 'em right on. Dey didn't meet 'cept when dey heard de Klu Kluxes was coming to get some of de colored folks. Den, de one who knowed dat tole de leader, an' he went round an' tole de others when an' where dey'd meet. Den, dey was ready for 'em. Dey'd hide in de cabins, an' when de Klu Kluxes come, dere dey was. Den's when dey found out who a lot of de Klu Kluxes was, 'cause a lot of 'em was killed. Dey wore dem long sheets, an' you couldn't tell who dey was. Dey even covered deir horses up, so you couldn't tell who dey belong to. Men you thought was your friends was Klu Kluxes. You deal wit' 'em in de stores in de daytime, an' at night dey come out to your house an' kill you.

— PIERCE HARPER

One of dem Kluxers come to our house and set down and talked to us 'bout how us ought to act, and how us was goin' to have to do, if us 'spected to live and do well. Us allus thought it was our own old marster, all dressed up in dem white robes, wid his face kivvered up, and a-talkin' in a strange, put-on lak, voice.

— ANDERSON FURR

I remembers one day when me an' anudder little nigger gal was goin' atter de cows down in de fiel', an' us seed what I reckon was de Ku Klux Klan. Us was so skeered us didn't know what to do. One of 'em walked up to us an' say, "Niggers, whar you a-goin'?"

"Us is jus' atter de cows, Mr. Ku Klux," us say. "Us ain't up to no debilment."

"All right, den," dey say, "jus' you be sho' dat you don't git into none."

Atter us got home, us told de massa 'bout de 'sperience, an' he jus' laugh. He told us dat us warn't goin' to be hurt, iffen us was good. He say dat it was only de bad niggers dat was goin' to be got atter by dem Ku Klux.

— NICEY PUGH

Dere am some trouble wid de Klux in my neighbahood. 'Twas an old cullud fellow named George. He don't trouble anybody, but one night, de white caps—dat's what dey am called—comes to his place. Now, George knows ob some folks dat am whupped fo' no cause, so he prepared fo' dem. When de Klux comes to his house, George am in de loft. He told dem dat he have done nothin' wrong, an' fo' dem to go 'way, or he would kill dem. Dey told him dat dey's gwine to show him what he would git if he did somethin' wrong. Sho', dey's gwine to give him de free sample.

Well, one ob de men stahts up de laddah to git George out ob de loft. When he gits part way up, George shoots de fellow dead. Den, atudder fellow stahts to shoot through de ceilin'. Co'se, dey can see George, an' George can see dem, through de cracks, an' he shoots atudder fellow. Dey leave, den, an' told him dat dey would be back. George run an' told his old marster, as soon as dey leaves. De marster tooks him to de lawmen, an' dere am never anythin' done 'bout de old cullud fellow shootin' an' killin' dem white caps.

—CHARLEY HURT

We lived in a log house during the Ku Klux days. Dey would watch you just like a chicken rooster watching fer a worm. At night, we was skeered to have a light. Dey would come around wid de "dough faces" on, and peer in de winders, and open de do'. Iffen you didn't look out, dey would skeer you half to death.

John Good, a darky blacksmith, used to shoe de horses fer de Ku Klux. He would mark de horseshoes with a bent nail or something like that. Then, atter a raid, he could go out in the road and see if a certain horse had been rode. So, he began to tell on de Ku Klux. As soon as de Ku Klux found out dey was being give away, dey suspicioned John. Dey went to him and made him tell how he knew who dey was. Dey kept him in hiding, and when he told his tricks, dey killed him.

When I was a boy on de Gilmore place, de Ku Klux would come along at night a-riding de niggers like dey was goats. Yes sir, dey had 'em down on all fours a-crawling, and dey would be on deir backs. Dey would carry de niggers to Turk Creek bridge, and make dem set up on de banisters of de bridge; den, dey would shoot 'em offen de banisters into de water.

—BRAWLEY GILMORE

I remembers one night, raght atter de War, when de Re'struction wuz a-goin' on. Dere wuz some niggers not far f'om our place dat said dey wuz a-goin' to take some lan' dat warn't deirs. Deir massa had been kilt in de War, an' warn't nobody 'ceptin' de mistis an' some chillun. Well, honey, dem niggers—mo' dan a hundred of 'em—commenced a riot an' wuz a-takin' things dat don't belong to 'em. Dat night, de white lady, she come ober to our place wid a wild look on her face. She tell Massa Bennett what dem niggers is up to, an' widout sayin' a word, Massa Bennett put his hat on an' lef' out de do'. 'Twarn't long atter dat when some hosses wuz heered down de road, an' I look out my cabin window, which wuz raght by de road, an' I saw a-comin' up through de trees a whole pack of ghosties—I thought dey wuz, anyways. Dey wuz all dressed in white, an' deir hosses wuz white, an' dey galloped faster dan de win' raght past my cabin. Den, I heered a nigger say, "De Ku Klux is atter somebody."

Dem Ku Klux went ober to dat lady's plantation an' told dem niggers dat iffen dey ever heered of 'em startin' anything mo', dat dey wuz a-goin' to tie 'em all to trees in de fores' till dey all died f'om being hongry. Atter dat, dese niggers all roun' Louisville, dey kept mighty quiet.

—HANNAH IRWIN

I stays with my folks till I's twenty-four year old, and den I's on my way to Galveston and gits work as de stevedore. I votes dere two times. Some white folks done come to us, and de boss, too, and gives us de ticket. It am all mark' up. Boss say us don't have to work de next day, and for us to report at a place. When us comes dere, 'twas a table with meat and bread and stuff for to eat, and whiskey and cigars. Dey give us something to eat and a cup or two of dat whiskey, and puts de cigar in de mouth. Us am 'portant niggers, ready to vote. With dat cup of whiskey in de stomach, and de cigar in de mouth, and de hat cock' on side de head, us march to de votin' place and does our duty. Fix up de way us was, us would vote to put us back in slavery.

—WILLIAM THOMAS

Ise never votes. De Lawd took care of slavery widout dem votin',
an' Him will lead de way now, fo' de cullud folks.

—BETTY POWERS

Most de cullud folks stays with Massa Buford after Surrender, and
works de land on shares. Dey have good times on dat place and don't
want to leave. Dey has dances and fun, till de Ku Klux org'nizes, and
den it am lots of trouble. De Klux comes to de dance and picks out a
nigger and whups him, jus' to keep de niggers scairt, and it git so
bad dey don't have no more dances or parties.

I 'members seein' Faith Baldwin and Jeb Johnson and Dan Hester
gittin' whupped by de Klux. Dey wasn't so bad after women. It am
allus after dark when dey comes to de house and catches de man, and
whups him for nothin'. Dey had de power, and it am done for to show
dey has de power. It gits so bad round dere dat de menfolks allus eats
supper befo' dark, and takes a blanket and goes to de woods for to
sleep. Alex Buford don't sleep in de house for one whole summer.

No one knowed when de Klux comin'. All a-sudden, up dey
gallops on hosses, all covered with hoods, and bust right into de
house. Just latches, 'stead of locks, was used, dem days. Dey comes
sev'ral times to Alex' house, but never cotches him. I'd hear dem
comin' when dey hit de lane, and I'd holler, "De Klux am comin'."
It was my job, after dark, listenin' for dem Klux. Den, I gits under
de bed.

—WILLIAM HAMILTON

I 'member de Klu Klux. Dey come to de house what I live in and
ax me is I scared? I tell 'em, "No." Dey say, "How come you ain't
scared?" I tell 'em I ain't done nobody nothin'. One man ax me,
"Does you know me?" And I tell him, "No." So dey tell me, "You
needn't be scared. You do like you do now, and ain't nothin' gwine ter
hurt you." Dey say dey ain't lookin' for me; dey lookin' for somebody
else.

—EVA MARTIN

De worsest time of all fer us darkies wuz when de Ku Klux killed Dan Black. We wuz little chillun a-playin' in Dan's house. We didn't know he had done nothin' 'ginst de white folks. Us wuz a-playin' by de fire jus' as nice, when something hit on de wall. Dan, he jump up and try to git outen de winder. A white spooky thing had done come in de do', right by me. I wuz so scairt dat I could not git up. I had done fell straight out on de flo'. When Dan stick his head outen dat winder, something say "bang," and he fell right down on de flo'.

I crawls under de bed. When I got dar, all de other chillun wuz dar, too, lookin' as white as ashed dough from hickory wood. Us peeped out, and den us duck under de bed agin. Ain't no bed eber done as much good as dat one. Den, a whole lot of dem come in de house. Day wuz all white and scary-lookin'. It still makes de shivers run down my spine, and here I is ole, and you all is a-settin' around wid me, and two mo' wars done gone since dat awful time. Dan Black, he wan't no mo', 'cause dey took dat nigger and hung him to a 'simmon tree. Dey would not let his folks take him down, either. He jus' stayed dar, till he fell to pieces.

—MILLIE BATES

After the War was over, we was afraid to move. Jes' like tarpins or turtles, after 'Mancipation. Jes' stick our heads out to see how the land lay.

—W. L. BOST

When the Yankees come to Marshall, after the War, they took charge of all the law business. They put ignorant Southern niggers in office. Here is the way it worked. A Yankee officer might come to me and say, "Allen, I'll give you sich-and-sich office, if you do what I tell you." I take the office, and set back like I was somebody. Then comes one of my Southern white men in to see me, and he say, "Allen, you got this office now?" I tell him I have, and he say, "Can you handle it?" I knowed he knowed I couldn't, and so I'd hire him as my clerk. When the Yankees found out I had a Southern clerk, they made a big fuss. That kind of business caused lots of trouble, but they got along tolerable well, after a while.

—ALLEN WILLIAMS

You wants me to tell you 'bout dat 'lection day at Woodward, South Carolina, in 1878? Well, you couldn't wet dis old man's whistle wid a swallow of red liquor, now?—couldn't you or could you?

Dis was de way of it. De 'lection was set for Tuesday. Monday, I drive de four-hoss wagon to dis very town. Marse John McCrory and Marse Ed Woodward come wid me. They was in a buggy. When us got here, us got twenty sixteen-shooters* and put dem under de hay us have in de wagon. Barrooms was here. I fetched my fiddle 'long, and played in Marse Fred Habernick's bar till dinnertime. Us leave town 'bout four o'clock. Roads was bad, but us got home 'bout dark. Us put de guns in Marse Andy Mobley's store. Marse Ed and me leave Marse John to sleep in de store and to take care of de guns.

De nex' mornin', de polls open in de little schoolhouse by de brick church. I was dere on time, help to fix de table by de window and set de ballot boxes on it. Voters could come to de window, put deir arms through, and tuck de vote in a slit in de boxes. Dere was two supervisors—Marse Thomas for de Democrats and Uncle Jordan for de Radicals [Republicans]. Marse Thomas had a book and a pencil; Uncle Jordan had de same.

Joe Foster, big buckra nigger, want to vote a stranger. Marse Thomas challenge dis vote. In dem times, colored preachers so 'furiate de women dat dey would put on breeches and vote de 'Publican Radical ticket. De stranger look lak a woman. Joe Foster 'spute Marse Thomas' word, and Marse Thomas knock him down wid de naked fist. Marse "Irish Billy" Brice, when him see four or five hundred blacks crowdin' round Marse Thomas, he jump through de window from de inside. When he lit on de ground, pistol went off, pow! One nigger drop in his tracks. Sixteen men come from nowhere, with sixteen sixteen-shooters. Marse Thomas hold up his hand to them and say, "Wait!" Him point to de niggers and say, "Git!" They

*Repeating rifles that carry sixteen bullets.

405

start to runnin' 'cross de railroad, over de hillside, and never quit runnin' till dey git half a mile away. De only niggers left on dat ground was me, old Uncle Kantz—you know, de old mulatto club-foot nigger—well, me and him and Albert Gladney, de hurt nigger dat was shot through de neck, was de only niggers left. Dr. Tom Douglas took de ball out Albert's neck, and de white folks put him in a wagon and sent him home. I drive de wagon.

When I got back, de white boys was in de graveyard gittin' names off de tombstones to fill out de tally sheets. Dere was so many votes in de box for de Hampton* ticket, dey had to vote de dead. I 'spect dat was one resurrection day, all over South Carolina.

—ANDY BRICE

The Reconstruction period has been hell on the Negro race, but we suffered it through, somehow. If we had another time like that to go through, believes I would hang myself, so es I would not suffer again.

—POLLY SHINE

*A former Confederate general, Wade Hampton was the victorious Democratic candidate for governor of South Carolina in 1878.

Narratives

———◇+ +◇———

MARY GRAYSON

WILLIAM COLBERT

MOLLIE DAWSON

MARY GRAYSON

I AM what we colored people call a "native." That means that I didn't come into the Indian country from somewhere in the Old South, after the War, like so many Negroes did, but I was born here in the old Creek Nation, and my master was a Creek Indian. That was eighty-three years ago, so I am told.

My mammy belonged to white people back in Alabama when she was born—down in the southern part, I think—for she told me that after she was a sizeable girl her white people moved into the eastern part of Alabama where there was a lot of Creeks. Some of them Creeks was mixed up with the whites, and some of the big men in the Creeks who come to talk to her master was almost white, it looked like. "My white folks moved around a lot when I was a little girl," she told me.

When mammy was about ten or twelve years old, some of the Creeks begun to come out to the [Indian] Territory in little bunches. They wasn't the ones who was taken out here by the soldiers and contractor men; they come on ahead by themselves, and most of them had plenty of money, too. A Creek come to my mammy's master and bought her to bring out here, but she heard she was being sold and run off into the woods. There was an old clay pit, dug way back into a high bank, where the slaves had been getting clay to mix with hog hair scrapings to make chinking for the big log houses that they built for the master and the cabins they made for themselves. Well, my mammy run and hid way back in that old clay pit, and it was way after dark before the master and the other men found her.

The Creek man that bought her was a kind sort of a man, Mammy said, and wouldn't let the master punish her. He took her away and was kind to her, but he decided she was too young to breed and he

409

PLATE 36: A former slave.

sold her to another Creek who had several slaves already. And he brought her out to the Territory.

The McIntosh men was the leaders in the bunch that come out at that time, and one of the bunch, named Jim Perryman, bought my mammy and married her to one of his "boys," but after he waited a while and she didn't have a baby, he decided she was no good as a breeder and he sold her to Mose Perryman.

Mose Perryman was my master, and he was a cousin to Legus Perryman, who was a big man in the tribe. He was a lot younger than Mose and laughed at Mose for buying my mammy, but he got fooled, because my mammy got married to Mose's slave boy, Jacob, the way slaves was married them days, and went ahead and had ten children for Mr. Mose.

Mose Perryman owned my pappy and his older brother, Hector, and one of the McIntosh men—Oona, I think his name was—owned my pappy's brother William.

I can remember when I first heard about there was going to be a war. The older children would talk about it, but they didn't say it was a war all over the country. They would talk about a war "back in Alabama," and I guess they had heard the Creeks talking about it that way.

When I was born, we lived in the Choska bottoms. Mr. Mose Perryman had a lot of land broke in, all up and down the Arkansas River, along there. After the War, when I had got to be a young woman, there was quite a settlement grew up at Choska, right across the river east of where Haskell now is, but when I was a child before the War, all the whole bottoms was marshy kind of wilderness except where farms had been cleared out. The land was very rich and the Creeks who got to settle there were lucky. They always had big crops. All west of us was high ground, toward Gibson Station and Fort Gibson, and the land was sandy. Some of the McIntoshes lived over that way, and my uncle William belonged to one of them.

We slaves didn't have a hard time at all before the War. I have had people who were slaves of white folks back in the old states tell me that they had to work awfully hard and their masters were cruel to them sometimes. But all the Negroes I knew who belonged to Creeks always had plenty of clothes and lots to eat, and we all lived in good log cabins we built. We worked the farm and tended to the horses and cattle and hogs. Some of the older women worked around the owner's house, but each Negro family looked after a part of the fields and worked the crops like they belonged to us.

When I first heard talk about the War, the slaves were allowed to go and see one another sometimes, and often they were sent on errands several miles with a wagon or on a horse. But pretty soon we were all kept at home, and nobody was allowed to come around to talk to us. But we heard what was going on.

The McIntosh men got nearly everybody to side with them about the War, but we Negroes got word somehow that the Cherokees over back of Fort Gibson was not going to be in the War, and that there were some Union people over there who would help slaves to get away. But we children didn't know anything about what we heard our parents whispering about, and they would stop if they heard us listening. Most of the Creeks who lived in our part of the country, between the Arkansas and the Verdigris [rivers], and some even south of the Arkansas, belonged to the Lower Creeks and sided with the South. But down below us, along the Canadian River, they were Upper Creeks, and there was a good deal of talk about them going with the North. Some of the Negroes tried to get away and go down to them, but I don't know of any from our neighborhood that went.

Some Upper Creeks came up into the Choska bottoms talking around among the folks there about siding with the North. They were talking, they said, for old man Gouge, who was a big man among the Upper Creeks. His Indian name was Opoeth-le-ya-hola, and he got away into Kansas with a big bunch of Creeks and Seminoles, during the War.

Before that time, I remember one night my uncle William brought another Negro man to our cabin and talked a long time with my pappy, but pretty soon some of the Perryman Negroes told them that Mr. Mose was coming down, and they went off into the woods to talk. But Mr. Mose didn't come down. When Pappy came back, Mammy cried quite a while, and we children could hear them arguing late at night. Then my uncle Hector slipped over to our cabin several times and talked to Pappy, and Mammy began to fix up grub, but she didn't give us children but a little bit of it, and told us to stay around with her at the cabin and not go playing with the other children.

Then, early one morning, about daylight, old Mr. Mose came down to the cabin in his buggy, waving a shotgun and hollering at the top of his voice. I never saw a man so mad in all my life, before nor since!

He yelled in at Mammy to "git them children together and git up to my house before I beat you and all of them to death!" Mammy began to cry and plead that she didn't know anything, but he acted like he was going to shoot sure enough, so we all ran to Mammy and started for Mr. Mose's house as fast as we could trot.

We had to pass all the other Negro cabins on the way, and we could see that they were all empty, and it looked like everything in them had been tore up—straw and corn shucks all over the place, where somebody had tore up the mattresses, and all the pans and kettles gone off the outside walls where they used to hang them.

At one place we saw two Negro boys loading some iron kettles on a wagon, and a little further on was some boys catching chickens in a yard, but we could see all the Negroes had left in a big hurry.

I asked Mammy where everybody had gone, and she said, "Up to Mr. Mose's house, where we are going. He's calling us all in."

"Will Pappy be up there, too?" I asked her.

"No. Your pappy and your uncle Hector and your uncle William, and a lot of other menfolks won't be here anymore. They went away. That's why Mr. Mose is so mad. So if any of you young-uns say anything about any strange men coming to our place, I'll break your necks!" Mammy was sure scared!

We all thought sure she was going to get a big whipping, but Mr. Mose just looked at her a minute and then told her to get back to the cabin and bring all the clothes and bed ticks and all kinds of cloth we had, and come back ready to travel.

"We're going to take all you black devils to a place where there won't no more of you run away!" he yelled after us. So we got ready to leave as quick as we could. I kept crying about my pappy, but Mammy would say, "Don't you worry about your pappy. He's free now. Better be worrying about us. No telling where we all will end up!" There was four or five Creek families, and their Negroes all got together to leave, with all their stuff packed in buggies and wagons and being toted by the Negroes or carried on horses, jackasses, mules, and milk cattle. I reckon it was a funny-looking sight, or it would be to a person now—the way we was all loaded down with all manner of baggage when we met at the old ford across the Arkansas that lead to the Creek Agency. The Agency stood on a high hill a few miles across the river from where we lived. We couldn't see it from our place down in the Choska bottoms, but as soon as we got up on the upland east of the bottoms we could look across and see the hill.

When we got to a grove at the foot of the hill near the Agency, Mr. Mose and the other masters went up to the Agency for a while. I suppose they found out up there what everybody was supposed to do and where they was supposed to go, for when we started on, it wasn't long until several more families and their slaves had joined the party, and we made quite a big crowd.

The little Negro boys had to carry a little bundle apiece, but Mr. Mose didn't make the little girls carry anything and let us ride if we could find anything to ride on. My mammy had to help lead the cows part of the time, but a lot of the time she got to ride an old horse, and she would put me up behind her. It nearly scared me to death, because I had never been on a horse before, and she had to hold on to me all the time to keep me from falling off.

Of course, I was too small to know what was going on then, but I could tell that all the masters and the Negroes seemed to be mighty worried and careful all the time. Of course, I know now that the Creeks were all split up over the War, and nobody was able to tell who would be friendly to us or who would try to poison us or kill us, or at least rob us. There was a lot of bushwhacking all through that country by little groups of men who was just out to get all they could. They would appear like they was the enemy of anybody they run across, just to have an excuse to rob them or burn up their stuff. If you said you was with the South, they would be with the North, and if you claimed to be with the Yankees, they would be with the South. So our party was kind of upset all the time we was passing through the country along the Canadian [river]. That was where old Gouge had been talking against the South. I've heard my folks say that he was a wonderful speaker, too.

We all had to move along mighty slow, on account of the ones on foot, and we wouldn't get very far in one day. Then we Negroes had to fix up a place to camp and get wood and cook supper for everybody. Sometimes we would come to a place to camp that somebody knew about, and we would find it all tromped down by horses and the spring all filled in and ruined. I reckon old Gouge's people would tear up things when they left, or maybe some Southern bushwhackers would do it. I don't know which.

When we got down to where the North Fork runs into the Canadian, we went around the place where the Creek town was. There was lots of Creeks down there who was on the other side, so we passed around that place and forded across west of there. The ford was a bad one, and it took us a long time to get across. Everybody got wet and a lot of the stuff on the wagons got wet. Pretty soon we got down into the Chickasaw country, and everybody was friendly to us, but the Chickasaw people didn't treat their slaves like the Creeks did. They was more strict, like the people in Texas and other places. The Chickasaws seemed of a lighter color than the Creeks, and they talked more in Indian among themselves and to their slaves. Our masters talked English nearly all the time, except when they were talking to Creeks who didn't talk good English, and we Negroes never did learn very good Creek. I could always understand it, and can yet, a little, but I never did try to talk it much. Mammy and Pappy used English to us all the time.

Mr. Mose found a place for us to stop close to Fort Washita, and got us places to stay and work. I don't know which direction we were from Fort Washita, but I know we were not very far. I don't know how many years we were down in there, but I know it was over two, for we worked on crops at two different places, I remember. Then, one day, Mr. Mose came and told us that the War was over and that we would have to root for ourselves after that. Then he just rode away, and I never saw him after that, until after we had got back up into the Choska country. Mammy heard that the Negroes were going to get equal rights with the Creeks, and that she should go to the Creek Agency to draw for us. So we set out to try to get back.

We started out on foot, and would go a little ways each day, and Mammy would try to get a little something to do to get us some food. Two or three times she got paid in money, so she had some money when we got back. After three or four days of walking, we came across some Negroes who had a horse, and Mammy paid them to let us children ride and tie with their children for a day or two. They had their children on the horse, so two or three little ones would get on with a larger one to guide the horse, and we would ride a while and get off and tie the horse and start walking on down the road. Then, when the others caught up with the horse, they would ride until they caught up with us. Pretty soon, the old people got afraid to let us do that, so we just led the horse and some of the little ones rode it.

We had our hardest times when we would get to a river or big creek. If the water was swift, the horse didn't do any good, for it would shy at the water and the little ones couldn't stay on. So we would have to just wait until someone came along in a wagon, and maybe have to pay them with some of our money or some of our goods we were bringing back, to haul us across. Sometimes, we had to wait all day before anyone would come along in a wagon.

We were coming north all this time, up through the Seminole Nation, but when we got to Weeleetka, we met a Creek family of freedmen who were going to the Agency, too, and Mammy paid them to take us along in their wagon. When we got to the Agency, Mammy met a Negro who had seen Pappy and knew where he was, so we sent word to him and he came and found us. He had been through most of the War in the Union army. He had got away into the Cherokee country, and some of them called the "Pins" helped to smuggle him on up into Missouri and over into Kansas; but he soon found that he couldn't get along and stay safe unless he went with the army. He went with them until the War was over, and was around Gibson quite a lot. When he was there he tried to find out where we had gone but said he never could find out. He was in the Battle of Honey Springs, he said, but never was hurt or sick. When we got back together, we cleared a selection of land a little east of the Choska bottoms, near where Clarksville now is, and farmed until I was a great big girl.

I went to school at a little school called Blackjack School. I think it was a kind of mission school and not one of the Creek Nation schools, because my first teacher was Miss Betty Weaver, and she was not a Creek but a Cherokee. Then we had two white teachers, Miss King and John Kernan, and another Cherokee was in charge.

When I got to be a young woman, I went to Okmulgee and worked for some people near there for several years. Then I married Tate Grayson. We got our freedmen's allotments on Mingo Creek, east of Tulsa, and lived there until our children were grown and Tate died. Then I came to live with my daughter in Tulsa.

WILLIAM COLBERT

S HO', I remember de slavery days. How could I forgits? We can jes' set in de swing effen you wants to hear a little 'bout dem ole days, 'kaze I can sho' tell it.

My name am William Colbert, and I's fum Jawja [Georgia]. I was born in 1844 on my massa's plantation, in Fort Valley. My massa's name wuz Jim Hodison. At one time, he had a hundred and sixty-five of us niggers.

Nawsuh, he warn't good to none of us niggers. All de niggers roun' dar hated to be bought by him, 'kaze he wuz so mean. When he wuz too tired to whup us, he had de overseer do it, and de overseer wuz meaner dan de massa. But, Mister, de peoples wuz de same as dey is now. Dere wuz good uns and bad uns. I jus' happened to belong to a bad un. One day, I remembers my brother, January, wuz cotched ober seein' a gal on de next plantation. He had a pass, but de time on it done gib out. Well, suh, when de massa found out dat he wuz a hour late, he got as mad as a hive of bees. So when brother January he come home, de massa took down his long mule skinner and tied him wid a rope to a pine tree. He strip his shirt off and said, "Now, nigger, I'm goin' to teach you some sense."

Wid dat, he started layin' on de lashes. January was a big, fine-lookin' nigger, de finest I ever seed. He wuz jus' four years older dan me, an' when de massa begin a-beatin' him, January neber said a word. De massa got madder and madder, 'kaze he couldn't make January holler.

"What's de matter wid you, nigger?" he say. "Don't it hurt?"

January he neber said nothin', and de massa keep a-beatin' till little streams of blood started flowin' down January's chest, but he

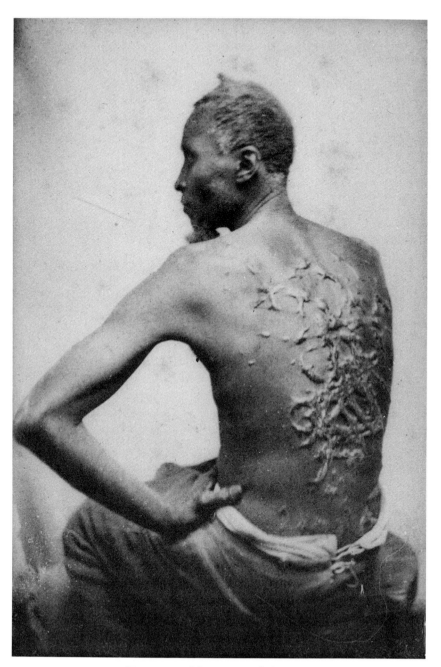

PLATE 37: The cause of the war.

neber holler. His lips wuz a-quiverin', and his body wuz a-shakin', but his mouf it neber open; and all de while, I sat on my mammy's and pappy's steps a-cryin'. De niggers wuz all gathered about, and some uv 'em couldn't stand it; dey hadda go inside deir cabins. Atter while, January, he couldn't stand it no longer hisself, and he say in a hoarse, loud whisper, "Massa! Massa! Have mercy on dis poor nigger."

Den, de War came. De Yankees come in, and dey pulled de fruit off de trees and et it. Dey et de hams and cawn, but dey neber burned de houses. Seem to me lak dey jes' stay aroun' long enough to git plenty somepin'-t'-eat, 'kaze dey lef' in two or three days, an' we neber seed 'em since. De massa had three boys to go to war, but dere wuzn't one to come home. All de chillun he had wuz killed. Massa, he los' all his money, and de house soon begin droppin' away to nothin'. Us niggers, one by one, lef' de ole place, and de las' time I seed de home plantation, I wuz a-standin' on a hill. I looked back on it for de las' time through a patch of scrub pines, and it look so lonely. Dere warn't but one person in sight—de massa. He was a-settin' in a wicker chair in de yard, lookin' out ober a small field of cotton and cawn. Dere wuz fo' crosses in de graveyard in de side lawn where he wuz a-settin'. De fo'th one wuz his wife. I lost my ole woman, too, thirty-seven years ago, and all dis time, I's been a-carryin' on like de massa—all alone.

MOLLIE DAWSON

THERE ain't much 'bout mah life dat would interest anybody 'ceptin' me, and dar is lots of dat I wish I could fergit and lots of it I wish I could live ovah again.

But, jest ter git acquainted first, mah name is Mollie Dawson, and ter de best of mah recollection, from de information mah maw give me, I is about eighty-five years old. You know us slavery niggers never did have no correct account of when we was bo'n and how ole we is. Puttin' it all together, we ain't got much sense, but we got more'n dese young niggers wid all deir edgecation. Slavery niggers didn't have no edgecation—only whut dey got by demselves.

Dat makes me bo'n in January sometime, of 1852, de bes' I kin figger out, in de fo'ks [forks] of Richland and Pin Oak creeks, in Navarro County, clost ter whar de Indians and dem surveyors had dat big fight when dey was surveyin' dis country. I's heard lots of talk of dem.

Mah maw was de slave of Nath Newman and dat made me his slave. Mah maw's name was Sarah Benjamin.

Mah father's name was Carrol Benjamin, and he belonged ter different white folks, and I never did know what his white folks' name was, and from whut I sees dat happen ovah dar one day, I nevah does wants ter know.

De plantation dat he worked on was j'inin' our'n. I would go ovah ter see him once in a while when I was little, and de last time I goes ovah dar dey whips a man wid a long whip dat looks sorter lak a blacksnake whip. Dey had dis man's hands and feet tied, and he was bent ovah wid a stick ovah his arms and undah his knees, and dey had him stripped off naked and he was layin' on de groun'. Dis white man

421

PLATE 38: A former slave.

was whippin' him and de blood was all ovah dis nigger and he was sayin', "Oh, Marser, oh, Marser, I pray you not to hit me anymore. Oh, Lo'dy, Lo'dy, has mercy on me. Marser, please has mercy on me, please has mercy." But dis man wouldn't stop a minute, and spits terbaccer juice and cusses him, and den starts in whippin' him agin. Dis nigger was jumpin' roun' on de groun' all tied up, jest lak a chicken when you chops his head off, when dis man was whippin' him, and when de white man would stop awhile, dis nigger would lay dar and roll from side ter side and beg for mercy.

I runs off a good piece when dis white man started whippin' him, and stopped and looks back at him. I was so skairt dat I jest stood dar and watched him till he quits. Den he tells some of de slaves ter wash him off and put salt in de cut places, and he stood dar ter watch dem ter see dat dey did. He was chewin' his terbaccer, spittin', and cussin' dat nigger, and when dey gits him washed off and puts salt in de raw places, he sho' did scream and groan. But when he groaned dey jest kept puttin' de salt inter de wounds on his po' ole beat-up body.

De first thing dat I knows, mah father was pattin' me on de back and sayin', "Honey, you better run along home, now," and I sho' did, and I didn't go back ovah dar anymo'. Dat was the only slave I ever seed gits a whippin', and I never did wants ter see dis white man anymo', nor I didn't wants ter know his name. I jest wants ter git away from dar and stay away.

Mah father told mah mother dat de white folks whipped dis nigger 'cause he had been lettin' de calves suck too much milk afore he 'gins to milkin'. Dat man was hard to please. I thinks dat he was a bully kin' of white man, from what I can remember about him.

Co'se, mah mother and father was slavery time married darkies. Dat didn't mean nuthin' dem days, but jest raisin' mo' darkies, and every slave darkie woman had ter do dat whether she wanted to or not. Dey would let her pick out a man, or a man pick him out a woman, and dey was married, and if de woman wouldn't have de man dat picks her, dey would take her ter a big stout high husky nigger somewhere and leave her a few days, jest lak dey do stock now'days, and she bettah begin raisin' chilluns, too. If she didn't, dey would works her ter death; dey say dat she no 'count and dey soon sells her.

Mah mother and father never did love each other lak dey ought to, so dey separated as soon as dey was free. Mah father married another woman by law. Mah mother married George Baldwin, and dey lives together fer about twelve years. Dey separated den, and she married Alfred Alliridge and dey lives together till she dies.

I didn't have no own brother or sister, but I had one half-brother and two half-sisters. Mah half-brother's name was George Baldwin. He was named after he's father, and mah two half-sisters' name was Mahailie and Annie Baldwin. Co'se, all dem was younger dan me.

When we lived on de plantation, as it was called—but dis one was a farm instead of a big plantation—we lived in a little ole one-room log house wid a shed clear 'crost de back. Dis house had puncheon floors in it, too, and all de houses had a giant stick-and-dirt chimney ter do de cookin' on and ter do de heatin' of de house. Dey all burned long wood, longer dan dey do now.

De beds in all de cabins was made in de corners and dey was made outen a rail er a pole wid bored holes in it. We took rawhide strings and run dem through de holes and across de bed; den we took some more rawhide strings and run dem longways and puts dem ovah and undah de ones runnin' across, weavin' dem lak a basket er a cane-bottom chair we had dem days. Den we would git some straw or grass and shucks and make a mattress outen dem, only it wasn't a mattress, it was jest a bed lak you beds down hogs er cows on now'days. But we was glad to gits to sleep on dis, when de day's work was did.

We done our cookin', eatin', sleepin', and ever'thin' in dis little one-room log house. All de cookin' was done ovah a fire in de big stick-and-dirt chimney. Dar was a big rod er a pole dat runs across up high, and some crooked irons er hooks hung down from dis ovah de fire, and we hung our kettles and pots on de end close ter de fire to do our b'ilin'.

When we done bakin' er roastin', we would git a big bed of coals and ashes in de fireplace and we would put our food in a pan wid a cover on it and drag back lots of de coals and ashes and put de pan and food in dar wid de cover on it and den cover it up wid de coals and ashes. But when we baked taters, we would bury dem in hot ashes and let dem stay dar till dey was done.

All de slave women done deir breakfas' and dinnah cookin' in de mornin' befo' dey went ter work, and carried deir dinnah ter de fiel' wid dem, and den come in at night and cook suppah.

We generally has plenty taters and peas ter eat de year roun', and in de spring we has some vegetables. Maser Newman would give us vegetables outen de garden. Dar was one big garden and all de vegetables was issued out by Maser Newman. He had lots of hogs dat run out in de timbah all de year. Dey was all marked, so in de wintah he would take some of de slaves wid him and kill a hog where dey runs onto it, and haul it in. Some slaves would be scrapin' and scaldin', and one would git de lard meat and dey would render de lard. All de meat was put down in salt for a while, and den it was took outen dat and hung up in de smokehouse and smoked good and proper. Meat done dis way is a lot bettah den de meat you buys at de grocery sto', now. Maser Newman would give out dis meat and some lard ter de slaves as dey needed it.

We had plenty of possum, coon, rabbit, squirrel, and hog, and sometimes we had beef and deer meat ter eat. But I was allus glad ter see hog-killin' time. I is yet, 'cause I sho' does lak good hog meat.

When all the slaves went to work, dey would send de small chilluns dat was too small ter take ter de field down ter de maser's yard to play. Maser Newman allus kept an old woman ter see after dem and do de cookin' and de housework for his family. He had a big yard and dar was plenty of room fer dem to play.

Chilluns dem days was under bettah control den dey is now. If any of de chilluns got out of line, dey got a good spankin', and dey didn't fergit it very soon. All mos' of de grown folks had ter do was ter look out de connah of de eye at dem kids and dey got good right quick.

Mah mother didn't have no father and mother ter raise her, as she was sold when she was a nursin' baby and she didn't ever remembah her folks. But, Maser Newman brought her up in Tennessee and brought her to Texas when he comes down here.

Mah father was not around very much, so I don't know much about him. I only saw his mother one time and never did see his father. I don't know where dey come from.

I was too young ter do much work durin' slavery time, but I picks lots of cotton, and all de pay we got fer it was a place ter stay, water ter drink, wood ter burn, food ter eat, and clothes ter wear, and we made de food and clothes ourselves. We eats corn pones three times a day, 'ceptin' Sunday and Christmas mornings; Maser Newman lets us have flour fer biscuits, den.

In de summah we wore cotton clothes. All of dem was made on de plantation. Some of de women would spin and some would weave and some would make clothes. All dis was usually done on rainy days, er cold days in de wintah time. A woman had ter spin so many cuts a day, and each one had ter weave so many knots a day. At the end of the day, Maser Newman would count dem to see dat each woman was doin' what she was s'posed to. Lots of de women could do lots mo' dan dey was s'posed to, but dey knew jest about how fast ter work ter gits done what dey was tasked to do. Dey jest gits a few mo' knots dan dey was s'posed ter gits and Maser Newman thought he got about all outen dem dey could do.

We wore jest plain homemade clothes all de time. When we went ter church er anywhere, we had a real nice dress and de menfolks had a nice shirt and pants made ter wear, and we kept dem to wear on special occasions.

We didn't wear no shoes, 'ceptin' in de wintah time and on special occasions, and dey was made on de plantation, too. Dey sho' was ugly-lookin' things. Dey was made outen hides dat was tanned on de plantation—what dey calls rawhide—and when dey gits wet dey was like tryin' ter hold a eel; sho' did feel messy and look messy, too. When de slaves was gittin' ready ter goes ter a dance er church, you could see dem all gittin' soot outen de chimney and mixin' it wid water ter make shoe polish. It didn't look nice and slick like it does now, but it made dem ole buckskin shoes look a lot bettah, though.

Maser Newman was a tall, slender man nearly six foot tall and was blue-eyed. He sho' was good ter all us slaves, but we all knew he means fer us ter work. He never whipped any of us slaves, but he hit one of de men wid a leather line 'bout two times once, 'cause dis slave kinda talked back ter him. He threatened to whip him good if he didn't go and do what he was told ter do without any backtalk. Dis slave danced around a little when he hit him wid dat line, and den trotted off ter git his job done befo' Maser Newman had time to say anything else to him.

Maser Newman was a slow easy-goin' sort of a man who took everything as it comes, takin' bad and good luck jest alak. He say not ter worry 'bout bad luck, 'cause worryin' won't do no good, and it would do you a lot of harm. He hardly ever did get mad, but when he did, you bettah leave him alone.

Maser Newman was tender-hearted, too. I know because 'bout de maddest I ever seen him was one evenin' when he comes in from one of de neighbor slave owners, and he sho' was mad; he was jest shakin'. Missus Jane—dat was his wife—went out ter his horse when he rode up, 'cause she could tell dat sumpin' was wrong, and she said, "Nath, what in de world is wrong?" And he begin tellin' her 'bout seein' dis feller whip one of his slaves unmercifully, and de slave beggin' him ter stop, and dis man laughin' and cussin'. Dis man keeps on whippin' him, and Maser Newman got on his horse and come home ter keep from jumpin' on him. I didn't hear all he was sayin'—I was afraid ter let Maser Newman see me listenin' ter what he was saying, while he was mad—but I heard enough ter tell dat it was 'bout dis man beatin' one his slaves nearly ter death.

Maser Newman was lots older dan his wife. She was a real young woman, and they 'peared ter think quite a bit of each other. Missus Newman was slender, like Maser Newman, and she had blue eyes, too. She hardly ever scolded any of us. She slapped me one time 'cause I spilled some hot coffee on her, but I didn't blame her fer dat. I would 'bout done de same thing if a big gawky gal spilled some on me. She slapped the housemaid one time ovah sumpin' 'bout cookin' dinner—I think it was about cookin' some food in a pan dat she hadn't washed clean. I got out of dar; I was skeered dat she would git hold of me, too. And I didn't stay ter hear what it was all about.

When Missus Newman got mad enough ter scold any of us, she had a good cause to do it. Jest lak anybody whippin' deir chilluns, dey don't whip dem unless dey needs it, and don't whip dem lots of times when dey do needs it. Dat was de way Missus Newman was by us slaves, and she sho' was good and kind when any of us got sick.

Maser and Missus Newman jest had two chilluns and both of dem was little girls. Martha was de oldest and Lizzie was de youngest. Both of dem looks jest lak deir mother. Dey sho' was pretty little gals and dey was smart, too. Dey played wid de little slave chilluns all de time, and course dey was de boss, same as deir mother and father.

Maser Newman was a poor man, compared wid some of de other slave owners. He only had about seven slaves big enough ter work all de year round in de fields, and he was de owner, overseer, and manager of his plantation. He didn't have no drivah; he would jest start dem all out ter work, and dey kept at it all day. But he generally worked around pretty close ter dem. I don't know how many acres was in his plantation, but he didn't has near as much land as de rest of de owners around him.

Didn't but one of us know how ter read and write, and he was one of de old slaves. He could write a little and he could read de Bible, and he reads it ter us a lot. De white folks never did try ter learn us ter read or write, either.

Dey was no slave weddin's or anything lak dat. Most all de slave weddin's was jest de maser says ter de man, "Slave Mose, you laks Nancy and wants ter marry her? Does you love her? Will you work fer her and bring home food ter her?" and some other foolish questions. And Mose says, "Yas, Sah." Den he ask Nancy, if she will obey Mose and love him and raise his chilluns, and lots mo' silly questions. And she says, "Yas, Sah." And den de maser says, "Now both of you jump over dis broomstick," and den he says, "You is married." Some of de masers would make de slaves git married by a preacher; dat would be about one slave owner out of ten, though. De rest would do de marryin' demselves and has a lot of fun out of de ones dat was gittin' married.

De slaves was about de same things as mules or cattle. Dey was bought and sold, and dey wasn't supposed ter be treated lak people, anyway. We all knew dat we was only a race of people, as our maser was, and dat we had a certain amount of rights, but we was jest property and had ter be loyal ter our masers. It hurt us sometimes ter be treated de way some of us was treated, but we couldn't help ourselves and had ter do de best we could, which nearly all of us done.

Some of de slaves tried ter run when dey was mistreated, and dey would put de bloodhoun's on deir trail and ketch dem and whip dem. Some of dem would git whipped nearly ter death, and some would git away. Some, I hears about, run away ter de North, and some would git killed by a lot of white folks dat was trailin' dem. Course dat would scare de rest of dem and dey wouldn't try it fer fear dey would git killed er whipped unmercifully wid de cat-o'-nine-tails, and dat was sumpin' awful.

De little chilluns was de only ones dat had things easy during slavery. Dey all knew dat dey was going ter git sumpin' ter eat, but now some of dem don't git enough ter eat. Some of de slave owners made de little chilluns do de chores, and dey all has ter pick cotton lak most of dem does now. Dey wasn't taught ter steal ter git sumpin' ter eat lak some of dem are now. And if any mother's chilluns wasn't sold, she knew whar dey was; and dat is more den some mothers can say dese days about deir chilluns.

Most all de young girls had what we called a charm string. Every one of deir friends and kinfolks dey would see dey would ask dem fer a pretty button ter put on dis charm string. I has seed some of dem charm strings five feet long, and some of de prettiest I ever seed in my life, dey was a lot prettier den dese beads dat we buys at de store now. Dis charm string was supposed ter bring good luck ter de owner of it.

All de menfolks carried a rabbit's foot fer good luck. A good luck charm lak dat would bring you plenty ter eat and you wouldn't git in no trouble wid de maser. But jest as sho' as you lose dat rabbit foot, you goin' ter have some bad luck. And iffen you is hoein' cotton er corn, you's goin' ter git a bad row and git behind, and de maser is goin' ter git on your neck and ball you out.

I allus keeps a horseshoe nailed up over my front do'. If I was ter take dat horseshoe down from my front do', I would either starves ter death or freeze, dis winter. My pension would be cut off and I knows I would starve den, sho' 'nuf.

I tells you all dem ole darkies back in slavery time has all de chilluns scared ter death 'bout Raw Head and Bloody Bones. Not jest little chilluns, great big chilluns, too, if dey done sumpin' deir mother and father didn't like, er wouldn't go ter sleep at night, all deir mother and father has ter say is, "Boy, you jest go on ter sleep er I will put you outside and let Raw Head and Bloody Bones git you," and dat would be de last of it. Er if de chilluns was makin' too much racket, some of de grown folks would say, "Listen, I thought I hears a racket roun' dis house outside somewhar," and he goes and peeps outside and slams de do' and says, "I sees ole Raw Head and Bloody Bones outside. Dey hears dese chilluns makin' racket and dey is waitin' fer one of dem ter come outside er ter be put outside," and dem kids would git quiet as a mouse and stay dat way. Our parents kept us chilluns scared ter death all de time 'bout first one thing and den another, but we all did mind better den de chilluns does dese days.

I remembahs one time in de winter, after I was a great big girl, we was all polishin' our shoes and hurryin' around gittin' our best clothes out and gittin' ready ter go ter a dance, and Maser Newman had give us all a pass ter go ter de dance at another plantation, close ter our'n. We was all thinkin' about what a good time we was goin' ter have ovah at de dance, and we couldn't hardly git dar fast enough. Well, we all got dar and de dance started. We was all in a big one-room log house wid a stick-and-dirt chimney in one end of it, and it had de ole puncheon floors in it. Couldn't so many couples git on de floor at one time fer de couples ter dance, but we all crowded in some way and had danced fer about two er three hours. I guess it was about ten er eleven o'clock when one of de men stepped out de door, and dar was three er four ghosts walkin' aroun' de house. Dey was about thirty er forty feet away from de house and jest walkin' in a circle around de house.

Dis man opened de door and started out, and he stopped jest outside de door when he saw dem ghosts, and stood dar. Directly, some of de others saw dese ghosts over dis man's head. Dese ghosts had done jest paralyzed dis man. He couldn't move; and some of de others caught hold of him and pulled him back inside and laid him on de floor. His eyes was big as my fist and was jest bulged out, and his face was white as de ghost. He was plum stiff. He laid dar and stared at de roof of de house. Everybody stopped dancin' and ganged up ter look at him, and somebody said ghosts was outside.

Some of us opens de door a little and peeps out, and dar was four of dem ghosts, and one of dem was a great tall one and could walk about as fast as de other ones could trot. We all knew dat we couldn't outrun dem, so we shut de door and got back in de house, and we begins talking about how we was going ter git out of dar and git rid of dem ghosts. Dar wasn't no window in de house, and we had ter look out de door. By dis time, dis cullud man dat first sees dem come from out under de spell de ghost had on him, and got up jest scared ter death. Some of dem wanted one ter start running out de door, and if he got away from de ghost we would all try it; but wouldn't no one go.

While we was talking and arguing, we heard dem ghosts on de roof. Dey was goin' ter jump off de house on our backs when we come out de door. About dat time, one of dem comes round ter de door and begins trying ter git in de door, but we holds it, and directly one of dem begins choppin' on de back side of de house. Dey was goin' ter chop a hole and come on in. Den dey knocks some chinks out de cracks where dey was choppin' and peeks through and says, "W-o-o-o-o," and 'bout dat time all us darkies hit dat front door and jest bust it into kindling wood, and out we goes. One of dem was standing at de corner of de house, and de tall one was out in front by a big ash tree, and de one at de corner of de house was saying, "Catch dat one. No, dis one," and on like dat. And dis tall one would try ter catch every one he told him to. He was jumping back and forth trying ter catch all of us. When I got up and started out, he told dat tall one ter catch me. I sho' did fly de opposite way from him.

We all got home together with a few scratches on us, and our clothes was tore up some where we run through de brush and climbed er jumped over some fences. De white folks come out wid deir guns and shot at dem ghosts, but course ain't no use trying ter shoot a ghost. You can drive dem away by shooting at dem, but you sho' can't shoot one.

De white folks sho' had lots of trouble wid deir slaves after dat. Dey finally jest had ter move deir quarters, but dey left dis log house where it was, 'cause it was haunted. Didn't anyone go around it anymore, and dey finally tore it down and burned it up—de white folks did, but didn't none of de darkies burn a stick of dat haunted wood. Some folks say dar ain't no ghosts, but I knows dar is, 'cause I's seed dem wid my own eyes, and what I sees I knows.

Dar wasn't very many slaves on our plantation, and we didn't have much sickness among us—bad colds in de winter and malaria in de spring of de year. We does most of de doctoring ourselves. If we got much sick, Maser Newman didn't wait very long to get a doctor out to see about us. He didn't have de doctor out but a very few times—

just when a bad cold was gittin' too bad. Mos' of de white folks was pretty good 'bout dat, 'cause dey had lots of money invested in us slaves.

We always used de barmonia weed ter make a tea, and drink dat fer chills and fever. It would always cure it, if you didn't wait too long. Asafoetida was 'bout de only thing dat any of us wore ter keep off any disease. Mostly jest chilluns wore dat, but some grown folks wore it, too, tied on a string roun' der neck, ter keep off common diseases, sech as whooping cough, measles, and chicken pox. We didn't have as much diseases den, and didn't so many people die den. Seems lak people was more healthy and strong dan dey is now, and people enjoyed life mo' dan dey does, dese days. People jest used home remedies den, when dey got ailin' a little. Now, dey calls a doctor and he looks at de person and leaves some pills er gives a prescription dat cost you a lot, and de person takes dat medicine and thinks he is gittin' well. Dat is why people now ain't as strong as dey was den. People dem days had jest enough sense ter tend ter deir selves and stay happy and healthy. Now dey got too much edgecation ter be sensible. Dey depends on someone else, and de other man depends on your money, if you got any. If you ain't, you don't git much 'tenshun and you think of the old remedies.

De War sho' begins changin' things. We raised mo' corn, and Maser Newman sold er sent off lots of hogs and corn, and we didn't have as much ter eat as we had been havin'. Our clothes and shoes had ter last us longer, as de hides and cotton had ter go ter make shoes and clothes fer de soldiers.

De day dat de news come dat de War was over, Maser Newman calls us slaves tergether and tole us dat we was as free as he was and dat we could go anywhar dat we wanted to and do anything we could, ter make a honest livin'. He said, "Now de War is over and times is hard, and all de slaves is free, and dar is goin' ter be jest lots of dem jest driftin' aroun', and work is goin' ter be hard ter get, and remembah, you is all on your own and has got ter hustle fer yourself. And if any of you leave, do your best ter get work as quick as you can. Don't wait till you get hungry befo' you tries ter get work, 'cause if you can't get it soon enough and have ter go and steal sumpin', dat will get you in trouble jest as sho' as you is standin' here in front of me, and den you will have ter get yourself out of it er go ter jail; fer remembah, you don't belong ter me er anybody else anymore.

"Now, I think I has tried ter treat you a little better den most of de slaves has been treated, and has tried ter learn you a few things while you was mah slaves. Now you is free ter leave, but if you want ter stay wid me, I will try ter think out some plan that I am able to finance, so we can all make some money out of it and make a good livin'; 'cause if I couldn't make a little money out of it and furnish everything, it wouldn't pay me ter make a trade wid you."

Now, we all knew dat he was tellin' us de truth 'bout everything. We all knew dat we was free all right, but even if we was, what was we goin' ter do if Maser Newman didn't help us. We didn't have no money and didn't know how we was goin' ter get any, and if we took a chance on trying ter git work other places, we might hire out ter a mean boss, and we knew dat dar was lots of dem around dar, too, and we figured dat if any slaves had a good maser lak ours, dey wouldn't all leave him. So we all decided ter stay wid Maser Newman if he would let us.

We all set aroun' dat place fer a couple of days, waitin' on Maser Newman and hopin' he would fix up fer us. I tell you dem two days was jest lak right after a funeral er bad accident. Sumpin' was missin' and we couldn't figure it all out. We was scared ter death he would come out and tells us he couldn't helps us none. Den one day we sees him comin' and we all held our breath, 'cause he didn't look very happy. We was all skeered ter death, and he comes up ter some of us, and when he looked at us he laughed and says, "What's de matter?" Mah mother says, "We 'fraid you ain't got no good news." He says, "Why, you don't want ter stay and work for me?" We all felt easy, den, and he says, "Well if you all wants ter stay and work and lets me pay you fer it in cash and meat and other things ter eat de rest of de year, I think we can git rigged up ter work on de halvers next year." We all jest hollered and hollered and laughed fer joy. So de next mornin' we all left de house goin' ter de fiel's a-hollerin' and singin' jest lak we allus did.

We worked on dat year fer Maser Newman jest lak we allus did. I don't know how much money he paid us. He paid in sweet and Irish potatoes, peas, beans, corn for meal, and hogs for meat, dat wintah, and he sold us some pigs so we could raise our own meat fer another year. He rented all de men wid families plenty of land on de halvers de next year, and worked two single men by de month and fed dem. He bought all de married folks groceries ter make a crop on, but course dey all had ter pay him back fer dem.

When we all started our crops dat year, we was all in a big way ter make more dan our neighbors did, and we started ter work as early as we could see how ter work and worked as late as we could see, and we worked hard while we was out dar. We all had ter work a team of oxens, and Maser Newman and his two hired hands worked de horses, 'cause he could handle a lot mo' land dan we could. But he didn't work his crop as good as we did.

Mah mother and stepfather worried all de time, 'cause we was havin' ter spend so much money ter make dat crop on de halvers, and dey thought dat we never git Maser Newman paid back. I hears mah mother and father talkin' 'bout Maser Newman spendin' so much money helpin' us all ter farm. Dey say he wasn't no poor man; he had to be rich ter keep us all goin', and payin' his hired hands, and keepin' his own family up, at de same time.

But dat fall comes and we made a good feed crop and made a good cotton crop, and got what we thought was a good price fer it. We paid Maser Newman ever' cent he loaned us dat year wid a little interest, and had lots of money left—mo' dan we had ever seed befo', and dat wasn't too much.

We raised lots of potatoes dat year, and beans and peas. We banked our potatoes, cabbage, beets, turnips, and things lak dat up fer de wintah. When we would bank up things lak dat, we would make a moun' of dirt up above de rest of de groun', close ter it, and den put some dry sand on it 'bout three er four inches deep, den haul up lots of dry cornstalks, straw, and grass. Den we would put each kind of potatoes ter itself on de moun' of dirt and sand, den place de cornstalks against de dirt at de bottom, and lean de tops in against de potatoes and other things, makin' a sorta Indian tepee, leavin' a small hole on de south side where we would git our hand and arms in and git dem things out when we wanted ter eats any of dem. Den we would place straw and grass on top of dese cornstalks all aroun', 'ceptin' de hole, ter keep de dirt from fallin' through. Den we begins pilin' dirt on dis. We would put dirt all aroun' dis, and on top of it, too, thick enough dat de rains in de wintah and spring wouldn't wash it off and seep through on de vegetables. Den we put a board er some elm bark ovah dis hole, and fit it down tight, and keep de rain and freezin' weather from gittin' into our vegetables. We would some-times have four er five sech mounds in de backyard all wintah and spring; and dey would keep, too, if you took care of dem and kep' de moun' built up after ever' rain.

Mah stepfather bought a cow and got some chickens and some hogs and got hold of some farmin' tools of his own dat year wid part of our money. Maser Newman would take my stepfather wid him, when he done de tradin', ter show him how ter trade. He told him how ter judge de price of anything, and he would talk ter my mother and stepfather lots of times tellin' dem how ter do and how ter keep der money and how and when ter buy. Good ole Maser Newman, I never will fergit him. I know de good Lord gives dat man a great reward fer his deeds done here on earth jest ter his slaves if fer nothin' else.

When de menfolks begins haulin' up wood fer de wintah fer ourselves, dey cuts Maser Newman plenty wood and hauls it up, too, 'cause he had helped us so much dat year. Dat wintah, we had plenty ter eat, and we had mo' biscuits dan we had been havin' while we still eats lots of corn bread. But lots of de other darkies round us got awful hungry dat wintah and begins doin' a lot of stealin', and de pad-daroles [patrollers] had ter ketch lots of 'em and flog 'em. De paddaroles was de Ku Klux Klan. Dese darkies wouldn't have done dis stealin' if de other white folks had helped 'em lak Maser New-man did.

Maser Newman went wid my stepfather and helped him rent a place on de third-and-fourths, close ter Pisgah Ridge. Dis place wasn't as good as Maser Newman's place. It was good, fresh upland and had a log house on it and had good pasture, but dar was plenty timber on it. After my stepfather rented de place, he bought a good team of horses from a white man dat us and Maser Newman knew.

Pisgah Ridge Village was named after a long high ridge in de south part of Navarro County, and it is covered wid big rocks and has caves and holes in it in lots of places, and low scrubby underbrush on both side. All de lawbreakers and thieves would run into dis county and de lawmen daresen ter go in dar after 'em, 'cause dey would sho' git kilt. After de War, it got worse and worse, till de farmers all got mad, 'cause dese cattle and horse thieves was stealin' everything dey had, and dey caught some of dem and hung dem ter trees. I remembahs one dey hung when I was jest a little girl. He was a horse thief, and he stole one of de best horses dat a farmer had dat lived out south of Corsicana. He was seen by another man—one of de neighbors of de man dat owned de horse—and he got some other men and dey ketched him. Dey said dey was a big bunch of men dat ketched him, and dey brought him back ter a big elm tree on Elm Creek, 'bout four miles south of Corsicana, and hung him ter a big limb. He sho' did look scary danglin' dar, and de wind blowin' 'im back and forth, and he hung dar till de rope broke in two and he fell ter de ground, and his hat lay on de ground fer a long time. Now, I tells you, dat put a stop ter horse stealin' roun' dar.

We made a good crop dat year at Pisgah Ridge, and my stepfather rented it again, and at de end of de second year I marries George Hunt. I had met him de first year we moves ovah dar. He had some kinfolks dat lived clost ter us, and he would come ovah ter see dem bout ever' two weeks er ever' month, and we got acquainted.

George Hunt lived at Brushy Prairie, where he had a small farm rented on de third-and-fourth. He had been batchin' and farmin', and he made a good crop er two and was fixed up pretty good, fer a young man. George and me worked hard and made good crops, and raised lots of chickens and had a few good cows. Our three chilluns was born here; we had two girls and one boy.

George and me worked hard on dis little farm all de time and had hopes of owning it someday. We built a good log crib, and built more fences, and cleared up more land down in de bottom. Part of it was bottom land and part was hillside. 'Bout de time we was gittin' where we could buy us a little home of our own, George took typhoid fever and died. Dat was before the doctors knew much about how to doctor it. There I was wid three chilluns to care for, and a doctor bill and funeral bill to pay, and nobody to work de place. So we buried George out dar, and me and de chilluns gathered de crop dat fall and sold de teams and all de cows but one. We killed enough stock for our meat and lard and sold de rest, and moved into town here in

Corsicana. I knew our money would play out some day, so I got a job doin' housework and cookin', on de west side, for some white folks. De chilluns was big enough ter keep house and go ter school.

When the T & B V Railroad comes through, I met a man by de name of Will Dawson. We went together for awhile and den marries. Will has a good job workin' fer de railroad, and he made me quit workin' out on de west side and takin' in washings, too. He said he was makin' enough money fer us ter live on, and I didn't have ter work. He followed de railroad fer a good ways and got on de repair crew here in Corsicana. De repair is what we all calls de section crew, and he worked fer dem a long time. He made a payment on our home when he first went ter work on de crew, and we got it paid off before he got laid off. When he got laid off, he begins ter look fer work here in town and finally Maser Ransom, dat runs de grocery store now, he was de one dat hires him. He told him if he had a horse and a hack, he would give him a job deliverin' groceries. So Will bought him a horse and delivery hack and went ter deliverin' groceries for Maser Ransom.

One mornin' in de early winter, like, Will got up and built a fire as he always did. Den I gits up ter git his breakfast, and he complained to me 'bout feeling so bad, and he did have a bad cold. I just thought de cold was makin' him feel bad, and I intended to put a flannel rag on his chest before he went ter work. He said he had ter go on and get the hack and started out fer de store. Dey said dat he staggered a little and fell dead in de middle of de store. Dey got a doctor but he couldn't do no good. He said Will died wid heart trouble.

After Will was buried I was flat broke and in debt, but de chilluns helped me along wid what washin's I could git ter do, and I done housework and cookin' again fer a long time. But as old as I was gittin', it gradually got ter whar I couldn't gits enough work ter keep me alive, so I tried rentin' out two of mah rooms ter some young married folks, er folks widout any chilluns. Well, dey would pay good fer awhile, and den dey would begin ter drop behind and finally quit payin'.

Den de Depression comes along, and I thought I would starve ter death, but as it happened de good people what elected our good President sho' knew what dey was doin', fer we sho' got a good

President dat helps de poor people dat needs helpin', 'stead helpin' all de rich people gittin' more money and robbin' de poor people of what little dey is got left, like most of de presidents. And de rich people all over de country is sho' cryin' 'bout it, too. Every paper you picks up somebody is tellin' a whole bunch of lies on our President.

Mr. Roosevelt has helped everybody. He ain't missed none of us, de rich and de poor, de young and de ole, and even de little chilluns. Dey took de money dat he either gives dem er loans dem—some of dem jest grabs it like a greedy hog—and den sneaks off and talks 'bout him breakin' de country. When dey gives all de ole folks a pension, some of de same people stands aroun' and hollers 'bout dat like a dog tied up at a strange place does.

Course, I is gittin' ole and can't work myself anymore. I jest lives by myself and on my little ole folks' pension, which ain't very much.

I ain't got no chilluns or grandchilluns livin', I jest gits de little neighbor girl ter come over and stay all night wid me, ever' night.

I still owns my home, but I ain't been able ter pay any taxes on it in a long time. Wid me not havin' ter pay any rent, and quiltin' a little fer other people, and de pension I gits, I jest barely live from one year ter de next.

I carries a little burial insurance policy dat will take care of me when I dies. Dat's one thing I done ever since Will died, so de county wouldn't have ter bury me.

I is a member of de First Independent Baptist Church and has been fer de past sixty years. I can't write much, but I can read de Bible, and I reads it ever' day, so I will be ready ter go any day er night de Lord calls fer me ter come fer my reward.

Voices

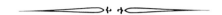

THE YOUNGER GENERATION,

REFLECTIONS AND CONCLUSIONS

Y ES, I was a slave. And I'll say this to the whole world: Slavery was the worst curse ever visited on the people of the United States.

—JOHN RUDD

Slavery wuzn't so good, 'cause it divided famblies an' done a heap o' other things dat wuz bad. But de wuk wuz good fer ever'body. It's a pity dat dese young-uns nowadays doan know de value o' wuk, lak we did. Why, when I wuz ten years old, I could do any kind o' housewuk an' spin an' weave, ter boot. I hope dat dese chillun will larn somethin' in school an' church.

—JOSEPHINE SMITH

Most ob de young niggers is headed straight fer hell. All dey think about is drinkin' hard liquor, goin' to dance halls, en' gittin' a ole rattletrap automobile. Dey piles in en' rides like dey been sont fer en' cain't go [fast enough]. Hit beats all how dey brags en' wastes things. Dey ain't one whit happier den de folks wuz in my day. I wuz ez proud to git a apple ez dey is wid a pint ob liquor. Course, schools has done a heap towards givin' colored folks book learnin'. But hit seems to me like all dey is studying 'bout is how to git out ob honest labor. I sees a heap o' fools what thinks because dey is wise in books dey is wise in all things.

—CHARLIE DAVENPORT

You asked me, son, about your young people. They does pretty well—that is, some of them do. I believes if times would ever get better, they would do lots better than they do.

The worst trouble with the young people is that they will not tell the truth. But that is not their fault. They have just learned more the ways of the world, as they have become more educated. They can read and write, and they have found out how the white people have "done" them. So, they have got to where they will steal and not tell the truth. And the white man—most of them—will beat the poor Negro out of everything he can, then make the Negro pay two or three prices for what he gets. And some of the store people will charge the Negro a higher price than they will their own color. I guess they think that is all right, but I don't.

—MARY GAFFNEY

I think the biggest run of this late generation is ignorant. Course, dey goes to school all right, but dey don't make no good of it. De people wid de Bible-and-God education is much better folks dan dese ignorant book-learned fools. Dat's all dey is, honey. Dey don't respect deirself, God, nor de devil. Dey jes' act like something wild-raised, turned loose in de swamps. Deir schooling makes me wish I could walk de streets wid my ears stopped up and eyes blindfolded, so I couldn't even hear nor see dis educated generation. Bless your soul, honey, I don't care a scrap 'bout schooling dat don't teach decency or common respect. De knee way is all de education dat 'mounts to anything, anyway. It makes you treat everybody in de world like you want to be treated by other folks, and dat's right, and everything else's wrong by dat.

—ALICE SEWELL

De young folks is making deir mark, now. One thing 'bout 'em is dat now dey get educated, but dere's nothing for 'em to do when dey get finished with school but walk de streets. I been always trying to help my people to rise 'bove deir station. Dey are rising all de time, an' some day dey'll be free.

—PIERCE HARPER

442

PLATE 39: A free black family in the rural South.

Free? Is anybody ever free? Ain't everybody you know a slave to someone or something-or-other?

—PATSY BLAND

I think slavery wus good, because I wus treated all right. I think I am 'bout as much a slave now, as ever. 'Bout half the folks, both black an' white, is slaves an' don't know it.

—JERRY HINTON

Look at me now—nothing to eat, nothing to wear. If I couldn't pay that two dollars rent, they would put me right out on the street. I gets 'shame' sometimes, begging. Ain't able to work. If it warn't for the government helping us some, I don't know what we would do. The neighbors brings in something to eat most every day, but if things was like the old times, I am telling you old Mollie would have a nice warm house, with no rent to pay, plenty of good food to eat, and nothing to do but set by a big log fire and care for the babies, while I smoke my old cob pipe in peace.

—MOLLIE EDMONDS

Mammy said dat she ain't cared 'bout bein' free, 'cause she had a good home. But, atter all, slavery wusn't de thing fer America.

—JULIA CRENSHAW

Everybody wants to be free, and they should be. I don't believe it's right to live in bondage, but I do say it bold and aboveboard that the slaves with good masters, like mine, was a heap better off. I can remember having everything I wanted, and it takes a long time to get used to not having nothing.

—MARK OLIVER

In slavery time, I had a tooth botherin' me. My mother say, "Emma, take dis egg an' go down to Doctor Busbee an' give it to him

444

an' git your tooth pulled." I give him one egg. He took it an' pulled my tooth. Try dat now, if you wants to, an' see what happens.

—EMMA BLALOCK

While for most colored folks freedom is de bes', dey's still some niggers dat ought to be slaves, now. Dese niggers dat's done clean forgot de Lawd— dose dat's always cuttin' an' fightin' an' gwine in white folks' houses at night—dey ought to be slaves. Dey ought to have an' ole marse wid a whip to make dem come when he say come, an' go when he say go, till dey learn to live right.

—SARAH DEBRO

These young folks doing every devilishment on earth they can. Look at that boy they caught the other day who had robbed twenty houses. This young race ain't goin' to stan' for what I stood for. They goin' to school every day, but they ain't learning nothin'. What will take us through this tedious journey through the world is our manners, our principles, and our behavior. Money ain't goin' to do it. You can't get by without principles, manners, and good behavior. Niggers can't do it, and white folks can't either.

—ISHE WEBB

Dar's one thing: We ole niggers wus raised right, an' de young niggers ain't. Iffen I had my say-so, dey'd burn down de nigger schools, gib dem pickaninnies a good spankin', an' put 'em in de patch ter wuk. Ain't no nigger got no business wid no edgercation, nohow.

—WILLIAM SYKES

I think that the majority of the young Negroes is going to hell. There is more educated Negroes in the penitentiary than there is in the church. Most of the young Negroes ain't got no time or use for religion. About ninety percent of them is in the church, with no religion.

—BERT STRONG

These young people, they is pretty good. They can read, write, and hold good jobs. Of course, I don't like the way some of them is doing, but if times were better, maybe they would do lots better. Some of them won't tell the truth, and I don't like that none too well. If this here government would quit feeding and sheltering them, these young bucks would go to work and behave themselves. Of course, I knows that times is hard, but not as hard as they were after the War, when the Negro was given freedom. They need to put more faith in the Good Book, quit their stealing and lying.

Some of our race have good homes, good cars, and good furniture in their homes, but they are mixing with the white people too much—so many half-breeds—and this shows that they are going backwards instead of forwards.

—LIZZIE ATKINS

I think slavery is a terrible system. I think slavery is the cause of mixing. If people want to choose somebody, it should be their own color. Many masters had children from their Negro slaves, but the slaves weren't able to help themselves.

—JULIA KING

Sometimes, I gits to ponderin', an' I thinks dem slavery days was jes' like human nature. When you has to listen, an' work, an' do things your missus an' marster say do, you think, "Oh, Lord-a'-mercy, wish I could git off to myself an' do as I please." An' den, when you is free to go out in de world an' do as you please, you gits to thinkin', "Oh, Lord-a'-mercy, wish I had someone to tell me what to do. I is lost in a fog, fer sho'. Yas, Suh!"

—ANDREW GILL

My mother always said, "Tillie, always tie to the bes' white folks—them that has inflooence—'cause if you gits into trouble, they can git you out." I've stuck to that. I've never had any traffic wid any but the blue bloods, an' now look at me. I'm not able to work, but I got a home an' plenty to eat. An' I ain't on no relief, an' Tillie can sho' hold her head up.

—ELLEN TRELL

We have had our ups and downs, in life. Sometimes, de livin' has been mighty hard, but dere has never been a time since I been free when I could not git a handout from de white folks' backyard.

—ADDY GILL

Pretty soon, all de old white folks be gone, an' den dey be no one to look after de ole-time slaves. So maybe hit jes' as well dey is passin' away, too.

—MOLLIE KIRKLAND

I likes to see my race gittin' educated an' goin' forward. It does my head good to see 'em ridin' in fine cars, an' a-ownin' deir own homes. But dey ought to live better. Dey is a-gwine too fas' an' a-thinkin' too little. Back in my days, us studied more 'bout religion. As us wukked, us sang ole songs, lak "Ole Time Religion" an' de ole nigger favorite, "Swing Low Sweet Chariot."

—LAURA FORD

Iffen you wants to know what I thinks of the young folks, I tells you. Look at that grandchile a-setting there. She fourteen and know more right now than I knowed in my whole life. Yes, ma'am! She can sew on a machine and make a dress in one day. She read in a book how to make somethin' to eat, and go hatch it up. They's fast, too. Ain't got no time for old folks, like me. Can't find no time to do nothin' for me.

447

People now makes more money than in the old days, but the way they makes it ain't honest. No'am, honey, it jest plain ain't. Old honest way was to bend the back and bear down on the hoe.

—MITTIE FREEMAN

Folks is too wise now—'specially chillun. Back in dem days, effen a lady got a baby, de chillun say, "Mammy, where you get dat baby?" An' she say, "I foun' it in a hollow log," or maybe, "I foun' it in de canebrake." Den, all de chillun runs out in de woods, lookin' in logs an' stumps an' behin' bushes, tryin' to fin' another baby. I jes' like to see you fool one of 'em, now.

—HENRI NECAISE

De young niggers has mo' education now dan de whites had when I growed up.

—ANDY SNOW

I don't think most of the young set of niggers nowadays is as smart as I was. Me and my man didn't have nothing when we left Nacogdoches County, but we worked hard and saved our money and bought us a farm. It 'pears like these young niggers don't try to 'cumulate nothing.

—LIZZIE HUGHES

We 'preciated our chance more'n de young folks does nowadays. Dey has so much dey don't have to try so hard. If we'd had what dey got, we'd thunk we was done died and gone to Glory Land.

—CLARISSA SCALES

De nigger come from Africa and other hot places. When he come here, de white man made him work, and he didn't like dat. He is natchally lazy, and when he had to work, then he began to get huffy and to conjure up in he mind hate and other bad things against de whites. Ever since de first time de nigger found out he had to work, he has silently despised de white man. If he had lived and done nothin', den he would be a 'tirely different person to dis very day. I knows dat.

—JANE JOHNSON

'Cordin' to my way of thinkin', Abraham Lincoln done a good thing when he sot us free. It's mighty good to do jus' as you please, and bread and water is heaps better dan dat somepin'-t'-eat us had to slave for.

—RACHEL ADAMS

Lady, if de nigger hadn't been set free, dis country wouldn't ever been what it is now! Poor white folks wouldn't never had a chance. De slaveholders had most of de money and de land, and dey wouldn't let de poor white folks have a chance to own any land or anything else to speak of. Dese white folks wasn't much better off dan we was. Dey had to work hard, and dey had to worry 'bout food, clothes, and shelter, and we didn't. Lots of slave owners wouldn't allow dem on deir farms among deir slaves, without orders from de overseer. I don't know why, unless dey was afraid dey would stir up discontent among de niggers.

White folks as well as niggers profited from Emancipation. Lincoln was a friend to all poor white folks, as well as black ones, and if he coulda lived, things woulda been different for ever'body.

—TOM WOODS

I think Lincoln was a mighty good man, and I think Roosevelt is trying to carry some of the good ideas Lincoln had. Lincoln would have done a heap more, if he had lived.

—MATTIE LOGAN

I believe Roosevelt's goin' to be President again. I believe he's goin' to run for a third term. He's goin' to be dictator. He's goin' to be king. He's goin' to be a good dictator. We don't want no more republic. The people are too hard on the poor. President Roosevelt lets everybody git somethin'. I hope he'll git it. I hope he'll be dictator. I hope he'll be king. Yuh git hold uh some money with him.

—JEFF BAILEY

De Lord not gwine to hold His hand any longer 'ginst us. Us cleared de forests, built de railroads, cleaned up de swamps, and nursed de white folks. Now, in our old age, I hopes they lets de old slaves like me see de shine of some of dat money I hears so much talk 'bout. They say it's free as de gift of grace from de hand of de Lord.

—ANNE BROOME

Yo' axes me what I thinks of Massa Lincoln? Well, I thinks he wuz doin' de wust thing dat he could ter turn all dem fool niggers loose, when dey ain't got no place ter go an' nothin' ter eat. Who helped us out den? Hit wuzn't de Yankees. Hit wuz de white folkses what wuz left wid deir craps [crops] in de fiel's, an' wuz robbed by dem Yankees, ter boot.

Slavery wuz a good thing den, but de world jist got better an' out-growed hit.

—HENRY BOBBITT

Abraham Lincoln was all right. I think slavery was wrong, because birds an' things are free, an' man ought to have the same privilege.

—SARAH DEBRO

De slaves, where I lived, knowed after de War dat dey had abundance of dat somethin' called freedom, what dey could not eat, wear, and sleep in. Yes, sir, dey soon found out dat freedom ain't nothin', 'less you got somethin' to live on and a place to call home. Dis livin' on liberty is lak young folks livin' on love, after dey gits married. It just don't work. No, sir, it las' so long, and not a bit longer. Don't

450

tell me! It sho' don't hold good when you has to work, or when you gits hongry. You knows dat poor white folks and niggers has got to work to live, regardless of liberty, love, and all dem things. I believes a person loves more better when dey feels good. I knows from experience dat poor folks feels better when dey has food in deir frame and a few dimes to jingle in deir pockets.

—EZRA ADAMS

One thing dat wus de matter wus de black man wudn't work as hard fer himself as he did fer his marster. If de black man wud work as hard fer himself now, as dey wus made to work when slaves, dat black man wud have as much as de white man. All de black men seem to be lazy, an' I is one uf dem.

—NELSON DICKERSON

Lord, when I thinks of de way we used to work—out in de field before day, and work till plumb dark. But what do dese young folks know 'bout work? Nothin'! Look at dat grandson of mine, just crossed de porch. Why, he's fourteen, and he can't even use a axe. Too young? Go on with you! When I's his age, I's working at anything I could find. I worked on a farm and on a steamboat, I carried cross-ties—just anything where I could earn money. And I saved money, too. When we bought dis house, I had $2,400 saved up. And men was stronger in dem days and had better health.

Dese young folks want too easy living. And dey ain't brung up to show respect to old folks, like we was. If I goes down de walk and a bunch of young folks is coming along, I knows I's got to step out of de way, 'cause dey won't give any. And if some little ones on roller skates is coming down de sidewalk, you better git off, or dey'll run right into you.

—GEORGE BOLLINGER

This new generation ain't got no strength. I think it is because they set around so much. What would a heap of them do? A long day's work in the field would kill some of them. It would! Some folks don't work 'nuf to be healthy. I don't know, but I really believes education and automobiles is the whole cause.

—LIDDIE BOECHUS

Sister, I just think dis younger generation is gone totally. Dey ain't taught right in de home, and de teachers can't do a thing with 'em. If it wasn't for de prayers goin' up to de throne of grace from all us old saints what's got sense enough to trust in nothin' else but Jesus, de whole business would be gone plum to rack. Dey ain't even got sense enough to know dat. De young folks' mind is on worldly goods and worldly pleasures, and dere ain't no good in none of it—just misery and woe, to all it touches. And still dey don't seem to see, and don't want to see, and nobody got any sense can make 'em see. God help dis generation, is all dat I can say.

—CHARLES ANDERSON

Times have changed so much, it is lak living in another world, now. Folks living in too much hurry. They getting too fast. They are restless. I see a heap of overbearing folks, now. Times is good for me, but I see old folks need things. I see young folks wasteful—both black and white. White folks setting the pace for us colored folks—it's mighty fast and mighty hard.

—ABSOLOM JENKINS

The young darkies these days says they are modern; sass their mammies, too. When I was raising up, the children minded their folks. My mammy was the boss, and she whip' me for something when I was twenty-seven year' old! The girls nowadays strip their shoulders and bare their legs, so's they can catch a man. That's the wrong way to live. I'm glad I'm a Christian. It makes your heart soft and kind—makes you do good things. It's the sacrificing of personal pleasure and time that please the Lord!

—HULDA WILLIAMS

452

The young niggers ain't got no sense, 'cause they ain't got no respect for age. One young buck walked up to me on the street last week and say, "Hello, son." I say to him, "How big do men grow where you come from?"

—GUS BRADSHAW

What does I think of these young niggers? Miss, I can't tell. My tongue just won't explain. It is like the time God was talking with his Disciples. God said to 'em, "I made you, but I know you not." That is the way with us and our chillun. When all the old wartime people die, I want to die, too. This up and coming generation is something terrible.

—JOSEPHINE COXE

Might as well tell the truth. Had just as good a time when I was a slave as when I was free. Had all the hog meat and milk and everything else to eat.

—HARDY MILLER

De white folks wuz good ter us, an' we loved 'em. But we wanted ter be free, 'cause de Lawd done make us all free.

—TOM WILCOX

There was no such thing as being good to slaves. Many white people were better than others, but a slave belonged to his master, and there was no way to get out of it.

—THOMAS LEWIS

We have been servants to the rest of the world, ever since old Noah's son laughed at his father's nakedness, and God turned his flesh black and told him for that act his race would always carry a curse, and that they would be servants of the people as long as this old world remained. Yes, and we was once sold into slavery. Then, they freed us, but we are still slaves to the white man, or worse. Because we have increased at a rapid rate, if one of us dies now, they don't care. The white people have lost nothing. There are plenty more servants at their door waiting for a handout of scraps. In other words, we are worse off than if we were a sorry cur dog; and if we gather anything together, there is some white man ready to take it away from us.

—LIZZIE GRANT

Better stay free, if you can stay straight. Slabery time was tough. It like looking back into de dark—like looking into de night.

—AMY PERRY

Slavery is pretty tough, but the Lard works all things for the better. I know He does. If it hadn't been for slavery, the niggers might still be in Africa. No telling where they would be.

—AARON JONES

Slaves prayed for freedom. Dey made me think of de crowd, one time, who prayed for rain, when it wus dry in crap time. De rain fell in torrents an' kept fallin', till it wus 'bout a flood. De fiel's wus so wet an' miry you could not go in 'em, an' water wus standin' in de fiel's middle of ebery row.

Den, one of de men who had been prayin' for rain up an' said, "I tell you, brothers, if it don't quit rainin', eberything goin' to be washed away." Dey all looked at de black rain cloud in de west wid sor'ful faces. Den, one of de brothers said to de other brothers kinder easy an' shameful-like, "Brothers, don't you think we overdone dis thing?" Dat's what many a slave thought 'bout prayin' for freedom.

Before two years had passed, after de Surrender, dere wus two out of every three slaves who wushed dey wus back wid deir marsters.

Slavery wus a bad thing, an' freedom, of de kin' we got, wid nothin' to live on, wus bad. Two snakes full of pisen—one lyin' wid

454

his head pintin' north, de other wid his head pintin' south. Deir names wus Slavery an' Freedom. Both bit de nigger, an' dey wus both bad.

—PATSY MITCHNER

What Ise lak bes', freedom or slavery? Well, 'tis dis away. In slavery, Ise owned nothin', an' never owed nothin', an', white man, Ise didn't know much. In freedom, Ise own de home, owe de people, an' raise de fam'ly. All dat cause me de worriment. In slavery, Ise have no worriment, but Ise takes de freedom.

—MARGRETT NILLIN

Here's the idea: freedom is worth it all.

—MOSES MITCHELL

I knowed a man name' Wyatt, who was free. He wanted to marry a slave girl name' Carrie, and he gave himself to Carrie's master, to marry her. He was crazy to do that. That love is an awful thing, I tell you. I don't think I would give my freedom away to marry anybody.

—ANONYMOUS

Love is a itchin' round the heart you can't get at to scratch.

—SALLY NEALY

Young folks of today don't love like they did in the olden days. Now, it is hot love, minute love, free love.

—SARAH SMILEY

Mother died near twenty years ago, and Father died four years later. He had not cared to live, since Mother left him.

I've heard some of the young people laugh about slave love, but they should envy the love which kept Mother and Father so close together in life, and even held them in death.

—ALONZO HAYWOOD

You knows, I believes I's mo' contented as a slave. I's treated kind all de time and had no frettin' 'bout how I gwine git on. Since I's been free, I sometimes have heaps of frettin'. Course, I don't want to go back into slavery, but I's paid for my freedom.

—JAMES HAYES

You used to be worth a thousand dollars then, but you're not worth two bits, now. You ain't worth nothin', when you're free.

—CAMPBELL ARMSTRONG

I thought slavery wuz right. I felt that this wuz the way things had to go—the way they were fixed to go. I wuz satisfied. The white folks treated me all right. My young missus loved me, and I loved her. She whupped me sometimes—I think, just for fun, sometimes.

—JOE HIGH

Some colored people say slavery was better, because they had no responsibility. It is true, they were fed, clothed, and sheltered, but I'm like the man that said, "Give me freedom or give me death!"

—BELLE CARUTHERS

I thought slavery wus a bad thing, 'cause all slaves did not fare alike. It wus all right for some, but bad for some. So it wus a bad thing.

—WILLIAM HINTON

I was riding on a streetcar, long after freedom, and I passed the cemetery where my [white] father was buried. I started cussing, "Let me get off this damn car and go see where my goddamn father is buried, so I can spit on his grave—a goddamn son of a bitch." I got no mercy on nobody who bring up their children like dogs. How could any father treat his child like that?—bring them up to be ignorant, like they did us. If I had my way with them all, I would like to have a chopping block and chop every one of their heads off. Of course, I don't hate them that is good. There are some good white folks. Mighty few, though. Old General [Andrew] Jackson said that before he would see niggers free, he would build a house nine miles long, and put them in it, and burn every one of them up. A dirty old rascal; now he is dead and gone.

—ANONYMOUS

God has been so good to me, to let me live all dese years. I just want to be ready to meet him, when he is ready for me. My only trouble will be to love white folks. Dey have treated my race so bad. My pastor, Reverend Fred McDonald, always tells me I will have to forgive dem and love dem, if I wants to go to Heaven. But, honey, dat's goin' to be a lifetime job. I don't care how long God lets me live, it will still be a hard job.

—LULA CHAMBERS

Boss, I is kinda glad I is a black man, 'cause, you know, dere ain't much expected of dem nohow, and dat, by itself, takes a big and heavy burden off deir shoulders. De white folks worries too much over dis and over dat. Dey worries 'cause dey ain't got no money, and when dey gits it, dey worries agin, 'cause dey is 'fraid somebody is gwine to steal it from dem. Yes, sir, dey frets and fumes, 'cause dey can't 'sociate wid big folks, and when dey does go wid dem, dey is bothered, 'cause dey ain't got what de big folks has got.

It ain't dat way wid most niggers. Nothin' disturbs dem much, 'cept a empty stomach and a cold place to sleep in. Give dem bread to eat and fire to warm by, and dey is sho' safe den. De possum in his hollow, de squirrel in his nest, and de rabbit in his bed is at home. So, de nigger, in a tight house wid a big hot fire in winter, is at home, too.

Some sort of ease and comfort is 'bout what all people, both white and black, is strivin' for in dis world. All of us laks dat somethin' called 'tentment, in one way or de other. Many white folks and some darkies thinks dat a pile of money, a fine house to live in, a 'spensive 'motorbile, fine clothes, and high 'ciety, is gwine to give dem dat. But, when dey has all dis, dey is still huntin' de end of de rainbow a little ahead of dem.

—CHARLIE DAVIS

White folks jes' naturally different from darkies. We's different in color, in talk, in 'ligion and beliefs. We's different in every way, and can never be 'spected to think o' to live alike.

—KATIE SUTTON

Though de slave question am settled, de race question will be wid us always, till Jesus come de second time. It's in our politics, in our justice courts, on our highways, on our sidewalks, in our manners, in our 'ligion, and in our thoughts, all de day and every day.

De Good Marster pity both sides. In de end, will it be settled by hate or by de policy of love your neighbor as you do yourself? Who knows. Dere's not much promise, at de 'mediate moment, for de risin' generation of either side, and I means no disrespect to you.

—CORNELIUS HOLMES

I think the time will soon be when people won't be looked on as regards to whether you are black or white, but all on the same equality. I may not live to see it, but it is on the way. Many don't believe it, but I know it.

—DELICIA PATTERSON

They say a rollin' stone gathers no moss, but I tell you, if I wasn't so old, I'd be rollin' right now. This is no place for colored people. The trouble with the people here is they don't know how to treat humanity, white or black. I know the sayin', when you're in Rome, do as the Romans do. But the Romans got the best of it.

—JAMES MARTIN

Bred an' bawn in Sumter County, wore out in Sumter County, 'spects to die in Sumter County, an' what is I got? Ain't got nothin', ain't got nothin', ain't got nothin'.

—ANK BISHOP

I always thought a lot of Lincoln, 'cause he had a heap of faith in de nigger ter think dat he could live on nothin' at all.

—JACOB THOMAS

My idea of life is to forget the bad and live for the good there is in it. This is my motto.

—THE REVEREND SQUIRE DOWD

Heah dat airplane gwine in de air? Well, co'se, when I's bo'n, we-uns don't have sich, an' don't dream of it. I 'membahs once I's lookin' at de hawk flyin', an' says to Mammy, "Mammy, I wish I could fly."

"Hush, chile," she tells me, "if de Lawd wanted folks to fly, he would give dem wings, lak de birds. Don't wish fo' what de Lawd don't want you to have." Now look, I's sat right heah an' see de folks flyin' in de air. An' right heah I's sat an' listen to de radio an' heah folks sing an' talk a thousand miles away, an' it sounds lak 'tis in de next room. When I's a young-un, de fartherest you could heah a person am 'bout half mile, an' den dey have to holler lak a stuck hawg. I wish I could live 'nother ninety yeahs to see what's a-comin'.

—ELSIE REECE

Yes, mum, I's happy enough. I got nothin' to worry over, 'cause 'tain't long, nohow. I eat every day, chew my tobacco. I rather have one meal a day and a-plenty o' tobacco. I's chewed for sixty year'. My somethin'-t'-eat'll hold out long as I do. De white folks is gwine feed us and clothes us. I ain't no 'count, 'cept to hobble round on my crutch and see what's gwine on. I takes my cheer [chair] outside and works de gyarden fur around as I's settin'; den, I moves it furder down de row and works fur as I can reach, till I gits to de end. Sometimes, in cold weather, when I gits wore out wid de house, I hobbles downtown and stands round de stores, lookin' at de passin'.

But dey's so many faces I misses, now. So many o' my white folks has done gone on. I's seed so many died. Dey's been so many changes. All dis here whole hill use' to be a solid block o' woods. I been a-livin' close round Seaboa'd seventy year', but 'twon't be many more days here for me. I's ready. I thinks about it most of de time, now. Yes, mum, I studies more about gwine dan I does stayin'.

—BERLE BARNES

We ole folks ain't got long tuh stay heah, now. We lives in de days dat's past. All we knows tuh talk 'bout is what we use' tuh do. When mah time is up, ah is ready tuh go, 'cause ah is done mah bes' fuh mah God, mah country, and mah race.

—TYLER FRAZIER

Dat was de beginnin', way back yonder, and de end is nigh. Soon, dere won't be nobody left livin' what was a sho'-'nuf slave. It's somepin' to think about, ain't it?

—CHARLIE HUDSON

Yes, sah! I sho does come from dat old stock who had de misfortune to be slaves, but who decided to be men, at one and de same time, and I's right proud of it.

—GEORGE CATO